iOS 13 Programming for Beginners

for Beginners

Fourth Edition

Get started with building iOS apps with Swift 5 and Xcode 11

Ahmad Sahar
Craig Clayton

BIRMINGHAM - MUMBAI

iOS 13 Programming for Beginners
Fourth Edition

Commissioning Editor: Pawan Ramchandani
Acquisition Editor: Ashitosh Gupta
Content Development Editor: Akhil Nair
Senior Editor: Mohammed Yusuf Imaratwale
Technical Editor: Jane Dsouza
Copy Editor: Safis Editing
Project Coordinator: Kinjal Bari
Proofreader: Safis Editing
Indexer: Pratik Shirodkar
Production Designer: Aparna Bhagat

First published: January 2017
Second published: January 2018
Third published: December 2018
Fourth published: January 2020

Production reference: 1230120

Published by Packt Publishing Ltd.
Livery Place
35 Livery Street
Birmingham
B3 2PB, UK.

ISBN 978-1-83882-190-6

www.packt.com

Packt.com

Subscribe to our online digital library for full access to over 7,000 books and videos, as well as industry leading tools to help you plan your personal development and advance your career. For more information, please visit our website.

Why subscribe?

- Spend less time learning and more time coding with practical eBooks and Videos from over 4,000 industry professionals

- Improve your learning with Skill Plans built especially for you

- Get a free eBook or video every month

- Fully searchable for easy access to vital information

- Copy and paste, print, and bookmark content

Did you know that Packt offers eBook versions of every book published, with PDF and ePub files available? You can upgrade to the eBook version at www.packt.com and as a print book customer, you are entitled to a discount on the eBook copy. Get in touch with us at customercare@packtpub.com for more details.

At www.packt.com, you can also read a collection of free technical articles, sign up for a range of free newsletters, and receive exclusive discounts and offers on Packt books and eBooks.

Contributors

About the authors

Ahmad Sahar is a trainer, presenter, and consultant at Tomafuwi Productions, specializing in conducting training courses for macOS and iOS, macOS Support Essentials certification courses, and iOS Development courses. He is a member of the DevCon iOS and MyCocoaHeads online communities in Malaysia, and has conducted presentations and talks for both groups. In his spare time, he likes building and programming LEGO Mindstorms robots.

Craig Clayton is a self-taught, senior iOS engineer at Adept Mobile, specializing in building mobile experiences for NBA and NFL teams. He also volunteered as the organizer of the Suncoast iOS meetup group in the Tampa/St. Petersburg area for 3 years, preparing presentations and hands-on talks for this group and other groups in the community. He has also launched Cocoa Academy online, which specializes in bringing a diverse list of iOS courses, ranging from building apps to games for all programming levels, to the market.

About the reviewers

Cecil Costa, also known as Eduardo Campos in Latin countries, is a Euro-Brazilian freelance developer who has been learning about computers since the time he got his first PC in 1990. From then on, he kept learning about programming languages, computer architecture, and computer science theory.

Learning is his passion as well as teaching; this is the reason why he worked as a trainer and a books author. He has been giving on-site courses for many companies.

He is also the author of three Swift books and two video courses.

Nowadays, Cecil Costa teaches through online platforms, helping people from every part of the world.

Chris Barker is a senior iOS developer and tech lead for fashion retailer N Brown, where he heads up the iOS team, building apps for their major brands. Having now worked in the IT industry for over 22 years, Chris has started developing .NET applications for retailer.

In 2014, he made his move into mobile app development with digital agency Openshadow at MediaCityUK. Here he worked on mobile apps for clients such as Louis Vuitton and L'Oréal Paris.

Chris often attends and speaks at his local iOS developer meetup - NSManchester. Most recently he attended Malaga Mobile in Spain where he spoke about accessibility in mobile apps. Over the past 2 years, Chris has been a regular speaker at CodeMobile and will be returning to speak again in 2020.

Packt is searching for authors like you

If you're interested in becoming an author for Packt, please visit authors.packtpub.com and apply today. We have worked with thousands of developers and tech professionals, just like you, to help them share their insight with the global tech community. You can make a general application, apply for a specific hot topic that we are recruiting an author for, or submit your own idea.

Table of Contents

Preface   1

Section 1: Swift

Chapter 1: Getting Familiar with Xcode   11
  Technical requirements   12
  Downloading and installing Xcode from the App Store   12
  Understanding the Xcode user interface   17
  Running the app in the Simulator   19
    Understanding the No Device and Build Only Device menu items   22
  Using an iOS 13 device for development   23
    Trusting the Developer App certificate on your iOS device   29
    Connecting an iOS device wirelessly   30
  Summary   32

Chapter 2: Simple Values and Types   33
  Technical requirements   34
  Understanding Swift playgrounds   34
    Customizing fonts and colors   38
  Exploring data types   39
    Storing integers   40
    Storing floating-point numbers   40
    Storing Booleans   41
    Storing strings   41
    Using common data types in the playground   41
  Exploring constants and variables   42
  Understanding type inference and type safety   44
    Using type annotation to specify a type   45
    Type safety   46
  Exploring operators   46
    Using arithmetic operators   47
    Using compound assignment operators   48
    Using comparison operators   49
    Using logical operators   49
    Performing string operations   50
  Using the print() instruction   51
  Summary   52

Chapter 3: Conditionals and Optionals   53
  Technical requirements   54

Introducing conditionals   54
  Using if statements   55
  Using switch statements   56
Introducing optionals   58
  Using optionals and optional binding   59
Summary   62

Chapter 4: Range Operators and Loops   63
Technical requirements   63
Range operators   64
Loops   65
  The for-in loop   66
  The while loop   67
  The repeat-while loop   68
Summary   69

Chapter 5: Collection Types   71
Technical requirements   71
Understanding arrays   72
  Creating an array   72
  Checking the number of elements in an array   73
  Adding a new item to an array   73
  Accessing an array element   74
  Assigning a new value to an index   74
  Removing an item from an array   74
  Iterating over an array   75
Understanding dictionaries   75
  Creating a dictionary   76
  Checking the number of elements in a dictionary   76
  Adding a new item to a dictionary   77
  Accessing a dictionary element   77
  Assigning a new value to a key   78
  Removing an item from a dictionary   78
  Iterating over a dictionary   79
Understanding sets   79
  Creating a set   80
  Checking the number of elements in a set   80
  Adding a new item to a set   80
  Checking whether a set contains an item   81
  Removing an item from a set   81
  Iterating over a set   82
  Set operations   82
  Set membership and equality   83
Summary   84

Chapter 6: Functions and Closures   85

Technical requirements 85
Understanding functions 86
Creating a function 86
Using custom argument labels 87
Using nested functions 88
Using functions as return types 89
Using functions as parameters 90
Using a guard statement to exit a function early 91
Understanding closures 92
Simplifying closures 93
Summary 94

Chapter 7: Classes, Structures, and Enumerations 95
Technical requirements 96
Understanding classes 96
Creating a class declaration 97
Making an instance of the class 98
Making a subclass 100
Overriding a superclass method 101
Understanding structures 103
Creating a structure declaration 104
Making an instance of the struct 105
Value types versus references types 105
Deciding which to use 107
Understanding enumerations 107
Creating an enumeration 108
Summary 110

Chapter 8: Protocols, Extensions, and Error Handling 111
Technical requirements 112
Understanding protocols 112
Creating a protocol declaration 113
Understanding extensions 115
Adopting a protocol via an extension 116
Creating an array of different types of objects 117
Exploring error handling 118
Summary 120

Section 2: Design

Chapter 9: Setting Up the Basic Structure 123
Technical requirements 124
Useful terms 124
Touring the Let's Eat app 130
Using the Explore screen 130
Using the Locations screen 131

Using the Restaurant List screen | 132
Using the Restaurant Detail screen | 133
Using the Review Form screen | 134
Using the Map screen | 135
Creating a new Xcode project | 136
Setting up a Tab Bar Controller Scene and Launch screen | 138
Setting the titles of the Tab Bar's buttons | 145
Embedding view controllers in navigation controllers | 147
Adding the Assets.xcassets file | 154
Configuring the Launch screen's background color | 156
Adding a logo and constraints to the Launch screen | 158
Adding the icons for the Explore and Map buttons | 163
Summary | 166

Chapter 10: Building Your App Structure in Storyboard | 167
Technical requirements | 168
Adding a collection view to the Explore screen | 168
Adding a Cocoa Touch Class file to your project | 172
Connecting outlets in storyboard to the view controller | 176
Configuring data source methods for the collection view | 182
Setting the delegate and data source properties of the collection view | 183
Adopting the UICollectionViewDataSource and UICollectionViewDelegate protocols | 184
Adding a section header to the collection view | 187
Creating a custom color | 190
Configuring the collection view cell and section header size | 193
Presenting a view modally | 195
Adding a button to the collection view header | 195
Adding a new view controller scene | 197
Adding the Cancel and Done buttons to the navigation bar | 205
Summary | 209

Chapter 11: Finishing Up Your App Structure in Storyboard | 211
Technical requirements | 212
Adding a table view to the Locations screen | 212
Implementing the Restaurant List screen | 217
Declaring the RestaurantListViewController class | 220
Adopting the delegate and data source protocols | 222
Presenting the Restaurant List screen | 228
Implementing the Restaurant Detail screen | 231
Implementing the Review Form screen | 236
Implementing the Map screen | 244
Summary | 249

Chapter 12: Modifying and Configuring Cells | 251

Technical requirements 252
Modifying the Explore screen section header 252
Adding Auto Layout to the Explore screen's section header 267
Modifying the exploreCell collection view cell 272
Modifying the restaurantCell collection view cell 279
Adding Auto Layout constraints to the restaurantCell collection view cell 292
Configuring the locationCell table view cell 301
Summary 302

Section 3: Code

Chapter 13: Getting Started with MVC and Collection Views 307
Technical requirements 308
Understanding the MVC design pattern 308
Exploring controllers and classes 309
Understanding collection views 310
Revisiting the Explore and Restaurant List screens 321
Summary 322

Chapter 14: Getting Data into Collection Views 323
Technical requirements 324
Understanding model objects 324
Understanding .plist files 327
Creating a structure to represent a cuisine 328
Implementing a data manager class to read data from a .plist 331
Using the data manager to initialize ExploreItem instances 334
Displaying data in a collection view 336
Connecting the outlets in exploreCell 338
Implementing additional data manager methods 342
Updating the data source methods in ExploreViewController 343
Summary 347

Chapter 15: Getting Started with Table Views 349
Technical requirements 350
Understanding table views 350
Creating LocationViewController 360
Connecting the table view to LocationViewController 363
Adding the data source and delegate methods 366
Adding location data for the table view 372
Creating a property list (.plist) file 375
Adding data to the .plist file 375
Creating LocationDataManager 379
Displaying data in a table view using LocationDataManager 380
Cleaning up the user interface 381

Summary 385
Chapter 16: Getting Started with MapKit 387
Technical requirements 388
Understanding and creating annotations 388
    Introducing MKAnnotation 389
    Creating the RestaurantItem class 390
    Creating MapDataManager 395
    Creating the DataManager protocol 397
    Refactoring MapDataManager 399
    Refactoring ExploreDataManager 400
Adding annotations to a map view 402
    Creating MapViewController 402
    Connecting the outlets for the map view to MapViewController 403
    Setting the map view region to be displayed 406
    Displaying annotations on the map view 407
    Creating custom annotations 410
Going from the Map screen to the Restaurant Detail screen 414
    Creating and configuring a storyboard reference 414
    Performing the showDetail segue 419
    Passing data to the Restaurant Detail screen 423
Organizing your code 427
    Refactoring ExploreViewController 427
    Using the // MARK: syntax 430
    Refactoring RestaurantListViewController 431
    Refactoring LocationViewController 432
    Refactoring MapViewController 434
Summary 437
Chapter 17: Getting Started with JSON Files 439
Technical requirements 440
Getting data from JSON files 440
    What is an API? 440
    Understanding the JSON format 441
    Creating RestaurantAPIManager 442
Using data from JSON files in your app 444
    Storing a user-selected location in LocationViewController 445
    Adding a view controller for the section header in the Explore screen 449
    Connecting the section header's label to ExploreViewController 450
    Adding an unwind action method to the Done button 452
    Selecting only one location in the Location screen 459
    Passing location and cuisine information to RestaurantListViewController 461
    Creating a view controller for the cells on the Restaurant List screen 472
    Connecting the outlets for RestaurantCell 472
    Creating RestaurantDataManager 476

Configuring MapDataManager to use RestaurantDataManager 480
Displaying a custom UIView to indicate no data available 481
Displaying a list of restaurants on the Restaurant List screen 486
Summary 494

Chapter 18: Displaying Data in a Static Table View 495
Technical requirements 496
Setting up outlets for RestaurantDetailViewController 496
Displaying data in the static table view 506
Passing data from RestaurantListViewController to RestaurantDetailViewController 509
Summary 517

Chapter 19: Getting Started with Custom UIControls 519
Technical requirements 520
Creating a custom UIControl object 520
Displaying stars in your custom UIControl object 524
Adding support for touch events 534
Implementing an unwind method for the Cancel button 540
Creating ReviewFormViewController 541
Summary 547

Chapter 20: Getting Started with Cameras and Photo Libraries 549
Technical requirements 550
Understanding filters 550
Creating a scrolling list of filters 555
Creating a view controller for the filter cell 557
Creating a View Controller for the Photo Filter screen 561
Getting permission to use the camera or photo library 573
Summary 578

Chapter 21: Understanding Core Data 579
Technical requirements 580
Introducing Core Data 580
Implementing Core Data components for your app 581
Creating a data model 582
Creating ReviewItem 586
Creating RestaurantPhotoItem 588
Creating a Core Data manager 589
Creating ReviewDataManager 594
Summary 596

Chapter 22: Saving and Loading from Core Data 597
Technical requirements 598
Understanding how saving and loading works 598
Adding a restaurantID property to RestaurantItem 601

Updating ReviewFormViewController to save reviews   601
  Passing RestaurantID to ReviewFormViewController   602
Updating PhotoFilterViewController to save photos   606
Displaying saved reviews and photos on the Restaurant Detail screen   611
Calculating a restaurant's overall rating   626
Summary   628

Section 4: Features

Chapter 23: Getting Started with Dark Mode   631
  Technical requirements   632
  Turning on Dark Mode in the simulator   632
  Updating the Launch screen to work with Dark Mode   635
  Updating the Explore screen to work with Dark Mode   640
  Updating the Restaurant List screen to work with Dark Mode   644
  Updating the Restaurant Detail screen to work with Dark Mode   647
    Updating the Reviews View Controller scene and NoDataView to work with Dark Mode   653
    Updating the Photo Reviews View Controller Scene to work with Dark Mode   655
  Summary   658

Chapter 24: Getting Started with Mac Catalyst   659
  Technical requirements   660
  Cleaning up the design   660
  Updating the app to work on iPad   670
    Checking device type   672
    Updating ExploreViewController for iPad   673
    Updating RestaurantListViewController for iPad   680
    Updating the Restaurant Detail screen for iPad   686
  Updating the app to work on macOS   690
  Summary   694

Chapter 25: Getting Started with SwiftUI   695
  Technical requirements   696
  Creating a SwiftUI project   696
  Working with text   700
  Combining Views using Stacks   704
  Working with images   710
  Using UIKit and SwiftUI Views together   713
  Composing the Restaurant Detail screen   717
  Summary   722

Chapter 26: Getting Started with Sign In with Apple   723

Technical requirements	724
Adding a login screen	724
Displaying a Sign in with Apple button	733
Implementing delegate methods and button actions	737
Passing user information to ExploreViewController	745
Summary	750
Chapter 27: Testing and Submitting Your App to the App Store	751
Technical requirements	752
Getting an Apple Developer account	752
Generating a certificate signing request	753
Creating development and distribution certificates	755
Registering an App ID	757
Registering your devices	759
Creating provisioning profiles	761
Creating icons for your app	766
Creating screenshots for your app	767
Creating an App Store listing	768
Creating an archive build	769
Completing the information in App Store Connect	775
Testing your app	781
Testing your app internally	781
Testing your app externally	783
Summary	788
Other Books You May Enjoy	791
Index	795

Preface

Welcome to iOS 13 Programming for Beginners. This book is the fourth edition of the iOS Programming for Beginners series, and has been fully updated for iOS 13, macOS 10.15 Catalina, and Xcode 11.

In this book, you will build a restaurant reservation app called *Let's Eat*. You will start off by exploring Xcode, Apple's programming environment, also known as its **Integrated Development Environment (IDE)**. Next, you will start learning the foundations of Swift, the programming language used in iOS apps, and see how it is used to accomplish common programming tasks.

Once you have a solid foundation of using Swift, you will start creating the visual aspects of the *Let's Eat* app. During this process, you will work with storyboards and connect your app's structure together using segues.

With your user interface complete, you will then add code to implement your app's functionality. To display your data in a grid, you will use collection views, and to display your data in a list, you will use table views. You will also look at how to add basic and custom annotations on to a map. Finally, it's time to get real data; you will look at what an **Application Programming Interface (API)** is and how you can get actual restaurant data into your collection views, table views, and map.

You now have a complete app, but how about adding some bells and whistles? The first place where you can add a feature will be the restaurant detail page, where users can add restaurant reviews. Here, users will be able to take or choose a picture and apply a filter to their picture. They will also be able to give the restaurant a rating as well as a review. You will save this data using Core Data.

After that, you will implement the latest iOS 13 features. You will make your app support Dark Mode, which gives your app a fresh and exciting user interface. Then, you will modify your app to work on both iPhone and iPad and make it work on the Mac Catalyst as well using Project Catalyst. After that, you will learn how to develop views using SwiftUI, a great new way of specifying what the user interface should look like. Finally you'll modify your app to use Sign in with Apple, to further personalize the app to a user.

When you have added some bells and whistles, you can test the app with internal and external testers, and finally get it into the App Store.

Who this book is for

This book is for you if you are a programmer who is completely new to Swift, iOS, or programming and want to make iOS applications. However, you'll also find this book useful if you're an experienced programmer looking to explore the latest iOS 13 features.

What this book covers

Chapter 1, *Getting Familiar with Xcode*, takes you through a tour of Xcode and talks about all the different panes that you will use throughout the book.

Chapter 2, *Simple Values and Types*, deals with how values and types are implemented by the Swift language.

Chapter 3, *Conditionals and Optionals*, shows how if and switch statements are implemented, and how to implement variables that may or may not have a value.

Chapter 4, *Range Operators and Loops*, shows how to work with ranges and the different ways loops are implemented in Swift.

Chapter 5, *Collection Types*, covers the common collection types, which are arrays, dictionaries, and sets.

Chapter 6, *Functions and Closures*, covers how you can group instructions together using functions and closures.

Chapter 7, *Classes, Structures, and Enumerations*, talks about how complex objects containing state and behaviour are represented in Swift.

Chapter 8, *Protocols, Extensions, and Error Handling*, talks about creating protocols complex data types can adopt, extending the capabilities of existing types, and how to handle errors in your code.

Chapter 9, *Setting Up the Basic Structure*, deals with creating the *Let's Eat* app, adding graphical assets, and setting up the initial screen the users will see.

Chapter 10, *Building Your App Structure in Storyboard*, covers setting up the main screen for the *Let's Eat* app.

Chapter 11, *Finishing Up Your App Structure in Storyboard,* covers setting up the remaining screens for the *Let's Eat* app.

Chapter 12, *Modifying and Configuring Cells,* is about designing the table and collection view cells in a storyboard.

Chapter 13, *Getting Started with MVC and Collection Views,* concerns working with collection views and how you can use them to display a grid of items.

Chapter 14, *Getting Data into Collection Views,* concerns the incorporation of data into collection views.

Chapter 15, *Getting Started with Table Views,* teaches you to work with table views and takes an in-depth look at dynamic table views.

Chapter 16, *Getting Started with MapKit,* deals with working with MapKit and adding annotations to a map. You will also create custom annotations for your map.

Chapter 17, *Getting Started with JSON Files,* involves learning how to use a data manager to read a JSON file and use the data inside your app.

Chapter 18, *Displaying Data in a Static Table View,* teaches you how to populate a static table view with data passed from one view controller to another using segues.

Chapter 19, *Getting Started with Custom UIControls,* takes a look at how to create your own custom views.

Chapter 20, *Getting Started with the Cameras and Photo Libraries,* talks about working with the device's camera and photo library.

Chapter 21, *Understanding Core Data,* teaches us the basics of using core data.

Chapter 22, *Saving and Loading from Core Data,* wraps up reviews and photos by saving them using core data.

Chapter 23, *Getting Started with Dark Mode,* shows how to add Dark Mode to your app.

Chapter 24, *Getting Started with Mac Catalyst,* deals with modifying your app to work well on the iPad's larger screen, and to make it work on a Mac.

Chapter 25, *Getting Started with SwiftUI,* is about building a custom UI using Apple's new SwiftUI technology.

Chapter 26, *Getting Started with Sign In with Apple,* provides instructions on how to implement Sign in with Apple into your app.

Chapter 27, *Testing and Submitting Your App to the App Store,* concerns how to submit apps for testing as well as submitting apps to the App Store.

To get the most out of this book

This book has been completely revised for iOS 13, macOS 10.15 Catalina, Xcode 11 and Swift 5. *Section 4* of this book also covers the latest technologies introduced by Apple during WWDC 2019, which are Dark Mode, Mac Catalyst, Swift UI and sign in with Apple.

To complete all the exercises in this book, you will need:

- A Mac computer running macOS 10.15 Catalina or later
- Xcode 11.2.1 or later

To check if your Mac supports macOS 10.15 Catalina, see this link: https://support. apple.com/en-us/HT210222. If your Mac is supported, you can update macOS using Software Update in System Preferences.

To get the latest version of Xcode, you can download it from the Mac App Store.

Most of the exercises can be completed without an Apple Developer account and use the iOS Simulator. If you wish to test the app you are developing on an actual iOS device, you will need a free or paid Apple Developer account, and the following chapters require a paid Apple Developer account:

Chapter 26, *Getting Started with Sign In with Apple*
Chapter 27, *Testing and Submitting Your App to the App Store*

Instructions on how to get a paid Apple Developer account are in Chapter 27, *Testing and Submitting Your App to the App Store.*

Download the example code files

You can download the example code files for this book from your account at www.packt.com. If you purchased this book elsewhere, you can visit www.packtpub.com/support and register to have the files emailed directly to you.

You can download the code files by following these steps:

1. Log in or register at www.packt.com.
2. Select the **Support** tab.
3. Click on **Code Downloads**.
4. Enter the name of the book in the **Search** box and follow the onscreen instructions.

Once the file is downloaded, please make sure that you unzip or extract the folder using the latest version of:

- WinRAR/7-Zip for Windows
- Zipeg/iZip/UnRarX for Mac
- 7-Zip/PeaZip for Linux

The code bundle for the book is also hosted on GitHub at https://github.com/PacktPublishing/iOS-13-Programming-for-Beginners. In case there's an update to the code, it will be updated on the existing GitHub repository.

We also have other code bundles from our rich catalog of books and videos available at https://github.com/PacktPublishing/. Check them out!

Download the color images

We also provide a PDF file that has color images of the screenshots/diagrams used in this book. You can download it here: https://static.packt-cdn.com/downloads/9781838821906_ColorImages.pdf.

Code in Action

Visit the following link to check out videos of the code being run:

http://bit.ly/2RhXuHk

Conventions used

There are a number of text conventions used throughout this book.

`CodeInText`: Indicates code words in text, database table names, folder names, filenames, file extensions, pathnames, dummy URLs, user input, and Twitter handles. Here is an example: "So, this is a very simple function, named `serviceCharge()`."

A block of code is set as follows:

```
func functionName(paramater1: parameterType, ...) -> returnType {
    code
}
```

Bold: Indicates a new term, an important word, or words that you see onscreen. For example, words in menus or dialog boxes appear in the text like this. Here is an example: "Launch **Xcode** and click **Create a new Xcode project**:"

Warnings or important notes appear like this.

Tips and tricks appear like this.

Get in touch

Feedback from our readers is always welcome.

General feedback: If you have questions about any aspect of this book, mention the book title in the subject of your message and email us at `customercare@packtpub.com`.

Errata: Although we have taken every care to ensure the accuracy of our content, mistakes do happen. If you have found a mistake in this book, we would be grateful if you would report this to us. Please visit `www.packtpub.com/support/errata`, selecting your book, clicking on the Errata Submission Form link, and entering the details.

Piracy: If you come across any illegal copies of our works in any form on the Internet, we would be grateful if you would provide us with the location address or website name. Please contact us at copyright@packt.com with a link to the material.

If you are interested in becoming an author: If there is a topic that you have expertise in and you are interested in either writing or contributing to a book, please visit authors.packtpub.com.

Reviews

Please leave a review. Once you have read and used this book, why not leave a review on the site that you purchased it from? Potential readers can then see and use your unbiased opinion to make purchase decisions, we at Packt can understand what you think about our products, and our authors can see your feedback on their book. Thank you!

For more information about Packt, please visit packt.com.

Section 1: Swift 1

Welcome to part one of this book. In this part, you will begin by exploring Xcode, Apple's programming environment, which is also known as the **Integrated Development Environment (IDE)**. Next, you will start learning the foundations of Swift 5, the programming language used in iOS apps, and see how it is used to accomplish common programming tasks.

This part comprises the following chapters:

- Chapter 1, *Getting Familiar with Xcode*
- Chapter 2, *Simple Values and Types*
- Chapter 3, *Conditionals and Optionals*
- Chapter 4, *Range Operators and Loops*
- Chapter 5, *Collection Types*
- Chapter 6, *Functions and Closures*
- Chapter 7, *Classes, Structures, and Enumerations*
- Chapter 8, *Protocols, Extensions, and Error Handling*

By the end of this part, you'll understand the process of creating an app and running it on a simulator or device, and you'll have a working knowledge of how to use the Swift programming language, in order to accomplish common programming tasks. This will prepare you for the next chapter, and will also enable you to create your own Swift programs. Let's get started!

Getting Familiar with Xcode 1

Welcome to *iOS 13 Programming for Beginners*. I hope you will find this a useful introduction to writing and publishing iOS 13 apps on the App Store.

This book is divided into four parts. Each is designed to accomplish a specific set of goals.

In *Section 1, Swift*, you start by learning Swift 5.1, which is the latest version of the Swift language. Swift is the programming language used to write apps for all Apple hardware. You'll see how common programming tasks are accomplished in Swift. At the end of this part, you should have a working knowledge of the Swift language.

In *Section 2, Design*, you'll create the design of an iOS 13 application from scratch using storyboards. This is accomplished using Xcode's Interface Builder, and coding is kept to a minimum. At the end of this part, you should have a clear idea of the app's user interface and flow.

Section 3, Code, will focus on coding. You will learn many important iOS app development concepts, and as you go along, you'll learn strategies and techniques that you can use in your own apps.

Section 4, Features, covers the exciting new technologies first introduced by Apple at WWDC 2019, such as Dark Mode, Catalyst, SwiftUI, and Sign In with Apple. You'll also learn how to create resources for App Store submission, submit your app to the App Store, and beta test your app.

The app you'll write is a restaurant reservation app named *Let's Eat*. This app was originally written by Craig Clayton, who wrote the previous edition of this book. I have updated this app for the latest version of Xcode and iOS.

In this chapter, we'll cover the following topics:

- Downloading and installing Xcode from the App Store
- Understanding the Xcode user interface
- Running the app in the Simulator
- Using an iOS 13 device for development

Technical requirements

To do the exercises for this chapter, you will need the following:

- An Apple Mac computer running macOS 10.15 Catalina
- An Apple ID (if you don't have one, you will create one in this chapter)
- Optionally, an iOS device running iOS 13

The Xcode project for this chapter is in the `Chapter01` folder of the code bundle for this book, which can be downloaded here:

`https://github.com/PacktPublishing/iOS-13-Programming-for-Beginners`.

You'll start by downloading Xcode, Apple's integrated development environment for developing iOS apps from the App Store.

Check out the following video to see the code in action:

`http://bit.ly/38B50D5`

Downloading and installing Xcode from the App Store

Before you begin writing iOS Apps, you need to download and install Xcode from the App Store. Perform the following steps:

1. Open the App Store on your Mac (it's in the Apple menu).
2. In the search field in the top-right corner, type `Xcode` and press the *Return* key.
3. You should see Xcode in the search results. Click **Get** and click **Install**.

4. If you have an Apple ID, type it in the **Apple ID** text box. If you don't have one, click the **Create Apple ID** button and follow the step-by-step instructions to create one:

 You can see more information on how to create an Apple ID at this link: `https://support.apple.com/en-us/HT204316#appstore`.

5. Once Xcode has been installed, launch it. You should see the following **Welcome to Xcode** screen:

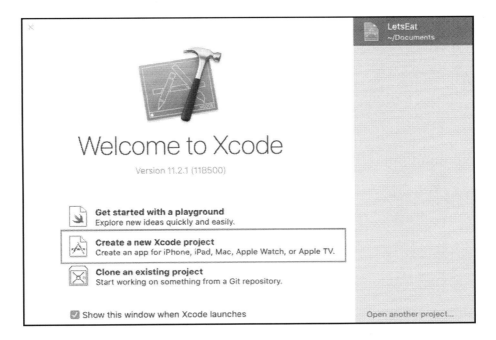

If this is the first time you have launched Xcode, you will see **No Recent Projects** in the right-hand panel. If you have previously created projects, then you will see them listed in the right-hand panel. Click **Create a new Xcode project** in the left-hand pane.

6. You will see the new project screen as follows:

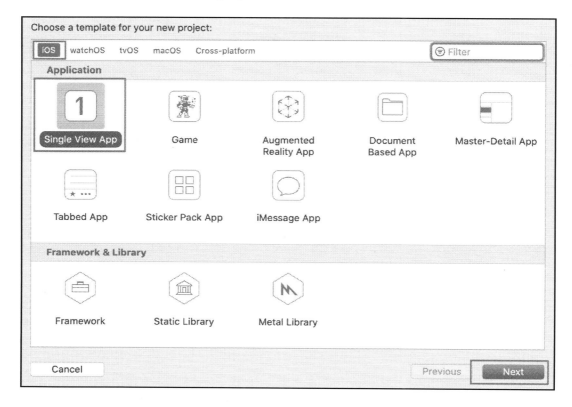

Across the top of this screen, you can select one of the following items: **iOS**, **watchOS**, **tvOS**, **macOS**, and **Cross-platform**. **iOS** should already be selected. Then, choose **Single View App** and click on **Next**.

7. You will see an options screen for a new project:

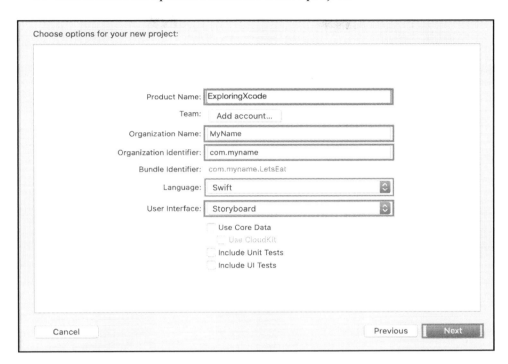

This options screen has the following eight items to complete or choose:

- **Product Name**: The name of your app. Enter `ExploringXcode` in the text field.
- **Team**: The Developer Account Team for this project. Leave it as it is for now.
- **Organization Name**: The name of your company. Just put your own name here for now.
- **Organization Identifier**: Used in conjunction with the **Product Name** to create a unique identifier for your app on the App Store. Normally, reverse DNS notation is used. Enter `com.myname` for now.
- **Bundle Identifier**: Automatically created by combining your **Product Name** and your **Organization Identifier**. Used to uniquely identify your app on the App Store.
- **Language**: The programming language to be used. Set this to **Swift**.

- **User Interface**: Set this to **Storyboard**.
- **Checkboxes**: These checkboxes are used to include code for core data, unit tests, and UI tests. Leave them unchecked for now.

Click **Next** when you're done.

8. Choose a location to save your project, such as the `Desktop` or `Documents` folder, and click **Create**:

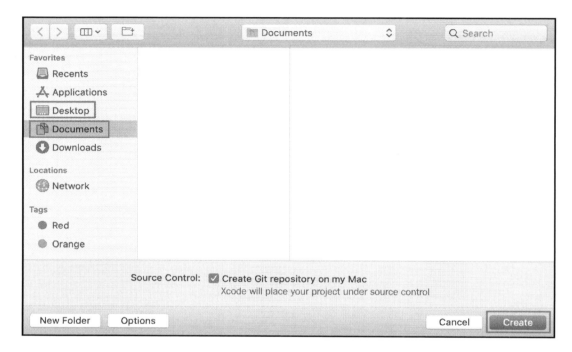

9. If you see a dialog box saying **No author information was supplied by the version control system**, click **Fix**.

 The reason why you see this dialog box is because **Source Control** checkbox is ticked. Apple recommends that **Source Control** be turned on. To learn more about version control and Git, see this link: `https://git-scm.com/video/what-is-version-control`.

10. You will see the **Source Control** preference screen as follows:

Enter the following information:

- **Author Name**: Your own name
- **Author Email**: Your email address

11. The Xcode main window will appear.

Fantastic! You have now successfully downloaded and installed Xcode, and in the next section, we will study the Xcode user interface.

Understanding the Xcode user interface

Xcode is the tool you use to write apps, and you will learn about the Xcode user interface in this section. You'll become familiar with the structure of a project in Xcode and learn how to navigate between and use basic project components.

Let's go over each of the different parts:

The following are the elements shown in the preceding screenshot:

- **Toolbar**: Used to build and run your apps, and view the progress of running tasks. Contains the **Play** button (1), the **Stop** button (2), the **Scheme** menu (3), and the **Activity View** (4):

- The **Play** button is used to build and run your app.
- The **Stop** button stops any currently running apps.
- The **Scheme** menu shows the specific target to be built (**Exploring Xcode**), and the destination (Simulator or device) to run the target on (**iPhone Simulator**). Schemes and destinations are distinct. Schemes specify the settings for building, running, testing, profiling, analyzing, and archiving your project. Destinations specify installation locations for your app. Typically, a scheme exists for each target in your project. Destinations exist for physical devices and simulators.

- The **Activity View** displays the progress of running tasks.
- **Window Pane buttons**: Used to configure your work environment. Contains the **Object library** (1), **Version Editor** (2), and **Navigator, Debug, and Inspector** buttons (3):

  - The **Library** button displays user interface elements, code snippets, and other resources.
  - The **Version Editor** button shows versions of the same file.
  - The **Navigator, Debug,** and **Inspector** buttons toggle the **Navigator area,** the **Debug area** and the **Inspector area** on and off.
- **Navigator area**: Provides quick access to the various parts of your project. The **Project navigator** is displayed by default.
- **Editor area**: Allows you to edit source code, user interfaces, and other resources.
- **Inspector area**: Allows you to view and edit information about items selected in the **Navigator area** or **Editor area**.
- **Debug area**: Contains the debug bar, the variables view, and the **Console**.

Don't be overwhelmed by all the different parts, you'll learn about them in more detail in later chapters. Now that you are familiar with the Xcode interface, we will run the app you just created in the Simulator, which displays a representation of your iOS device.

Running the app in the Simulator

The Simulator gives you an idea of how your app would look and behave if it were running on a device. It can model a number of different types of hardware—all the screen sizes and resolutions for both iPad and iPhone—so you can simulate your app on every device you're developing for.

To run the app in the Simulator, perform the following steps:

1. Click the **Scheme** menu in the toolbar and you will see a list of Simulators. Choose **iPhone 11** from this menu:

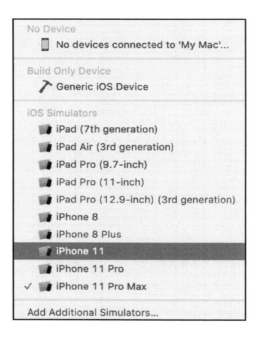

2. Click the Play button to install and run your app on the currently selected Simulator. You can also use the *command + R* keyboard shortcut.

3. If you see the **Developer Tools Access** dialog box, enter the Mac's admin **Username** and **Password** and click **Continue**:

4. The Simulator app will launch and show a representation of an **iPhone 11**. Your app displays a white screen, as you have not yet added anything to your project:

5. Switch back to Xcode and click on the Stop button (or type `Command - .`) to stop the currently running project.

You have just created and run your first iOS app in the Simulator! Great job!

If you look at the **Scheme** menu, you may be wondering about what the **No Device** and **Build Only Device** menu items are for. Let's take a look at them.

Understanding the No Device and Build Only Device menu items

You learned how to choose a Simulator in the **Scheme** menu to run your app in the previous section. But what are the **No Device** and **Build Only Device** menu items for? Well, Xcode not only allows you to run apps on the Simulator, but it also allows you to run apps on actual iOS devices, and prepare apps for submission to the App Store.

By clicking the **Scheme** menu in the toolbar, you will see the entire menu, and at the top of the menu are the **No Device** and **Build Only Device** sections:

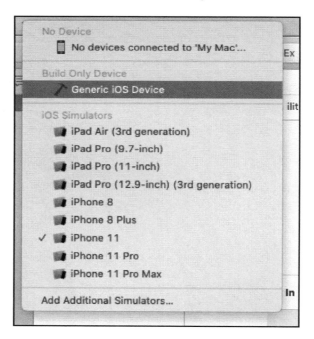

The **No Device** section currently displays text stating **No devices connected to 'My Mac'...** because you currently don't have any iOS devices connected to your computer. If you were to plug in an iOS device, it would appear in this section, and you would be able to run the apps you develop on it for testing. Running your apps on an actual device is recommended as the Simulator will not accurately reflect the performance characteristics of an actual iOS device, and does not have some hardware features and software APIs that actual devices have.

The **Build Only Device** section has only one option, **Generic iOS Device**. This is used when you need to archive your app prior to submitting it to the App Store. You'll learn how to do this in the last chapter of this book.

Now let's see how to build and run your app on an actual iOS 13 device. The vast majority of the instructions in this book do not require you to have an iOS device though, so if you don't have one, skip the next section and go straight to Chapter 2, *Simple Values and Types*.

Using an iOS 13 device for development

Although you'll be able to go through most of the exercises in this book using the Simulator, it is recommended to build and test your apps on an actual iOS device, as the Simulator will not be able to simulate some hardware components and software APIs.

 For a comprehensive look at all the differences between the Simulator and an actual device, see this link: https://help.apple.com/simulator/mac/current/#/devb0244142d.

In addition to your device, you'll need an Apple ID or a paid Apple Developer account to build and run your app on your device. You'll use the same Apple ID that you used in the App Store for now:

1. Use the USB cable to connect the iOS device to your Mac.
2. In the **Scheme** menu, choose your device (**iPhone** in this case):

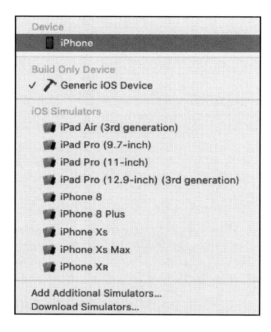

3. Wait for Xcode to finish indexing and processing, which will take a while. Once complete, **Ready** will be displayed in the status window.
4. Run the project by hitting the **Play** button (or use *command + R*). You will get the following error: **Signing for "Exploring Xcode" requires a development team**:

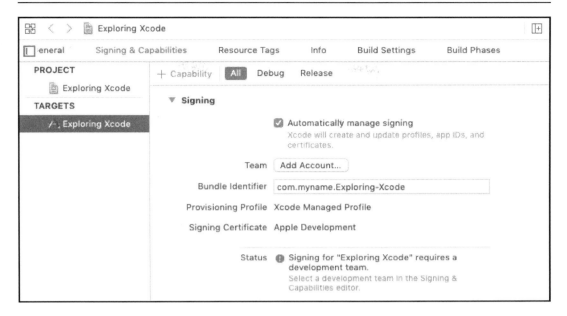

This is because a digital certificate is required to run the app on an iOS 13 device, and you need to add an Apple ID or a Developer account to Xcode so the digital certificate can be generated.

Certificates ensure that the only apps that run on your device are the ones you authorize. This helps to protect against malware. You can also learn more about them at this link: `https://help.apple.com/xcode/mac/current/#/dev60b6fbbc7`.

5. Click the **Add Account...** button:

6. The Xcode **Preferences** window appears with the **Accounts** pane selected. Enter your **Apple ID** and click **Next**. Note that you can create a different **Apple ID** if you wish using the **Create Apple ID** button:

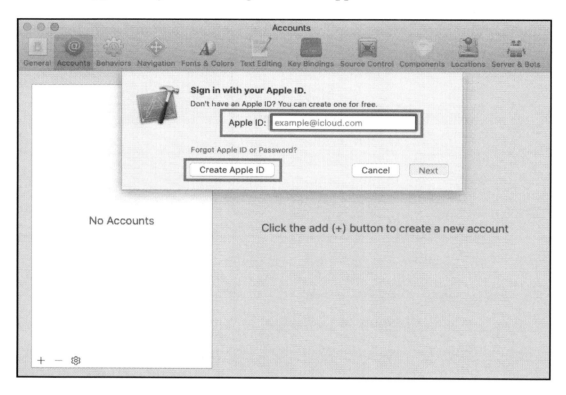

7. Enter your password when prompted. After a few minutes, the **Accounts** pane will display your account settings:

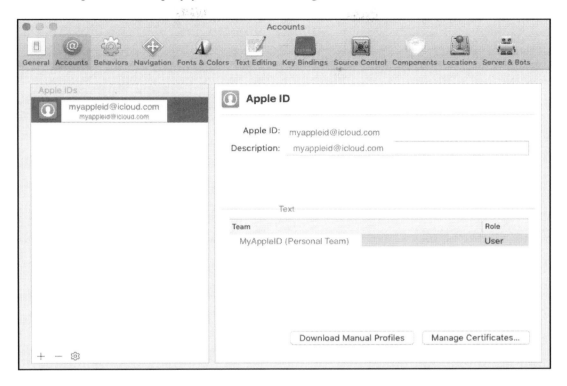

8. Close the **Preferences** window when you're done by clicking the red button in the top-left corner.

9. In Xcode's editing area, Click **Signing & Capabilities**. Make sure **Automatically manage signing** is ticked and **Personal Team** is selected from the **Team** pop-up menu:

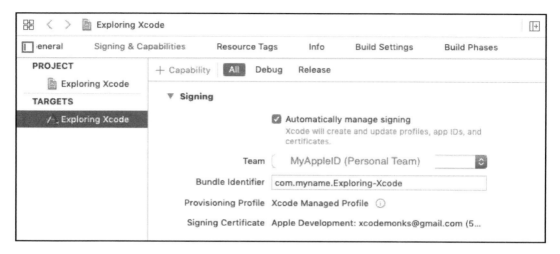

10. If you still see errors in this screen, try changing your **Bundle Identifier** by typing some random characters into it, for example, `com.12345myname.Exploring-Xcode`.

11. Everything should work now when you build and run, and your app will be installed on your iOS device. However, it will not launch and you will see the following message:

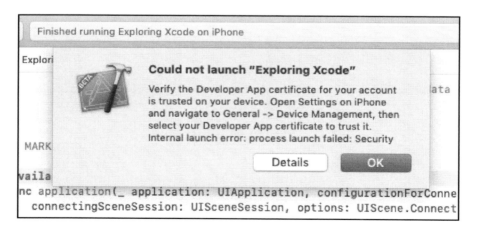

This means you need to trust the certificate that has been installed on your device.

You can also access Xcode preferences by choosing **Preferences** in the **Xcode** menu.

In the next section, we will see how to do that.

Trusting the Developer App certificate on your iOS device

A **Developer App** certificate is a special file that gets installed on your iOS device along with your app. Before your app can run, you need to trust it. Let's do that now:

1. On your iOS 13 device, tap **Settings**.
2. Tap **General**.
3. Tap **Device Management**:

4. Tap **Apple Development**:

5. Tap **Trust "Apple Development: "**:

6. Tap **Trust**:

7. You should see the following, which shows the app is now trusted:

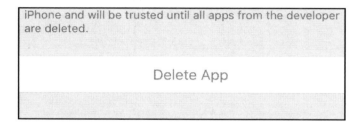

8. Click the Play button in Xcode to build and run again. You'll see your app launch and run on your iOS device.

Congratulations! Note that you have to connect your iOS 13 device to your Mac using the USB cable to build and run your app, so in the next section we'll see how we can connect over Wi-Fi.

Connecting an iOS device wirelessly

Unplugging and replugging your iOS device using USB gets pretty cumbersome after a while, so you'll configure Xcode to connect to your iOS device over Wi-Fi as follows:

1. Make sure your Mac and iOS device are on the same wireless network.
2. Choose **Window | Devices and Simulators** from the menu bar:

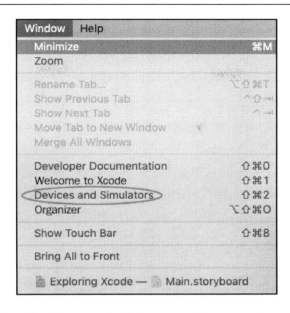

3. Click on the checkbox marked **Connect via network**:

Awesome! Your iOS device is now connected wirelessly to Xcode, and you no longer need the USB cable connected.

Summary

In this chapter, you learned how to download and install Xcode on your Mac. You familiarized yourself with the different parts of the Xcode user interface. You created your first iOS app, selected a Simulator, and built and ran the app. You learned what the **Generic iOS Device** menu item is for. You also learned how to connect an iOS device to Xcode via USB so that you can run the app on it, how to add an Apple ID to Xcode so the necessary digital certificates can be created and installed on your device, and how to trust the certificate on your device. Finally, you learned how to connect to your device over Wi-Fi, so you no longer need to plug and unplug your device every time you want to run an app.

You now know how to download and install Xcode from the App Store, the different panels in Xcode, how to add Developer credentials, and how to connect an iOS device for development using USB and Wi-Fi.

In the next chapter, we'll start exploring the Swift language using Swift Playgrounds, and learn how simple values and types are implemented in Swift.

2
Simple Values and Types

Now that you have had a short tour of Xcode, let's look at the Swift programming language.

 For more information about the latest version of the Swift language, visit `https://docs.swift.org/swift-book/`.

First, you'll explore Swift playgrounds, an interactive environment where you can type in Swift code and have it execute and display results immediately. You'll study how Swift stores various types of data, and how it performs operations on that data. You'll also look at some cool Swift features such as type inference and type safety, which help you to write code more concisely and avoid common errors. Finally, you'll learn how to perform common operations on data and how to print messages to the Debug area to help you troubleshoot issues.

By the end of this chapter, you should be able to write simple programs that can process letters and numbers.

The following topics will be covered:

- Understanding Swift playgrounds
- Exploring data types
- Exploring constants and variables
- Understanding type inference and type safety
- Exploring operators
- Using the `print()` function

Technical requirements

To do the exercises for this chapter, you will need the following:

- An Apple Mac computer running macOS 10.15 Catalina
- Xcode 11 installed (refer to `Chapter 1`, *Getting Familiar with Xcode*, for instructions on how to install Xcode)

The Xcode playground for this chapter is in the `Chapter02` folder of the code bundle for this book, which can be downloaded here:

`https://github.com/PacktPublishing/iOS-13-Programming-for-Beginners`.

You'll start by creating a new playground in the next section, where you can type in the code presented in this chapter.

Check out the following video to see the code in action:

`http://bit.ly/36prN3j`

Understanding Swift playgrounds

Playgrounds are an interactive coding environment. You type code in the left-hand pane, and the results are displayed immediately in the right-hand pane. You can also use `print()` to display anything you like in the Debug area. It's a great way to experiment with code and to explore system APIs. Let's get started!

1. To create a playground, launch Xcode. Click **Get started with a playground**:

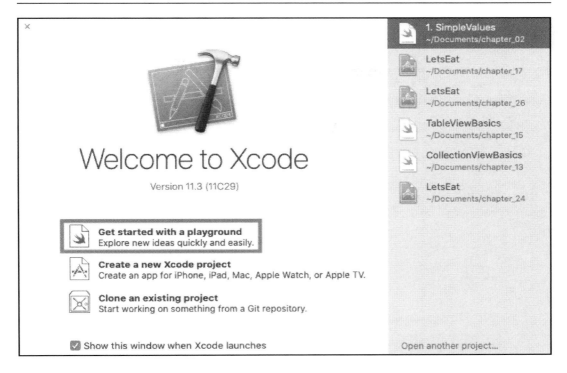

2. If you don't see the welcome screen, you can also choose
   File | New | Playground... from the Xcode menu bar to create a new
   playground.

3. The template screen appears. **iOS** should already be selected. Choose **Blank** and click **Next**:

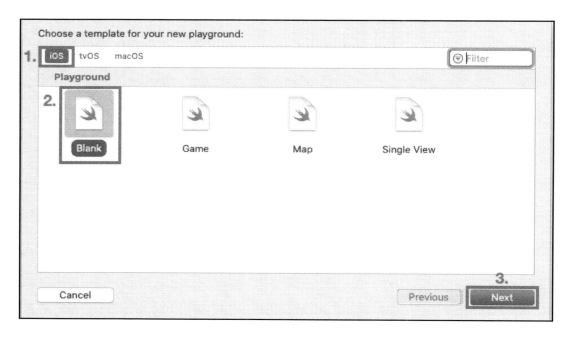

4. Name your playground `SimpleValues` and save it anywhere you like. Click **Create** when done:

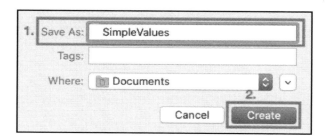

5. You should see the playground on the screen:

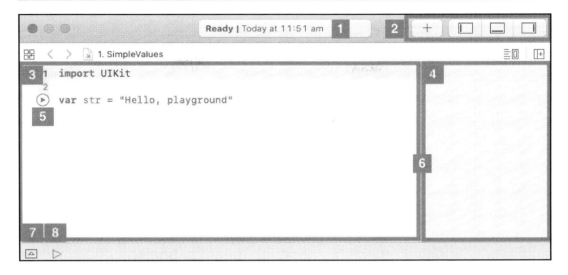

As you can see, it's much simpler than an Xcode project. Let's look at the interface in more detail:

- **Activity View** (1): Shows the current operation or status.
- **Window pane buttons** (2): As we saw in the previous chapter, the first button displays the Library. The remaining three buttons toggle the Navigator, Debug, and Inspector areas.
- **Editor area** (3): You write code here.
- **Results area** (4): Provides immediate feedback to the code you write.
- **Play button** (5): Executes code from a selected line.
- **Border** (6): This border separates the Editor and Results areas. If you find the results displayed in the Results area are truncated, drag the border to the left to increase the size of the Results area.
- **Debug Toggle** (7): Shows and hides the Debug area.
- **Play/Stop button** (8): Executes or stops the execution of all code in the playground.

You may find the code in the playground a bit too small. Let's see how to change that in the next section.

Customizing fonts and colors

Xcode has extensive customization options available. You can access them in the **Preferences...** menu. If you find that the text is small and hard to see, do the following:

1. Choose **Preferences...** from the **Xcode** menu.
2. Click **Fonts & Colors** and choose **Presentation (Light)**:

3. This makes your text larger and easier to read. Close the preferences window to return to the playground. Note that the text is larger than before.
4. Click the Play/Stop button in the bottom-left corner of the playground. You may see the following dialog box:

5. Enter the **Username** and **Password** for your Mac's administrator, and click **Continue**. You will see **"Hello, playground"** displayed in the Results area:

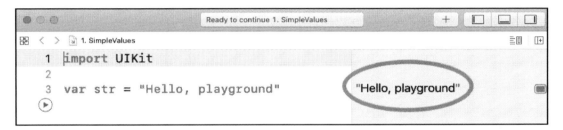

6. Remove the line of code `var str = "Hello, playground"` from the playground.
7. As you go along, type the code shown in this chapter into the playground, and click the Play/Stop button to run it.

Now that you've changed the size of the fonts to make your code easier to read, let's dive into the simple data types used in Swift.

Exploring data types

All programming languages can store numbers, words, and logic conditions, and Swift is no different. Even if you're an experienced programmer, you may find that Swift implements storage for numbers, words, and logic conditions differently from other languages that you might be familiar with. Let's walk through the Swift versions of these simple data types, which are as follows:

- Integers
- Floating-point numbers

- Booleans
- Strings

After this, you will also take a look at how to use constants and variables to store these data types in the playground.

 For more information on data types, visit: `https://docs.swift.org/swift-book/LanguageGuide/TheBasics.html`.

Storing integers

Let's say you want to store the following:

- The number of restaurants in a city
- Passengers in an airplane
- Rooms in a hotel

You would use integers, which are numbers with no fractional component.

Integers in Swift are represented by the `Int` type. Negative numbers are included.

Storing floating-point numbers

Let's say you want to store the following:

- Pi (3.14159...)
- Absolute zero (-273.15 °C)

You would use floating-point numbers, which are numbers with a fractional component. The default type for floating-point numbers in Swift is `Double`, which uses 64 bits, including negative numbers. You can also use `Float`, which uses 32 bits, but `Double` is preferred.

Storing Booleans

Sometimes, you need to store answers to simple yes/no questions, such as the following:

- Is it raining?
- Are there any available seats at the restaurant?

For this, you use Boolean values. Swift provides a `Bool` type that can be assigned `true` or `false`.

Storing strings

A string is a series of characters. You use strings to store things such as the following:

- The name of a restaurant, such as `"Bombay Palace"`
- A job description, such as `"Accountant"` or `"Programmer"`
- A kind of fruit, such as `"banana"`

Swift strings are represented by the `String` type, which is fully Unicode-compliant.

Using common data types in the playground

Now that you know about Swift's implementation of these common data types, let's use them in the playground we created. Perform the following steps:

1. Type the following code into the Editor area of your playground and click the Play/Stop button when done:

```
// Examples of integers
42
-23

// Examples of floating-point numbers
3.14159
0.1
-273.15

// Examples of booleans
true
false
```

```
// Examples of strings
"hello, world"
"albatross"
```

Note that any word with `//` in front of it is a **comment**. Comments are a great way to create notes or reminders to yourself and that will be ignored.

2. Wait a few seconds. You should see the values displayed in the Results area.

Cool! You have just created and run your first playground. Let's look at how to store different data types in the next section.

Exploring constants and variables

Now that you know about the different simple data types that Swift supports, let's look at how to store them, so you can do operations on them later.

You can use **constants** or **variables**. Both are containers that have a name and can store values, but a constant's value can only be set once and can't be changed once it's set.

You must declare constants and variables before you use them. Constants are declared with the `let` keyword and variables with the `var` keyword.

You may have noticed that the names for constants and variables start with a lowercase letter, and if there is more than one word in the name, every subsequent word starts with a capital letter. This is known as **camel case.** You don't have to do this, but this is encouraged, as most experienced Swift programmers adhere to this convention.

Now, let's explore how constants and variables work by implementing them in your playground:

1. Add the following code to your playground and click the Play/Stop button to run it:

```
// Examples of constants
let theAnswerToTheUltimateQuestion = 42
let pi = 3.14159
let myName = "Ahmad Sahar"
```

These are examples of **constants**. In each case, a container is created and named, and the assigned value stored.

2. Enter the following code and run it:

```
// Examples of variables
var currentTemperatureInCelsius = 27
var myAge = 50
var myLocation = "home"
```

These are examples of **variables**. Similar to constants, a container is created and named in each case, and the assigned value stored.

You should see the stored values displayed in the Results area.

3. Add the following code and run it:

```
// Value of a constant can't be changed once it is set
let isRaining = true
isRaining = false
```

As you're typing the second line of code, note that a pop-up menu will appear with suggestions:

```
34   // Value of a constant can
35   let isRaining = true
36   isR|
 V         Bool isRaining
```

Use the up and down arrow keys to choose the `isRaining` constant, and press the *Tab* key to select it. This feature is called **autocomplete** and helps to prevent typing mistakes when you're entering code.

When you have finished typing, wait a few seconds. On the second line, you should see a red circle with a white dot in the middle appear:

```
30   // Value of a constant can't be changed once it is set
31   let isRaining = true
 ▶   isRaining = false   ⊘ Cannot assign to value: 'isRaining' is a 'let'
```

This means there is an error in your program, and Xcode thinks it can be fixed. The error appears because you are trying to assign a new value to a constant after its initial value has been set. Click the red circle.

4. After you have clicked the red circle, you should see the following box with a **Fix** button:

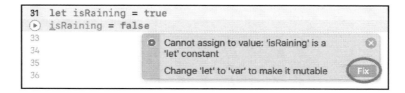

Xcode tells you what the problem is (**Cannot assign to value: 'isRaining' is a 'let' constant**) and suggests a correction (**Change 'let' to 'var' to make it mutable**). Click the **Fix** button.

5. After you have clicked the **Fix** button, you should see the following:

```
29
30   // Value of a constant can't be changed once it is set
31   var isRaining = true
     isRaining = false
33
```

Hey presto! No more errors! Do note, however, that the suggested correction might not be the best solution.

If you look at the code you typed in, you might be wondering how Xcode knows what type of data is stored in a variable or constant. You'll look at that in the next section.

Understanding type inference and type safety

In the previous section, you declared constants and variables and assigned values to them. Swift determines the constant or variable type based on the value you supplied. This is called **type inference**. You can see the type of a constant or variable by holding down the *Option* key and clicking its name:

1. Enter the following code and run it:

```
// Type inference
// Hold down option and click on the variable or constant name
```

```
// to disclose the type should be on one line
let cuisine = "American"
```

2. Now hold down the *Option* key and click `cuisine`. You should see the following:

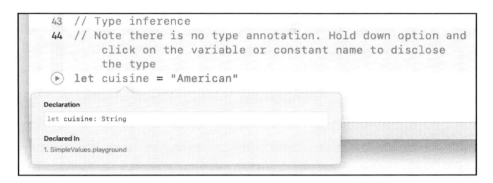

As you can see, `cuisine` is of the `String` type.

What if you want to set a specific type for a variable or constant? You'll see how to do that in the next section.

Using type annotation to specify a type

You've seen that Xcode tries to automatically determine the variable or constant type based on the value provided. However, at times, you may want to specify a type instead. To do this, type a colon after a constant or variable name, followed by the desired type.

Enter the following code and run it:

```
//Type annotation
var restaurantRating: Double = 3
```

Here, you specified `restaurantRating` has a specific type, `Double`. Even though you assigned an integer to `restaurantRating`, it will be stored as a floating-point number.

Now you'll look at how Xcode helps you reduce the number of errors in your program by enforcing type safety.

Type safety

Swift is a type-safe language. It checks to see whether you're assigning values of the correct type to variables and flags mismatched types as errors. Let's see how this works:

1. Enter the following code and run it:

```
// Type safety
restaurantRating = "Good"
```

Here, you are trying to assign a string to a variable of type `Double`. This is a type mismatch and you'll see a red circle with an exclamation mark inside it:

```
38  // Type safety
39  // Uncomment the line to see the error
    restaurantRating = "Good"
41
42          Cannot assign value of type 'String' to type
43          'Double'
```

The exclamation mark means Xcode can't suggest a fix for this.

2. Comment out the line by typing two / characters in front of it so it no longer causes an error in your program:

```
// Type safety
// restaurantRating = "Good"
```

Now that you know how to store data in constants and variables, let's look at how to perform operations on them.

Exploring operators

You can perform arithmetic, comparison, and logical operations in Swift. Arithmetic operators are for common mathematical operations. Comparison and logical operators check an expression's value and return `true` or `false`.

Let's look at each operator type in more detail.

For more information on operators, visit `https://docs.swift.org/swift-book/LanguageGuide/BasicOperators.html`.

Using arithmetic operators

You can perform mathematical operations on integer and floating-point numbers by using the standard **arithmetic operators**:

+	Addition
-	Subtraction
*	Multiplication
/	Division

Let's see how these operators are used:

1. Enter the following code and run it:

    ```
    // Operations with numbers
    // (+) operator for addition
    let sum = 23 + 20
    // (-) operator for subtraction
    let result = 32 - sum
    // (*) operator for multiplication
    let total = result * 5
    // (/) operator for division
    let divide = total/10
    ```

    The results displayed in the Results area will be 43, −11, −55, and −5, respectively. Note that 55 divided by 10 returns 5 instead of 5.5, as both numbers are integers.

2. Operators can only work with operands of the same type. Enter the following code and run it:

    ```
    // Operators can only work with operands of the same type
    let a = 12
    let b = 12.0
    let c = a + b
    ```

You'll get an error message, **Binary operator '+' cannot be applied to operands of type 'Int' and 'Double'.** This is because a and b are different types. Note that Xcode can't fix this automatically, so it does not display any *fix-it* suggestions.

3. To fix it, modify the program as follows:

```
let c = Double(a) + b
```

This will convert the value in a to a floating-point number so that you can add the value in b to it. The result, 24, will be displayed in the Results area.

This concludes the section on arithmetic operators. We'll look at compound assignment operators next.

Using compound assignment operators

You can perform an operation on a value and assign the result to the variable using **compound assignment operators**:

+=	Adds a value and assigns the result to the variable
-=	Subtracts a value and assigns the result to the variable
*=	Multiplies with the value and assigns the result to the variable
/=	Divides with the value and assigns the result to the variable

Let's see how these operators are used. Enter the following code and run it:

```
// compound assignment operators
var aa = 1
aa += 2
// aa is now equal to 3
aa -= 1
// aa is now equal to 2
```

The a += 2 expression is shorthand for a = a + 2, so the value in a is now 1 + 2, and 3 will be assigned to a. In the same way, a -= 1 is shorthand for a = a - 1, so the value in a is now 3 - 1, and 2 will be assigned to a.

Now that you are familiar with compound assignment operators, let's look at comparison operators.

Using comparison operators

You can compare one value to another using **comparison operators**, and the result will be `true` or `false`. You can use the following comparison operators:

Operators	Description
==	Equal to
!=	Not equal to
>	Greater than
<	Less than
>=	Greater than or equal to
<=	Less than or equal to

Let's see how these operators are used. Enter the following code and run it:

```
//comparison operators
1 == 1 // equal to, true because 1 is equal to 1
2 != 1   // not equal to, true because 2 is not equal to 1
2 > 1  // greater than, true because 2 is greater than 1
1 < 2  // less than, true because 1 is less than 2
1 >= 1 // greater or equal to, true because 1 is greater than or equal
to 1
2 <= 1 // less or equal to, false because 2 is not less than or equal
to 1
```

All the statements except for the last one will return `true`. The last statement will return `false`. The returned Boolean values will be displayed in the Results area.

What happens if you want to check more than one condition? That's where logical operators come in. You'll study those in the next section.

Using logical operators

Logical operators are handy when you have to deal with two or more conditions. For example, if you are at a convenience store, you can pay for items if you have cash or a credit card. **Or** is the logical operator in this case.

You can use the following logical operators:

&&	Logical AND—returns `true` only if all conditions are true
||	Logical OR—returns `true` if any condition is true
!	Logical NOT—returns the opposite Boolean value

To see how these operators are used, enter the following code and run it:

```
// logical operators
(1 == 1) && (2 == 2) // logical AND operator, true because both
                        operands are true, so true AND true
                        returns true
(1 == 1) && (2 != 2) // logical AND operator, false because one
                        operand is false, so true AND false
                        returns false
(1 == 1) || (2 == 2) // logical OR operator, true because both
                        operands are true, so true OR true
                        returns true
(1 == 1) || (2 != 2) // logical OR operator, true because one operand
                        is true, so true OR false returns true
(1 != 1) || (2 != 2) // logical OR operator, false because both
                        operands are false, so false OR false
                        returns false
!(1 == 1) // logical NOT operator, false because 1==1 is true,
            so NOT true returns false
```

The returned Boolean values are `true`, `false`, `true`, `true`, `false`, and `false`, and will be displayed in the Results area.

So far, you've only worked with numbers. In the next section, you'll see how you can perform operations on strings.

 For more information on strings, visit: `https://docs.swift.org/swift-book/LanguageGuide/StringsAndCharacters.html`.

Performing string operations

You can join two strings together using the `'+'` operator:

1. Enter the following code and run it:

   ```
   // you can concatenate two string using the '+' operator
   let greeting = "Good" + " Morning"
   ```

   The `"Good"` string is concatenated with the string `" Morning"`, and `"Good Morning"` is displayed in the Results area.

   You can combine strings with constants and variables of other types by casting them as strings.

2. Enter the following code and run it:

```
// you can cast an integer or real as a string to concatenate
it with another string
let rating = 3.5
var ratingResult = "The restaurant rating is " +
String(rating)
```

The `rating` object contains `3.5`, a value of type `Double`. Putting `rating` in `String()` converts the floating-point number into a string, `"3.5"`, which is combined with the string in `ratingResult`, returning the string `"The restaurant rating is 3.5"`.

There is a simpler way of combining strings though, called **string interpolation**. String interpolation is done by typing the name of a constant or variable between `"\("` and `")"` in a string.

3. Enter the following code and run it:

```
// you can also use string interpolation
ratingResult = "The restaurant rating is \(rating)"
```

As in the previous example, the value in `rating` is converted into a string, `"3.5"`, returning the string `"The restaurant rating is 3.5"`.

It is often very useful if you can display the contents of variables and constants to make sure your program is working as it should. In the next part, you'll see how to print stuff to the Debug area.

Using the print() instruction

Using the `print()` command will print anything between the brackets to the Debug area.

Enter the following code and run it:

```
// This will print the ratingResult to the Debug area
print(ratingResult)
```

The value of `ratingResult` appears in the Debug area:

```
98  //This will print the ratingResult to the Debug area
99  print(ratingResult)                                    "The restaurant rating is 3.5\n"

The restaurant rating is 3.5
```

When you're just starting out, feel free to use as many `print()` statements as you like. It's a really good way to understand what is happening in your program.

Summary

In this lesson, you learned how to create and use playground files, which allow you to explore and experiment with Swift. The more you explore and experiment, the more you will learn. You saw how Swift implements data types, and how to use constants and variables to store numbers, words, and logic statements in your program. You also learned about type inference, type annotation, and type safety, which help you to write code concisely and with fewer errors. You looked at how to perform operations on numbers and strings, how to fix errors, and how to print to the Debug area to help you understand how your program works.

At this point, you can now write simple programs that process letters and numbers. You now know how to create and save playgrounds, the different data types, how to create and use variables and constants, how to use type inference to assign variable types, and how to perform common operations. Good job!

In the next chapter, you'll look at options and conditionals. Options deal with cases where a variable may or may not have a value, and conditionals deal with branching in your program.

Conditionals and Optionals

3

In the last chapter, you looked at data types, constants and variables, and operations. At this point, you are able to write simple programs that process letters and numbers. However, in many cases, programs are not linear, which is to say they don't always proceed in sequence. Oftentimes, you will need to execute different instructions based on a condition. Swift allows you to do this by using **conditionals**, and you will learn how to use them in this chapter.

Another thing you may have noticed is that, in the last chapter, each variable or constant was immediately assigned a value. What if you require a variable where the value may not be present initially? You will need a way to create a variable that may or may not have a value. Swift allows you to do this by using **optionals**, and you will also learn about them in this chapter.

By the end of this chapter, you should be able to write programs that do different things based on different conditions, and to handle variables that may or may not have a value.

The following topics will be covered:

- Introducing conditionals
- Introducing optionals

Please spend some time understanding optionals. They can be daunting for the novice programmer.

Technical requirements

The Xcode playground for this chapter is in the `Chapter03` folder of the code bundle for this book, which can be downloaded here:

`https://github.com/PacktPublishing/iOS-13-Programming-for-Beginners.`

If you wish to start from scratch, create a new playground and name it `ConditionalsAndOptionals`.

You can type in and run all the code in this chapter as you go along. You'll start by learning about conditionals.

Check out the following video to see the code in action:

`http://bit.ly/3aKLiGS`

Introducing conditionals

At times, you want to execute different code blocks based on a condition, such as in the following scenarios:

- Choosing between different room types at a hotel. The room price for bigger rooms would be higher.
- Switching between different payment methods at an online store. Procedures for different payment methods would be different.
- Deciding what to order at a fast-food restaurant. Preparation procedures for each food item would be different.

To do this, you would use conditionals. In Swift, this is implemented using `if` and `switch` statements. Let's take a look at them now.

 For more information on conditionals, visit `https://docs.swift.org/swift-book/LanguageGuide/ControlFlow.html`.

Using if statements

A basic if statement looks like this:

```
if condition {
code
}
```

The code in the curly braces is executed if the condition is true.

Let's implement an if statement now to see this in action:

1. Type in and run the following code:

```
// If statements execute code in curly braces if the condition
is true
let isPictureVisible = true
// if the value is changed to false nothing would be printed
if isPictureVisible {
 print("Picture is visible")
}
```

First, you created a constant, isPictureVisible, and assigned true to it. Next, you have an if statement that checks the value stored in isPictureVisible. Since the value is true, the print statement is executed and Picture is visible is printed in the Debug area.

2. Try changing the value of isPictureVisible to false and run your code again. As the condition is now false, nothing will be printed.

3. You can also execute statements if a condition is false. Type in and run the following code:

```
// isRestaurantFound == false returns true, so the print
statement is executed
let isRestaurantFound = false
// if the value is changed to true nothing will be printed
if isRestaurantFound == false {
print("Restaurant was not found")
}
```

The constant isRestaurantFound is set to false. Next, the if statement is checked. The isRestaurantFound == false condition returns true, and "Restaurant was not found" is printed in the Debug area.

4. Try changing the value of `isRestaurantFound` to `true` and run your code again. As the condition is now false, nothing will be printed.

What if you want to do one set of statements if a condition is true, and another set of statements if a condition is false? You use the `else` keyword.

5. Type in and run the following code:

```
// if-else statement. Code after the else keyword is executed
if the condition is false
let drinkingAgeLimit = 21
var customerAge = 19
// experiment by changing the customer age to a value greater
than 21
if customerAge < drinkingAgeLimit {
print("Under age limit")
} else {
print("Over age limit")
}
```

Here, `drinkingAgeLimit` is assigned the value 21 and `customerAge` is assigned the value 19. In the `if` statement, `customerAge < drinkingAgeLimit` is checked. Since 19 < 21 returns true , `Under age limit` is printed in the Debug area.

If you change `customerAge` value to 22, `customerAge < drinkingAgeLimit` will return false, so `Over age limit` will be printed in the Debug area.

Up to now, you have only been dealing with single conditions. What if there are multiple conditions? That's where `switch` statements come in, and you will see them in the next section.

Using switch statements

Let's say you're programming a traffic light. There are three possible conditions for the traffic light—red, yellow, or green—and you want something different to happen based on the color of the light. To do this, you can chain multiple `if` statements together:

1. Type in and run the following code:

```
// Implementing a traffic light program using multiple if
statements
var trafficLight = "Yellow"
// Try changing the value of trafficLight to get different
```

```
results
if trafficLight == "Red" {
    print("Stop")
} else if trafficLight == "Yellow" {
    print("Caution")
} else if trafficLight == "Green" {
    print("Go")
} else {
    print("Invalid Color")
}
```

The first `if` condition, `trafficLight == "Red"`, returns `false`, so the statement after `else` is executed. The second `if` condition, `trafficLight == "Yellow"`, returns `true`, so `Caution` is printed in the Debug area and no more `if` conditions are evaluated. Try changing the value of `trafficLight` to see different results. This works, but it's a little hard to read.

In this case, a `switch` statement works better. A basic `switch` statement looks like this:

```
switch value {
    case firstValue:
    code
    case secondValue:
    code
    default:
    code
}
```

The `value` is checked and matched to a `case`, and code for that case is executed. If none of the cases match, the code in `default` is executed.

2. Here's how to write the `if` statement shown earlier as a `switch` statement. Type in and run the following code:

```
// the same traffic light program implemented using a switch
statement
// Note: you can't fall-through to the next case once a case
is matched
// Note: switch statements must cover all possible cases
trafficLight = "Yellow"
switch trafficLight {
case "Red":
    print("Stop")
case "Yellow":
```

```
        print("Caution")
case "Green":
        print("Go")
default:
        print("Invalid color")
}
```

The code here is much easier to read and understand when compared to the prior implementation, which used the `if` statement. The value in `trafficLight` is "Yellow", so `case "Yellow":` is matched and "Caution" is printed in the Debug area. Try changing the value of `trafficLight` to see different results.

There are two things to remember about `switch` statements:

- First, `switch` statements in Swift do not fall through the bottom of each case and into the next one by default. In the example shown previously, once `case "Red":` is matched, `case "Yellow":`, `case "Green":`, and `default:` will not execute.
- Second, a `switch` must cover all possible cases. So in the example shown previously, any `trafficLight` color other than "Red", "Yellow", or "Green" will be matched to `default:` and `Invalid color` will be printed in the Debug area.

This concludes the section on `if` and `switch` statements. In the next section, you'll learn about optionals, which allow you to create variables without initial values, and optional binding, which allows instructions to be executed if an optional has a value.

Introducing optionals

Up until now, every time you declare a variable or constant, you assign a value immediately. As you will see, Swift does not allow you to declare a variable or constant without a value. But what if you want to declare a variable first and assign a value later? In this case, you would use optionals.

 For more information on optionals, visit `https://docs.swift.org/swift-book/LanguageGuide/TheBasics.html`.

Let's take a look at how to create and use optionals now, and see how they may be used in a program.

Using optionals and optional binding

Imagine you're writing a program where the user needs to enter the name of their spouse. Of course, if the user is not married, there would be no value for this. So you can use an optional to represent the spouse name. Let's see how this works:

1. Type in and run the following code:

```
// optionals
var spouseName: String
print(spouseName)
```

Since Swift is type-safe, it will display an error, **Variable 'spouseName' used before being initialized.**

2. You could assign an empty string to spouseName as follows. Modify your code as shown:

```
// optionals
var spouseName: String = ""
print(spouseName)
```

This makes the error go away, but an empty string is still a value, and we don't want spouseName to have a value.

In cases like these, we can use optionals. An optional may have one of two possible states. Either it does not contain a value, or it contains a value, and you can access the value by a process called **unwrapping**.

3. To make spouseName an optional, type a question mark after the type annotation and run your program:

```
// optionals
var spouseName: String?
print(spouseName)
```

Even though there is a warning, the program will execute. Ignore the warning for now:

```
57  // optionals
58  var spouseName: String?                                                    nil
59  print(spouseName)    ⚠  Expression implicitly coerced from 'String?' to 'Any'  "nil\n"
```

The value of `spouseName` is shown as `"nil\n"` in the Results area, and `nil` is printed in the Debug area. `nil` is a special keyword that means the optional has no value.

4. Let's assign a value to `spouseName`. Modify the code as shown:

```
// optionals
var spouseName: String?
spouseName = "Lydia"
print(spouseName)
```

When you run this, you would expect `Lydia` to appear in the Debug area. Instead, `Optional("Lydia")` is printed, showing that the optional has not been unwrapped.

5. Add one more line of code as follows:

```
// optionals
var spouseName: String?
spouseName = "Lydia"
print(spouseName)
let greeting = "Hello, " + spouseName
```

You'll get an error, and the Debug area shows you where the error occurred.

This happened because you can't use an optional's value without unwrapping it first.

6. Click on the red circle to display possible fixes, and you'll see the following:

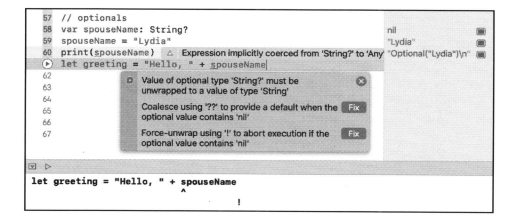

7. Click the second fix, and you'll see an exclamation mark appear after `spouseName` in the last line of code. The program runs fine now, and the value of `greeting` is `Hello, Lydia` as shown in the Results area. **Force-unwrapping** unwraps an optional whether it contains a value or not. It works fine if `spouseName` has a value, but if `spouseName` is `nil`, your program will crash.

8. To see this, modify your program as shown and run it:

```
// optionals
var spouseName: String?
spouseName = nil
print(spouseName)
let greeting = "Hello, " + spouseName!
```

Your program crashes, and you can see what caused the crash in the Debug area:

```
57  // optionals
58  var spouseName: String?
59  spouseName = nil
60  print(spouseName)      ⚠ Expression implicitly coerced from 'String?' to 'Any'
⏵  let greeting = "Hello, " + spouseName!   ⓧ error: Execution was...  ⓧ error
62
⌄ ▷
Caution
nil
Fatal error: Unexpectedly found nil while unwrapping an Optional value: file 2.
Conditionals and optionals.playground, line 61
```

Since `spouseName` is now `nil`, the program crashed while attempting to force-unwrap `spouseName`.

A better way of handling this is to use optional binding. In optional binding, we attempt to assign the value in an optional to a temporary variable (we can name it whatever we like). If the assignment is successful, a block of code is executed.

9. Modify your program as follows and run it:

```
// optionals
var spouseName: String?
spouseName = "Lydia"
print(spouseName)
// optional binding
if let spouse = spouseName {
```

```
        let greeting = "Hello, " + spouse
        print(greeting)
    }
```

Here's how it works. If `spouseName` has a value, it will be unwrapped and assigned to `spouse`, and the `if` statement will return true. The statements between the curly braces will be executed and the constant `greeting` will then be assigned to the value `"Hello, Lydia"`. Then, `Hello, Lydia` will be printed in the Debug area. Note that `spouse` is not an optional.

If `spouseName` does not have a value, no value can be assigned to `spouse` and the `if` statement will return `false`. In this case, the statements in the curly braces will not be executed at all.

10. Modify your program as follows and run it:

```
// optionals
var spouseName: String?
spouseName = nil
print(spouseName)
if let spouse = spouseName {
    let greeting = "Hello, " + spouse
    print(greeting)
}
```

You'll notice that nothing appears in the Debug area, and your program no longer crashes even though `spouseName` is `nil`.

This concludes the section on optionals and optional binding. Awesome!

Summary

You're doing great! You learned how to use `if` and `switch` statements, and you also learned about optionals and optional binding.

You are now able to write your own programs that use `if` and `if-then` statements to do different things based on different conditions, use optionals to handle variables in your programs that may or may not have a value, and to use optional binding to execute instructions if a variable or constant's value is present.

In the next chapter, you will study how to use a range of values instead of single values, and how to repeat program statements using loops.

Range Operators and Loops

4

In the last chapter, you looked at conditionals, which allow you to do different things based on different conditions, and optionals, which enable you to create variables that may or may not have a value. You were able to create more complex programs.

Sometimes, you will need to represent a range of numbers instead of discrete values. Swift uses **range operators** for this, which makes it easy to specify the start and end points for a range. You will learn about the different types of range operators in this chapter.

In programming, you frequently need to repeat an operation over and over again. Swift handles this by using **loops**. You can repeat a sequence a fixed number of times, or repeat a sequence until a condition is met. You will learn about the different types of loops in this chapter.

By the end of this chapter, you'll have learned how to use ranges, and how to create and use the different types of loops (`for-in`, `while`, and `repeat-while`).

The following topics will be covered:

- Range operators
- Loops

Technical requirements

The Xcode playground for this chapter is in the `Chapter04` folder of the code bundle for this book, which can be downloaded here:

`https://github.com/PacktPublishing/iOS-13-Programming-for-Beginners`

If you wish to start from scratch, create a new playground and name it `RangeOperatorsAndLoops`.

You can type in and run all the code in this chapter as you go along. Let's start with how to specify a range of numbers using range operators.

Check out the following video to see the code in action:

`http://bit.ly/2GgwXE8`

Range operators

Imagine you need to write a program for a department store. This program will automatically send a discount voucher to customers between the ages of 18 and 30. It would be very cumbersome if you needed to set up an `if` or `switch` statement for each age. It's much more convenient if there was a way to specify a range of numbers, and that is what a **range operator** does.

 For more information on range operators, visit: `https://docs.swift.org/swift-book/LanguageGuide/BasicOperators.html`.

Let's say you want to represent a sequence of numbers from 10 to 20. You don't need to specify every value; you can just specify the first number and the last number in this way:

`firstNumber...lastNumber`

Let's try this out in the playground. Do the following steps.

1. Type the following into the playground and run it:

   ```
   // closed range operator
   let myRange = 10...20
   ```

   This will assign a number sequence that starts with `10` and ends with `20`, including both numbers, to the constant, `myRange`. This is known as a **closed range operator**.

   Note that the result displayed in the Results area may be truncated.

2. Click the square icon to the right of the result. It will be displayed inline in the Editor area:

If you don't want to include the last number in the sequence in the range, use . . < in place of . . . .

3. Type in and run the following code:

```
// half-open range operator
let myRange2 = 10..<20
```

This will store the sequence starting with 10 and ending with 19 in myRange2, and is known as a **half-open range operator**.

There is one more type of range operator, the **one-sided range operator**, and you will learn about that in the next chapter.

Now that you know what range operators are, you will study loops and see how they are used in for-in loops to determine how many times the loop body is executed.

Loops

In programming, you frequently need to do the same thing over and over again. For example, each month, the company you work for will need to generate payroll slips for each employee. If you have 10,000 employees, it would be inefficient to write 10,000 instructions. Repeating a single instruction 10,000 times would be better, and loops are used for this.

There are three types of loop; the `for-in` loop, the `while` loop, and the `repeat-while` loop. Let's look at each type in turn, starting with the `for-in` loop, which is used when you know how many times a loop should be repeated.

 For more information on loops, visit: `https://docs.swift.org/swift-book/LanguageGuide/ControlFlow.html`.

The for-in loop

The `for-in` loop steps through every value in a sequence. You can assign each value to a variable in turn. Here is what it looks like:

```
for item in sequence {
     code
  }
```

The number of times the loop repeats is dictated by the number of items in the sequence.

Let's begin by creating a `for-in` loop to display all the numbers in `myRange`:

1. Type in and run the following code:

```
for number in myRange {
    print(number)
}
```

You should see each number in the sequence displayed in the Debug area. Note that the statements inside the loop are executed 11 times since `myRange` includes the last number in the range. Let's try the same program, but this time with `myRange2`.

2. Modify the code as follows and run it:

```
for number in myRange2 {
    print(number)
}
```

The statements inside the loop are executed 10 times, and the last value printed is **19**.

You can even use a range operator directly after the `in` keyword.

3. Type and run the following code:

```
for number in 0...5 {
print(number)
}
```

If you want the sequence to be reversed, use the `reversed` keyword.

4. Modify the code as follows and run it:

```
for number in (0...5).reversed() {
print(number)
}
```

Great job! Let's check out `while` loops next, which are used when you're not sure how many times a loop sequence should be repeated.

The while loop

A `while` loop contains a condition and a set of statements in curly braces. The condition is checked first; if `true`, the set of statements are executed, and the loop repeats until the condition is `false`. Here is what it looks like:

```
while condition == true {
  code
  }
```

Type and run the following code:

```
// while loop
// condition is checked, and if true, the set of statements in the
curly braces are executed
var y = 0
while y < 50 {
 y += 5
 print("y is \(y)")
}
```

Initially, `y` is set to 0. The `y < 50` condition is checked and returns `true`, so the statements inside the curly braces are executed. The value of `y` is incremented by 5, and `y is 10` is printed in the Debug area. The loop repeats, and `y < 50` is checked again. Since `y` is now 10 and `10 < 50` still returns true, the statements inside the curly braces are executed again. This is repeated until the value of `y` is 50, at which point `y < 50` returns `false` and the loop stops.

If the `while` loop's condition is `false`, to begin with, the statements inside the curly braces will never be executed. Try changing the value of `y` to `100` to see this.

Now you'll study `repeat-while` loops. These are also used when you don't know how many times a loop should repeat, but the loop condition is only checked after the statements have been executed.

The repeat-while loop

A `repeat-while` loop also contains a condition and a set of statements in curly braces, but it executes the statements first before checking the condition, repeating until the condition returns `false`. Here is what it looks like:

```
repeat {
    code
} while condition == true
```

Type and run the following code:

```
// repeat loop
// set of statements is executed, then the condition is checked
var x = 0
repeat {
    x += 5
    print("x is \(x)")
} while x < 50
```

Initially, `x` is set to `0`. The statements inside the curly braces are executed. The value of `x` is incremented by 5, so now `x` contains 5, and `x is 5` is printed to the Debug area. The `x < 50` condition is checked, and since it returns `true`, the loop is repeated. The value of `x` is incremented by 5, so now `x` contains 10, and `x is 10` is printed to the Debug area. The loop is repeated until `x` contains 50, at which point `x < 50` returns `false` and the loop stops.

The statements in the curly braces will be executed at least once, even if the condition is `false`, to begin with. Try changing the value of `x` to `100` to see this.

This concludes the section on loops.

Summary

In this chapter, you looked at closed and half-open range operators, which allow you to specify a range of numbers rather than specifying every individual number discretely. You also learned about the three different loop types, the `for-in` loop, the `while` loop, and the `repeat-while` loop, and how best to use them depending on the situation.

You are now able to write your own programs that uses range operators to specify a range of numbers, and uses loops to easily perform repetitive tasks. You are also able to determine which type of loop is best suited to your program. Great job!

In the next chapter, you will study collection types, which allow you to store a collection of data that can be referenced by an index, and a collection of key-value pairs.

Collection Types 5

So far you've learned quite a lot! You can now create a program that stores data in constants or variables and performs operations on them, and you can control the flow using conditionals and loops. But so far, you've mostly been storing single values. Now you will learn ways to store collections of values. Swift has three collection types: **arrays**, which store an ordered list of values; **dictionaries**, which store a list of key-value pairs; and **sets**, which store an unordered list of values.

By the end of this chapter, you'll have learned how to create arrays, dictionaries, and sets and how to perform operations on them.

The following topics will be covered:

- Understanding arrays
- Understanding dictionaries
- Understanding sets

Technical requirements

The Xcode playground for this chapter is in the `Chapter05` folder of the code bundle for this book, which can be downloaded here:

`https://github.com/PacktPublishing/iOS-13-Programming-for-Beginners`.

If you wish to start from scratch, create a new playground and name it `CollectionTypes`.

You can type in and run all of the code in this chapter as you go along. The first collection type you will learn about are arrays, which allow you to store information in an ordered list.

Check out the following video to see the code in action:

```
http://bit.ly/2utxHmk
```

Understanding arrays

Let's say you want to store the following:

- List of items to buy at the supermarket
- Chores that you have to do every month

You would use an array for this.

An array stores values in an ordered list. Here's what it looks like:

Index	Value
0	value1
1	value2
2	value3

Values must be of the same type. You can access any value in an array by using the array index, which starts with 0.

If you create an array using the `let` keyword, its contents can't be changed after it has been created. If you want to change the contents after creation, use the `var` keyword.

Let's look at how to work with arrays. You'll start by creating an array.

Creating an array

You can create an array by assigning some initial values to it. Type the following into your playground and run it:

```
// Arrays
// Creating an array
var shoppingList = ["Eggs", "Milk"]
```

Next, you'll learn how to find out how many items there are in an array.

Checking the number of elements in an array

To find out how many items there are in an array, use `count`. Type and run the following code:

```
// count returns the number of items in an array
shoppingList.count
```

`2` is displayed in the Results area.

You can check whether an array is empty by using `isEmpty`. Type and run the following code:

```
// isEmpty returns true if an array is empty
shoppingList.isEmpty
```

`false` is displayed in the Results area.

Now, let's see how to add items to arrays.

Adding a new item to an array

You can add a new item to the end of an array by using `append(_:)`. Type and run the following code:

```
// Add "Cooking Oil" to the end of the array
shoppingList.append("Cooking Oil")
shoppingList
```

The array now has three items, `"Eggs"`, `"Milk"`, and `"Cooking Oil"`, and this can be seen in the Results area.

You can add a new item at a particular index using `insert(_:at:)`. Type and run the following code:

```
// Add "Chicken" at index 1 in the array
shoppingList.insert("Chicken", at: 1)
shoppingList
```

This inserts `"Chicken"` at index 1, so now the array contains `"Eggs"`, `"Chicken"`, `"Milk"`, and `"Cooking Oil"`, and this can be seen in the Results area.

Next, you'll see how to access specific elements in an array.

Accessing an array element

You can use the array index to access its elements. Type and run the following code:

```
// Access the element at index 2 ("Milk")
shoppingList[2]
```

`"Milk"` is displayed in the Results area.

Let's see how to assign new values to an index next.

Assigning a new value to an index

You can also assign a new value to an index. Type and run the following code:

```
// Assign a new value, "Soy Milk" to index 2
shoppingList[2] = "Soy Milk"
shoppingList
```

`ShoppingList` now consists of `"Eggs"`, `"Chicken"`, `"Soy Milk"`, and `"Cooking Oil"`, and you can see this in the Results area.

Note that the index used must be valid.

Now, let's learn how to remove items from arrays.

Removing an item from an array

You can remove an item from an array by using `remove(at:)`. Type and run the following code:

```
// Remove the item at index 1, "Chicken", from the array
shoppingList.remove(at: 1)
shoppingList
```

This removes `"Chicken"` from the array, so now it consists of `"Eggs"`, `"Soy Milk"`, and `"Cooking Oil"`.

If you're removing the last item from the array, use `removeLast()` instead.

Finally, let's see how to iterate over an array.

Iterating over an array

Remember the `for-in` loop you studied in the previous chapter? You can use it to iterate over every item in an array. Type and run the following code:

```
// Iterating over an array
for shoppingListItem in shoppingList {
print(shoppingListItem)
}
```

This prints out every item in the array to the Debug area.

You can also use **one-sided range operators**. These are range operators with the value only on one side, for example, `1....`. Type in and run the following code:

```
// one-sided range operators
for shoppingListItem in shoppingList[1...] {
print(shoppingListItem)
}
```

This prints out items starting with index `1`, and continuing till the end of the array, to the Debug area.

This concludes the section on arrays, so now let's look at the second collection type, dictionaries. Dictionaries allow you to store a list of key-value pairs.

Understanding dictionaries

Let's say you're writing a *contacts* app. You would need to store a list of names and their corresponding contact numbers. A dictionary would be perfect for this.

A dictionary stores key-value pairs in an unordered list. Here's what it looks like:

Key	Value
Key 1	Value 1
Key 2	Value 2
Key 3	Value 3

All **Keys** must be of the same type and must be unique. All **Values** must be of the same type. **Keys** and **Values** don't have to be of the same type, though. You use the **Key** to get the corresponding **Value**.

If you create a dictionary using the `let` keyword, its contents can't be changed after it has been created. If you want to change the contents after creation, use the `var` keyword.

Let's look at how to work with dictionaries. You'll start by creating a dictionary.

Creating a dictionary

You can create a dictionary by assigning some initial values to it. Type the following into your playground and run it:

```
// Dictionaries
// Creating a dictionary
var contactList = ["Shah" : "+60123456789", "Akhil" : "+0223456789" ]
```

This creates a dictionary variable, `contactList`, with two key-value pairs inside it. Each key-value pair is a combination of a unique key and a value. You don't have to specify a type because Swift uses type inference to figure out the type based on the values you assigned. Note that the `var` keyword was used; this means you can change the contents of the dictionary after it has been created.

Now, let's see how to find out how many items there are in a dictionary.

Checking the number of elements in a dictionary

To find out how many items there are in a dictionary, use `count`. Type and run the following code:

```
// count returns the number of items in a dictionary
contactList.count
```

2 is displayed in the Results area.

You can check whether a dictionary is empty by using `isEmpty`. Type and run the following code:

```
// isEmpty returns true if a dictionary is empty
contactList.isEmpty
```

`false` is displayed in the Results area.

Now, let's see how to add new items to a dictionary.

Adding a new item to a dictionary

To add a new item to a dictionary, provide a key and assign a value to it. Type in and run the following code:

```
// Add a new item, with key "Kajal" and value "+0229876543"
contactList["Kajal"] = "+0229876543"
contactList
```

This adds a new item with the `"Kajal"` key and the `"+0229876543"` value to the dictionary. `contactList` now consists of `"Shah"` : `"+60126789345"`, `"Akhil"` : `"+0223456789"`, and `"Kajal"` : `"+0229876543"`. You can see this in the Results area.

Next, you'll see how to access dictionary elements.

Accessing a dictionary element

You can use the dictionary key to access its corresponding value. Type and run the following code:

```
// Access the element with key "Shah"
contactList["Shah"]
```

`"+60123456789"` is displayed in the Results area.

Let's now see how to assign new values to a key.

Assigning a new value to a key

You can also assign a new value to a key. Type and run the following code:

```
// Assign a new value, "+60126789345" to key "Shah"
contactList["Shah"] = "+60126789345"
contactList
```

contactList now consists of "Shah" : "+60126789345", "Akhil" :
"+0223456789", and "Kajal" : "+0229876543". You can see this in the Results
area.

Let's see how to remove items from a dictionary next.

Removing an item from a dictionary

To remove an item from a dictionary, assign nil to an existing key. Type in and run
the following code:

```
// Removing "Kajal" from the dictionary
contactList["Kajal"] = nil
contactList
```

contactList now consists of "Shah" : "+60126789345" and "Akhil" :
"+0223456789". You can see this in the Results area.

If you want to assign the value you are removing to a variable or constant, use
removeValue(for:Key) instead. Modify your code as follows:

```
// Removing "Kajal" from the dictionary
var oldDictValue = contactList.removeValue(forKey: "Kajal")
oldDictValue
contactList
```

oldDictValue ("+0229876543") and contactList ("Shah" :
"+60126789345" and "Akhil" : "+0223456789") are displayed in the Results
area.

Finally, let's look at how to iterate over a dictionary.

Iterating over a dictionary

You can use a `for-in` loop to iterate over every item in a dictionary. Type in and run the following code:

```
// Iterating over a dictionary
for (name, contactNumber) in contactList {
print("\(name) : \(contactNumber)")
}
```

This will print every item in the dictionary to the Debug area. Since dictionaries are unsorted, you may get the results in a different order when you run this code again.

This concludes the section on dictionaries. Let's look at the third collection type, sets. Sets are used to store an unordered list of values.

Understanding sets

Let's say you're writing a *movie* app and you want to store a list of movie genres. You could implement this using a set.

A set stores values in an unordered list. Here's what it looks like:

Value
Value 1
Value 2
Value 3

All values must be of the same type.

If you create a set using the `let` keyword, its contents can't be changed after it has been created. If you want to change the contents after creation, use the `var` keyword.

Let's look at how to work with sets. You'll start by creating a set.

Creating a set

You can create a set by assigning some initial values to it. Type the following into your playground and run it:

```
// Sets
// Creating a set
var movieGenres: Set = ["Horror", "Action", "Romantic Comedy" ]
```

This creates a set variable, `movieGenres`, with three values inside it. You have to specify the type for `movieGenres` because, otherwise, Swift will create an array variable and not a set variable. Note that the `var` keyword was used; this means you can change the contents of the set after it has been created.

Now, let's learn how to find the number of elements in a set.

Checking the number of elements in a set

To find out how many items there are in a set, use `count`. Type and run the following code:

```
// count returns the number of items in a set
movieGenres.count
```

`3` is displayed in the Results area.

You can check whether a set is empty by using `isEmpty`. Type and run the following code:

```
// isEmpty returns true if a set is empty
movieGenres.isEmpty
```

`false` is displayed in the Results area.

Next, you'll learn how to add new items to a set.

Adding a new item to a set

To add a new item to a set, use `insert(_:)`. Type in and run the following code:

```
// Add "War" to the set
movieGenres.insert("War")
movieGenres
```

That adds a new item, `"War"`, to the set. `{"Horror", "Romantic Comedy", "War", "Action"}` is displayed in the Results area.

Next, you'll learn how to check whether a set contains a specific item.

Checking whether a set contains an item

To check whether a set contains an item, use `contains(_:)`. Type in and run the following code:

```
// Check if the set contains "War"
movieGenres.contains("War")
```

`true` is displayed in the Results area.

Let's see how to remove items from a set next.

Removing an item from a set

To remove an item from a set, use `remove(_:)`. The value you are removing can be assigned to a variable or a constant. If the value doesn't exist in the set, `nil` will be returned. Type in and run the following code:

```
// Remove "Action" from the set
var oldSetValue = movieGenres.remove("Action")
oldSetValue
movieGenres
```

`oldSetValue` (`"Action"`) and `movieGenres` (`{"Horror", "Romantic Comedy", "War"}`) are displayed in the Results area.

To remove all of the values from a set, use `removeAll()`.

Next, let's learn how to iterate over a set.

Iterating over a set

You can use a `for-in` loop to iterate over every item in a set. Type in and run the following code:

```
// Iterating over a set
for genre in movieGenres {
print(genre)
}
```

You should see each set item in the Debug area. Since sets are unsorted, you may get the results in a different order when you run this code again.

In the next section, you will learn about the various operations that you can do with sets in Swift.

Set operations

It's easy to perform `Set` operations such as **union, intersection, subtracting,** and **symmetric difference**. Type in and run the following code:

```
// Set operations
// movieGenres contains "Horror", "Romantic Comedy", "War"
let movieGenres2: Set = ["Science Fiction", "War", "Fantasy"]

// union
movieGenres.union(movieGenres2)
// ["Horror", "Romantic Comedy", "War", "Science Fiction", "Fantasy"]

// intersection
movieGenres.intersection(movieGenres2)
// ["War"]

// subtracting
movieGenres.subtracting(movieGenres2)
// ["Horror", "Romantic Comedy"]

// symmetricDifference
movieGenres.symmetricDifference(movieGenres2)
// ["Horror", "Romantic Comedy", "Science Fiction", "Fantasy"]
```

Let's see how each `Set` operation works:

- `union(_:)` turns a new set containing all of the values in both sets. `{"Horror", "Romantic Comedy", "War", "Science Fiction", "Fantasy"}` will be displayed in the Results area.

- `intersection(_:)` returns a new set containing only the values common to both sets. `{"War"}` will be displayed in the Results area.

- `subtracting(_:)` returns a new set without the values in the specified set. `{"Horror", "Romantic Comedy"}` will be displayed in the Results area.

- `symmetricDifference(_:)` returns a new set without the values common to both sets. `{"Horror", "Romantic Comedy", "Science Fiction", "Fantasy"}` will be displayed in the Results area.

In the next section, you'll learn how to check a set is equal to another set, is part of another set, or has nothing in common with another set.

Set membership and equality

It's easy to check whether a set is equal to the subset, superset, or disjoint of another set. Type in and run the following code:

```
// Set membership and equality
// movieGenres contains "Horror", "Romantic Comedy", "War"
// movieGenres2 contains "Science Fiction", "War", "Fantasy"
let movieGenresSubset: Set = ["Horror", "Romantic Comedy"]
let movieGenresSuperset: Set = ["Horror", "Romantic Comedy", "War",
                                "Science Fiction", "Fantasy"]
let movieGenresDisjoint: Set = ["Bollywood"]

movieGenres == movieGenres2
// false
movieGenresSubset.isSubset(of: movieGenres)
// true
movieGenresSuperset.isSuperset(of: movieGenres)
// true
movieGenresDisjoint.isDisjoint(with: movieGenres)
// true
```

Let's see how this code works:

- The isEqual operator (==) checks whether all the members of one set are the same as those of another set. false will be displayed in the Results area.
- isSubset(of:) checks whether a set is a subset of another set. true will be displayed in the Results area.
- isSuperset(of:) checks whether a set is a superset of another set. true will be displayed in the Results area.
- isDisjoint(of:) checks whether a set has no values in common with another set. true will be displayed in the Results area:

This concludes the section on sets.

To find out more about arrays, dictionaries, and sets, visit https://docs.swift.org/swift-book/LanguageGuide/CollectionTypes.html.

Summary

In this chapter, you looked at collection types in Swift. You learned how to store ordered lists using arrays and how to perform array operations. Next, you learned how to store key-value pairs in dictionaries and how to perform dictionary operations. Finally, you learned about storing unordered lists using sets and how to perform set operations. Great job!

You now know how to write your own programs that use arrays, dictionaries, and sets to store data, and how to perform operations on them.

In the next chapter, you will study how to group a set of instructions together using functions. This is handy when you want to execute a set of instructions multiple times in your program.

6
Functions and Closures

In the `Chapter 4`, Range Operators and Loops, you learned about how to repeat instruction sequences using loops. Note that each sequence has a number of instructions, and if there are a lot of instructions, then it becomes unclear what the sequence is supposed to do. Swift allows you to combine a number of instructions together and execute them by calling a single name. This is called a **function**. It is also possible to combine a number of instructions together without a name and assign it to a constant or variable. This is called a **closure**.

By the end of this chapter, you'll have learned how to create and use functions, nested functions, functions as return types, and functions as arguments. You'll also have learned how to create and use closures.

The following topics will be covered:

- Understanding functions
- Understanding closures

Technical requirements

The Xcode playground for this chapter is in the `Chapter06` folder of the code bundle for this book, which can be downloaded here:

`https://github.com/PacktPublishing/iOS-13-Programming-for-Beginners.`

If you wish to start from scratch, create a new playground and name it `FunctionsAndClosures`.

You can type in and run all of the code in this chapter as you go along. Let's start with functions.

Check out the following video to see the code in action:

```
http://bit.ly/38rlHk6
```

Understanding functions

Let's say you want to do the following:

- Calculate the 10% service charge for a meal at a restaurant.
- Calculate the monthly payment for a car that you wish to purchase.

You would use a **function** for this.

A function contains a number of instructions that perform a specific task. You give it a name and call it by this name when needed. You can also define what it takes as input and what it outputs. Function inputs are called **parameters**, and the function output is called the **return type**.

Here's what a function looks like:

```
func functionName(paramater1: parameterType, ...) -> returnType {
    code
}
```

Both parameters and return types are optional. You can have more than one parameter, but you can only have one value returned.

Let's see how to create a function.

Creating a function

In its simplest form, you can write a function that just executes some instructions without any parameters or return types:

1. Type the following into your playground and run it:

```
// Functions
// Computing a service charge
func serviceCharge() {
    let mealCost = 50
```

```
    // serviceCharge is 10% of mealCost
    let serviceCharge = mealCost / 10
    // print to the Debug area
    print("Service charge is \(serviceCharge)")
}

// call the function
serviceCharge()
```

So, this is a very simple function, named `serviceCharge()`. All it does is calculate the 10% service charge for a meal costing $50, which is `50 / 10`, returning 5. You'll see `Service charge is 5` in the Debug area.

This function is not very useful because `mealCost` is always `50` every time you call this function, and the result, `5`, is only printed in the Debug area and can't be used elsewhere in your program. Let's add some parameters and a return type to this function to make it more useful.

2. Modify your code, as shown:

```
// Functions
// Computing a service charge
func serviceCharge(mealCost: Int) -> Int {
    // serviceCharge is 10% of mealCost, which is the value
returned
    return mealCost / 10
}
// call the function and print to the Debug area
let serviceChargeAmount = serviceCharge(mealCost: 50)
print(serviceChargeAmount)
```

This is much better. Now, you can set the meal cost when you call the `serviceCharge(mealCost:)` function, and the result can be assigned to a variable or constant. It looks a bit awkward, though. Let's see what you can do about that next, where you'll make custom argument labels for your function.

Using custom argument labels

Note that the `serviceCharge(mealCost:)` function is not very English-like. You can add a custom label to the parameter, so the purpose of the function is easier to understand.

Modify your code as shown:

```
// Functions
// Computing a service charge
func serviceCharge(forMealPrice mealCost: Int) -> Int {
    // serviceCharge is 10% or mealCost, which is the value returned
    // forMealPrice is used when calling the function
    // mealCost is used in the function itself
    return mealCost / 10
}

// call the function and print to the Debug area
let serviceChargeAmount = serviceCharge(forMealPrice: 50)
print(serviceChargeAmount)
```

The function works exactly the same as before, but it's more readable now. Another thing you can do to make functions easier to comprehend is to use several smaller functions within a function, and these are known as nested functions. You will study that next.

Using nested functions

It's possible to have a function within another function, and the inner function can use the variables of the enclosing function. These are called **nested functions**.

Type in and run the following code:

```
// Calculating monthly payments for a car loan
func calculateMonthlyPayments(carPrice: Double, downPayment: Double,
   interestRate: Double, paymentTerm: Double) -> Double {
    // loanAmount() calculates the total loan amount
    func loanAmount() -> Double {
        return carPrice - downPayment
    }
    // totalInterest() calculates the total interest amount
       incurred for the payment term
    func totalInterest() -> Double {
        return interestRate * paymentTerm
    }
    // noOfMonths() calculates the total number of months in
      the payment term
    func noOfMonths() -> Double {
        return paymentTerm * 12
    }
    return ((loanAmount() + (loanAmount() * totalInterest() / 100))
           / noOfMonths())
```

```
}

// calculate monthly payments for a car costing 50,000,
   with a downpayment of 5000
// interestRate of 3.5 and 7 years payment term
calculateMonthlyPayments(carPrice: 50000, downPayment: 5000,
    interestRate: 3.5, paymentTerm: 7.0)
// result is 666.96
```

As you can see, there are three functions within
`calculateMonthlyPayments(carPrice:, downPayment:, interestRate:,`
`paymentTerm:)`.

The first nested function, `loanAmount()`, calculates the total loan amount. It returns
`50000 - 5000 = 45000`.

The second nested function, `totalInterest()`, calculates the total interest amount
incurred for the payment term. It returns `3.5 * 7 = 24.5`.

The third nested function, `noOfMonths()`, calculates the total number of months in
the payment term. It returns `7 * 12 = 84`. The value returned is (`45000 + (`
`45000 * 24.5 / 100 ) ) / 84 = 666.96`, which is the amount you have to pay
each month for 7 years to buy this car.

As you can see, functions in Swift are similar to functions in other languages, but they
have a cool feature. Functions in Swift are a first-class type, so they can be used as
parameters and return types. Let's see how that is done in the next section.

Using functions as return types

A function can return another function as its return type.

Type in and run the following code:

```
// functions can return other functions
func makePi() -> (() -> Double) {
    // this is the function that will be returned
    func generatePi() -> Double {
        return 22.0/7.0
    }
    return generatePi
}
// the function is assigned to a constant
let pi = makePi()
```

```
print(pi())
// 3.142857142857143 will appear in the Debug area
```

The `makePi()` function's return type is a function that takes no parameters and returns `Double`. `generatePi()` is a function that takes no parameters and returns `Double` and will be the function that is returned. So, `pi` will be assigned `generatePi()` and will return `22.0/7.0` when called. `3.142857142857143` will be printed in the Debug area.

Now, let's see how a function can be used as a parameter.

Using functions as parameters

A function can take a function as a parameter.

Type in and run the following code:

```
// functions can have functions as parameters
func isThereAMatch(listOfNumbers: [Int], condition:
    (Int) -> Bool) -> Bool {
    for item in listOfNumbers {
        if condition(item) {
            return true
        }
    }
    return false
}
// this function determines if a number is an odd number
func oddNumber(number: Int) -> Bool {
    // number % 2 returns 1 for odd, 0 for even
    return (number % 2) > 0
}
var numbersList = [2, 4, 6, 7]
isThereAMatch(listOfNumbers: numbersList, condition: oddNumber)
// since numbersList has 7 in it, true will be returned
```

`isThereAMatch(listOfNumbers:, condition:)` takes two parameters: an array of integers and a function. The function provided as a parameter must take an integer value and return a Boolean. `oddNumber(number:)` takes an integer and returns `true` if the number is an odd number, which means it can be a `condition:` parameter for `isThereAMatch(listOfNumbers:, condition:)`. `numbersList`, an array containing an odd number, is used for the `listOfNumbers:` parameter. Since `numbersList` contains an odd number, `isThereAMatch(listOfNumbers:, condition:)` will return `true` when called.

In the next section, you'll see how you can perform an early exit on a function if the parameters used are not suitable.

Using a guard statement to exit a function early

Sometimes, you need to exit a function early if there is something wrong with the input data. Consider the following code:

```
func buySomething(itemValueField: String, cardBalance: Int) -> Int {
    guard let itemValue = Int(itemValueField) else {
        print("error in item value")
        return cardBalance
    }
    let remainingBalance = cardBalance - itemValue
    return remainingBalance
}
print(buySomething(itemValueField: "10", cardBalance: 50))
print(buySomething(itemValueField: "blue", cardBalance: 50))
```

When you run the code in the playground, you should see this result in the Debug area:

```
40
error in item value
50
```

Here, you have a function that may be used in an online purchasing terminal. This function will calculate the remaining balance of a debit or credit card when you buy something. The price of the item that you want to buy is entered in a text field. The value in the text field is converted into an integer so that you can calculate the remaining card balance.

Here, you can see the use of a guard statement. A guard statement checks to see whether a condition is true; if not, it exits the function. Here, it is used to check and see whether the user entered a valid price in the online purchasing terminal. If he did, the value can be converted successfully into Int, and you can calculate the remaining card balance. Otherwise, the let statement fails and an error message is printed to the Debug area and the unchanged card balance is returned.

For this statement, `print(buySomething(itemValueField: "10", cardBalance: 50))`, the item price is deducted successfully from the card balance, and `40` is returned.

For this statement, `print(buySomething(itemValueField: "blue", cardBalance: 50))`, the `guard` statement's condition fails and its `else` clause is executed, resulting in an error message being printed to the Debug area and `50` being returned.

 To learn more about functions, visit `https://docs.swift.org/swift-book/LanguageGuide/Functions.html`.

This concludes the section on functions. Let's look at **closures** next. Like functions, closures allow you to combine a number of instructions together, but closures do not have names and can be assigned to a constant or a variable.

Understanding closures

A closure, like a function, contains a sequence of instructions and can take parameters and return values. However, closures don't have names. The sequence of instructions in a closure is surrounded by curly braces (`{ }`), and the `in` keyword separates the arguments and return type from the body.

Closures can be assigned to a constant or variable, so they're handy if you need to pass them around inside your program. For instance, let's say you have an app that downloads a file from the internet, and you need to do something to the file once it has finished downloading. You can put a list of instructions to process the file inside a closure and have your program execute it once the file finishes downloading. You'll see how closures are used in `Chapter 16`, *Getting Started with MapKit*.

Type in and run the following code:

```
// Closures
// var numbersList = [2, 4, 6, 7]
let myClosure = { (number: Int) -> Int in
 let result = number * number
 return result
}
let mappedNumbers = numbersList.map(myClosure)
```

This assigns a block of code that calculates a number's power of two to `myClosure`. The `map()` function then applies this closure to every element in `numbersList`. [4, 16, 36, 49] appears in the Results area.

It's possible to write closures in a more concise fashion and you'll see how to do that in the next section.

Simplifying closures

One of the things that new developers have trouble with are closures written by experienced Swift programmers, who employ a very concise way of writing them. Consider the code in the example shown in the following code snippet:

```
var numbers = [2, 4, 6, 7]
let mappedNumbers = numbers.map({ (number: Int) -> Int in
let result = number * number
return result
})
print(mappedNumbers)
// Prints "[4, 16, 36, 49]"
```

Here, you have an array of numbers, and you use the `map(_:)` function to map a closure to each element of the array in turn. The code in the closure multiplies the number by itself, generating the square of that number. The result is then printed to the Debug area. As you will see, you can write the closure code much more simply.

When a closure's type is already known, you can remove the parameter type, return type, or both. Single statement closures implicitly return the value of their only statement, which means you can remove the return statement as well. So, you can write the closure as follows:

```
var numbers = [2, 4, 6, 7]
let mappedNumbers = numbers.map({ number in number * number })
print(mappedNumbers)
// Prints "[4, 16, 36, 49]"
```

When a closure is the only argument to a function, you can omit the parentheses enclosing the closure. See the code sample here:

```
var numbers = [2, 4, 6, 7]
let mappedNumbers = numbers.map { number in number * number }
print(mappedNumbers)
// Prints "[4, 16, 36, 49]"
```

You can refer to parameters by number instead of by name, as shown in the code sample here:

```
var numbers = [2, 4, 6, 7]
let mappedNumbers = numbers.map { $0 * $0 }
print(mappedNumbers)
// Prints "[4, 16, 36, 49]"
```

So, the closure here is very concise indeed, but will be challenging for new developers to understand. Feel free to write closures in a way that you are comfortable with.

 To learn more about closures, visit https://docs.swift.org/swift-book/LanguageGuide/Closures.html.

This concludes the section on closures.

Summary

In this chapter, you studied how to group statements together into functions. You learned how to use custom argument labels, functions inside other functions, functions as return types, and functions as parameters. This will be useful later when you need to accomplish the same task at different points in your program.

You also learned how to create closures. This will be useful when you need to pass around blocks of code within your program.

You now know how to create and use functions, nested functions, functions as return types, and functions as arguments. You also know how to create and use closures.

In the next chapter, we will study classes, structures, and enumerations. Classes and structures allow for the creation of complex objects that can store state and behavior, and enumerations can be used to limit the values that can be assigned to a variable or constant, reducing the chances for error.

7
Classes, Structures, and Enumerations

At this point, you can write fairly sophisticated programs that use conditionals to determine which path to take and loops to repeat sequences over and over. You've learned how to group instruction sequences together using functions and pass bits of code around using closures.

It's time to think about how to represent complex objects in your code. For example, think about a car. You could use a string constant to store a car name and a double variable to store a car price, but these constants or variables are not associated with one another.

You've seen that you can group instructions together to make functions and closures. Can you group constants and variables together in a single entity? Indeed, you can, and you will learn two ways of doing so: **classes** and **structures**.

Finally, you'll also learn how to use **enumerations** to group a set of related values together.

By the end of this chapter, you'll have learned how to create and initialize a class, create a subclass from an existing class, create and initialize a structure, understand the difference between classes and structures, and create an enumeration.

The following topics will be covered in this chapter:

- Understanding classes
- Understanding structures
- Understanding enumerations

Technical requirements

The Xcode playground for this chapter is in the Chapter07 folder of the code bundle for this book, which can be downloaded here:

https://github.com/PacktPublishing/iOS-13-Programming-for-Beginners.

If you wish to start from scratch, create a new playground and name it Classes, StructuresAndEnumerations.

You can type in and run all of the code in this chapter as you go along. Let's start with classes.

Check out the following video to see the code in action:

http://bit.ly/36gRG4X

Understanding classes

Let's say you want to store the following:

- Individual employee information for a company
- Items for sale at an e-commerce site
- Date on the toys belonging to your children

You would use a **class** for this.

A class groups together variables or constants used to represent an object. Variables or constants associated with a class are called **properties**.

A class can also contain functions that perform specific tasks. Functions associated with a class are called **methods**.

Once you have a class, you can create instances of that class. Imagine you are creating an app for a zoo. If you have an Animal class, you can use instances of that class to represent animals at the zoo. Each of these instances will have different property values.

Here's what a class declaration looks like:

```
class className {
    property1
    property2
    property3
    method1() {
    code
    }
    method2() {
    code
    }
}
```

Let's look at how to work with classes. You'll learn how to declare classes, create instances based on the class declaration, and how to manipulate them. You'll start by creating a class declaration.

Creating a class declaration

Let's create a class that can store details about animals.

Type the following into your playground and run it:

```
// Classes
// Creating a class declaration

class Animal {
    var name: String = ""
    var sound: String = ""
    var numberOfLegs: Int = 0
    var breathesOxygen: Bool = true

    func makeSound() {
        print(self.sound)
    }
}
```

So, this is a very simple class, `Animal`. Class names normally start with a capital letter. This class has properties to store the name of the animal, the sound it makes, the number of legs it has, and whether it breathes oxygen or not. This class also has a method, `makeSound()`, that prints the noise it makes to the Debug area.

Now that we have a class declaration, let's use it to create some instances.

Making an instance of the class

Once you have a class declaration, you can use it to create instances of that class. You will now create an instance of the `Animal` class that represents a cat. Do the following steps:

1. Type the following after your class declaration and run it:

```
// Making an instance of the class
let cat = Animal()

// Printing out the property values
print(cat.name)
print(cat.sound)
print(cat.numberOfLegs)
print(cat.breathesOxygen)

// Calling an instance method
cat.makeSound()
```

You access the instance properties and methods by typing a dot after the instance name, followed by the property or method you want. You will see that the values for all of the instance properties will be listed in the Debug area. Since the values are the default values assigned when the class was created, you'll see name and sound are empty strings, numberOfLegs is 0, and breathesOxygen is true. After the cat.makeSound() method is called, an empty string is printed in the Debug area.

Let's assign some values to this instance's properties.

2. Modify your code as shown:

```
// Making an instance of the class
let cat = Animal()

// Assigning some values to the properties in the instance
cat.name = "Cat"
cat.sound = "Mew"
cat.numberOfLegs = 4
cat.breathesOxygen = true

// Printing out the property values
print(cat.name)
print(cat.sound)
print(cat.numberOfLegs)
print(cat.breathesOxygen)
```

```
// Calling an instance method
cat.makeSound()
```

That's better. Now, when you run the program, the following is displayed in the Debug area:

```
Cat
Mew
4
true
Mew
```

Note that we have to create an instance and, after that, assign the values. Is it possible to assign the values when the instance is created? Indeed, it is, and you do this by implementing an initializer in your class declaration. An initializer is responsible for ensuring all of the instance properties have valid values when a class is created.

3. Modify your class declaration as shown:

```
// Classes
// Creating a class declaration
class Animal {
    var name: String
    var sound: String
    var numberOfLegs: Int
    var breathesOxygen: Bool = true

    // Class initializer
    init(name: String, sound: String, numberOfLegs: Int,
        breathesOxygen: Bool) {
      self.name = name
      self.sound = sound
      self.numberOfLegs = numberOfLegs
      self.breathesOxygen = breathesOxygen
    }

    func makeSound() {
        print(self.sound)
    }
}
```

As you can see, an initializer starts with the init keyword and has a list of parameters that will be used to set the property values. Note the use of the self keyword to distinguish the property names from the parameters, for instance, self.name refers to the property and name refers to the parameter. At the end of the initialization process, every property in the class should have a value.

You'll see some errors in your code at this point. You will need to update your function call to address this.

4. Modify your code as shown and run it:

```
// Making an instance of the class
let cat = Animal(name: "Cat", sound: "Mew", numberOfLegs: 4,
breathesOxygen: true)

// Printing out the property values
print(cat.name)
print(cat.sound)
print(cat.numberOfLegs)
print(cat.breathesOxygen)

// Calling an instance method
cat.makeSound()
```

The results are the same as before, but you created the instance and set its properties in a single step. Excellent!

Now, there are different types of animals, such as mammals, birds, reptiles, and fish. You could create a class for each type, but you could also create a subclass based on an existing class. Let's see how to do that.

Making a subclass

A subclass of a class inherits all of the methods and properties of an existing class:

1. Type in the following code just after the class declaration:

```
// Mammal class, subclass of Animal
class Mammal: Animal {
    let hasFurOrHair: Bool = true
}
```

2. Modify your code that creates an instance of your class, as shown, and run it:

```
// Making an instance of the class
let cat = Mammal(name: "Cat", sound: "Mew", numberOfLegs: 4,
        breathesOxygen: true)
```

As you can see, the results displayed in the Debug area are the same as before. There is an additional property, `hasFurOrHair`, which has not been displayed. Let's fix that.

3. Type in the following code after all other code in your playground and run it:

```
// displaying the subclass property
print(cat.hasFurOrHair)
```

`true` will be displayed in the Debug area.

You have seen that a subclass can have additional properties. A subclass can also have additional methods, and methods in a subclass can differ from the superclass implementation. Let's see how to do that next.

Overriding a superclass method

So far, we just used multiple `print()` statements to display the values of the class instance. Instead of using multiple `print()` statements, we will implement a `description()` method to display all of the instance properties in the Debug area:

1. Modify your class declaration to implement a `description()` method, as shown:

```
// Classes
// Creating a class declaration
class Animal {
    var name: String
    var sound: String
    var numberOfLegs: Int
    var breathesOxygen: Bool = true

    // Class initializer
    init(name: String, sound: String, numberOfLegs: Int,
      breathesOxygen: Bool) {
        self.name = name
        self.sound = sound
```

```
        self.numberOfLegs = numberOfLegs
        self.breathesOxygen = breathesOxygen
    }

    func makeSound() {
        print(self.sound)
    }

    func description() -> String{
        return("name: \(self.name) sound: \(self.sound)
          numberOfLegs: \(self.numberOfLegs) breathesOxygen:
          \(self.breathesOxygen)")
    }
}
```

2. Modify the rest of your code, as shown, and run the program:

```
// Making an instance of the class
let cat = Mammal(name: "Cat", sound: "Mew", numberOfLegs: 4,
        breathesOxygen: true)

// Printing out the property values
print(cat.description())

// Calling an instance method
cat.makeSound()
```

You will see the following in the Debug area:

```
name: Cat sound: Mew numberOfLegs: 4 breathesOxygen: true
Mew
true
```

As you can see, even though the description() method is not
implemented in the Mammal class, it is implemented in the Animal class.
This means it will be inherited by the Mammal class, and the instance
properties are printed to the Debug area.

Note that hasFurOrHair is missing, and we can't put it in because
hasFurOrHair is not a property for the Animal class. We can, however,
change the implementation in the subclass, so that the hasFurOrHair value
is displayed.

3. Add the following code to your `Mammal` class declaration and run it:

```
// Mammal class, subclass of Animal
class Mammal: Animal {
    let hasFurOrHair: Bool = true
    // overrides the description method in the superclass
    override func description() -> String {
        return("Class: Mammal name: \(self.name) sound:
            \(self.sound) numberOfLegs: \(self.numberOfLegs)
            breathesOxygen: \(self.breathesOxygen)
hasFurOrHair:
            \(self.hasFurOrHair) ") }
}
```

The `override` keyword is used here to specify that the description method declared here is to be used in place of the superclass implementation. You will see the following in the Debug area:

```
Class: Mammal name: Cat sound: Mew numberOfLegs: 4
    breathesOxygen: true hasFurOrHair: true
Mew
true
```

`hasFurOrHair` is displayed in the Debug area, showing that we are using the subclass implementation of the `description()` method, instead of the class implementation.

You've created a class declaration and implemented your first instance of a class! Cool! Let's look at structures next.

Understanding structures

Like classes, **structures** also group together properties used to represent an object. They can also contain methods that do specific tasks.

You can also create instances of a structure. Remember the `Animal` class you created? You can also use a structure to accomplish the same thing. There are differences between classes and structures though, and you will learn more about those later.

Here's what a structure declaration looks like:

```
struct structName {
    property1
    property2
    property3
```

```
method1() {
    code
}
method2(){
    code
}
}
```

Let's look at how to work with structures. You'll learn how to declare structures, create instances based on the structure declaration, and how to manipulate them. You'll start by creating a structure declaration.

Creating a structure declaration

Continuing with the animal theme, let's declare a structure that can store details of reptiles.

Type the following into your playground and run it:

```
// Structures
// Creating a structure declaration
struct Reptile {
    var name: String
    var sound: String
    var numberOfLegs: Int
    var breathesOxygen: Bool
    let hasFurOrHair: Bool = false
    func makeSound() {
        print(sound)
    }
    func description() -> String {
        return("Class: Reptile name: \(self.name) sound:
        \(self.sound) numberOfLegs: \(self.numberOfLegs)
        breathesOxygen: \(self.breathesOxygen) hasFurOfHair:
        \(self.hasFurOrHair) ") }
}
```

As you can see, this is almost the same as the class declaration you did earlier. Structure names also normally start with a capital letter, and this structure has properties to store the name of the animal, the sound it makes, how many legs it has, whether it breathes oxygen, and whether it has fur or hair. This structure also has a method, makeSound(), that prints the sound it makes to the Debug area.

Now we have a structure declaration, let's use it to create an instance.

Making an instance of the struct

Now that you have a structure declaration, you can use it to create instances of that structure. You will now create an instance of the `Reptile` structure that represents a snake. Do the following steps:

Type the following after your structure declaration and run it:

```
// Making an instance of the struct
var snake = Reptile(name: "Snake", sound: "Hiss", numberOfLegs: 0,
          breathesOxygen: true)

// Printing out the property values
print(snake.description())

// Calling an instance method
snake.makeSound()
```

Note that you did not need to implement an initializer; structures automatically get an initializer for all of their properties, called the **memberwise initializer**. Neat! The following will be displayed in the Debug area:

```
Class: Reptile name: Snake sound: Hiss numberOfLegs: 0
    breathesOxygen: true hasFurOfHair: false
Hiss
```

You can see this is very similar to the class implementation you did earlier.

There are two differences between a class and a structure, though:

- First, structures cannot inherit from another structure.
- Second, classes are **reference** types, while structures are **value** types.

Let's look at the difference between value types and reference types.

Value types versus references types

Structures are **value** types. This means when you assign a structure to a variable or constant, that structure is copied, and whatever changes you make to the original structure do not affect the copy. Now, you will create an instance of a class and a structure and observe the differences between them.

Perform the following steps:

1. Type in the following code and run it:

```
// Value types vs reference types
// Value type
struct SampleValueType {
    var sampleProperty = 10
}
var a = SampleValueType()
var b = a
b.sampleProperty = 20
print(a.sampleProperty)
print(b.sampleProperty)
```

In this example, you declared a structure, SampleValueType, that contains one property, sampleProperty. Then, you created an instance of that structure and assigned it to a. After that, you assigned a to b. Next, you changed the sampleProperty value of b to 20. When you print out the sampleProperty value of a, 10 is printed in the Debug area, showing that any changes made to the sampleProperty value of b do not affect the sampleProperty value of a.

Classes, however, are **reference** types. This means when you assign an instance to a variable or constant, the variable or constant will refer to the original instance and not a copy of it.

2. Type in the following code and run it:

```
// Reference type
class SampleReferenceType {
    var sampleProperty = 10
}
let c = SampleReferenceType()
let d = c
c.sampleProperty = 20
print(c.sampleProperty)
print(d.sampleProperty)
```

In this example, you declared a class, `SampleReferenceType`, that contains one property, `sampleProperty`. Then, you created an instance of that class and assigned it to c. After that, you assigned c to d. Next, you changed the `sampleProperty` value of d to 20. When you print out the `sampleProperty` value of c, 20 is printed in the Debug area, showing that any changes made to c or d are affecting the same `SampleReferenceType` instance.

Now, the question is, which should you use, classes or structures? Let's explore that next.

Deciding which to use

You've seen that you can use either a class or a structure to represent a complex object. So, which should you use?

It is recommended to use structures unless you need something that requires classes, such as subclasses. This actually helps to prevent some subtle errors that may occur due to classes being reference types.

 To learn more about structures and classes, see the page at `https://docs.swift.org/swift-book/LanguageGuide/ClassesAndStructures.html`.

Fantastic! Now that you have learned about classes and structures, let's take a look at the final collection type in this chapter, enumerations.

Understanding enumerations

Let's say you want to store the following:

- Compass directions (E, W, N, and S)
- Traffic light colors
- The colors of a rainbow

You would use an enumeration for this. You can group together related values in an enumeration.

Let's say you want to program a traffic light. You can use an integer variable to represent different traffic light colors, like this:

```
// Traffic light variable, 0 is red, 1 is yellow, and 2 is green
var trafficLight = 2
```

Although this is a possible way to represent a traffic light, what happens when you assign 3 to `trafficLight`? This will cause problems as 3 does not represent a valid traffic light color. So, it would be better if we could limit the possible values of `trafficLight` to the colors it can display.

Here's what an enumeration declaration looks like:

```
enum enumName {
case value1
case value2
case value3
}
```

Let's look at how to work with enumerations. You'll learn to create and manipulate them. You'll start by creating one to represent a traffic light.

Creating an enumeration

Let's create an enumeration to represent a traffic light. Perform the following steps:

1. Type the following code as shown into your playground and run it:

```
// Enumerations
// Traffic light enumeration
enum TrafficLight {
    case red
    case yellow
    case green
}
var trafficLight = TrafficLight.red
```

This creates an enumeration named `TrafficLight`, which groups together the `red`, `yellow`, and `green` values. As you can see, now the value for `trafficLight` is limited to `red`, `yellow`, and `green`; if you were to try to set the values as anything else, an error will be generated.

Enumerations can contain methods. Let's add a method to `trafficLight`. This method will return a string representing the `trafficLight` color.

2. Modify your code as shown and run it:

```
// Enumerations
// Traffic light program with enumerations
enum TrafficLight {
    case red
    case yellow
    case green

    func trafficLightDescription() -> String {
        switch self {
        case .red:
            return "red"
        case .yellow:
            return "yellow"
        default:
            return "green"
        }
    }
}

var trafficLight = TrafficLight.red
print(trafficLight.trafficLightDescription())
```

`red` will appear in the Debug area.

To learn more about enumerations, visit `https://docs.swift.org/swift-book/LanguageGuide/Enumerations.html`.

As you can see, enumerations are great when you need to represent an object that only has a specific set of values. This concludes this section on enumerations and concludes this chapter. As you will discover, you will frequently use all three collection types in the programs that you write.

Summary

Good job! You've learned how to declare complex objects using a class, create instances of a class, create a subclass, and override a class method. You've learned how to declare a structure, create instances of a structure, and understand the difference between reference and value types and which to use. You've learned how to use enumerations to represent a specific set of values.

You now know how to create and initialize a class, create a subclass from an existing class, create and initialize a structure, understand the difference between classes and structures, and create an enumeration.

In the next chapter, you will study how to specify common traits in classes and structures using protocols, extend the capability of built-in classes using extensions, and handle errors in your programs.

8

Protocols, Extensions, and Error Handling

In the last chapter, you've learned how to represent complex objects using classes or structures and how to use enumerations to create a set of related values.

To finish the section on Swift, you need to understand some concepts that are important in developing iOS applications. You'll begin by learning about **protocols**, which define a blueprint of methods, properties, and other requirements that can be adopted by a class, structure, or enumeration. Next, you'll learn about **extensions**, which provide new functionality for an existing class, structure, or enumeration. Finally, you'll learn error handling, which covers how to respond to or recover from errors in your program.

By the end of this chapter, you'll be able to write your own protocols to meet the requirements of your apps, use extensions to add new capabilities to existing types, and handle error conditions in your apps gracefully.

The following topics will be covered:

- Understanding protocols
- Understanding extensions
- Exploring error handling

Technical requirements

The Xcode playground for this chapter is in the `Chapter08` folder of the code bundle for this book, which can be downloaded here:

`https://github.com/PacktPublishing/iOS-13-Programming-for-Beginners.`

If you wish to start from scratch, create a new playground and name it `Protocols,ExtensionsAndErrorHandling`.

You can type in and run all of the code in this chapter as you go along. Let's start with protocols.

Check out the following video to see the code in action:

`http://bit.ly/2RhHEwq`

Understanding protocols

Imagine an app used by a fast food restaurant. The management has decided to show calorie counts for the meals being served. The app currently has the following class, structure, and enumeration, and none of them have calorie counts implemented:

- A `Burger` class
- A `Fries` structure
- A `Sauce` enumeration

Let's see how you can add calorie counts to all three, and later write a function to calculate the total calorie count.

Type in the following code and run it:

```
class Burger {
}

struct Fries {
}

enum Sauce {
    case chili
    case tomato
}
```

These represent the existing class, structure, and enumeration in the app. Don't worry about the empty implementations, as they are not required for this lesson. As you can see, none of them have calorie counts.

You will solve this problem by using **protocols**. A protocol is like a blueprint that determines what properties or methods an object should have. After you've declared a protocol, classes, structures, and enumerations can adopt this protocol, and provide their own implementation for the required properties and methods.

Here's what a protocol declaration looks like:

```
protocol protocolName {
    property1
    property2
    property3

    method1()
    method2()
}
```

Note that you just have method names. The implementation is done within the adopting class, structure, or enumeration.

Let's look at how to work with protocols. You'll start by creating a protocol declaration.

Creating a protocol declaration

Let's create a protocol that specifies a required variable, `calories`, and a method, `description()`.

Each class, structure, or enumeration that adopts it must implement a `calories` variable and a `description()` method.

Type the following into your playground above the class, structure, and enumeration declarations:

```
// Protocols and extensions
// CalorieCountProtocol
protocol CalorieCountProtocol {
    // To adopt this protocol these methods must be implemented
    var calories: Int { get }
    func description() -> String
}
```

```
class Burger {
}

struct Fries {
}

enum Sauce {
    case chili
    case tomato
}
```

This protocol is named `CalorieCountProtocol`. It specifies that any object that adopts it must have a variable, `calories`, that holds the calorie count, and a function, `description()`, that returns a string. The `{ get }` code means that you only need to be able to read the value, and you don't need to write it. Note that the implementation of the function is not specified as that will be done in the class, structure, or enumeration.

Now, you will make `Burger` adopt this protocol. To do so, modify your code for the `Burger` class as follows:

```
// CalorieCountProtocol adopted by a class
class Burger : CalorieCountProtocol {
    let calories = 800
    func description() -> String {
        return "This burger has \(calories) calories"
    }
}
```

All you need to do to adopt a protocol is the following:

- Type a colon after the name of the class, followed by the name of the protocol.
- Implement the required properties and methods.

As you can see, the `calories` constant and the `description()` function has been added. Even though the protocol specifies a variable, we can use a constant here because the protocol only requires that you can get the value for `calories` and not to set it.

Now, the `Burger` class conforms to `CalorieCountProtocol`. Next, let's make `Fries` adopt this protocol as well. To do, so modify your code for the `Fries` class as follows:

```
// CalorieCountProtocol adopted by a structure
struct Fries : CalorieCountProtocol {
    let calories = 500
    func description() -> String {
        return "These fries has \(calories) calories"
    }
}
```

The same process that was used for `Burger` is used for `Fries`. Now, `Fries` conforms to `CalorieCountProtocol` as well.

 For more information on protocols, visit: `https://docs.swift.org/ swift-book/LanguageGuide/Protocols.html`.

You could modify the `Sauce` enumeration in the same way, but let's look at another way to do it, using extensions—they are called so because they extend an object's capabilities. You'll add `CalorieCountProtocol` to the `Sauce` enumeration using an extension in the next section.

Understanding extensions

Sometimes, you need to provide extra capabilities to an object without modifying the object declaration. For this, we use **extensions**.

Here's what an extension looks like:

```
extension existingType : protocolName {
    property1
    property2
    property3

    method1()
    method2()
}
```

Let's look at how to work with extensions. You'll start by adopting a protocol via an extension.

Adopting a protocol via an extension

Let's make the `Sauce` enumeration conform to `CalorieCountProtocol` using extensions.

Add the following code after the declaration for `Sauce`:

```
// Sauce enum
enum Sauce {
    case chili
    case tomato
}

// Sauce adopting CalorieCountProtocol via extension
extension Sauce : CalorieCountProtocol {
    // enums can't have stored variables, only computed variables
    var calories : Int {
    switch self {
        case .chili:
            return 20
        case .tomato:
            return 15
        }
    }
    func description() -> String {
        return "This sauce has \(calories) calories"
    }
}
```

As you can see, no changes are made to the declaration for `Sauce`. You just added the required properties and methods to conform to `CalorieCountProtocol` in an extension. This is also really useful if you want to extend the capabilities of existing Swift types.

Enumerations can't have stored properties, so a `switch` statement is used to return the number of calories. The `description()` method is the same as the one in `Burger` and `Fries`.

At this point, all three food items have a `calories` property and a `description()` method. Great!

Let's see how we can put them in an array and perform an operation to get the total calorie count.

Creating an array of different types of objects

Ordinarily, it is not possible to create an array of different object types. However, since `Burger`, `Fries`, and `Sauce` all conform to `CalorieCountProtocol`, we can make an array that contains them:

1. Type in the following code after all of the protocol and object declarations and run it. Since all of the food items conform to the `CalorieCountProtocol` protocol, you can add them to `foodArray`.

```
// create instances of each type
let burger = Burger()
let fries = Fries()
let sauce = Sauce.tomato

// print the descriptions
print(burger.description())
print(fries.description())
print(sauce.description())

// since all items have adopted the same protocol, you can add them
    to a single array
let foodArray : [CalorieCountProtocol] = [burger, fries, sauce]
```

2. All you need to do is to use a loop to calculate the total calorie count. Add in the following code after the line where you created the array and run the code:

```
// calculate the total number of calories
var totalCalories = 0
for food in foodArray {
    totalCalories += food.calories
}
print(totalCalories)
```

The `calories` value for each food item will be successively added to `totalCalories`, and the total amount, `1315`, will be displayed in the Debug area.

 For more information on extensions, visit `https://docs.swift.org/swift-book/LanguageGuide/Extensions.html`.

This concludes the section on protocols and extensions. Let's look at error handling next, which looks at how to respond to or recover from errors in your program.

Exploring error handling

Things don't always go as you would expect, so you need to keep that in mind as you write apps. You need to think of ways that your app might fail, and what to do if it does.

Let's say you have an app that needs to access a web page. However, if the server where that web page is located is down, it is up to you to write the code to handle the error—for example, trying an alternative web server or informing the user that the server is down.

First, you need an object that conforms to Swift's `Error` protocol:

1. Type in the following code into your playground:

```
// Error handling
// Create an enum that adopts the error protocol
enum WebpageError: Error {
    case success
    // associate server response value of type Int with
failure
    case failure(Int)
}
```

The code you entered declares an enumeration, `WebpageError`, that has adopted the `Error` protocol. It has two values, `success`, and `failure(Int)`. You can associate `Int` with the failure value, which will be used to store the server response code.

2. Type in the following code after the `WebpageError` declaration:

```
// getWebpage will throw an error if the site is down
func getWebpage(uRL: String, siteUp: Bool) throws -> String {
    if siteUp == false {
        throw WebpageError.failure(404)
    }
    return "Success"
}
```

This function, `getWebpage(url:siteUp:)`, takes two parameters:

- uRL contains a `String` representing a URL, such as `http://www.apple.com`.
- `siteUp` is a `Bool` that is used to check whether a website is online. It is set to `true` if the website is online and `false` if the website is not.

If `siteUp` is `true`, `getWebpage` returns `"Success"`. If `siteUp` is `false`, the program will throw an error with the server response code.

3. Type in the following code after the function declaration and run it:

```
let webpageURL = "http://www.apple.com"
let websiteUp = true

try getWebpage(uRL: webpageURL, siteUp: websiteUp)
```

Since `websiteUp` is `true`, `"success"` will appear in the Results area.

4. Change the value of `websiteUp` to `false` and run it. Your program crashes and the error is displayed in the Debug area. Of course, it is always better if you can handle errors without making your program crash. One way to do this is by using `do-catch`.

5. Modify your code as shown and run it:

```
do {
    let status = try getWebpage(uRL: webpageURL, siteUp:
websiteUp)
    print(status)
} catch {
    print(error)
}
```

The `do` block tries to execute the `getWebpage(url:siteUp:)` function and prints the status if successful. If there is an error, instead of crashing, the statements in the `catch` block are executed, and the error appears in the Debug area.

For more information on error handling, visit `https://docs.swift.org/swift-book/LanguageGuide/ErrorHandling.html`.

Summary

In this chapter, you learned how to write protocols and how to make classes, structures, and enumerations conform to them. You also learned how to extend the capabilities of a class by using an extension. Finally, you learned how to handle errors gracefully.

You're now able to write your own protocols to meet the requirements of your apps, use extensions to add new capabilities to existing types, and handle error conditions in your apps gracefully.

It may seem rather abstract and hard to understand now, but as you will see in *Section 3* of this book, you will use protocols to implement common functionalities in different parts of your program instead of writing the same program over and over. You will see how useful extensions are in organizing your code, which makes it easy to maintain. Last but not least, you'll see how good error handling makes it easy to pinpoint the mistakes you made while coding your app.

Give yourself a pat on the back; you have completed the first part of this book!

In the next chapter, you will start writing your first iOS application by creating the screens for it using storyboards, which allow you to rapidly prototype an application without having to type a lot of code.

Section 2: Design

Welcome to second section of this book. At this point, you're familiar with the Xcode user interface, and you have a solid foundation of using Swift. In this part, you'll start creating the user interface of a restaurant reservation app, named *Let's Eat*. You will use Interface Builder to build the screens that your app will use, add elements such as buttons, labels, and fields to them, and connect them together, using segues. As you will see, you can do this with a minimum of coding.

This part comprises the following chapters:

- Chapter 9, *Setting Up the Basic Structure*
- Chapter 10, *Building Your App Structure in Storyboard*
- Chapter 11, *Finishing Up Your App Structure in Storyboard*
- Chapter 12, *Modifying and Configuring Cells*

By the end of this part, you'll be able to navigate the various screens of your app in the iOS Simulator, and you will know how to prototype the user interface of your own apps. Let's get started!

9
Setting Up the Basic Structure

In *Section 1* of this book, you studied the Swift language. Now that you have a good working knowledge of the language, you can learn how to develop an iOS application.

In this part, you will focus on building the user interface of a restaurant reservation app, *Let's Eat*. You will use Xcode's **Interface Builder** for this, and coding will be kept to a minimum.

You'll start by learning useful terms used in iOS app development, which are used extensively throughout this book. Not only will this help you to understand the rest of this book, but it will also be useful when you're reading other books or online resources on iOS app development.

Next, you will tour the screens used in the *Let's Eat* app and learn how the user would use the app. This will be useful for comparison purposes as you recreate the app's **user interface (UI)**.

Finally, you will begin recreating the app's UI with Interface Builder, starting with the **tab bar**, which allows the user to select between the **Explore** and **Map** screens. You'll add **navigation bars** to the top of both screens. You'll also learn how to configure the **Launch** screen that is displayed when the app is started and how to use custom icons for the **Launch** screen and the **tab bar buttons**.

By the end of this chapter, you'll have learned common terms used in iOS app development and how to create a new Xcode project, delete files from a project and add assets to a project, use storyboards to prototype an app's screens, and use tab bar and navigation controllers.

The following topics will be covered:

- Useful terms
- *Let's Eat* app tour
- Creating a new Xcode project
- Setting up a Tab Bar Controller Scene and **Launch** screen

Technical requirements

You will create a new Xcode project, `LetsEat`, in this chapter.

The resource files and completed Xcode project for this chapter are in the `Chapter09` folder of the code bundle for this book, which can be downloaded here:

`https://github.com/PacktPublishing/iOS-13-Programming-for-Beginners`.

Check out the following video to see the code in action:

`http://bit.ly/2urONRC`

Useful terms

Here are some common terms used in iOS app development. Just read through them for now. Even though you may not understand everything yet, it will become clearer as you go along:

- **View**: A view is an instance of the `UIView` class or one of its subclasses. Anything you see on your screen (buttons, text fields, labels, and so on) is a view. You will use views to build your UI.
- **Stack View**: A stack view is an instance of the `UIStackView` class, which is a subclass of `UIView`. It is used to group views together in a horizontal or vertical stack. This makes them easier to position on the screen using **Auto Layout**, which is described later in this section.
- **View Controller**: A view controller is an instance of the `UIViewController` class. It determines what a view displays to the user, and what happens when a user interacts with a view. Every view controller has a `view` property, which contains a reference to a view.

- **Table View Controller**: A table view controller is an instance of the `UITableViewController` class, which is a subclass of the `UIViewController` class. Its `view` property has a reference to a table view instance, which displays a single column of **table view cells.**

The **Settings** app displays settings in a table view:

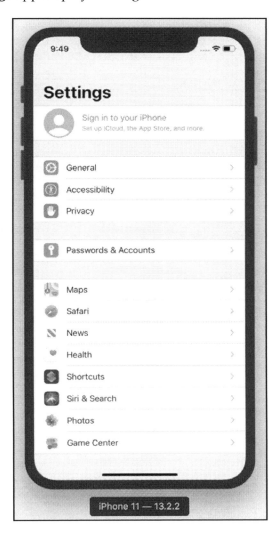

As you can see, all of the different settings (**General**, **Privacy**, and so on) are displayed in table view cells inside the table view.

- **Collection View Controller**: A collection view controller is an instance of the `UICollectionViewController` class, which is a subclass of the `UIViewController` class. Its `view` property has a reference to a collection view instance, which displays a grid of **collection view cells**.

The **Photos** app displays photos in a collection view:

As you can see, each thumbnail picture is displayed in a collection view cell, inside the collection view.

- **Navigation Controller**: A navigation controller is an instance of the `UINavigationController` class, which is a subclass of the `UIViewController` class. It has a `viewControllers` property that holds an array of view controllers. The view of the last view controller in the array appears onscreen, along with a navigation bar at the top of the screen.

The table view controller in the **Settings** app is embedded in a navigation controller:

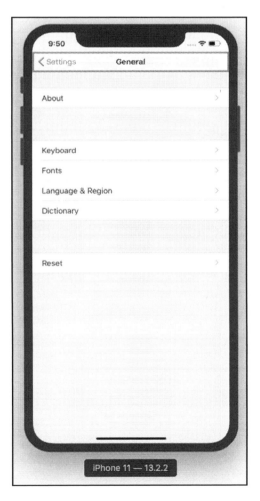

When you tap on a setting, the view controller for that setting is added to the array of view controllers assigned to the `viewControllers` property. The user sees the view for that view controller slide in from the left. Note the navigation bar at the top of the screen, which can hold a title and buttons. Here, a button to return to the previous screen appears in the navigation bar.

- **Tab Bar Controller**: A tab bar controller is an instance of the `UITabBarController` class, which is a subclass of the `UIViewController` class. It has a `viewControllers` property that holds an array of view controllers. The view of the first view controller in the array appears onscreen, along with a tab bar with buttons at the bottom. Each button corresponds to a view controller in the array. When you tap a button, the corresponding view controller is loaded and its view appears on screen.

The **Photos** app uses a tab bar controller to display a row of buttons at the bottom of the screen:

Tapping each button in the tab bar will take you to a different screen.

- **Model-View-Controller (MVC)**: This is a very common design pattern used in iOS app development. The user interacts with views onscreen. Controllers manage the flow of information between an app's data model and the views the user interacts with. Most importantly, there is no direct communication between the views and the data model.
- **Storyboard**: A storyboard file contains a visual representation of what the user sees. Each screen of information is called a **scene**.

Open the `Exploring Xcode` project and click `Main.Storyboard`:

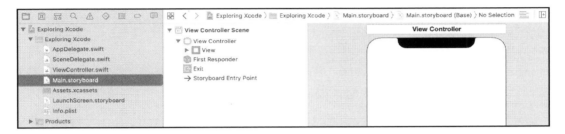

You'll see one scene in it, and when you run your app in the Simulator, the contents of this scene will be displayed. You can have more than one scene in a storyboard file.

- **Segue**: If you have more than one scene in an app, you use segues to move from one scene to another. The `Exploring Xcode` project does not have any segues since there is just one scene in its storyboard, but you will see them in a later part of this chapter.
- **Auto Layout**: As a developer, you have to make sure that your app looks good on devices with different screen sizes. Auto Layout helps you lay out your user interface based on constraints you specify. For instance, you can set a constraint to make sure a button is centered on the screen regardless of screen size or make a text field expand when the device is rotated from portrait to landscape.

Now that you are familiar with the terms used in iOS app development, let's take a tour through the app you will build.

Touring the Let's Eat app

The *Let's Eat* app is a restaurant reservation app that allows users to explore a list of restaurants categorized by cuisine or view a map showing all restaurants in a particular area. Let's take a look at the overall flow of the app.

Using the Explore screen

When the app launches, you will see the **Explore** screen:

Let's study the different parts of this screen.

A **tab bar** at the bottom of the screen displays **Explore** and **Map** buttons. The **Explore** button is selected, and you see a **Collection View** displaying a list of cuisines in collection view cells. A **Collection View Header** containing a **LOCATION** button is at the top of the screen.

Before you can pick a cuisine, you have to select a location by tapping the **LOCATION** button.

Using the Locations screen

When you tap the **LOCATION** button, you will see the **Locations** screen:

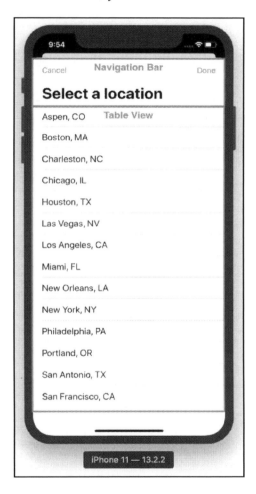

Let's study the different parts of this screen.

A **Navigation Bar** at the top of the screen contains **Cancel** and **Done** buttons. A **Table View** displays a list of locations in table view cells.

You have to tap a row to select a location and tap the **Done** button to confirm. Once you tap **Done**, you are returned to the **Explore** screen and can then pick a cuisine. You can also tap **Cancel** to return to the **Explore** screen without choosing a location.

Using the Restaurant List screen

Once a location has been set (**ASPEN, CO** in this case), you can tap a cuisine. This displays the **Restaurant List** screen:

Let's study the different parts of this screen.

A **Navigation Bar** at the top of the screen contains a **Back** button. A Collection View displays a list of restaurants at a selected location, offering the cuisine you picked, in collection view cells.

You have to tap a restaurant to see its details. You can also tap the **Back** button to return to the **Explore** screen without choosing a restaurant.

Using the Restaurant Detail screen

Tapping on a restaurant on the **Restaurant List** screen displays details of that restaurant on the **Restaurant Detail** screen:

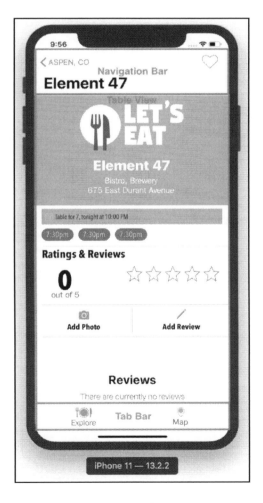

Let's study the different parts of this screen.

A **Navigation Bar** at the top of the screen contains a button showing the location (**ASPEN, CO** in this case). A **Table View** displays the restaurant's location, rating, customer reviews, photo reviews, and a location map in table view cells.

You can tap the **ASPEN, CO** button to return to the **Restaurant List** screen or tap the **Add Review** button.

Using the Review Form screen

Tapping on the **Add Review** button displays the **Review Form** screen:

Let's study the different parts of this screen.

A **Navigation Bar** at the top of the screen contains **Cancel** and **Save** buttons. A **Table View** displays a rating and text fields in table view cells.

You can set a rating and write a review for the restaurant on this screen. You can then tap the **Save** button to save your rating and review or the **Cancel** button to return to the **Restaurant Detail** screen without saving.

Using the Map screen

Tapping the **Map** button in the tab bar displays the **Map** screen:

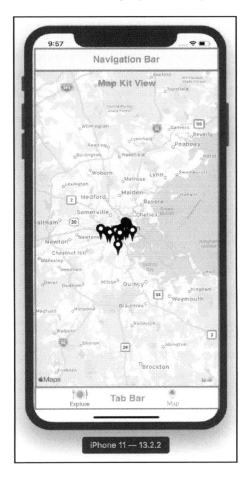

Let's study the different parts of this screen.

A **Tab Bar** at the bottom of the screen displays **Explore** and **Map** buttons. The **Map** button is selected, and you see a **Map Kit View** displaying a map on the screen, with pins indicating restaurant locations.

Tapping a pin will display an annotation, and tapping the button in the annotation will display the **Restaurant Detail** screen for that restaurant.

This completes the tour of the app. You did not cover everything on this tour, but you will in later chapters. For now, it's time to start building the UI for your app!

Creating a new Xcode project

Now that you know what the screens of the app are going to look like, let's start. You'll create a new Xcode project and use Interface Builder to create a new project, make the **Explore** and **Map** screens, add graphical assets to the project, and configure the **Launch** screen and tab bar button icons.

 The process of creating a new project is the same process used to create the `Exploring Xcode` project in `Chapter 1`, *Getting Familiar with Xcode*.

Let's create a new project now:

1. Launch Xcode and click **Create a new Xcode project**.
2. **iOS** should already be selected. Choose **Single View App** and click **Next.**

3. The **Choose options for your new project:** screen is displayed:

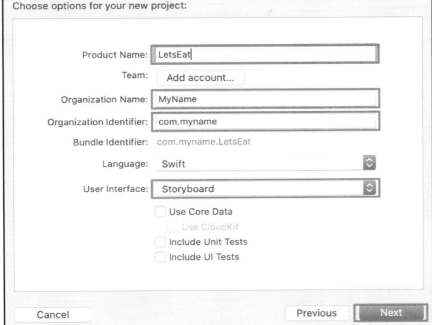

Enter the information as shown:

- **Product Name:** LetsEat
- **Organization Name:** Your own name.
- **Organization Identifier:** com. followed by your own name, as shown in the screenshot.
- **User Interface:** Storyboard

Leave the rest of the settings at their default values. Click **Next**.

4. Choose a location to save your project and click **Create.**
5. In the **Scheme** menu, choose the **iPhone 11** Simulator.

If you build and run the app now, all you will see is a blank white screen. If you click Main.storyboard in the Project navigator, you will see that it contains a single scene containing a blank view. This is why you only see a blank white screen when you run the app.

To configure the UI, you will modify `Main.storyboard` using Interface Builder. Interface Builder allows you to add and configure scenes. Each scene represents a screen the user will see. You can add UI objects such as views and buttons to a scene and link those objects to code. You will learn how to link objects to code in *Section 3* of this book.

 For more information on how to use Interface Builder, visit this link: `https://help.apple.com/xcode/mac/current/#/dev31645f17f`.

To begin, you will add a tab bar controller scene to your project, which displays a Tab Bar with two tabs at the bottom of the screen. Tapping a tab will display the screen associated with it. This corresponds to the **Explore** and **Map** screens shown in the app tour. You'll also configure the screen that is displayed to the user when the app is launched.

Setting up a Tab Bar Controller Scene and Launch screen

As you saw in the app tour, the *Let's Eat* app has a Tab Bar with two buttons at the bottom of the screen, which are used to display the **Explore** and **Map** screens. In this section, you will remove the existing **View Controller Scene** and `ViewController.swift` file and add a **Tab Bar Controller Scene** with two buttons to your project. Perform the following steps:

1. Click `Main.storyboard` in the Project navigator:

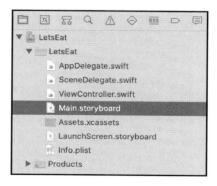

2. The contents of `Main.storyboard` appear in the Editing area. Click the Document Outline button to collapse the document outline. This gives you more room to work with:

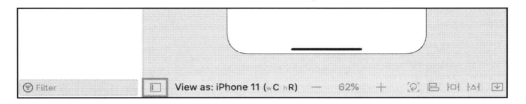

3. Click the + button to open the Object library:

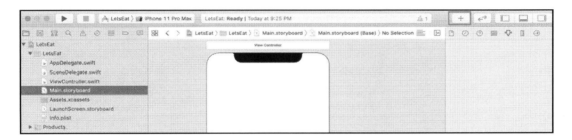

4. The Object library allows you to pick UI objects that you can add to a scene. Type `tabbar` in the filter field. A **Tab Bar Controller** object will appear in the list of results:

5. Drag the **Tab Bar Controller** object to the storyboard. It's okay if it covers the existing **View Controller Scene**. You can see it consists of a scene with two arrows leading to two more scenes. These arrows represent segues:

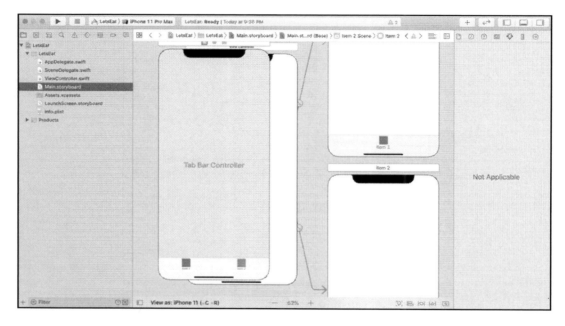

6. Click the - button to zoom out, and rearrange the scenes in the storyboard so the **Tab Bar Controller Scene** is not covering the **View Controller Scene**:

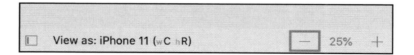

7. Drag the arrow from the **View Controller Scene** to the **Tab Bar Controller Scene** as shown. This will set the **Tab Bar Controller** as the initial **View Controller** of your project, making the Tab Bar appear when you launch your app:

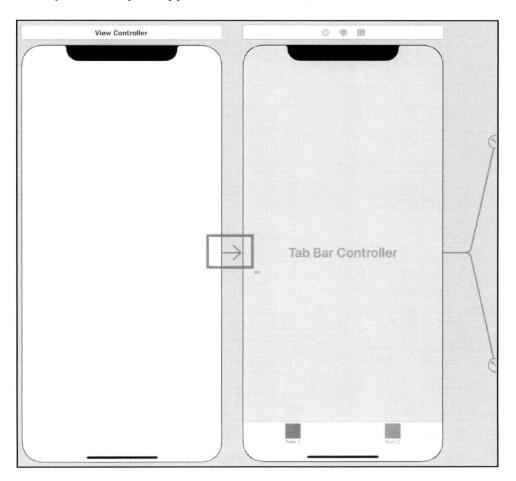

8. Select the existing **View Controller Scene** and press *Delete* on the keyboard to remove it, as you won't be using it for this project:

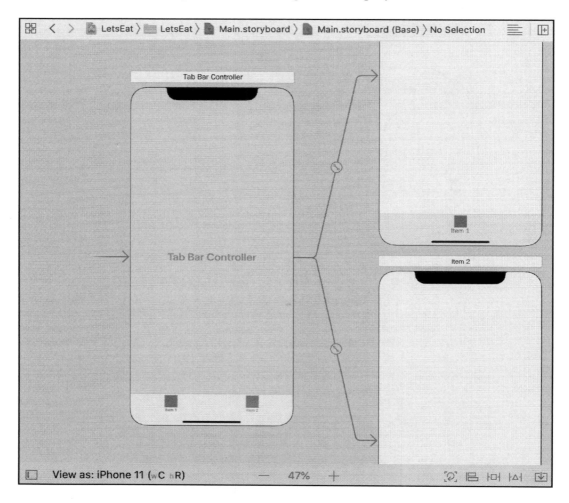

9. Select `ViewController.swift` in the Project navigator and press *Delete* on the keyboard to remove it, as you won't be using it for this project:

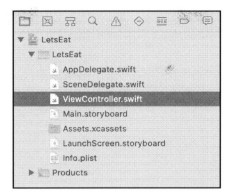

10. Click **Move to Trash** in the dialog box that pops up:

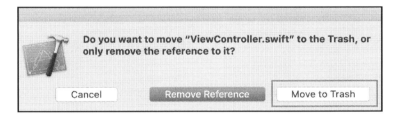

11. If you see a second editor window appear, click the Adjust Editing Option button and choose **Show Editor Only**:

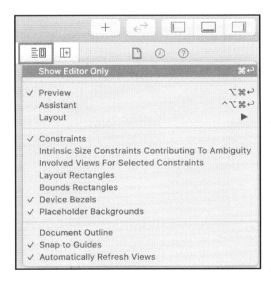

When you build and run your app in the Simulator, you'll see the tab bar with two buttons at the bottom of the screen:

You have successfully added a Tab Bar to your project, but as you can see, the button titles are currently **Item 1** and **Item 2**. You will change them to **Explore** and **Map** in the next section.

Setting the titles of the Tab Bar's buttons

You now have a tab bar at the bottom of the screen, but the button titles do not match those shown in the app tour. You will configure the button titles in the Attributes Inspector so they match. Follow these steps to change the button titles to **Explore** and **Map**:

1. Click `Main.storyboard` in the Project navigator. Click the Document Outline button to show the document outline. Click **Item 1 Scene** in the document outline:

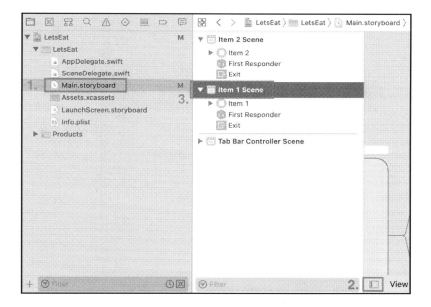

2. Click the **Item 1** button under **Item 1 Scene**. Click the Attributes Inspector button:

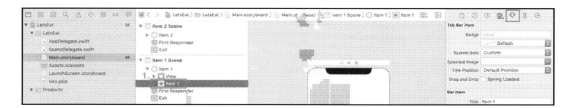

3. Under **Bar Item**, set **Title** to `Explore`:

4. Click the **Item 2** button in the **Item 2** scene and under **Bar Item**, set **Title** to `Map`:

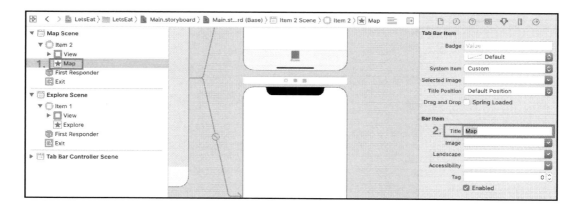

When you build and run your app in the Simulator, you'll see the titles for the buttons have changed to **Explore** and **Map**, respectively. Great!

Tapping the **Explore** and **Map** buttons will display the scenes for the **Explore** and **Map** screens. As shown in the app tour, if you tap the **LOCATION** button on the **Explore** screen, you will see a navigation bar at the top of the **Locations** screen containing the **Cancel** and **Done** buttons. You'll also see an empty navigation bar at the top of the **Map** screen. You will learn how to add navigation bars to your screens in the next section.

Embedding view controllers in navigation controllers

As you saw in the app tour, many screens have a navigation bar at the top of the screen. To get this, you will embed the view controller of the **Explore** and **Map** scenes in a navigation controller. This will make navigation bars appear at the top of the screen when the **Explore** and **Map** screens are displayed:

1. Click **Explore Scene** in the document outline:

2. Choose **Editor** | **Embed In** | **Navigation Controller**:

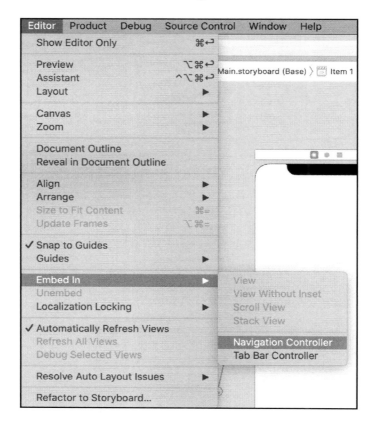

3. A **Navigation Controller Scene** appears between the **Tab Bar Controller Scene** and the **Explore Scene:**

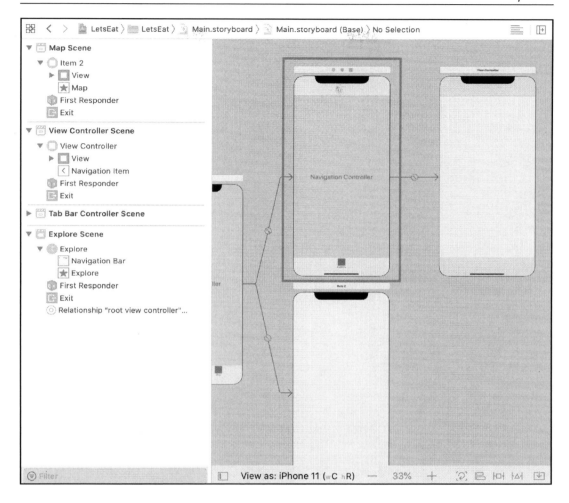

4. Build and run your app. Note that the **Explore** screen now has a navigation bar:

Embedding a view controller in a navigation controller adds that view controller to the navigation controller's `viewControllers` array. The navigation controller then displays the view controller's view on the screen. The navigation controller also displays a navigation bar at the top of the screen. If you tap the **Map** button in the Tab Bar, you'll see the **Map** screen does not have a navigation bar yet.

5. Click **Map Scene** in the document outline:

6. Choose **Editor | Embed In | Navigation Controller**:

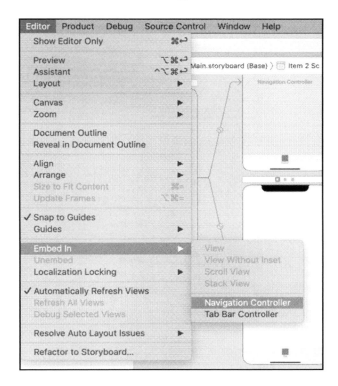

7. A **Navigation Controller Scene** appears between the **Tab Bar Controller Scene** and the **Map View Controller Scene**:

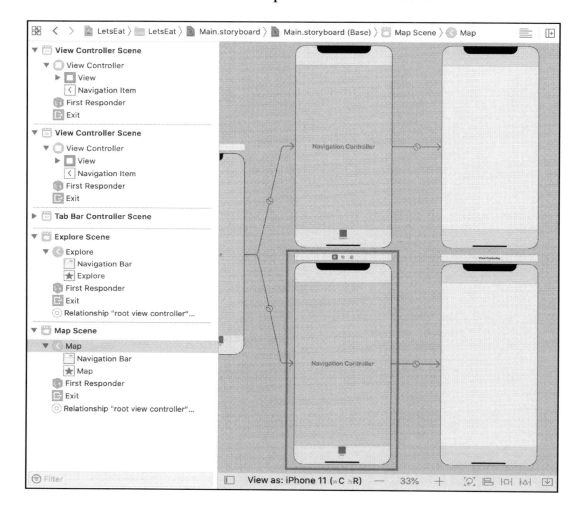

Build and run your app. Both screens now have a navigation bar:

The Tab Bar buttons can switch between the **Explore** and **Map** screens, and each screen now has a navigation bar. The button titles are correct but the buttons themselves do not have icons. To get the button icons, you will add a file containing all of the graphics assets required for your project in the next section.

Adding the Assets.xcassets file

The `Assets.xcassets` file is used to hold all of the graphic files for your project. It is currently empty as you just created this project. You will need to download the `Assets.xcassets` file in the `Chapter09` folder (which contains all of the graphic files for the *Let's Eat* app) from this link if you have not yet done so:

`https://github.com/PacktPublishing/iOS-13-Programming-for-Beginners`.

Once you have downloaded the file, you can add it to your project by following these steps:

1. First, you have to remove the existing `Assets.xcassets` file from your project. Select it in the Project navigator and press the *Delete* key to remove it:

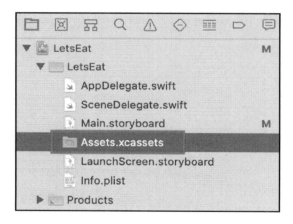

2. Click **Move to Trash** when this dialog appears:

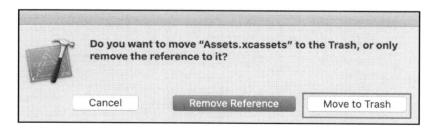

3. Open the `Chapter09` folder inside the code bundle files you downloaded. You will see `Assets.xcassets` inside:

4. Drag the new `Assets.xcassets` file to the Project navigator area. The **Choose options for adding these files** dialog appears. Tick the **Copy items if needed** checkbox. Tick the **Create groups** radio button. Leave the rest of the settings at their default values. Click **Finish**:

5. The `Assets.xcassets` file has been added to your project:

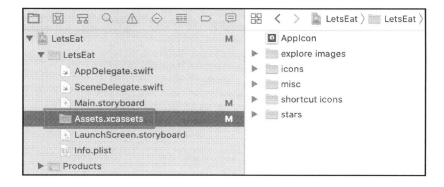

You can click it to see what it contains.

Among the graphic files included is a logo that will appear onscreen when the app is launched, and icons for the tab bar buttons.

Before you add the icons for the tab bar buttons, you will configure the **Launch** screen for your app. This screen is displayed briefly as the app is starting up. You will create a new custom color and add an icon from the `Assets.xcassets` folder to this screen. Creating a new custom color is discussed in the next section.

Configuring the Launch screen's background color

You can configure a custom **Launch** screen when your app is started. This screen is automatically created when you create a project and is contained in `LaunchScreen.storyboard`. It will appear briefly onscreen before the UI is displayed. First, let's set a custom color for this screen, as follows:

1. Click `Launchscreen.storyboard` in your Project navigator:

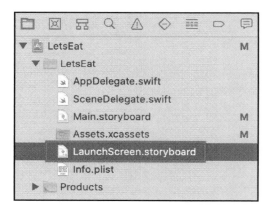

2. Select **View** in the document outline. Select the Attributes Inspector, and click the **Background** menu in the Attributes Inspector:

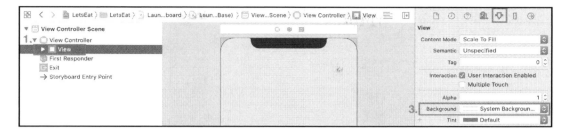

3. Choose **Custom...** from the pop-up menu:

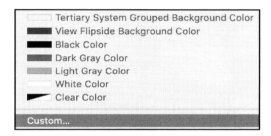

4. In the color picker, choose the second tab (the one with the three sliders):

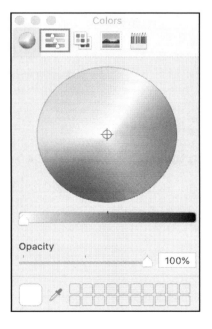

5. Select **RGB Sliders** from the pop-up menu and enter 4A4A4A in the **Hex Color** # box:

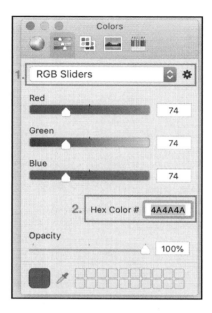

Build and run your app. You should briefly see a dark gray screen before the Tab Bar appears. Cool!

The next thing you will do is add a logo to this screen and position the logo so that it is in the exact center of the screen regardless of the device and orientation. You will do that in the next section.

Adding a logo and constraints to the Launch screen

Your **Launch** screen is rather plain, so let's add a logo to it. You will find this logo inside the Assets.xcassets file you added to your project earlier. You'll also learn how to use constraints to position the logo in the center of the screen.

Perform the following steps:

1. `LaunchScreen.storyboard` should still be selected in the Project navigator. Click the Object library button to display the Object library:

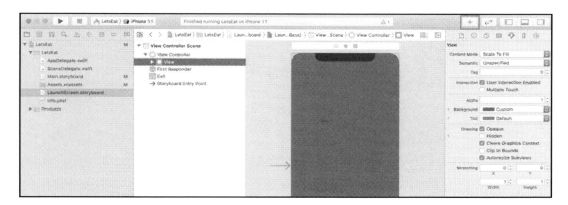

2. Click the Media button to show all of the graphic files in your project:

3. Type `detail` in the filter field. You'll see `detail-logo` in the results:

4. Drag `detail-logo` into the **View** of your **View Controller Scene** and center it vertically and horizontally. You'll see blue guidelines to help you. Click the Align button when you're done:

5. Tick **Horizontally in Container** and **Vertically in Container**. Click **Add 2 Constraints**:

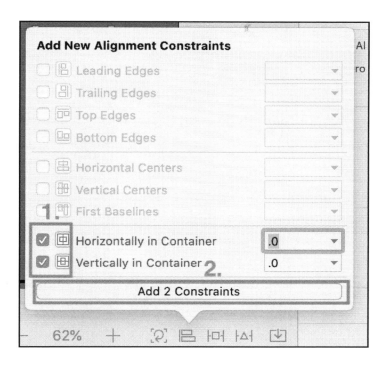

6. The constraints have been added to `detail-logo` and are visible in the document outline:

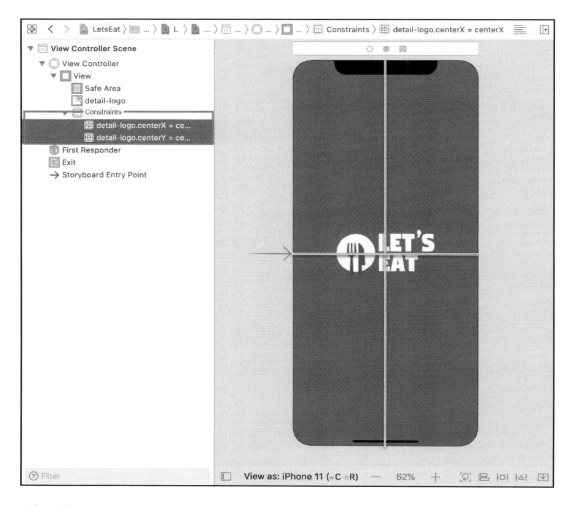

What the constraints do is specify the position of the logo in relation to the view controller's view. The view controller's view is the container in this case. **Horizontally in Container** calculates the logo's horizontal position relative to the left and the right sides of the container, and **Vertically in Container** calculates the logo's vertical position relative to the top and bottom of the container.

Build and run your app. You'll see the logo in the middle of the screen. Even if you try running the app in the Simulator with a different screen size, the logo will still be in the exact center of the screen.

 For more information on Auto Layout and how to use it, see this link: `https://developer.apple.com/library/archive/documentation/UserExperience/Conceptual/AutolayoutPG/`.

Now that you have completed configuring the **Launch** screen, you will configure the **Explore** and **Map** buttons to use the icons from the `Assets.xcassets` file you imported in the next section.

Adding the icons for the Explore and Map buttons

The **Explore** and **Map** buttons currently do not have icons. These icons are in the `Assets.xcassets` folder. Let's add them to the buttons now:

1. Click `Main.storyboard`. Click **Explore** under **Explore Scene**. Click the Attributes Inspector button:

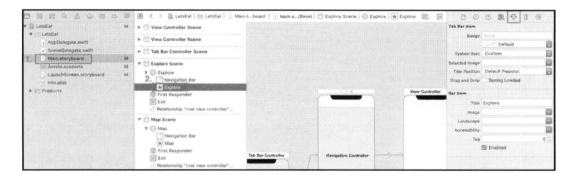

2. In the Attributes Inspector, set **Bar Item | Image** to `icon-explore-on`:

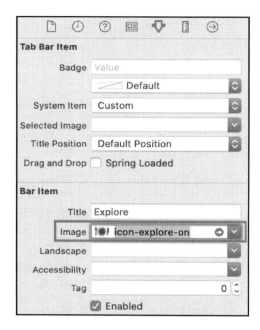

3. Click the **Map** button under **Map Scene** and, in the Attributes Inspector, set **Bar Item | Image** to `icon-map-on`:

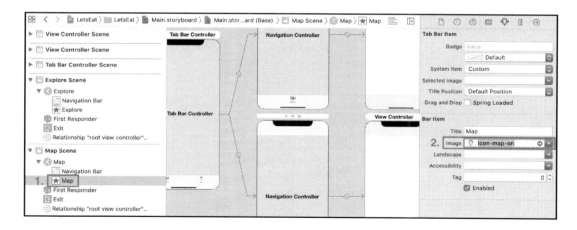

Build and run your app. When the app has finished launching, you can see the
Explore and **Map** buttons now have icons:

Congratulations! You have successfully configured the **Launch** screen and the tab
bar of your app!

Summary

In this chapter, you learned some useful terms used in iOS app development. You also learned about the different screens used in the *Let's Eat* app and how the user would use the app. As you recreate the app's user interface from scratch, you'll be able to compare what you're doing to the actual app. Next, you learned how to use Interface Builder and storyboards to add a tab bar controller scene to your app, configure the button titles, and configure the navigation bar for the **Explore** and **Map** screens. You added an `Assets.xcassets` file that contains all of the graphic files required for your project, configured the **Launch** screen for your app with a custom color and icon, and configured custom tab bar button icons.

Since you now know useful terms used in iOS app development, you will find it easier to understand the remainder of this book, as well as other books or online resources on the subject. You will also be able to create your own Xcode projects, delete files from a project, add assets to a project, use storyboards to prototype an app's screens, and use tab bar and navigation controllers, which will be useful when you write your own apps.

In the next chapter, you will continue setting up your app's user interface and become familiar with more UI elements. You will configure the **Explore** screen to display a collection view displaying collection view cells and a collection view section header containing a button that displays another view when tapped.

10
Building Your App Structure in Storyboard

In the previous chapter, you created a new Xcode project and started building the UI for the *Let's Eat* app. You added a tab bar to your app that allowed the user to select between the **Explore** and **Map** screens, added navigation bars to both screens, added custom graphics files to your app, made a custom color for the **Launch** screen, and added custom icons for the **Launch** screen and tab bar buttons. The **Explore** screen is displayed initially when your app is launched, but it is currently blank.

As you saw in the *Touring the Let's Eat app* section in `Chapter 9`, *Setting Up the Basic Structure*, the **Explore** screen should display a collection view showing a list of cuisines in collection view cells and have a collection view section header containing a **LOCATION** button. Tapping the **LOCATION** button should display a **Locations** screen containing a list of locations.

In this chapter, you will make the **Explore** screen display a **collection view** containing 20 empty **collection view cells**, as well as a **collection view section header** containing a button that will display a view representing the **Locations** screen when tapped. You'll also configure a **Cancel** button to dismiss this view and return you to the **Explore** screen.

You'll be adding a small amount of code to your app to link UI elements to outlets, but don't worry too much about this—you'll learn more about the code in your app in the next part of this book.

By the end of this chapter, you'll have learned how to add view controllers to a storyboard scene, link outlets in view controllers to scenes, create custom colors, set up collection view cells and collection view section headers, and present a view controller modally.

In this chapter, we will cover the following topics:

- Adding a collection view to the **Explore** screen
- Connecting storyboard elements to an outlet in a view controller
- Configuring data source methods for the collection view
- Adding a collection view section header to the collection view
- Creating a custom color
- Configuring the collection view cell and collection view section header size
- Presenting a view modally

Technical requirements

You will continue working on the `LetsEat` project that you created in the previous chapter.

The completed Xcode project for this chapter is in the `Chapter10` folder of the code bundle for this book, which can be downloaded here:

`https://github.com/PacktPublishing/iOS-13-Programming-for-Beginners`.

Let's start by adding a collection view to the **Explore** scene, which will eventually display the list of cuisines and the **LOCATION** button.

Check out the following video to see the code in action:

`http://bit.ly/2tHlxq0`

Adding a collection view to the Explore screen

A collection view is an instance of the `UICollectionView` class. Like a spreadsheet program, it displays a grid of cells. Each cell in a collection view is a collection view cell, which is an instance of the `UICollectionViewCell` class. In this section, you will add a collection view to the view for the **Explore** scene.

A collection view needs a view controller to tell it what to display and to handle user interactions. Let's create a new **Cocoa Touch Class** file and implement `ExploreViewController`, a subclass of the view controller class, to act as the collection view's view controller.

Open the `LetsEat` project you created in the previous chapter and run the app to make sure everything still works as it should. The tab bar and navigation bar are visible and the **Explore** screen is blank. Stop the app.

Let's begin by adding a collection view to the view controller scene for the **Explore** screen in `Main.storyboard`:

1. Click `Main.storyboard`. Then, click the Object library button:

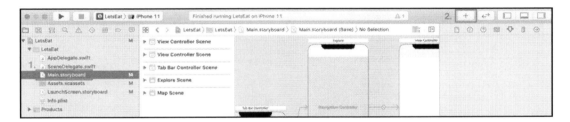

2. The Object library window will appear. Type `collec` in the filter field. A **Collection View** object will appear as one of the results. Drag it to the middle of the **View** of the **View Controller Scene** for the **Explore** screen, as shown in the following screenshot:

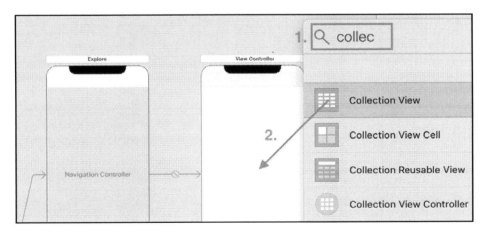

The **Collection View** has been added, but it only takes up a small part of the screen. As shown in the app tour in Chapter 9, *Setting Up the Basic Structure*, it should take up the entire screen. As you may recall, in the previous chapter, you used the Auto Layout Align button to make the *Let's Eat* app icon appear at the center of the **Launch** screen. This time, you will use the Auto Layout Add New Constraints button to bind the edges of the collection view to the edges of its enclosing view.

3. Make sure the collection view is selected. Click the Auto Layout Add New Constraints button:

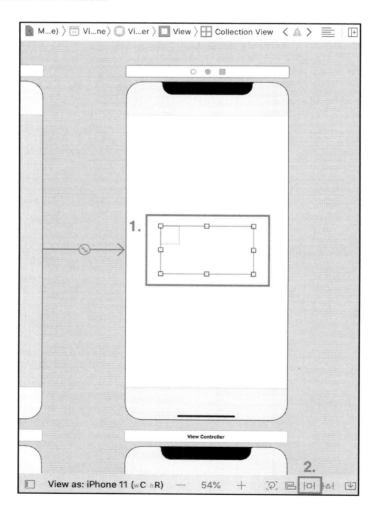

4. Type 0 in the top, left, right, and bottom edge constraint fields and click all the struts. Make sure all the struts are bright red. Click **Add 4 constraints.** This action sets the space between the edges of the collection view and the edges of the enclosing view to 0. This binds the edges of the collection view to those of the enclosing view. The collection view will take up the whole of the screen, regardless of device and orientation.

5. Now, all four sides of the collection view are bound to the edges of the screen:

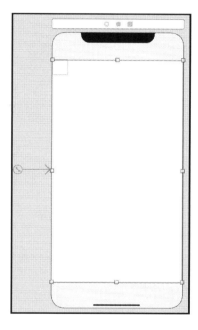

In this section, you added a collection view to the view of the view controller scene for the **Explore** screen and used Auto Layout to make it fill the screen completely.

 For more information on Auto Layout and how to use it, go to `https://developer.apple.com/library/archive/` `documentation/UserExperience/Conceptual/AutolayoutPG/.`

In the next section, you will add a **Cocoa Touch Class** file to your project so that you can implement the code for the `ExploreViewController` class, which determines what the collection view will display.

Adding a Cocoa Touch Class file to your project

First, you will make a new `Explore` group in your project to keep things organized. Next, you will add a **Cocoa Touch Class** file, `ExploreViewController.swift`, to this group. This is where you will declare and define the `ExploreViewController` class, which will contain the properties and methods that control the collection view that you added to the **View Controller Scene** earlier. Follow these steps to do so:

1. Right-click on the `LetsEat` group in the Project navigator and choose **New Group.**

2. The name of the group will be highlighted. Change it to `Explore` and press *Return* on the keyboard when you're done:

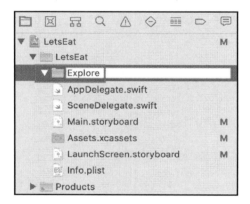

If you make a mistake, press *Return* once more. This makes the field editable so that you can make changes to the name.

3. Right-click on the `Explore` group in the Project navigator and choose **New File...**:

4. **iOS** should already be selected. Choose **Cocoa Touch Class** and click **Next**:

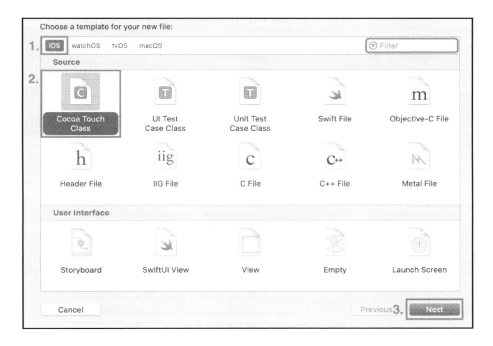

5. The **Choose options for your new file** screen will appear:

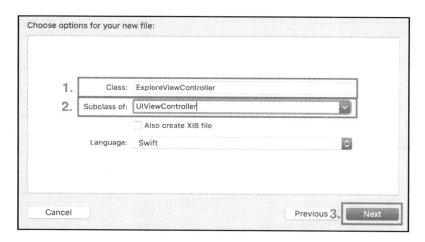

Enter the following in the **Class** and **Subclass of** fields:

- **Class**: `Explore`
- **Subclass of**: `UIViewController`

  The name in the **Class** field is automatically changed to `ExploreViewController`

- Click **Next**

6. Click **Create** to add the file to your project.

7. You will see that `ExploreViewController.swift` has been added to the project inside the `Explore` folder in the Project navigator. Review the code in the Editing area. You'll see that `ExploreViewController` is a subclass of `UIViewController`, which means it inherits properties and methods from the `UIViewController` class. There is one function, `viewDidLoad()`, inside the class definition, but it won't be used right now.

8. Remove the remaining code from the `ExploreViewController.swift` file so that it looks like this:

```
//
//  ExploreViewController.swift
//  LetsEat
//
//  Created by admin on 28/11/2019.
//  Copyright © 2019 MyName. All rights reserved.
//

import UIKit

class ExploreViewController: UIViewController {

    override func viewDidLoad() {
        super.viewDidLoad()

        // Do any additional setup after loading
            the view.
    }

}
```

Now, you have a collection view in the view controller scene for the **Explore** screen, as well as an `ExploreViewController.swift` file containing the `ExploreViewController` class definition in your app.

The next step is to assign `ExploreViewController` as the view controller for the view in your **View Controller Scene**, and assign an outlet for the collection view in `ExploreViewController`, which allows you to manage what the the collection view displays.

Connecting outlets in storyboard to the view controller

Let's review where you are now. In `Main.storyboard`, you have a **View ControllerScene** that has a view containing a collection view. In `ExploreViewController.swift`, you have code that declares and defines the `ExploreViewController` class. You need to assign the `ExploreViewController` class as the view controller for the view containing the collection view. To do this, you will use the Identity inspector.

After that, you need to be able to manage the collection view from `ExploreViewController`. You'll create a connection between the collection view to an outlet in `ExploreViewController`.

To assign the identity of the view controller scene in the **Explore** screen to the `ExploreViewController` class, follow these steps:

1. Click on `Main.storyboard`. Make sure the **View Controller Scene** for the **Explore** screen is selected. Click the **View Controller** icon in the document outline. Then, click on the Identity inspector:

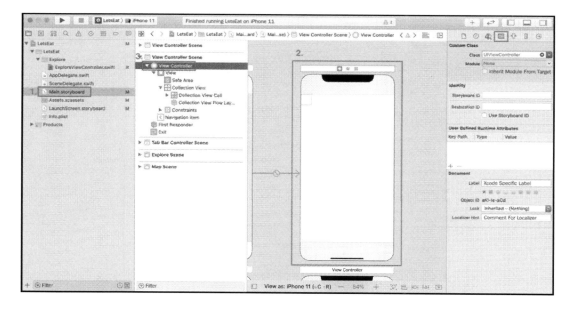

2. In the **Class** field, choose `ExploreViewController`:

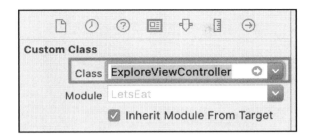

Now, the view controller for this scene has been set to `ExploreViewController`. Note that the scene name has changed from **View Controller Scene** to **Explore View Controller Scene**. Now let's create the outlet for the collection view.

3. Click the Navigator and Inspector buttons to hide the Navigator and Inspector areas:

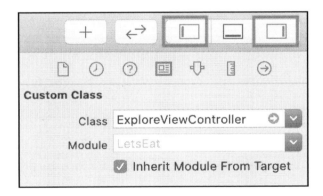

4. Click on the Adjust Editor Options button:

5. Choose **Assistant** from the pop-up menu:

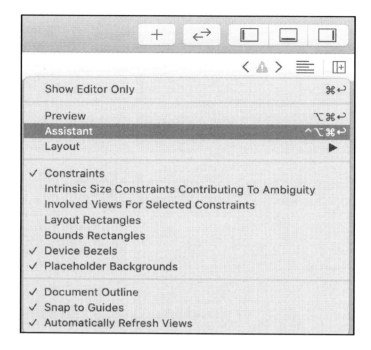

This will display any Swift files associated with this scene.

6. As you can see, the `Main.storyboard` file's content appears on the left and some code appears on the right, but it doesn't look like the `ExploreViewController` class. Look at the bar just above the code. You will see that `UIResponder.h` has been selected, which is incorrect:

```
1  #if (defined(USE_UIKIT_PUBLIC_HEADERS) &&
       USE_UIKIT_PUBLIC_HEADERS) ||
       !__has_include(<UIKitCore/UIResponder
       .h>)
```

7. Click on `UIResponder.h` and choose `ExploreViewController.swift` from the pop-up menu:

The `ExploreViewController` class definition appears on the right-hand side of the Editing area. Now, you need to connect the collection view in the **Explore View Controller Scene** to an outlet in the `ExploreViewController` class.

8. *Ctrl + Drag* from the **Collection View** in the **Explore View Controller Scene** to the `ExploreViewController` file, just below the class name declaration:

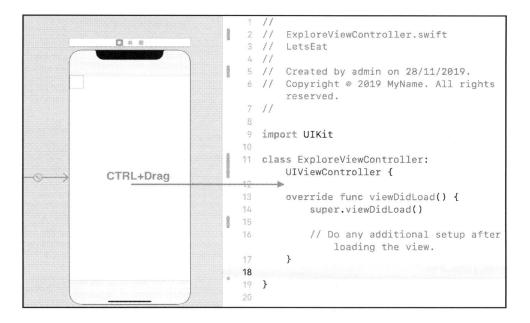

9. Type the name of the outlet, `collectionView`, into the **Name** text field and click **Connect**:

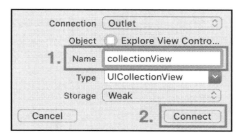

10. Now, you will see that the code that creates the `collectionView` outlet has been automatically added to the `ExploreViewController.swift` file. Note the `IBOutlet` keyword, which indicates that `collectionView` is an outlet. Click the **x** to close the **Assistant** window:

```
 1  //
 2  //  ExploreViewController.swift
 3  //  LetsEat
 4  //
 5  //  Created by admin on 28/11/2019.
 6  //  Copyright © 2019 MyName. All rights
        reserved.
 7  //
 8
 9  import UIKit
10
11  class ExploreViewController:
        UIViewController {
12
        @IBOutlet weak var collectionView:
            UICollectionView!
14
15      override func viewDidLoad() {
16          super.viewDidLoad()
```

`ExploreViewController` now has an outlet, `collectionView`, for the collection view. This means `ExploreViewController` can manage what the collection view displays.

It is common to make mistakes when using *Ctrl + Drag* to drag from an object in a storyboard scene to the Swift file. This may cause a crash to occur when the app is launched. To check if there are any errors in the connection between the collection view and `ExploreViewController`, follow these steps:

1. Click the Navigator and Inspector buttons to display the Navigator and Inspector areas.

2. With **Explore View Controller** in **Explore View Controller Scene** selected, click the Connections inspector:

You should be able to see the outlet, `collectionView`, connected to the collection view in the **Outlets** section.

3. If you see a tiny error icon, click on the **x** to break the connection:

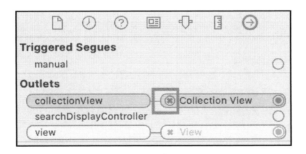

4. Drag from the **collectionView** outlet back to the **Collection View** to re-establish the connection:

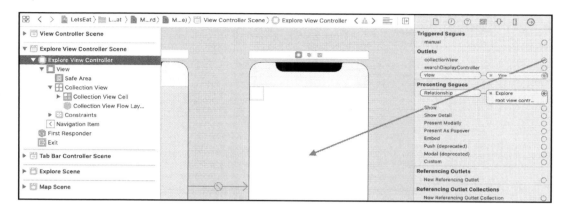

Now, you've assigned `ExploreViewController` as the view controller for the **Explore View Controller Scene** and created an outlet in `ExploreViewController` for the collection view.

Next, in order to display collection view cells on screen, you will need to implement **data source** methods for the collection view by adding some code to `ExploreViewController`. You will do this in the next section.

Configuring data source methods for the collection view

The collection view needs to know how many cells to display and what to display in each cell. Normally, the view controller for the collection view is responsible for providing this information. Apple has already defined the **collection view data source protocol** for this purpose. All you need to do is connect the collection view's data source outlet to `ExploreViewController` and implement the required methods of the collection view data source protocol.

The collection view also needs to know what to do if the user taps on a collection view cell. Again, the view controller for the collection view is responsible, and Apple has defined the **collection view delegate protocol** for this purpose. You will connect the collection view's delegate outlet to `ExploreViewController`, but you won't be implementing any methods from the collection view delegate protocol yet.

You will need to type in a small amount of code in this chapter. Don't worry about what it means; you'll learn more about **collection view controllers** and their associated protocols in `Chapter 13`, *Getting Started with MVC and Collection Views*.

In this section, we'll set the delegate and data source outlets of the collection view, which is easily done using Interface Builder.

Setting the delegate and data source properties of the collection view

`ExploreViewController` will provide the data that the collection view will display, as well as the methods that will be executed when the user interacts with the collection view. You need to connect the collection view's data source and delegate outlets to `ExploreViewController` for this to work. Follow these steps to do so:

1. Click the Navigator and Inspector buttons to display the Navigator and Inspector areas again if you haven't done so already.

2. `Main.storyboard` should still be selected. Click the **Collection View** for the **Explore View Controller Scene** in the document outline to select it. Click the Connections inspector. Look at the **Outlets** section. Note that there are two empty circles next to the **dataSource** and **delegate** outlets. Drag from each empty circle to the `ExploreViewController` icon in the document outline, as shown in the following screenshot:

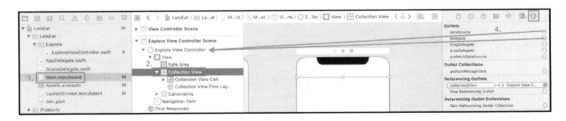

3. The **dataSource** and **delegate** properties of **Collection View** have been connected to `ExploreViewController`:

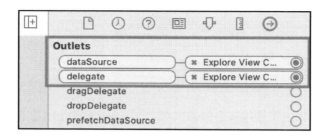

Now, you will add some code to make `ExploreViewController` conform to the collection view data source protocol, and tell the collection view to display 20 collection view cells when you run your app.

Adopting the UICollectionViewDataSource and UICollectionViewDelegate protocols

So far, you've made `ExploreViewController` the data source and delegate for the collection view. The next step is to adopt the collection view data source and delegate protocols and implement any required methods. You'll also change the color of the collection view cell so that it will be easy to see on screen. Follow these steps to do this:

1. The default color of the **Collection View Cell** is white and will be invisible when you run the app. Click **Collection View Cell** in the document outline. This represents the cells that the **Collection View** will display. Make sure the Attributes inspector is selected:

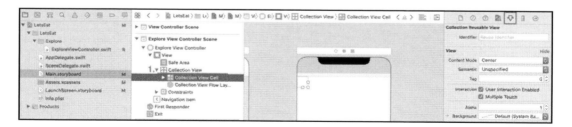

2. Change the **Identifier** to `exploreCell` and press *Return*. Note that the name **Collection View Cell** has been changed to `exploreCell`. Set the **Background** color to `Light Grey Color` so that it will be visible when you run the app:

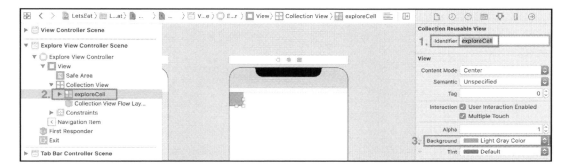

3. Click on `ExploreViewController.swift` in the Project navigator. Type in the following code after the class declaration to make `ExploreViewController` adopt the `UICollectionViewDataSource` and `UICollectionViewDelegate` protocols:

    ```
    class ExploreViewController: UIViewController,
    UICollectionViewDataSource, UICollectionViewDelegate {
    ```

    After a few seconds, an error will appear. Click on it.

4. The error message says that **Type 'ExploreViewController' does not conform to protocol 'UICollectionViewDataSource'
    Do you want to add protocol stubs?**
    What this means is that, if you wish to adopt the `UICollectionViewDataSource` protocol, then you'll need to implement the methods that are required by this protocol. Click **Fix.**

5. The methods that are required by the `UICollectionViewDataSource` protocol are automatically inserted into `ExploreViewController.swift`:

```
12
13      func collectionView(_ collectionView:
            UICollectionView, numberOfItemsInSection
            section: Int) -> Int {
14          code
15      }
16
17      func collectionView(_ collectionView:
            UICollectionView, cellForItemAt
            indexPath: IndexPath) ->
            UICollectionViewCell {
18          code
19      }
```

The first method tells the collection view how many cells to display, while the second method tells the collection view what to display in each collection view cell.

6. Replace the `code` text in the first method with `20`. This tells the collection view to display 20 cells:

```
12
13      func collectionView(_ collectionView:
            UICollectionView, numberOfItemsInSection
            section: Int) -> Int {
14          20
15      }
```

7. Replace the `code` text in the second method with the following code:

```
let cell =
collectionView.dequeueReusableCell(withReuseIdentifier:
        "exploreCell", for: indexPath)
return cell
```

Don't worry about what this means for now as you'll learn more about collection views in `Chapter 13`, *Getting Started with MVC and Collection Views.*

Build and run the app. You should see the Simulator display a grid of 20 light grey collection view cells:

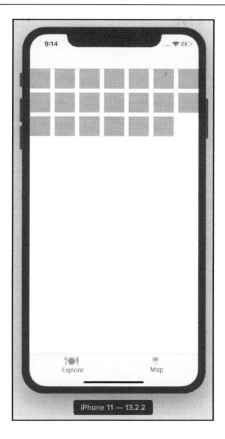

As you saw in the app tour in Chapter 9, *Setting Up the Basic Structure*, there should be a **LOCATION** button at the top right of this screen. You will implement a collection view section header for the collection view, so that you have a place to put this button, in the next section.

Adding a section header to the collection view

Now, you need to add the **LOCATION** button to the **Explore** screen. A collection view can have a section header and a section footer. For now, you just need the section header, which will provide a space for the **LOCATION** button.

Follow these steps to add one:

1. Click on `Main.storyboard` and click on the **Collection View** in the document outline. Click on the Attributes inspector. Then, tick the checkbox for **Section Header**:

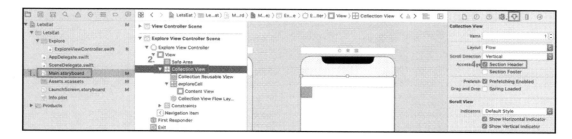

2. Note that **Collection Reusable View** appears in the document outline. This is the collection view section header. The Attributes inspector should still be selected. Click on **Collection Reusable View** in the document outline and type `header` into the **Identifier** field, pressing *Return* when you're done:

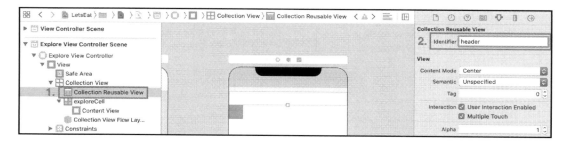

3. Click on `ExploreViewController.swift` in the Project navigator. Just before the data source methods, type in the following code:

```
func collectionView(_ collectionView: UICollectionView,
viewForSupplementaryElementOfKind kind: String, at indexPath:
IndexPath)
-> UICollectionReusableView {
 let headerView =
collectionView.dequeueReusableSupplementaryView(ofKind: kind,
 withReuseIdentifier: "header", for: indexPath)
 return headerView
}
```

The preceding code creates and returns an instance of the collection view section header to be displayed on the screen.

Build and run the app. You should see the collection view section header as a white space between the collection view cells and the navigation bar:

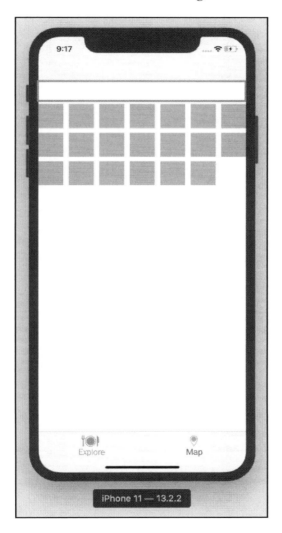

Before you add the button to the collection view section header, take a look at the collection view cells. Currently, you're using a standard light grey color for the cell background. Let's make a custom color for the cell background that can be reused for other objects you will add later.

Creating a custom color

In the previous chapter, you used a custom color for the **Launch** screen. You can actually create custom colors and assign them a name in the `Assets.xcassets` file. This makes them really easy to reuse and ensures consistency in your project. In this section, you will create a custom color and assign it to the collection view cells. Follow these steps to do so:

1. Click on the `Assets.xcassets` folder in the Project navigator and right-click in the clear white space of the document outline, as shown in the following screenshot:

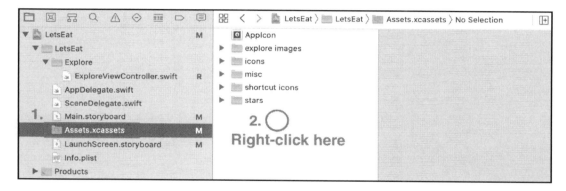

2. Choose **New Folder** from the pop-up menu:

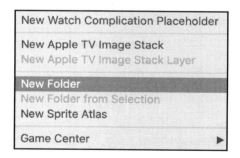

3. Change the name of the folder to `colors`:

If you make a mistake while renaming the folder, remember that you can always select the name and press *Return* to make it editable.

4. Right-click on the `colors` folder and choose **New Color Set**:

5. Click on the **Color Set** and click the Attributes inspector. Set the name of the color to `Demo Grey`, pressing *Return* when you're done:

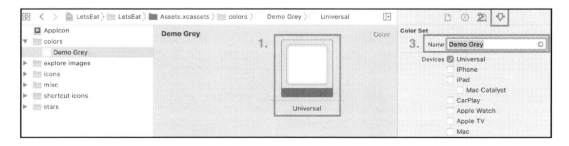

6. In the **Color** section of the Attributes inspector, set the **Input Method** to **8-bit Hexadecimal** and type #AAAAAA into the **Hex** field, pressing *Return* when you're done:

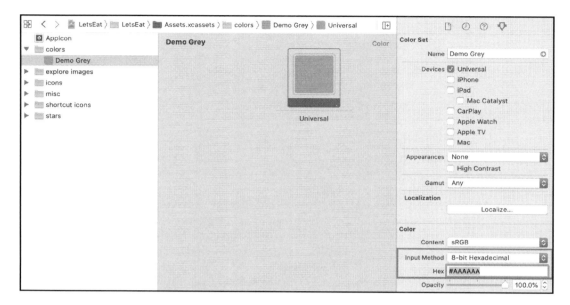

7. Click on Main.storyboard. Then, click on exploreCell in the document outline. In the Attributes inspector, set the **Background** color of the cell to your newly created Demo Grey color:

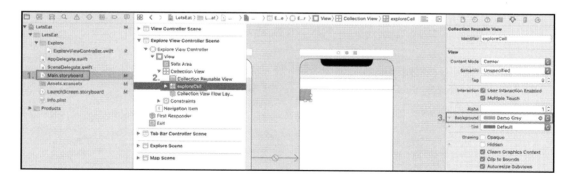

You've set the color of the collection view cells, but you'll need to change their size to match the size of the cells shown in the app tour in Chapter 9, *Setting Up the Basic Structure*. You also need to make the collection view section header taller. You will set the cell and header size in your app using the Size inspector in the next section.

Configuring the collection view cell and section header size

Now, you need to change the size of the collection view cell and collection view section header so that it more closely resembles the **Explore** screen that was shown in the app tour in Chapter 9, *Setting Up the Basic Structure*. To set the layout of the collection view cells, you use the Size inspector. Follow these steps:

1. Select **Collection View** in the document outline. Click the Size inspector:

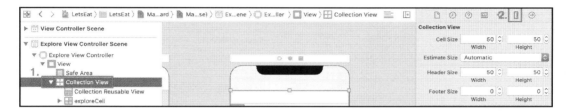

2. The **Collection View** size settings will be displayed:

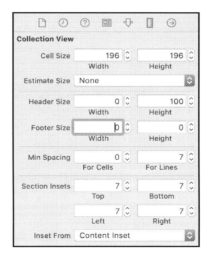

Configure the **Collection View** size settings, as follows:

- **Cell Size**: The width is 196 and the height is 196.
- **Estimate Size**: None.
- **Header Size**: The width is 0 and the height is 100.

- **Min Spacing**: For cells, this is 0, while for lines, this is 7.
- **Section Insets**: Set the top, bottom, left, and right to 7.

Remember to press *Return* after changing each value.

The units that are used in the Size inspector are points. Each point may refer to one or more pixels on the device screen. For the iPhone 11, the screen is 414 points wide and 896 points high, although the actual screen resolution is 828 x 1,792 pixels.

Cell Size determines the size of the collection view cell. **Header Size** determines the size of the collection view section header. **Min Spacing** determines the space between cells. **Section Insets** determines the space between the section containing the cells to the sides of the enclosing view. These settings are specific to the iPhone 11. In Chapter 24, *Getting Started with Mac Catalyst,* you will calculate the optimum cell size based on the dimensions of the device screen.

Build and run your project:

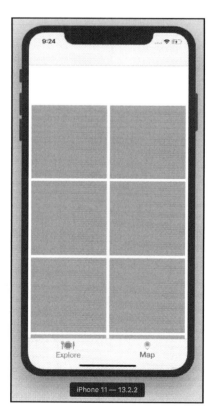

Note that, although there is no data in the cells and no button in the header, it looks similar to the **Explore** screen that was shown in the app tour in Chapter 9, *Setting Up the Basic Structure*. You will configure the cells to display data in the next part of this book. For now, let's add a button to the collection view section header, which will be used later to display the **Locations** screen.

Presenting a view modally

In this section, you will add a button to the collection view section header. When tapped, this button will display a view representing the **Locations** screen. This view will be from a new view controller scene embedded in a navigation controller, which you will add to the project. The view will be presented **modally**, which means you won't be able to do anything else until it is dismissed. To dismiss it, you'll add a **Cancel** button to the view's navigation bar. You'll also add a **Done** button, but you'll implement its functionality in a Chapter 17, *Getting Started with JSON Files.*

Adding a button to the collection view header

As shown in the app tour in Chapter 9, *Setting Up the Basic Structure*, there is a **LOCATION** button at the top right-hand side of the screen. In this section, you'll add a button to the collection view section header, which will eventually become the **LOCATION** button. Follow these steps to do so:

1. Make sure the **Explore View Controller Scene** is selected. Then, click the Object library button:

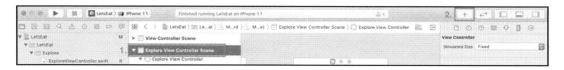

2. Type button in the filter field:

Button will appear in the results.

3. Drag the **Button** object to the **Collection Reusable View**:

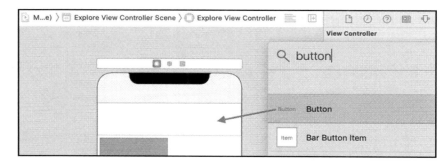

4. Position the **Button** object to the right-hand side of the **Collection Reusable View**:

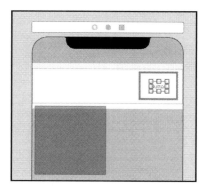

Its exact placement isn't important right now as you will customize the button's position in `Chapter 12`, *Modifying and Configuring Cells.* You now have a button in your collection view section header. Next, you will add a view controller scene to represent the **Locations** screen that will appear when the button is tapped.

Adding a new view controller scene

As shown in the app tour in `Chapter 9`, *Setting Up the Basic Structure,* when you tap the **LOCATION** button, a list of locations will appear in the **Locations** screen. You'll use a new view controller scene to represent this screen. Follow these steps to add it to the project:

1. Click the Object library button and type `view con` in the filter field. A **View Controller** object will be among the search results. Drag the **View Controller** object onto the storyboard:

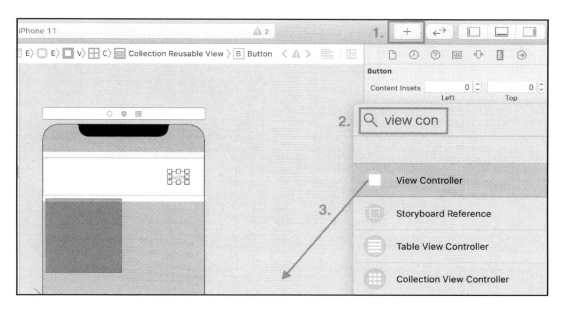

2. Position it to the right of the **Explore View Controller Scene**:

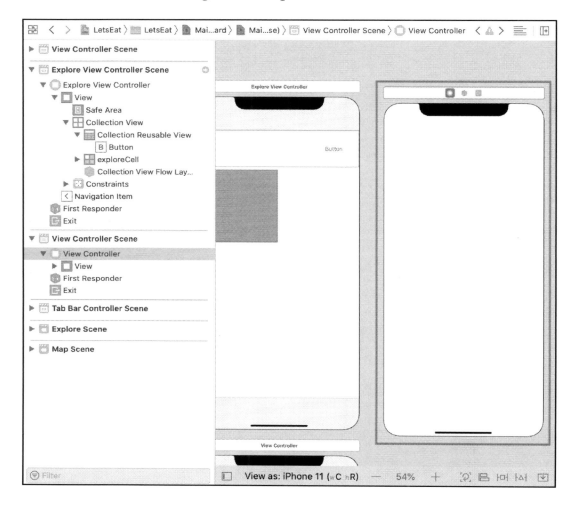

3. The newly added **View Controller Scene** should already be selected. In the document outline, click on the **View Controller** icon for this scene:

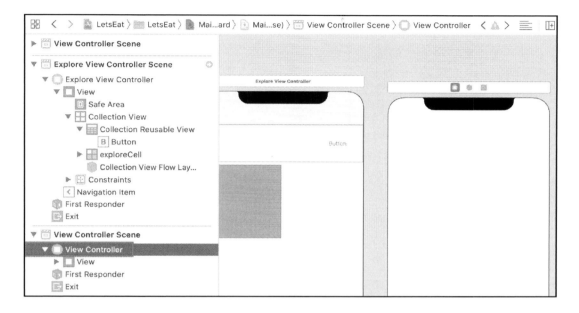

4. You will need space for the **Cancel** and **Done** buttons, so you will need to embed this **View Controller Scene** in a navigation controller to provide a navigation bar where the buttons can be placed. Choose **Embed In | Navigation Controller** from the **Editor** menu:

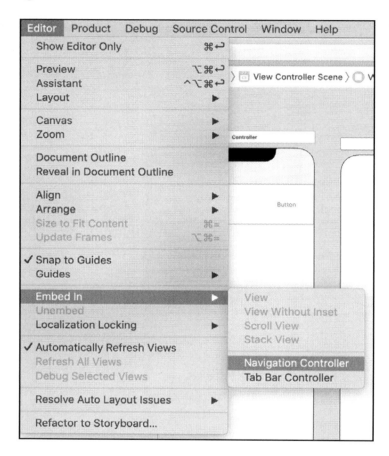

5. A **Navigation Controller Scene** will appear to the left of the **View Controller Scene**:

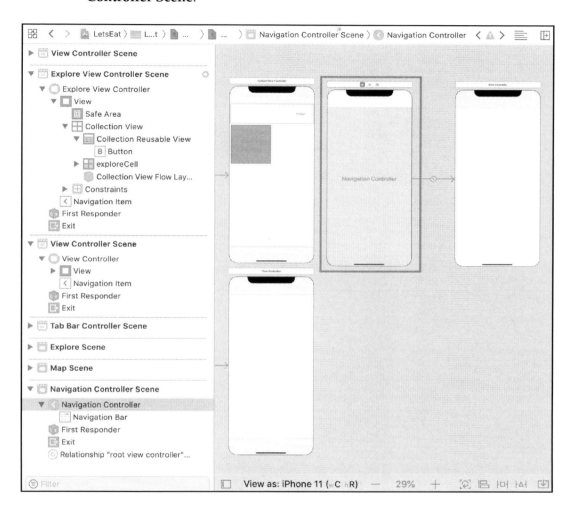

6. *Ctrl + Drag* from the **Button** to the **Navigation Controller Scene**:

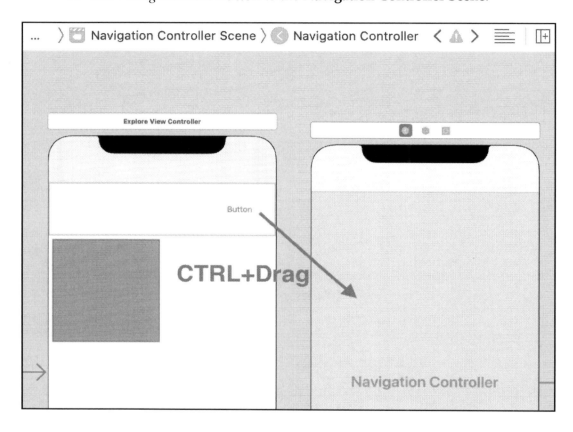

7. The **Segue** pop-up menu will appear. Choose **Present Modally**. This makes the view controller's view slide up from the bottom of the screen when the button is clicked. You won't be able to interact with any other view until this view is dismissed:

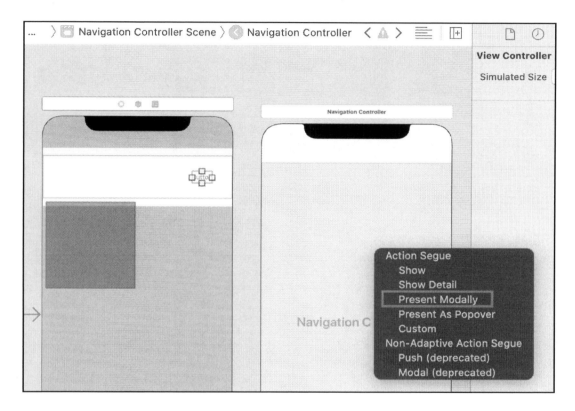

8. Note that a segue has linked the **Explore View Controller Scene** and the **Navigation Controller Scene** together:

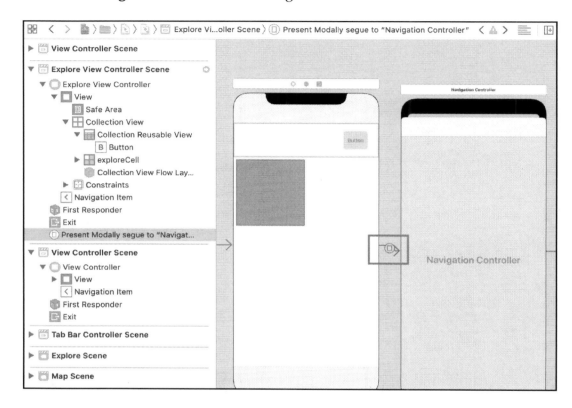

Build and run. If you click **Button**, the new view controller's view should slide up from the bottom of the screen:

At the moment, you can't dismiss this view. In the next section, you will add a **Cancel** button to the navigation bar and program it so that it dismisses the view.

Adding the Cancel and Done buttons to the navigation bar

One of the benefits of embedding a view controller in a navigation controller is the navigation bar at the top of the screen. You can place buttons on its left- and right-hand sides.

Follow these steps to add the **Cancel** and **Done** buttons to the navigation bar:

1. Click the **Navigation Item** in the **View Controller Scene**. Then, click the Object library button:

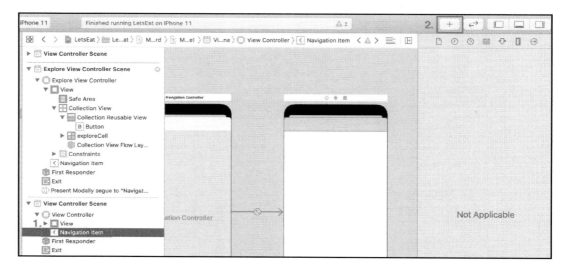

2. Type `bar b` into the filter field and drag two **Bar Button Item** objects to each side of the navigation bar:

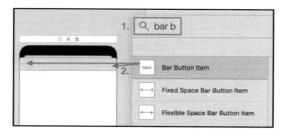

3. Click the **Item** button on the right:

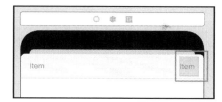

4. Click the Attributes inspector. Choose Done from the **System Item** menu:

5. Click the **Item** button on the left and choose Cancel from the **System Item** menu:

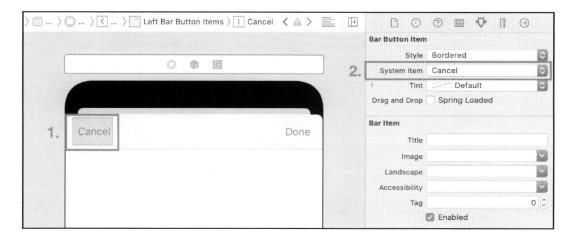

Remember that the navigation controller has a property that holds an array of view controllers. When you click the button in the **Explore** screen, the new view controller is added to the array and its view appears from the bottom of the screen, covering the collection view. To dismiss the view, you will need to link the **Cancel** button to the scene exit and implement an unwind method in `ExploreViewController` that will be executed after the scene exits.

6. In the Project navigator, click `ExploreViewController.swift` and add the following code at the bottom of the file, just before the last curly brace:

```
@IBAction func unwindLocationCancel(segue:UIStoryboardSegue){
}
```

7. Click on `Main.storyboard` in the Project navigator. *Ctrl + Drag* from the **Cancel** button to the Scene exit icon and choose `unwindLocationCancelwithSegue:` from the pop-up menu:

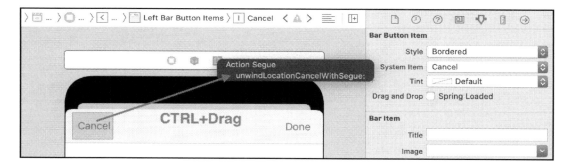

This will remove the view controller from the navigation controller's array of view controllers, making the view that is presented modally go away and execute the `unwindLocationCancel(segue:)` method.

Build and run your app and click the button. The new view will appear onscreen. If you click the **Cancel** button, the view disappears:

Congratulations! You've completed the basic structure for the **Explore** screen.

Summary

In this chapter, you added a collection view to the **Explore** screen in `Main.storyboard` and added a new file, `ExploreViewController.swift`, which contains the implementation of the `ExploreViewController` class. You made `ExploreViewController` the view controller for the scene containing the collection view. Then, you added an outlet to connect the collection view to `ExploreViewController` and made `ExploreViewController` the data source and delegate for the collection view. You added a collection view section header to the collection view, configured a custom color that was used as the color for the collection view cells, and set the size for the collection view cells and collection view section header. Finally, you added a button to display a second view and configured a **Cancel** button to dismiss it.

When you run the app in the Simulator, your **Explore** screen will now display 20 empty collection view cells and have a button in the collection view section header, which presents another view modally when tapped. Tapping the **Cancel** button in the presented view will return the user to the **Explore** screen. These cells in the **Explore** screen are blank for now but will be used later to display cuisines. We've done a lot of work! You should be proud of yourself.

At this point, you should be fairly proficient in using Interface Builder to add views and view controllers to a storyboard scene, link view controller outlets to UI elements in storyboards, create custom colors, set up collection view cells and section headers, and present views modally. This will be very useful when you're designing the user interface for your own apps.

In the next chapter, you'll configure the new view controller to display a table view, and you'll implement a map view for the **Map** screen.

11

Finishing Up Your App Structure in Storyboard

In the previous chapter, you configured the **Explore** screen so that it displayed 20 empty collection view cells in a collection view, added a button to the collection view section header to present a view representing the **Locations** screen modally, and added a **Cancel** button to dismiss this view.

In this chapter, you will implement the remaining screens that were shown in the app tour shown in `Chapter 9`, *Setting Up the Basic Structure*.

First, you'll add a blank **table view** to the **Locations** screen.

Next, you'll add the **Restaurant List** screen. This will be displayed when a cell in the **Explore** screen is tapped. This screen will contain a collection view with a single collection view cell.

After that, you'll add the **Restaurant Detail** screen. This will be displayed when the cell in the **Restaurant List** screen is tapped. This screen will contain a table view with **static table view cells**. You'll also add a button to one of the cells that displays a view representing the **Review Form** screen when tapped.

Finally, you'll make the **Map** screen display a map.

By the end of this chapter, you'll have learned how to add and configure a table view to a storyboard scene, how to add segues between scenes, and how to add a map view to a scene. The basic structure of your app will be complete and you will be able to walk through all the screens in the Simulator. None of the screens will be displaying data, but you will finish their implementation in Section three of this book.

The following topics will be covered:

- Adding a table view to the **Locations** screen
- Implementing the **Restaurant List** screen
- Implementing the **Restaurant Detail** screen
- Adding a map view to the **Map** screen

Technical requirements

You will continue working on the LetsEat project that you created in the previous chapter.

The completed Xcode project for this chapter is in the Chapter11 folder of the code bundle for this book, which can be downloaded here:

https://github.com/PacktPublishing/iOS-13-Programming-for-Beginners.

Let's start by adding a table view to the **Locations** screen, which is needed to display the list of restaurant locations. You'll do this in the next section.

Check out the following video to see the code in action:

http://bit.ly/2Gk1WyM

Adding a table view to the Locations screen

When you tap the button in the collection view section header of the **Explore** screen, another view representing the **Locations** screen will be presented modally, but it will be blank. Let's add a table view to this view. Go through the following steps:

1. Build and run the *Lets Eat* app to make sure everything still works as it should. Tap the **Button** in the **Collection Reusable View** of the **Explore** screen. A second view will appear showing the **Cancel** and **Done** buttons. Note that the screen is blank. Tap the **Cancel** button and stop the app.

2. Click `Main.storyboard` and select the **View Controller** icon in the **View Controller Scene,** which is presented modally by the button in the **Explore View Controller Scene.** Click the Object library button:

3. Type `table` into the filter field. A **Table View** object will appear in the results.

4. Drag the **Table View** object to the view in the **View Controller Scene:**

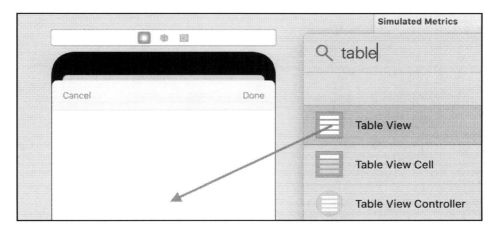

5. With the **Table View** selected, click the Add New Constraints button:

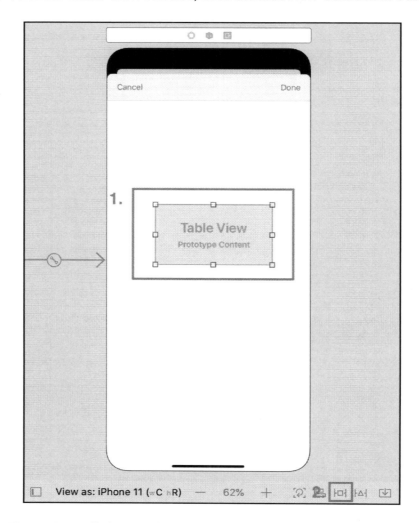

6. Type 0 into all the **Spacing to nearest neighbor** fields and make sure that the red struts are selected (they will turn bright red when selected). Click the **Add 4 Constraints** button.

7. The table view's edges are now bound to the edges of the view in the view controller scene:

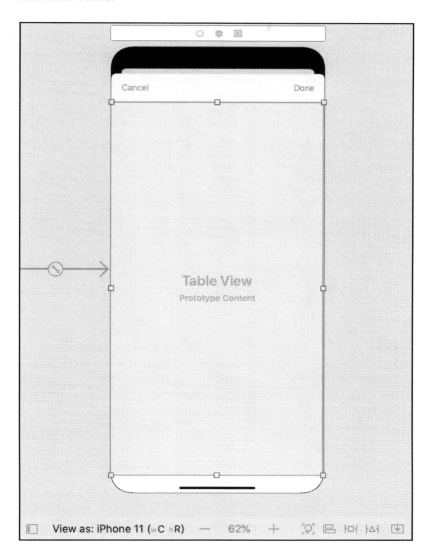

Build and run your app and tap the button in the section header. You'll see an empty table view in the **Locations** screen. Note that it takes up the whole of the screen:

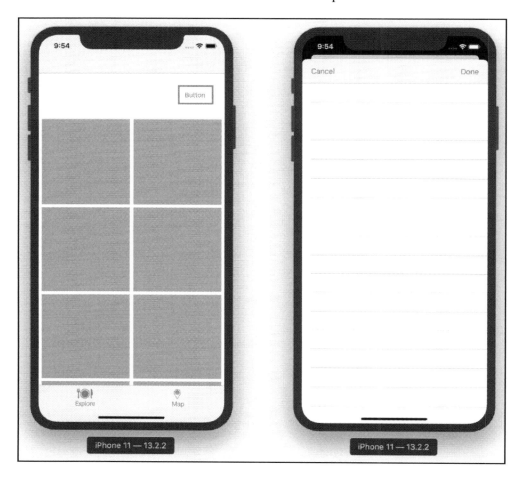

You won't be implementing the view controller class for this table view just yet. Eventually, this table view will display a list of restaurant locations, as shown in the app tour.

As you can see, this process is similar to adding a collection view to the **Explore** screen, which is what you did in the previous chapter. In the next section, you will add a view controller scene to your storyboard. This will be used for the **Restaurant List** screen.

Implementing the Restaurant List screen

As can be seen in the app tour in `Chapter 9`, *Setting Up the Basic Structure*, once you've set a location and tapped a cuisine in the **Explore** screen, the **Restaurant List** screen will appear, showing a list of restaurants.

To implement the **Restaurant List** screen, you'll need to add a new view controller scene to your storyboard. You'll add a collection view to the view in this scene. To do this, you'll also add a new **Cocoa Touch Class** file containing the `RestaurantListViewController` class definition, make it the view controller for the view controller scene's view, and connect the outlets of the collection view to this class. This process is very similar to the one we followed in the previous chapter for `ExploreViewController`.

Let's start by adding the new view controller scene. Go through the following steps:

1. In `Main.storyboard`, move the **Navigation Controller Scene** and **View Controller Scene** that you added in the previous chapter upward to make room for the new view controller scene that you will add:

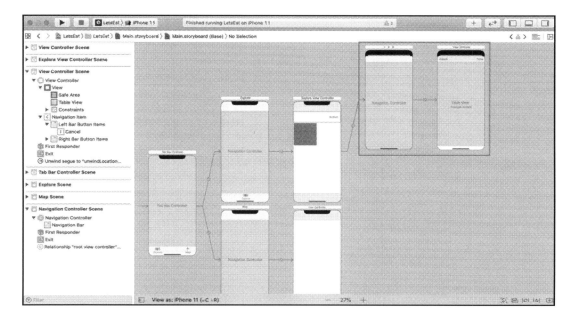

2. Click the Object library button and type `view con` into the filter field. A **View Controller** object will be in the results.

3. Drag the **View Controller** object into the storyboard, as shown in the following screenshot:

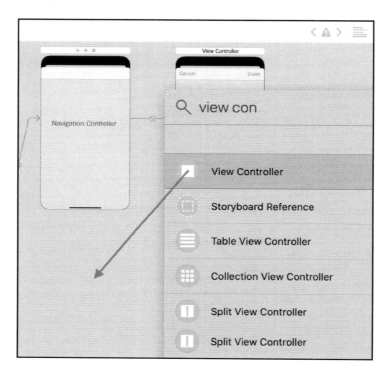

4. Click the Object library button and type `colle` into the filter field. A **Collection View** object will be in the results.

5. Drag the **Collection View** object to the **View** in the **View Controller** scene:

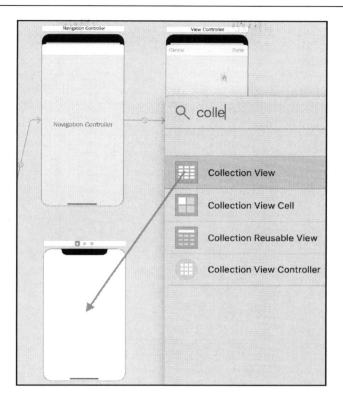

6. Make sure that the **Collection View** is selected. Then, click the Add New Constraints button:

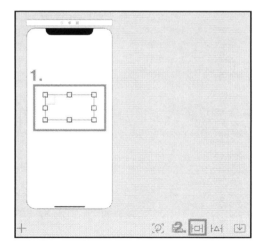

7. Type 0 into all the **Spacing to nearest neighbor** fields and make sure that the red struts are selected (they will turn bright red). Click the **Add 4 Constraints** button.

8. The edges of **Collection View** are now bound to the edges of the **View** in the **View Controller Scene**:

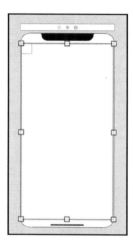

The view controller scene for the **Restaurant List** screen has been added, but it does not have a view controller yet. In the next section, you'll add a new **Cocoa Touch Class** file to your app so that you can declare and define the RestaurantListViewController class.

Declaring the RestaurantListViewController class

As you did in the previous chapter, you'll add a new **Cocoa Touch Class** file to your project, but this time, it will be used to implement the RestaurantListViewController class. Follow these steps:

1. Click the Navigator and Inspector buttons to turn on the **Navigator** and **Inspector** areas.

2. Right-click on the LetsEat group and choose **New Group** from the pop-up menu.

3. Name this new group `Restaurants`. If you make a mistake, click the name and press *Return* on your keyboard to make it editable again.

4. Right-click the `Restaurants` group and select **New File...**:

5. **iOS** should already be selected. Select **Cocoa Touch Class** and click **Next.**

6. The **Choose options for your new file screen** window will appear. Type the following into the **Class** and **Subclass of** fields:

   - **Class**: `RestaurantListViewController`
   - **Subclass of**: `UIViewController`

   Click **Next** when you're done.

7. On the next screen, click **Create.**

8. Now, the `RestaurantListViewController.swift` file has been added to the project, and you will see the boilerplate code for the `RestaurantListViewController` class in it. The `RestaurantListViewController` class is a subclass of `UIViewController` and contains a single method, `viewDidLoad()`. Like you did previously, remove all the extra code in the `RestaurantListViewController` class until only the code shown in the following screenshot remains:

As you did before for ExploreViewController, you'll make
RestaurantListViewController the view controller for the view in the view
controller scene and adopt the collection view data source and delegate protocols.
Now, you need to add an outlet for the collection view manually in the class
definition and use the Connections inspector to connect the outlet to the collection
view in the storyboard. You'll do this in the next section.

Adopting the delegate and data source protocols

You will modify RestaurantListViewController in order to adopt the collection
view data source and delegate protocols and add the required protocol methods.
You'll also add an outlet for the collection view and make
RestaurantListViewController the view controller for the view. Go through the
following steps:

1. Modify the RestaurantListViewController class declaration, as shown
    in the following code, to adopt the UICollectionViewDataSource and
    UICollectionViewDelegate protocols:

    ```
    class RestaurantListViewController: UIViewController,
    UICollectionViewDataSource, UICollectionViewDelegate {
    ```

2. When the error icon appears, click it.
3. You can see this error because the methods that are required to conform to
    the protocols you just added are not present in the class definition. Click
    the **Fix** button to add protocol stubs to your class.

4. Now, the stubs for the required methods have been added to the file. Rearrange everything so that the stubs will be at the bottom of the file, as shown in the following screenshot:

```
< >  ) ) ) RestaurantListViewController.swift > [M] collectionView(_:numberOfItemsInSection:)  < ⚠ >  ≣🔲  🗔

10
11    class RestaurantListViewController:
          UIViewController, UICollectionViewDataSource,
          UICollectionViewDelegate {
12
13
14        override func viewDidLoad() {
15            super.viewDidLoad()
16
17            // Do any additional setup after loading
                  the view.
18        }
19
20        func collectionView(_ collectionView:
              UICollectionView, numberOfItemsInSection
              section: Int) -> Int {
21            code
22        }
23
24        func collectionView(_ collectionView:
              UICollectionView, cellForItemAt
              indexPath: IndexPath) ->
              UICollectionViewCell {
25            code
26        }
```

5. Modify the code, as shown in the following code fragment, to make the collection view display a single collection view cell on the screen when the app is run:

```
func collectionView(_ collectionView: UICollectionView,
  numberOfItemsInSection section: Int) -> Int {
    1
}

func collectionView(_ collectionView: UICollectionView,
  cellForItemAt indexPath: IndexPath) -> UICollectionViewCell
```

```
    {
        return
    collectionView.dequeueReusableCell(withReuseIdentifier:
            "restaurantCell", for: indexPath)
    }
```

6. Your code should look like this:

```
19
20  func collectionView(_ collectionView:
        UICollectionView, numberOfItemsInSection
        section: Int) -> Int {
21      1
22  }
23
24  func collectionView(_ collectionView:
        UICollectionView, cellForItemAt
        indexPath: IndexPath) ->
        UICollectionViewCell {
25      return
            collectionView
            .dequeueReusableCell
            (withReuseIdentifier:
            "restaurantCell", for: indexPath)
26  }
```

7. Add an outlet, `collectionView,` **just under the class declaration. You will link this to the collection view in the storyboard later:**

```
@IBOutlet weak var collectionView: UICollectionView!
```

8. Your code should look like this:

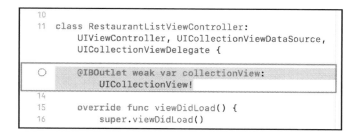

```
10
11  class RestaurantListViewController:
        UIViewController, UICollectionViewDataSource,
        UICollectionViewDelegate {

    ◯   @IBOutlet weak var collectionView:
            UICollectionView!
14
15      override func viewDidLoad() {
16          super.viewDidLoad()
```

Note that you won't be using the *assistant editor* like you did in the previous chapter. This is a matter of personal preference—you are free to choose whichever method suits you best.

9. Click `Main.storyboard` and click the **View Controller** icon of the newly added **View Controller Scene** in the Document Outline. Then, click the **Identity inspector**:

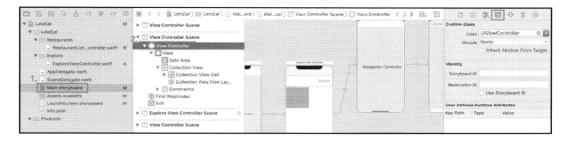

10. Select `RestaurantListViewController` in the **Class** field:

11. Note that the name of the **View Controller Scene** has changed to **Restaurant List View Controller Scene**. Click the **Connections inspector**. In the **Outlets** section, drag the circle next to the **collectionView** outlet to the **Collection View** in the **Restaurant List View Controller Scene**:

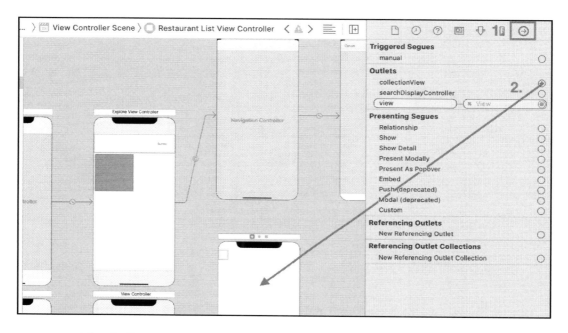

12. The **Collection View** in the **Restaurant List View Controller Scene** and the `collectionView` outlet in `RestaurantListViewController` are now connected:

13. Click the **Collection View** in the document outline. In the **Outlets** section of the Connections inspector, drag from the circles next to the **dataSource** and **delegate** outlets to the **Restaurant List View Controller** icon in the document outline:

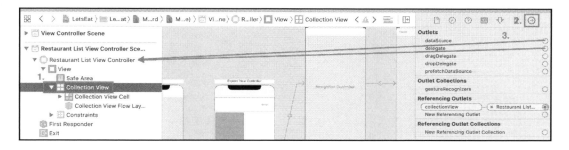

14. The **dataSource** and **delegate** outlets are now connected:

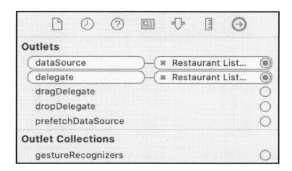

15. Click the **Collection View Cell** in the document outline. Click the Attributes inspector:

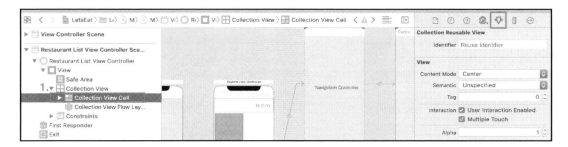

16. Set the **Identifier** of the **Collection View Cell** to `restaurantCell` and set the **Background** color to `Demo Grey`:

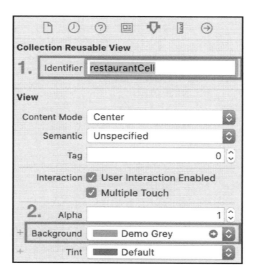

The **Restaurant List View Controller Scene** setup is now complete. Now, you need to display this screen when a cell in the **Explore** screen is tapped. To do this, you will need to add a segue to `exploreCell`, which you will do in the next section.

Presenting the Restaurant List screen

To display the **Restaurant List** screen when a cell in the **Explore** screen is tapped, go through the following steps.

1. Click **Explore View Controller Scene** in the document outline. Hold down *Ctrl* and drag from the `exploreCell` in the document outline to the **Restaurant List View Controller** scene:

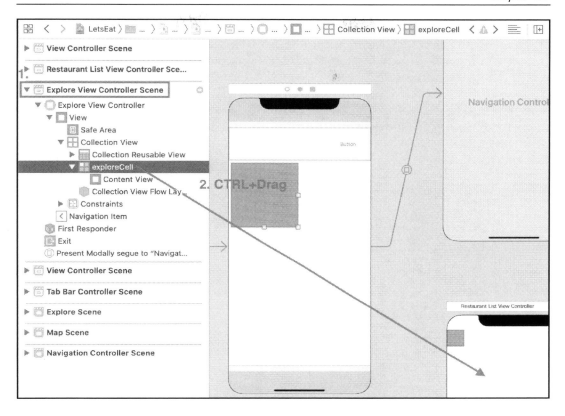

2. The **Segue** menu will appear. Choose **Show** from the menu. This makes the **Restaurant List** screen slide in from the right when the `exploreCell` is tapped and will display a **<Back** button in the navigation bar:

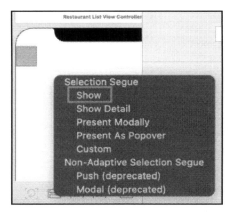

3. Build and run the app. In the **Explore** screen, tap a cell. You should see the **Restaurant List** screen appear with a collection view containing a single cell inside it. Tapping the **<Back** button in the navigation bar will dismiss the **Restaurant List** screen:

4. Eventually, this collection view will display a list of restaurants at a particular location, as shown in the app tour in `Chapter 9`, *Setting Up the Basic Structure.*

Great! The next thing you need to do is add a view controller scene to represent the **Restaurant Detail** screen. This screen will be displayed when a cell in the **Restaurant List** screen is tapped. You'll do this in the next section.

Implementing the Restaurant Detail screen

As shown in the app tour, when you tap a restaurant in the **Restaurant List** screen, a **Restaurant Detail** screen containing the details of that restaurant will appear. Tapping the **Add Review** button will display the **Review Form** screen where you can add reviews.

In this section, you'll add a new table view controller scene to your storyboard to represent the **Restaurant Detail** screen and add a second view controller scene to represent the **Review Form** screen. You'll place a button in one of the table view cells to present the second view.

Let's start by adding the new view controller scene. Go through the following steps:

1. Click the **Object library** button, search for `table`, and drag a **Table View Controller** object to the storyboard next to the **Restaurant List View Controller Scene**:

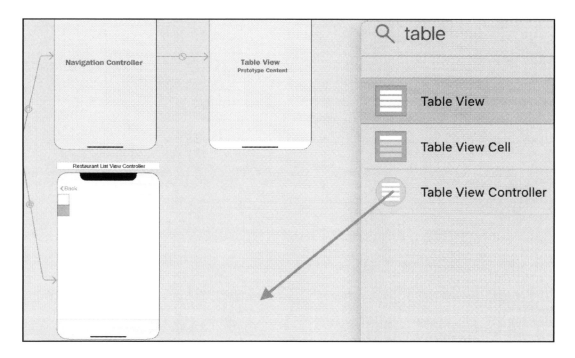

2. This is what the **Table View Controller Scene** looks like. Note that it already has a **Table View** inside it:

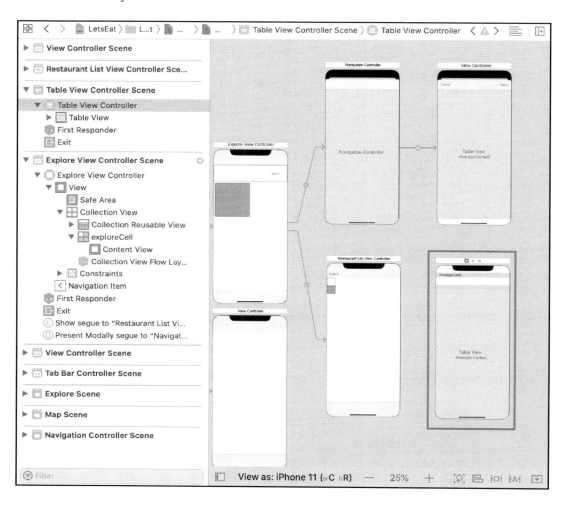

3. To display the **Restaurant Detail** screen when a cell in the **Restaurant List** screen is tapped, press and hold *Ctrl* and drag it from `restaurantCell` (inside the **Restaurant List View Controller Scene**) to the **Table View**:

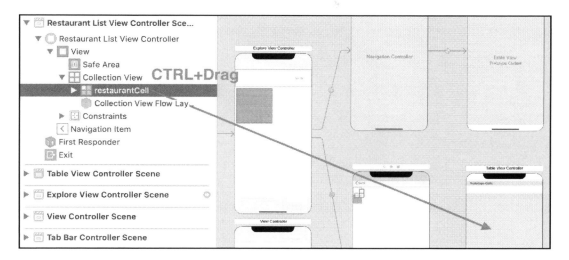

4. Select **Show** from the pop-up menu:

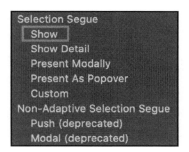

5. A segue will appear between the two scenes:

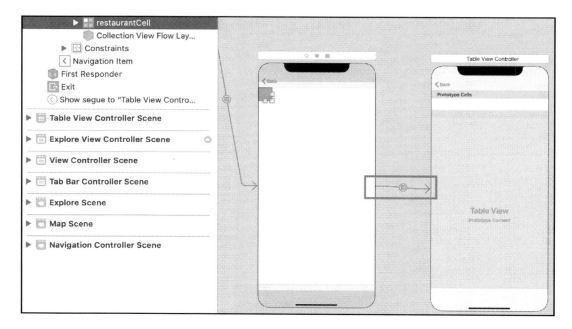

6. Click **Table View** in the document outline of the **Table View Controller Scene** and click the Attributes inspector:

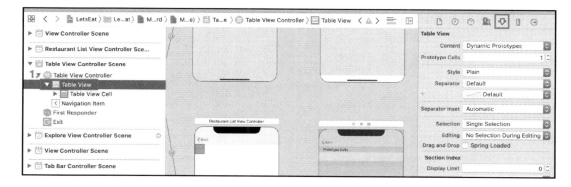

7. Set **Content** to **Static Cells**:

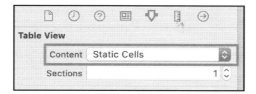

We're doing this because the **Restaurant Detail** screen always uses the same number of cells to display restaurant details. Build and run your app. Click on a cell in the **Explore** screen. Then, click on a cell in the collection view to display the **Restaurant Detail** screen:

Click the **Back** button to go back.

In the next section, you will implement a button inside one of the table view cells to display a **Review Form** screen.

Implementing the Review Form screen

In this section, you will implement a new view controller scene to represent the **Review Form** screen. Then, you will add a button to one of the table view cells in the scene representing the **Restaurant Detail** screen to display it. Go through the following steps:

1. Click the Object library button and type button into the filter field. A **Button** object appears as one of the results. Drag it to the top static cell in the **Table View Controller Scene**:

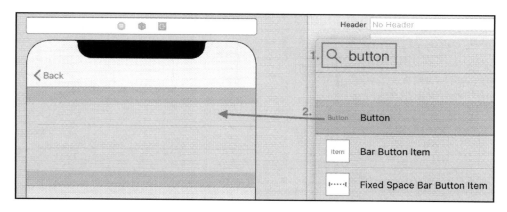

2. Position it on the right-hand side of the cell:

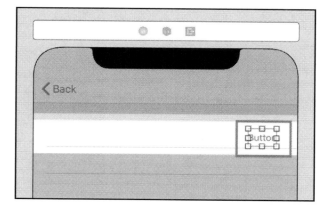

3. Click the Object library button and type `view con` in the filter field. A **View Controller** object will appear as one of the results. Drag it next to the **Table View Controller** scene:

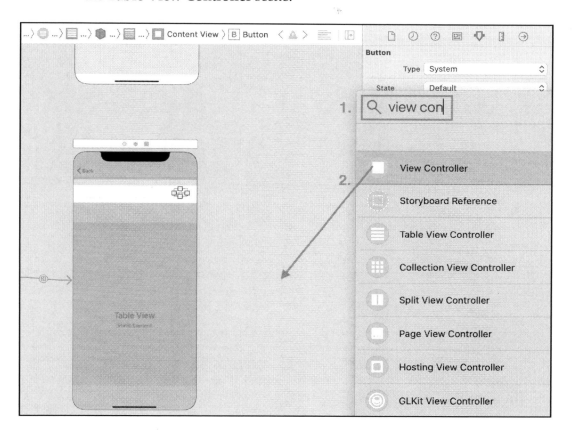

4. A new **View Controller** scene will appear:

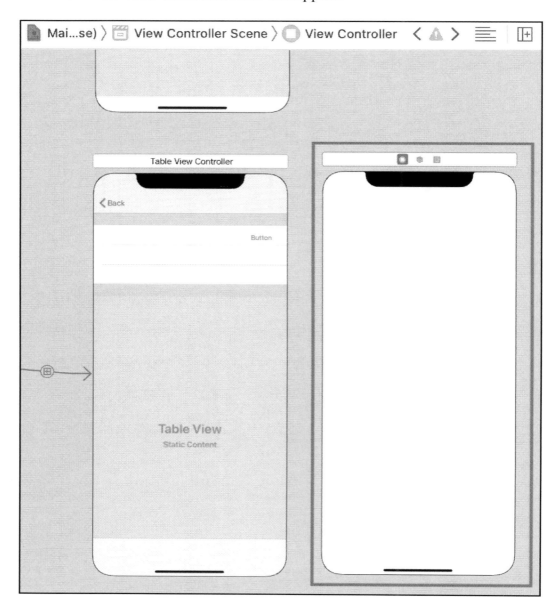

5. Click the Object Library button and type `label` in the filter field.
   A **Label** object appears as one of the results. Drag it to the center of the new
   View Controller scene:

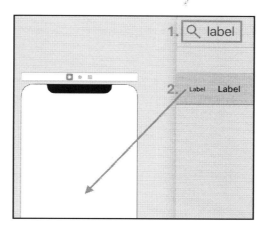

6. Change the **Label** text to `Reviews`. Then, click the Align button:

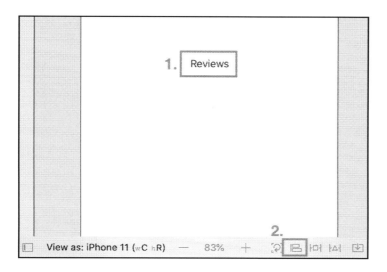

7. Check the **Horizontally in Container** and **Vertically in Container** checkboxes. Then, click the **Add 2 Constraints** button:

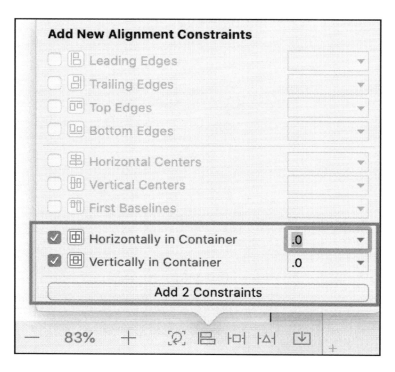

8. These constraints ensure that the **Reviews** label will always be in the middle of the screen when the app is run, regardless of orientation or screen size:

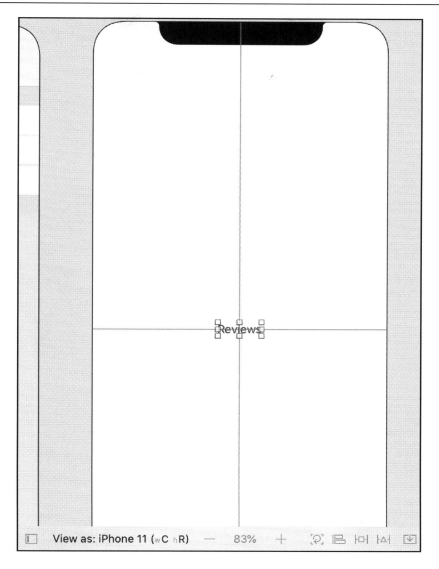

View as: iPhone 11 (wC hR)   —   83%   +

9. *Ctrl* + Drag from the **Button** in the **Table View** cell to the newly added **View Controller Scene**, and select **Show** from the pop-up menu:

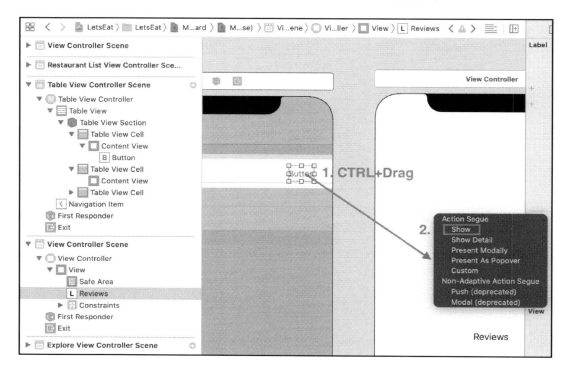

Build and run the app. Click on a cell in the **Explore** screen, then click on a cell in the collection view. Click the button in the table view to display the **Reviews** screen:

Fantastic! All the screens that are accessible from the **Explore** tab have now been implemented, with hardly any coding required! The last thing that you have to do is make the **Map** screen display a map. You'll do this in the next section.

Implementing the Map screen

To make the **Map** screen display a map, you have to add a map view to the view in the view controller scene for the **Map** screen. Go through the following steps:

1. Select the **View Controller Scene** for the **Map** screen:

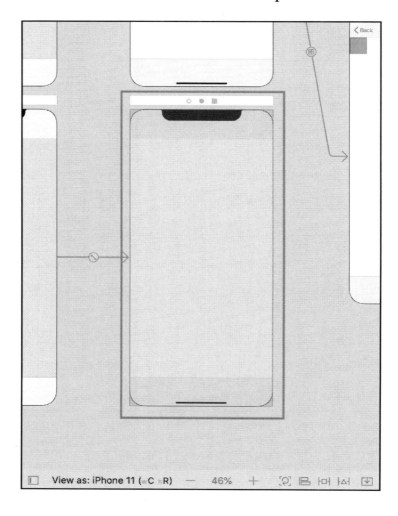

2. Click the Object library button and type map in the filter field. A **Map Kit View** object appears as one of the results. Drag it to the **View** in the **View Controller Scene**:

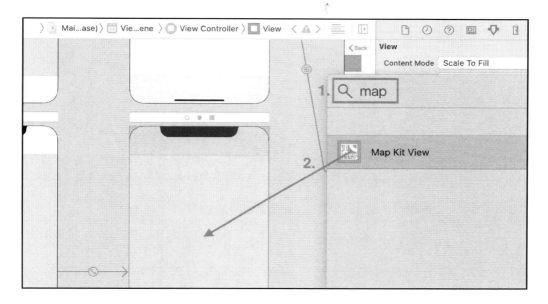

3. With the **Map Kit View** selected, click the Add New Constraints button:

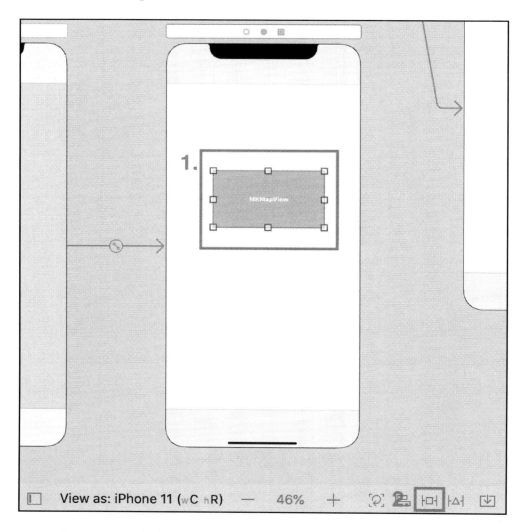

4. Type 0 into all the **Spacing to nearest neighbor** fields and make sure that the red struts are selected (they will turn bright red). Click the **Add 4 Constraints** button.

5. The **Map Kit View** now fills the entire screen:

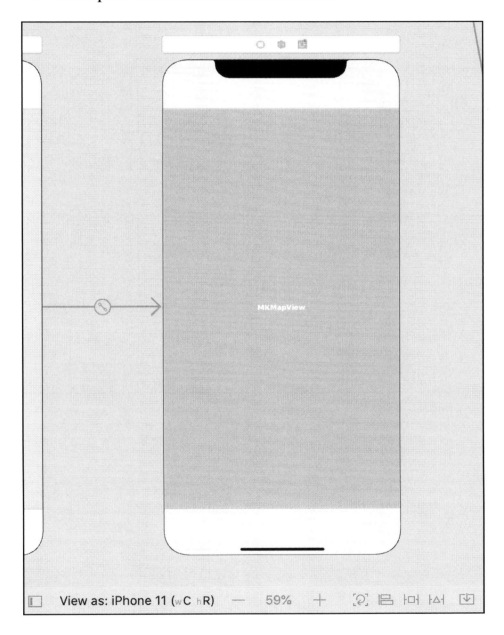

View as: iPhone 11 (wC hR) — 59% +

6. Build and run your app. Click the **Map** button. You should see a map similar to the following one:

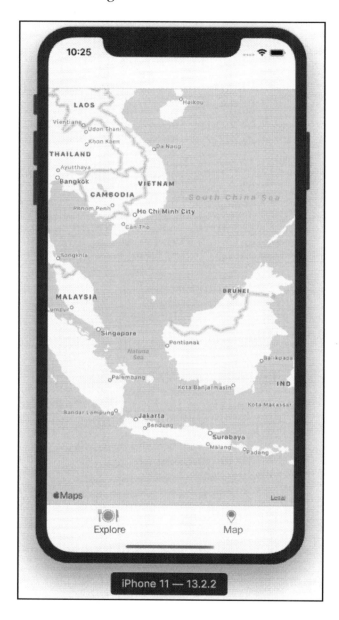

7. Wonderful! You've now completed the basic structure of your app!

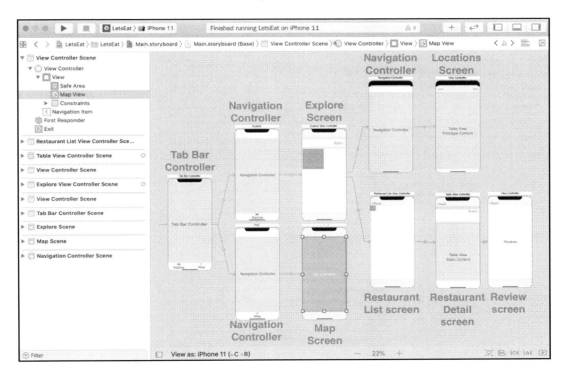

Summary

In this chapter, you completed the basic structure of your app. First, you added a blank table view to the **Locations** screen. You also added a new view controller scene to your storyboard to represent the **Restaurant List** screen, configured a collection view to this screen, and implemented a segue that will display this screen when a cell in the **Explore** screen is tapped. You added a new table view controller scene to represent the **Restaurant Detail** screen, configured a table view with static cells for this screen, and implemented a segue that will display this screen when a cell in the **Restaurant List** screen is tapped. Then, you also added a button to one of the rows in the table view that will display another view controller scene when tapped, simulating the **Review Form** screen. Finally, you added a map view to the view controller scene for the **Map** screen, and it now displays a map.

When you run your app in the simulator, you'll be able to see every screen that your app should have and test the flow of the app. Great!

At this point, you should be quite proficient with Interface Builder. You now know how to add and configure a table view to a storyboard scene, how to add segues between scenes and how to add a map view to a scene. This will be useful as you implement your own apps that contain table views, use segues to navigate between different screens, and display maps.

In the next chapter, you'll modify the cells inside the **Explore** screen, the **Restaurant List** screen, and the **Locations** screen so that they match the designs that were shown in the app tour.

12
Modifying and Configuring Cells

In the previous chapter, you completed the basic structure of your storyboard. You implemented all of the screens required for your app, but the content on each screen still needs work. For example, the **Explore** screen has a collection view section header containing a button and a collection view that displays a grid of exploreCell collection view cells, but the collection view section header and exploreCell collection view cells do not match the design shown in the app tour in Chapter 9, *Setting Up the Basic Structure*.

In this chapter, you'll modify the **Explore**, **Restaurant List**, and **Locations** screens to match the design shown in the app tour.

For the **Explore** screen, you'll add labels and a view to the collection view section header, and configure the button's appearance. You'll also modify the exploreCell collection view cell by adding an image view and a label to it.

For the **Restaurant List** screen, you'll modify the restaurantCell collection view cell by adding labels, buttons and an image view to it. You'll also configure the image view to show a default image.

For the **Locations** screen, you'll configure a prototype cell for the table view and set an identifier, locationCell, for the table view cells.

By the end of this chapter, you will be proficient in adding and positioning user interface elements and will know how to use constraints to determine their position relative to one another.

The following topics will be covered:

- Modifying the **Explore** screen's collection view section header
- Modifying the `exploreCell` collection view cell
- Modifying the `restaurantCell` collection view cell
- Configuring the `locationCell` collection view cell

Technical requirements

You will continue working on the `LetsEat` project that you modified in the previous chapter.

The completed Xcode project for this chapter is in the `Chapter12` folder of the code bundle for this book, which can be downloaded here:

`https://github.com/PacktPublishing/iOS-13-Programming-for-Beginners.`

Let's start by adding UI elements to the collection view section header in the **Explore** screen, to make it match the collection view section header shown in the app tour.

Check out the following video to see the code in action:

`http://bit.ly/3719Ync`

Modifying the Explore screen section header

Let's take a look at what the collection view section header for the **Explore** screen looks like in the app tour:

There are four elements in this collection view section header: two labels (title and subtitle), a button, and a view (the gray line underneath the title and button).

You have already added a button to the collection view section header of the **Explore** screen's collection view in `Chapter 10`, *Building Your App Structure in Storyboard*. You will now add two labels and a view, and revise all elements to match the app tour design.

First, you'll add a view that will act as a container for the four elements. Perform the following steps:

1. In `Main.storyboard`, find the **Explore View Controller Scene**. Select the collection view's **Collection Reusable View** in the document outline (remember, this is the collection view section header). Click the Size inspector. Update the values in the **Size** section if required:

   - **Width**: 0
   - **Height**: 100

   Remember that the units used are points. Setting the width of the **Collection Reusable View** to 0 will automatically make it the same width as the screen:

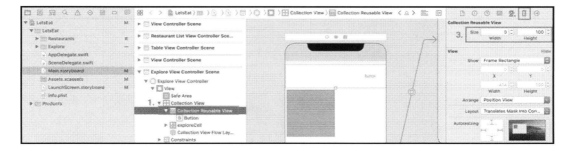

 The Storyboard may not update properly after you have made these changes. Click on a different file and come back; the Storyboard should fix itself.

2. Click the Object library button. Type `uiview` in the filter field.
   A **View** object will appear in the results. Drag it to the **Collection Reusable View**:

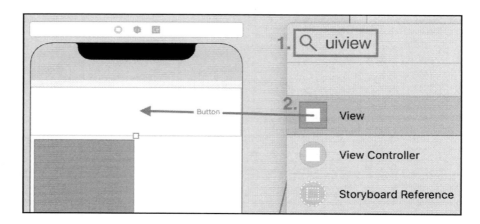

3. In the document outline, drag the **View** so it becomes the first item in the **Collection Reusable View's** list of subviews, as shown in the following screenshot. This is to ensure it doesn't obscure the **Button**:

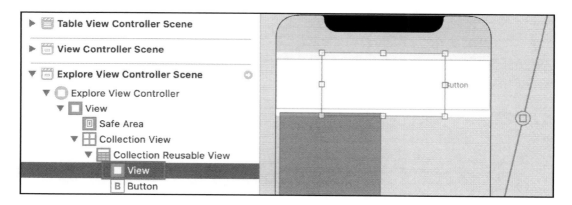

4. With the **View** selected, click the Size inspector. In the **View** section, update the following values:

- **X**: 0
- **Y**: 0
- **Width**: 414
- **Height**: 100

The **X** and **Y** values determine the horizontal and vertical offset of the **View** relative to the top-left corner of the **Collection Reusable View**, and the **Width** and **Height** values determine the width and height of the **View**. This makes the position of the top-left corner of this **View** the same as the top-left corner of the **Collection Reusable View**, sets the width of the **View** to the same width as the screen (414 points), and sets the height of the **View** to 100 points:

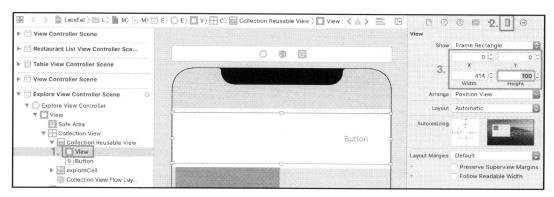

5. Click the Object library button. Type `label` in the filter field.
   A **Label** object will appear in the results. Drag two **Label** objects into the
   View you dragged in earlier:

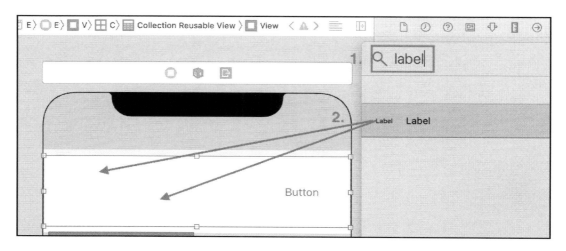

6. Note that the two **Labels** are subviews of the **View**, and the **View** is a
   subview of the **Collection Reusable View**:

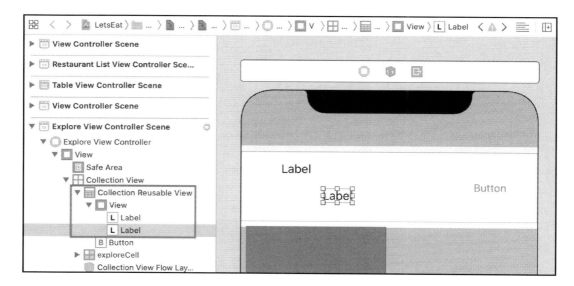

7. Select the **Button** in the document outline and drag it to the **View**, to make it a subview of the **View** as well. When you are done, it should look like the following:

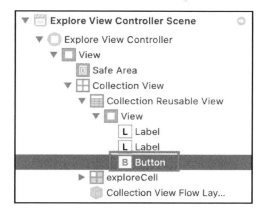

8. One of the **Labels** in the **Collection Reusable View** should be grey. You will need a create a new color for it, and rename the existing color to follow the same naming convention. Click `Assets.xcassets` and click `Demo Grey`:

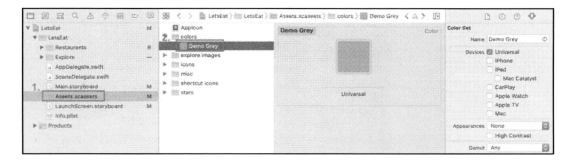

9. Click the Attributes inspector. Set the **Name** to LetsEat Dark Grey:

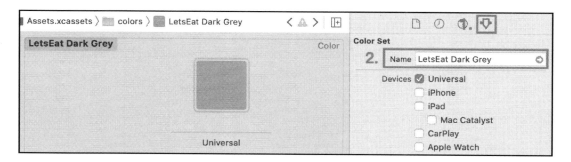

10. Right-click the colors folder and choose **New Color Set**:

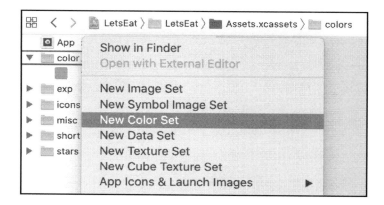

11. Click the newly created color set. In the Attributes inspector, name the color LetsEat Light Grey and set the **Hex in Color** section to #AFAFB2:

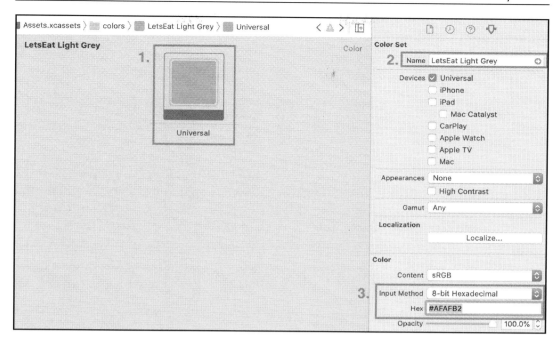

12. Click `Main.storyboard`. Select one of the **Labels**. You'll make this the subtitle. Click the Attributes inspector. Update the following values:

- **Color**: `LetsEat Light Grey`
- **Font**: `System Semibold 13.0`

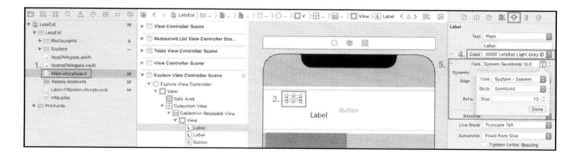

13. With the **Label** still selected, click the Size inspector. Update the following values in the **View** section:

- **X**: 8
- **Y**: 24
- **Width**: 398
- **Height**: 21

This **Label** is a subview of the **View** you added earlier to the **Collection Reusable View**. This means the position of the **Label** will be relative to this **View**. The top-left corner of the **Label** will be offset by 8 points horizontally and 24 points vertically, appearing below and to the right of the top-left corner of **Collection Reusable View**. The **Width** of the **Label** will be 398 points and the **Height** will be 21 points:

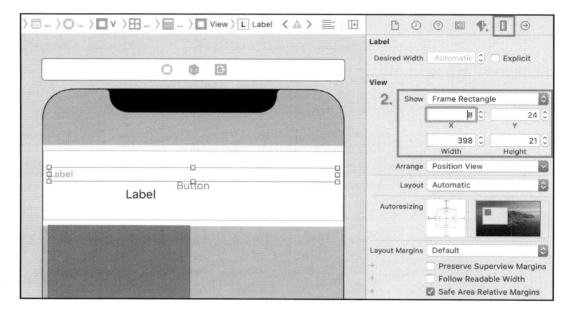

14. Select the other **Label**. You'll make this the title. Click the Attributes inspector. Update the **Font** as follows to make the **Label** more prominent: **Font:** System Heavy 40.0:

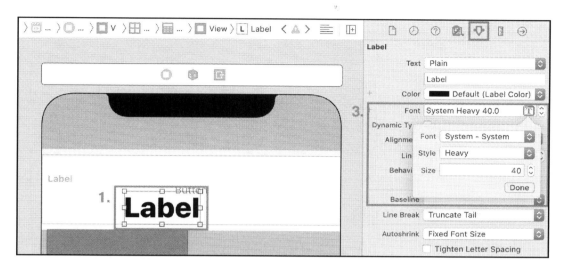

15. With the **Label** still selected, click the Size inspector. Update the following values in the **View** section:

- **X:** 8
- **Y:** 45
- **Width:** 294
- **Height:** 37

These settings offset this **Label** by 8 points to the right and 45 points below the top-left corner of the enclosing **View**, positioning it just below the first **Label**. Note that it does not extend all of the way to the right, leaving some space for the **Button** later:

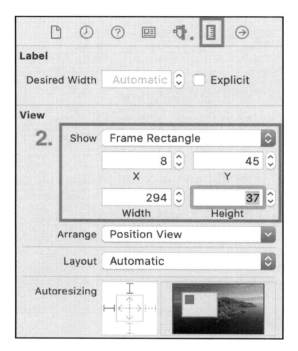

16. Select the **Button**. In the Attributes inspector, update the following values in the **Button** section to make it use a custom image:

   - **Type**: Custom
   - Remove the text from the field under the **Title** pop-up menu
   - **Image**: btn-location

This image is included in the Assets.xcassets file you added to your app in Chapter 9, *Setting Up the Basic Structure*:

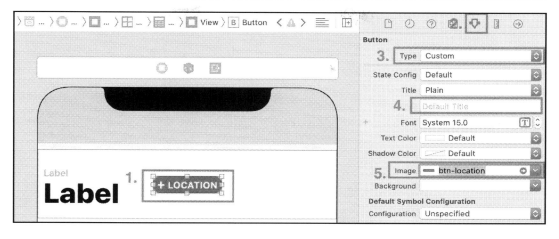

17. With the **Button** still selected, click the Size inspector. Update the following values in the **View** section:

- **X:** 310
- **Y:** 50

You don't need to change the width and height because the width and height of the custom image will be used automatically:

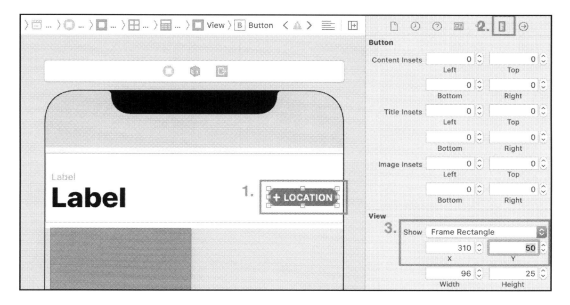

18. Click the Object library button. Type `uiview` in the filter field. A **View** object will appear in the results. Drag a **View** into the container **View**. This will become the thin gray line at the bottom of the **Collection Reusable View**:

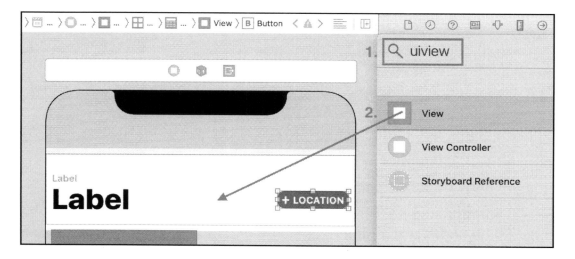

19. With the newly added **View** selected, click the Size inspector. Update the following values in the **View** section:

- **X**: 8
- **Y**: 89
- **Width**: 398
- **Height**: 1

This places the **View** below all of the other elements, but it is invisible:

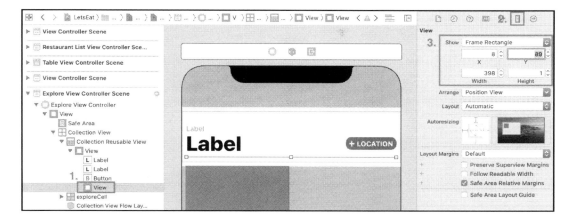

20. With the **View** still selected, click the Attributes inspector. Change the background color to LetsEat Light Grey:

Build and run your app. Your **Collection Reusable View** should now look like this:

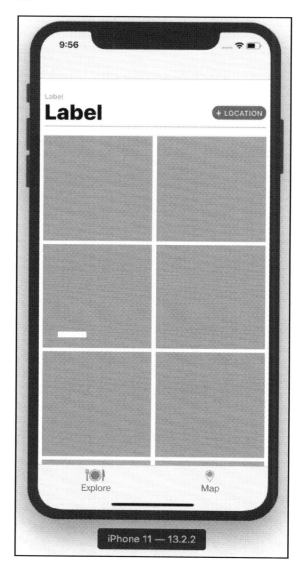

As you can see, the collection view section header now matches the design shown in the app tour. It works great using the iPhone 11 Simulator, but to make sure it works in other screen sizes, you will add Auto Layout constraints. You'll do this in the next section.

Adding Auto Layout to the Explore screen's section header

If you build and run your app now in the iPhone 11 Simulator, the collection view section header will look great, but if you switch to a simulator with a smaller screen, you'll see some graphic elements have been cut off. As you have seen in previous chapters, Auto Layout ensures that the UI adapts to the device's screen size and orientation. For example, the *Let's Eat* app logo stays in the exact center of the screen regardless of device, and the table view in the **Locations** screen takes up all of the available screen space even when the device is rotated.

So far, you've only used Auto Layout with single UI elements. In this section, you will add Auto Layout constraints to multiple UI elements inside the collection view section header.

You will begin by adding constraints to the container view, then proceed to add constraints to all of the other items inside it. Perform the following steps:

1. Select the container **View**:

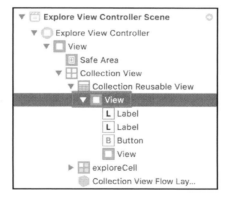

2. Click the **Add New Constraints** button and enter the following values:

   - **Top**: 0
   - **Left**: 0
   - **Right**: 0
   - **Height**: 90

When done, click **Add 4 Constraints**. This binds the top, left, and right edges of the container **View** to the edges of the **Collection Reusable View**. The height of the **View** is set to 90 points, which determines the position of the bottom edge.

3. Select the **Label** used as a subtitle:

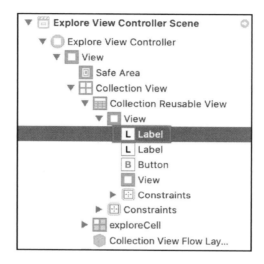

4. Click the **Add New Constraints** button and enter the following values:

- **Top**: 24
- **Left**: 8
- **Right**: 16
- **Height**: 21

When done, click **Add 4 Constraints**. The space between the top, left, and right edges of the **Label** and the corresponding edges of the container **View** are set to 24 points, 8 points, and 16 points respectively. Note the width of the **Label** is not set, allowing it to change if you run it on a simulator with a smaller or larger screen. As before, setting the height constraint determines the position of the bottom edge of the **Label.**

5. Select the **LOCATION** button:

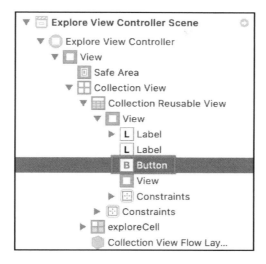

6. Click the **Add New Constraints** button and enter the following values:

- **Top**: 5
- **Right**: 8
- **Width**: 96
- **Height**: 25

When done, click **Add 4 Constraints**. Since the **LOCATION** button is under the subtitle **Label**, the top constraint determines the space between the top edge of the **LOCATION** button and the bottom edge of the **Label**, not the top edge of the container **View**. The space between the right edge of the **LOCATION** button and the right edge of the container **View** is set to 8 points, and the width and height constraints determine the position of the **LOCATION** button's left and bottom edges.

7. Select the gray line **View** (it may be easier to do this in the document outline):

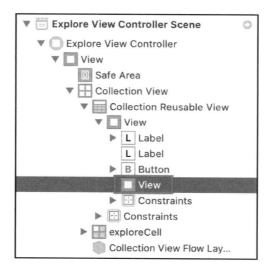

8. Click the **Add New Constraints** button and enter the following values:

- **Left**: 8
- **Right**: 8
- **Bottom**: 0
- **Height**: 1

When done, click **Add 4 Constraints**. The space between the left and right edges of the **View** and the left and right edges of the container **View** are set to 8 points, and the bottom edge of the **View** is bound to the bottom edge of the container **View**. The height constraint determines the position of the top edge of the **View.**

9. Select the **Label** used as a title:

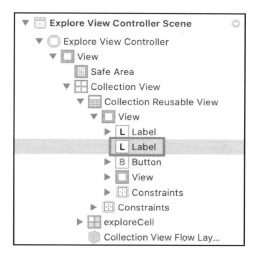

10. Click the **Add New Constraints** button and enter the following values:

- **Top:** 0
- **Left:** 8
- **Right:** 8
- **Height:** 37

When done, click **Add 4 Constraints**. The top edge of the **Label** is bound to the bottom edge of the subtitle **Label**. The space between the left edge of the **Label** and the left edge of the container **View** is 8 points. The space between the right edge of the **Label** and the left edge of the **LOCATION** button is 8 points. The height constraint determines the position of the bottom edge of the **Label.**

You have completed adding Auto Layout constraints to all of the views in the **Explore** screen's collection view section header. Cool!

You may be wondering why you needed to set the position of the UI elements using the Size inspector before adding constraints. Actually, you don't have to, but, by doing that, it makes it much easier to add constraints, as the constraint values that you see when you click the **Add New Constraints** button are derived from the current space between the UI elements.

Working with Auto Layout can be challenging for novice developers. Take your time doing it. If it doesn't work properly, clear all of the constraints and start over. To do this, click the **Resolve Auto Layout Issues** button at the bottom of the screen and choose **Clear Constraints**:

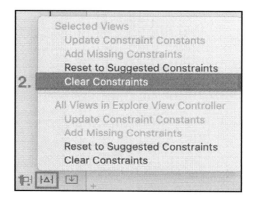

Now that you've completed modifying the collection view section header, let's modify the `exploreCell` collection view cell in the next section. You'll add some UI elements to make it match the cell shown in the app tour.

Modifying the exploreCell collection view cell

Let's take a look at what the `exploreCell` collection view cell looks like in the app tour:

Bar / Lounge

In the previous chapter, you set the background color for the `exploreCell` collection view cell and configured the collection view to display a grid of 20 `exploreCell` collection view cells. You'll now add some more graphic elements to the `exploreCell` collection view cell to match the design shown in the app tour. Perform the following steps:

1. Select `exploreCell` in the document outline of the **Explore View Controller Scene**. Click the Attributes inspector. Confirm **Identifier** is set to `exploreCell`. Change **Background** to `White Color`:

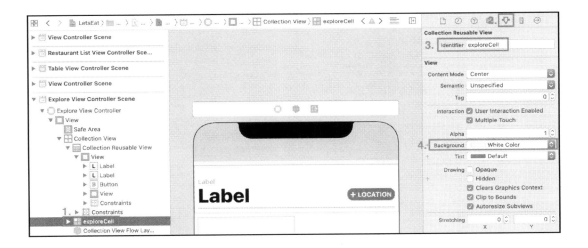

2. Click the Object library button. Type `uiview` into the filter field. A **View** object will appear in the results. Drag it into the prototype cell:

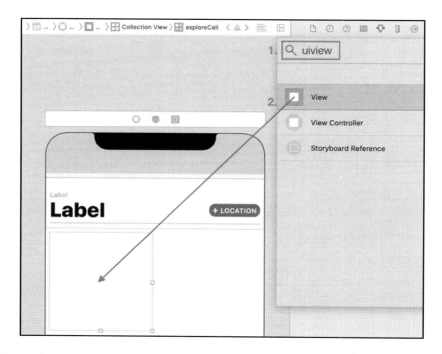

3. Make sure the **View** you just added is selected and is a subview of the **exploreCell Content View**:

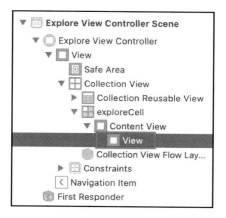

4. Click the **Add New Constraints** button and enter the following values.

- **Top**: 0
- **Left**: 0
- **Right**: 0
- **Height**: 156

When done, click **Add 4 Constraints**. This binds the view top, left, and right edges to corresponding edges of the exploreCell collection view cell. The position of the bottom edge is determined by the height constraint, which sets the distance between the top and bottom edges of the view.

5. Click the Object library button. Type image into the filter field. An **Image View** object will appear in the results. Drag it on top of the **View** you added earlier:

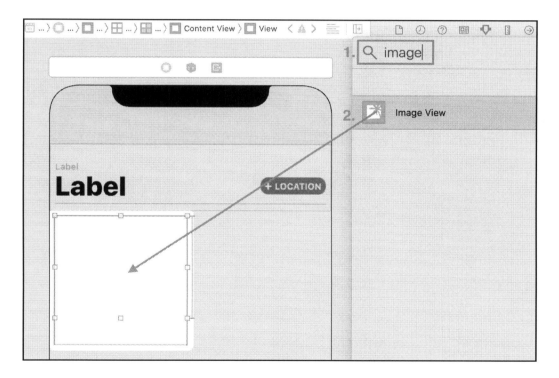

6. Make sure the **Image View** is selected and is a subview of the **View** you added earlier:

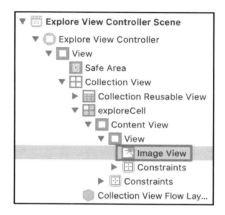

7. Click the **Add New Constraints** button and enter the following values:

- **Top**: 0
- **Left**: 0
- **Right**: 0
- **Bottom**: 0

When done, click **Add 4 Constraints**. This binds the edges of the image view to the edges of the view you added earlier.

8. Click the Object library button. Type `label` into the filter field.
A **Label** object will appear in the results. Drag it to the space between the **View** you just added and the bottom of the cell:

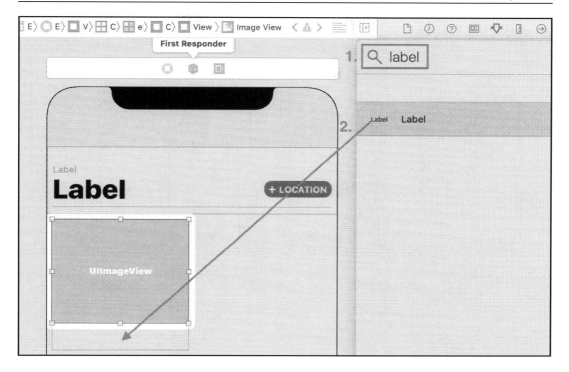

9. Make sure the **Label** is selected and is a subview of the `exploreCell` collection view cell's **Content View**, not the **View** you added earlier:

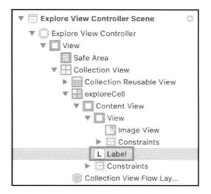

10. Click the **Add New Constraints** button and enter the following values:

- **Top**: 9
- **Left:** 8

- **Right:** 8
- **Height:** 21

When done, click **Add 4 Constraints**. The space between the top edge of the label and the bottom edge of the view you added earlier is set to 9 points. The space between the left and right edges of the label and the corresponding edges of the exploreCell content view are both set to 8 points. The height constraint determines the position of the bottom edge of the **Label** by setting the space between the top and bottom edges of the label.

Build and run the app:

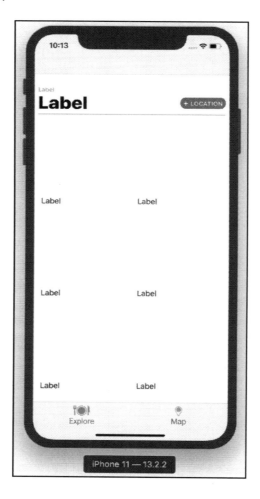

As you can see, the **Explore** screen now more closely matches the design shown in the app tour. Each cell now has an image view and a label just under it, and all of the necessary constraints have been added. Fantastic!

Note that unlike the previous section, you did not set the position of the UI elements using the Size inspector before adding constraints. You can do this as you are only adding a few elements in this section, and the relative positions of each element to one another is not ambiguous.

Now that you've completed modifying the `exploreCell` collection view cell, let's modify the `restaurantCell` collection view cell next by adding some UI elements to it in the next section.

Modifying the restaurantCell collection view cell

Let's take a look at what the `restaurantCell` collection view cell looks like in the app tour:

As you can see, `restaurantCell` has many elements. You will now modify `restaurantCell` to match the design shown in the app tour. A summary of the changes required is as follows:

- Change the size of `restaurantCell` to make it larger and change the background color to white.
- Add a view, then add a label and a stack view containing three buttons to show the available reservation times.

- Add a view, then add an image view to it in order to show a picture of the restaurant.
- Add a label at the top-left corner to show the restaurant's name.
- Add a label just under the name label to show the restaurant's address.

You'll be using the Size inspector to position all of the elements, and this will make it easier to add the necessary Auto Layout constraints later. Take your time doing this to reduce the chances of making a mistake:

1. In `Main.storyboard`, click the **Collection View** for the **Restaurant List View Controller** scene in the document outline. Click the Size inspector. Under **Cell Size**, set **Width** to 375 and **Height** to 312. Set **Estimate Size** to `None`:

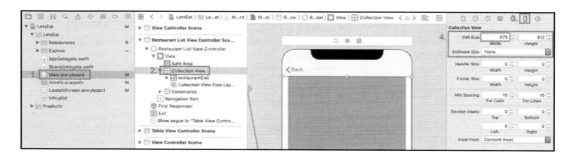

2. Click `restaurantCell` in the document outline. Click the Attributes inspector. Confirm the **Identifier** is set to `restaurantCell`. Set **Background** to `White Color`:

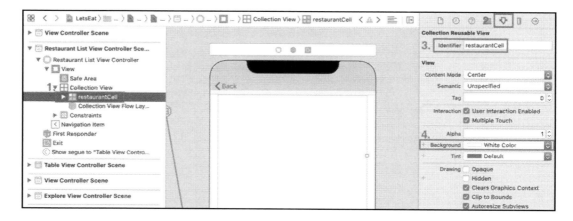

3. Click the Object library button. Type `uiview` in the filter field.
   A **View** object will appear in the results. Drag it into the prototype cell:

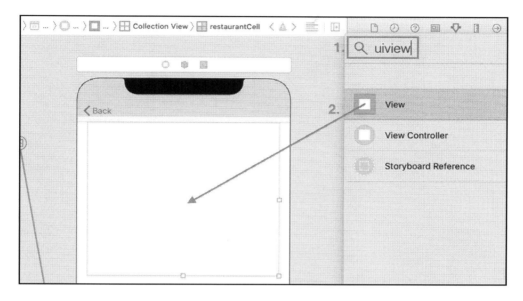

4. With the **View** selected, click the Size inspector. Update the following values for the **View** section:

- **X**: 75.5
- **Y**: 245
- **Width**: 224
- **Height**: 56

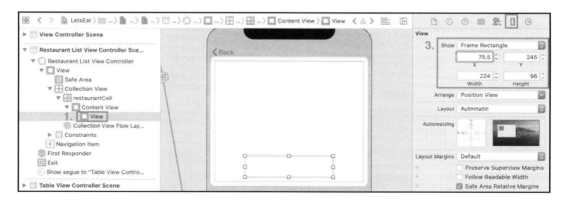

5. Click the Object library button. Type `label` in the filter field.
    A **Label** object will appear in the results. Drag it into the **View** you just
    added:

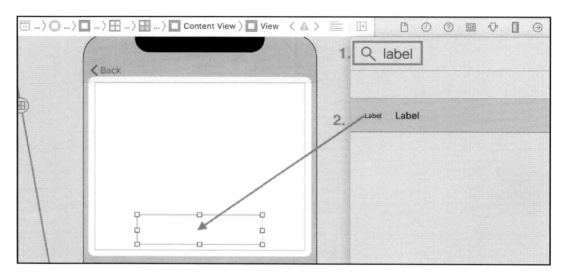

6. With the **Label** selected, click the Size inspector. Update the following
    values in the **View** section:

    - **X:** 0
    - **Y:** 2
    - **Width:** 224
    - **Height:** 21

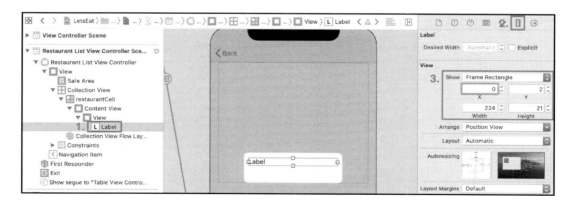

7. Click the Attributes inspector. Update the following values:

- **Text**: `Plain` and then add `Available Times` in the empty text field below it
- **Alignment**: `Center`
- **Font**: `System Bold 17.0`

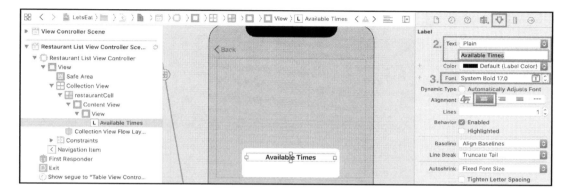

8. Click the Object library button. Type `button` in the filter field. A **Button** object will appear in the results. Drag it into the same **View** where the **Label** was:

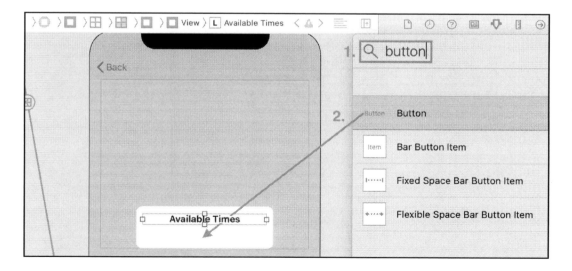

9. With the **Button** selected, click the Attributes inspector. Update the following values:

- **Type**: System
- **Title**: Plain and then add 7:30pm in the empty text field below it
- **Font**: System Bold 15.0
- **Text Color**: White Color
- **Background**: time-bg

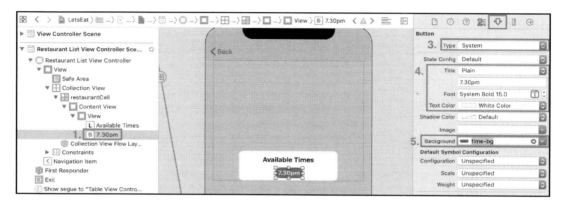

10. Click the Size inspector. Update the following values in the **View** section if necessary:

- **Width**: 68
- **Height**: 27

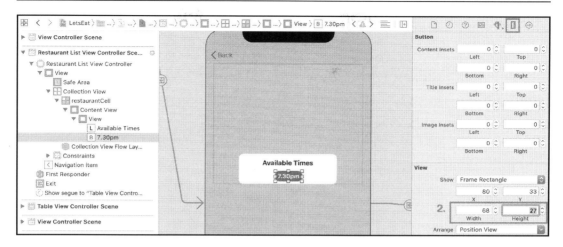

11. Select the **Button** and hit *command* + *C* to copy. Hit *command* + *V* twice to paste. You should now have three **Buttons**. Arrange them as follows:

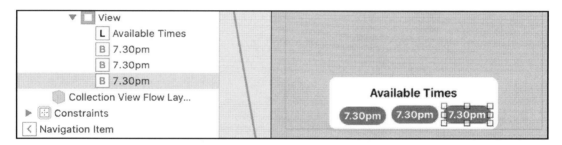

12. Click one **Button,** then press *Shift* and click the other two. All three **Buttons** should now be selected:

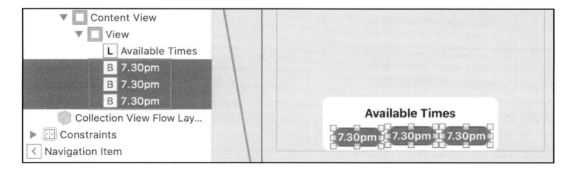

13. Choose **Embed | Stack View** from the **Editor** menu. This will put all three **Buttons** into a **Stack View** that has a grid of cells with 1 row and 3 columns.

14. All of the **Buttons** are now subviews in the **Stack View**:

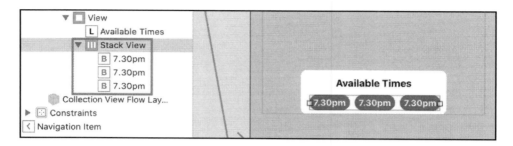

15. Select the **Stack View** in the document outline. Click the Attributes inspector. Update the following values:

- **Axis**: Horizontal
- **Alignment**: Fill
- **Distribution**: Equal Spacing
- **Spacing**: 10

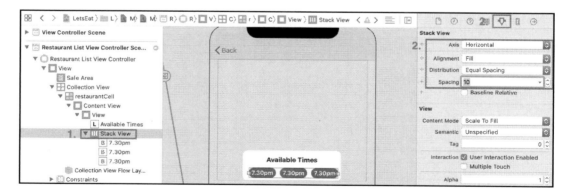

16. Click the Size inspector. Update the following values in the **View** section:

- **X**: 0
- **Y**: 29

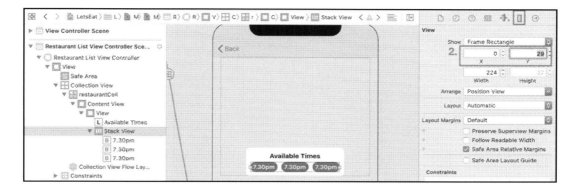

17. Click the Object library button. Type `uivie` in the filter field. A **View** object will appear in the results. Drag it into the prototype cell:

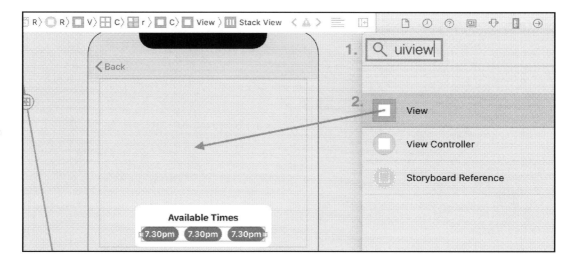

18. With the **View** selected, click the Size inspector. Update the following values in the **View** section:

- **X**: 11
- **Y**: 42
- **Width**: 353
- **Height**: 200

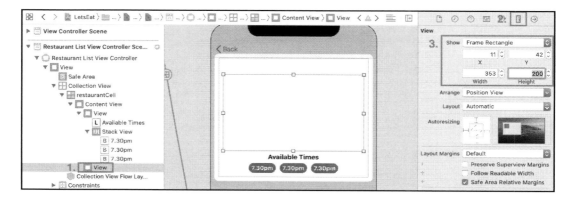

19. Click the Object library button. Type image into the filter field. **Image View** will appear in the results. Drag it into the **View** you just added:

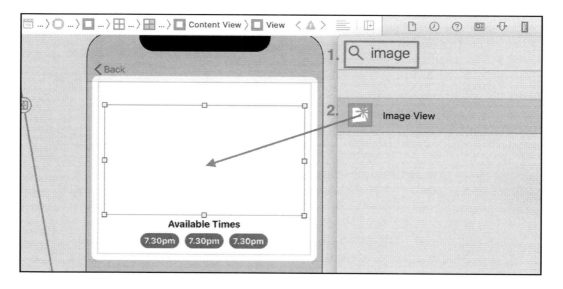

20. With the **Image View** selected, click the Attributes inspector. Set **Image** to american. This is just a placeholder; later, you will load images using code:

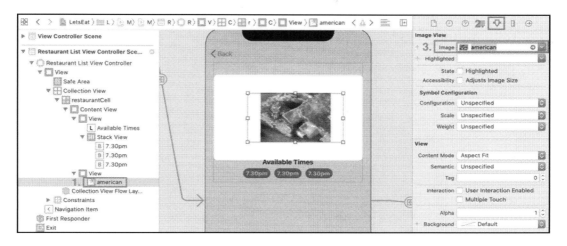

21. With the **Image View** selected, click the Size inspector. Update the following values in the **View** section:

- **X**: 0
- **Y**: 0
- **Width**: 353
- **Height**: 200

22. Click the Object library button. Type `label` into the filter field. A **Label** object will appear in the results. Drag two **Labels** into the prototype cell:

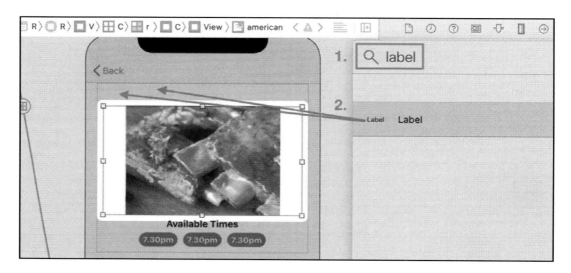

23. Select a **Label** and click the Attributes inspector. Set the **Font** to `System Bold 17.0`:

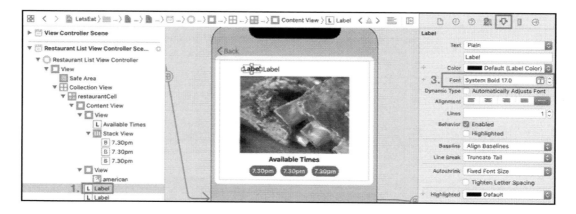

24. With the **Label** selected, click the Size inspector. Update the following values in the **View** section:

- **X**: 10
- **Y**: 3
- **Width**: 355
- **Height**: 19

25. Select the other **Label** and click the Attributes inspector. Update the following values:

- **Color**: LetsEat Dark Grey
- **Font**: System 14.0

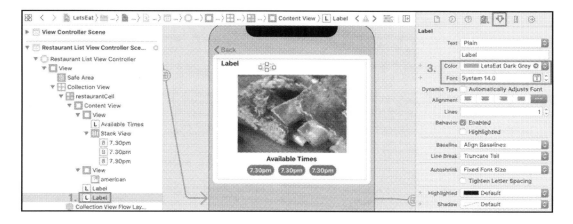

26. With the **Label** selected, click the Size inspector. Update the following values in the **View** section:

- **X**: 10
- **Y**: 22
- **Width**: 355
- **Height**: 16

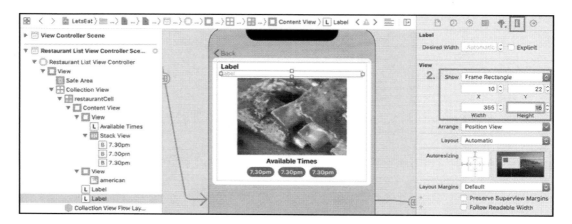

You have added all of the elements for `restaurantCell` and set their positions using the Size inspector. Now, you need to add Auto Layout constraints to them to ensure the user interface adapts to device screen size and orientation. You'll do this in the next section.

Adding Auto Layout constraints to the restaurantCell collection view cell

As you did before for the `exploreCell` collection view cell, you will now add Auto Layout constraints to all of the elements in `restaurantCell`. Since you have used the Size inspector to position the elements, their positions relative to one another and the values of the constraints should already be correctly set, making it easy for you to add the constraints.

Since there are many elements in `restaurantCell`, take your time during this section:

1. Select the top **Label**:

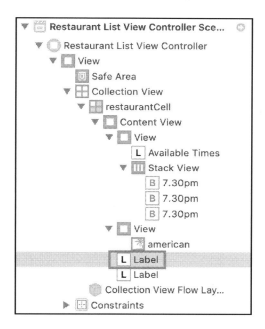

2. Click the **Add New Constraints** button and enter the following values:

    - **Top**: 3 (sets a space between the top edge and the top edge of the **Content View**)
    - **Left**: 10 (sets a space between the left edge and the left edge of the **Content View**)
    - **Right**: 10 (sets a space between the right edge and the right edge of the **Content View**)
    - **Height**: 19 (sets a space between the top and bottom edges)

    Click **Add 4 Constraints** when done.

3. Select the **Label** under the previous **Label**:

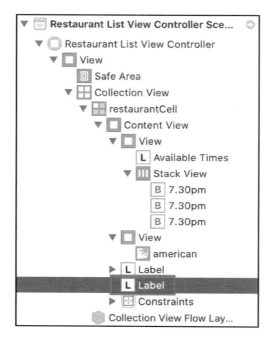

Click the **Add New Constraints** button and enter the following values:

- **Top**: 0 (sets a space between the top edge and the previous bottom edge of the **Label**)
- **Left**: 10 (sets a space between the left edge and the left edge of the **Content View**)
- **Right**: 10 (sets a space between the right edge and the right edge of the **Content View**)
- **Height**: 16 (sets a space between the top and bottom edges)

Click **Add 4 Constraints** when done.

5. Select the **View** that contains the **Image View**:

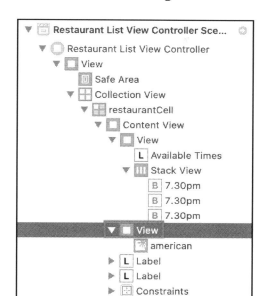

6. Click the **Add New Constraints** button and enter the following values:

- **Top**: 4 (sets a space between the top edge and the bottom edge of the **Label**)
- **Width**: 353 (sets a space between the left and right edges)
- **Height**: 200 (sets a space between the top and bottom edges)

Click **Add 3 Constraints** when done. Note that the position of the left and right edges are not set yet.

7. Click the **Align** button, tick **Horizontally in Container** and enter the following value: 0. Click **Add 1 Constraint** when done. This sets the horizontal position of the **View** to the center of the **Content View**. Since the width of this **View** is set, the position of the left and right edges can be determined.

8. Select the **Image View**:

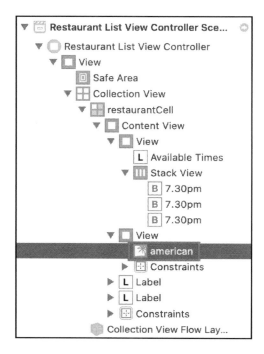

9. Click the **Add New Constraints** button and enter the following values:

- **Top**: 0
- **Left**: 0
- **Right**: 0
- **Bottom**: 0

Click **Add 4 Constraints** when done. This binds the edges of the **Image View** to the enclosing **View.**

10. Select the **View** containing the `Available Times` **Label** and the **Stack View**:

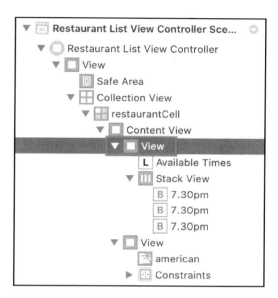

11. Click the **Add New Constraints** button and enter the following values:

- **Top**: 3 (sets a space between the top edge and the **View** containing the bottom edge of the **Image View**)
- **Width**: 224 (sets a space between the left and right edges)
- **Height**: 56 (sets a space between the top and bottom edges)

Click **Add 3 Constraints** when done. Note that the position of the left and right edges are not set yet.

12. Click the **Align** button. tick **Horizontally in Container** and enter the following value: 0. Click **Add 1 Constraint** when done. This sets the horizontal position of the **View** to the center of the **Content View**. Since the width of this **View** is set, the position of the left and right edges can be determined.

13. Select the **Stack View**:

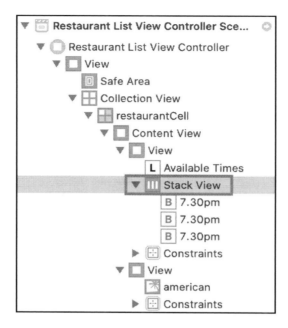

14. Click the **Add New Constraints** button and enter the following values:

- **Top**: 6 (sets a space between the top edge and the bottom edge of the `Available Times` **Label**)
- **Left**: 0 (sets a space between the left edge and the left edge of the enclosing **View**)
- **Right**: 0 (sets a space between the right edge and the right edge of the enclosing **View**)
- **Height**: 27 (sets a space between the top and bottom edges)

Click **Add 4 Constraints** when done.

15. Select the `Available Times` **Label**:

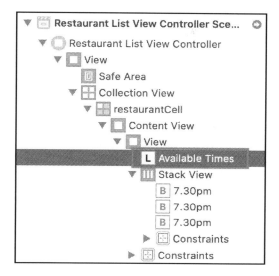

16. Click the **Add New Constraints** button and enter the following values:

- **Top**: 2 (sets a space between the top edge and the top edge of the enclosing **View**)
- **Left**: 0 (binds the left edge to the left edge of the enclosing **View**)
- **Right**: 0 (binds the right edge to the right edge of the enclosing **View**)
- **Height**: 21 (sets a space between the top and bottom edges)

Click **Add 4 Constraints** when done.

All of the Auto Layout constraints for `restaurantCell` have been set up.

Build and run your app and go to the **Restaurant List** screen. You should now see the following:

As you can see, the **Restaurant List** screen now more closely matches the design shown in the app tour. The `restaurantCell` table view cell now looks just like the app tour design, and all of the necessary constraints have been added. Awesome!

Now that you've completed modifying `restaurantCell`, let's modify the table view cells in the **Locations** screen in the next section.

Configuring the locationCell table view cell

The last thing to do in this chapter is to configure the table view cells inside the **Locations** screen. As you have seen in the app tour, each table view cell just contains text, so all you need to do now is to enable the prototype cell for the table view and set the identifier for the table view cell to `locationCell`. Perform the following steps:

1. Find the **View Controller** scene triggered by the button in the **Explore View Controller Scene**. Select the **Table View**. Click on the Attributes inspector. Set **Prototype Cells** to 1:

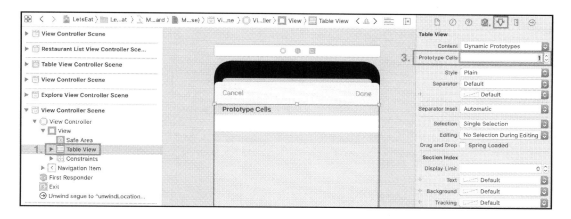

2. Select the prototype cell. Click the Attributes inspector and enter the following values:

- **Style**: Basic
- **Identifier**: locationCell

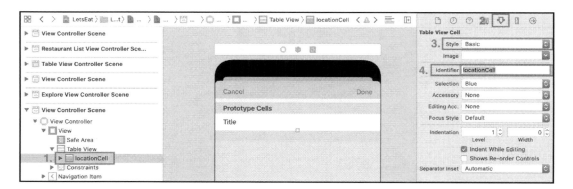

When you change the style from **Custom** to **Basic**, the word **Title** should appear in the cell. The word **Title** is just a placeholder. You will change this value in code later.

If you build and run your app now and go the **Locations** screen, it will still appear blank, as you have not yet added any code to display data in the cells. You will do so in Chapter 15, *Getting Started with Table Views*.

Summary

In this chapter, you modified the cells inside the **Explore**, **Restaurant List**, and **Locations** screens to match the design shown in the app tour.

For the **Explore** screen, you added labels and a view to the collection view section header, configured the button with a custom image, and modified the exploreCell collection view cell by adding an image view and a label to it, as well as the required constraints.

For the **Restaurant List** screen, you modified the restaurantCell collection view cell by adding labels, buttons and an image view to it, configured it to show a default image, and added the necessary constraints.

For the **Locations** screen, you configured a prototype cell for the table view and set the identifier for the table view cells to `locationCell`.

You now have experience on how to use Interface Builder to add and configure multiple user interface elements, set their sizes and positions using the Size inspector, and apply the necessary constraints using the **Add New Constraints** and **Align** buttons to ensure compatibility with different screen sizes and orientations. This will be useful when you design your own user interfaces. You should also be able to easily prototype the appearance and flow of your own apps.

At this point, you're now finished with the storyboard and design setup. You can go through every screen that your app is supposed to have and see what they look like, even though none of the screens have actual data in them. If this app was a house being built, it's as though you've built all of the walls and floors, and the house is now ready to have the interior done. Great job!

This concludes *Section 2* of this book. In the next part, you'll begin to type in all of the code required for your app to work. In the next chapter, you'll start by learning more about the **Model-View-Controller** design pattern. You'll also learn how collection views work, which are crucial for understanding how the **Explore** and **Restaurant List** screens work.

Section 3: Code

3

Welcome to section three of this book. With your user interface complete, you will then add code to implement your app's functionality. To display your data in a grid, you will use collection views, and to display your data in a list, you will use table views. You will also look at how to add basic and custom annotations to a map. After that, you will look at what an **Application Programming Interface (API)** is, and how you can get actual restaurant data into your collection views, table views, and map. Next, you will add code that allows users to add restaurant reviews and photos, and to rate a restaurant. Finally, you'll make restaurant reviews and photos persistent, using Core Data.

This part comprises the following chapters:

- Chapter 13, *Getting Started with MVC and Collection Views*
- Chapter 14, *Getting Data into Collection Views*
- Chapter 15, *Getting Started with Table Views*
- Chapter 16, *Getting Started with MapKit*
- Chapter 17, *Getting Started with JSON Files*
- Chapter 18, *Displaying Data in a Static Table View*
- Chapter 19, *Getting Started with Custom UIControls*
- Chapter 20, *Getting Started with Cameras and Photo Libraries*
- Chapter 21, *Understanding Core Data*
- Chapter 22, *Saving and Loading from Core Data*

By the end of this part, you'll have completed the *Let's Eat* app. You'll have the experience of building a complete app from scratch, which will be useful as you build your own apps. Let's get started!

13
Getting Started with MVC and Collection Views

In the previous chapter, you modified the cells inside the **Explore** screen, the **Restaurant List** screen, and the **Locations** screen to match the app tour in Chapter 9, *Setting Up the Basic Structure*.

You're now finished with the structure of the *Let's Eat* app, and this concludes *Section 2* of this book.

This chapter begins *Section 3* of this book, where you will focus on the code that makes your app work. In this chapter, you will learn about the **Model-View-Controller (MVC)** design pattern and how the different parts interact with one another. Then, you'll implement a collection view **programmatically** (which means implementing it using code instead of storyboards) using a playground, to understand how collection views work. Finally, you'll revisit the collection views you implemented in the **Explore** and **Restaurant List** screens, so you can see what the differences are between implementing them in storyboard and implementing them programmatically.

By the end of this chapter, you'll understand the MVC design pattern, learn how a create a collection view controller programmatically and learn how to use collection view delegate and data source protocols.

The following topics will be covered:

- Understanding the MVC design pattern
- Exploring controllers and classes

Technical requirements

The resource files and completed Xcode project for this chapter are in the `Chapter13` folder of the code bundle for this book, which can be downloaded here:

`https://github.com/PacktPublishing/iOS-13-Programming-for-Beginners`.

Create a new playground and call it `CollectionViewBasics`. You can use this playground to type in and run all the code in this chapter as you go along.

Before you do this, let's take a look at the MVC design pattern, which describes an approach commonly used in writing iOS apps.

Take a look at the following video to see the code in action:

`http://bit.ly/2TSLNZh`

Understanding the MVC design pattern

A common way to build iOS apps is by using the MVC design pattern.

MVC divides an app into three different parts:

- **Model**: This handles data storage and representation, and data processing tasks.
- **View**: This includes all the things that are on the screen that the user can interact with.
- **Controller**: This manages the flow of information between model and view.

One feature of MVC is that view and model do not interact with one another; instead, all communication is managed by the controller.

For example, imagine you're at a restaurant. You look at a menu and choose something you want. Then, a waiter comes, takes your order, and sends it to the cook. The cook prepares your order, and, when it is done, the waiter takes the order and brings it out to you. In this scenario, the menu is the view, the waiter is the controller, and the cook is the model. Also, note that all interactions between you and the kitchen are only through the waiter; there is no interaction between you and the cook.

To find out more about MVC, you can refer to https://en.wikipedia.org/wiki/Model-view-controller.

To see how MVC works, let's learn a little more about controllers and classes. You will see what it takes to implement a view controller that is required to manage a collection view, which is used in the **Explore** screen and the **Restaurant List** screen.

Exploring controllers and classes

So far, you have implemented view controller scenes in Main.storyboard using Interface Builder. You added ExploreViewController, a UIViewController subclass to manage the collection view inside the **Explore** screen, and RestaurantListViewController, a UIViewController subclass subclass to manage the collection view inside the **Restaurant List** screen. However, you still haven't learned how the code you added to each of them works.

A collection view displays an ordered collection of collection view cells using customizable layouts.

To learn more about collection views, you can refer to https://developer.apple.com/documentation/uikit/uicollectionview.

The layout for the collection view is dictated by UICollectionViewFlowLayout.

To learn more about UICollectionViewFlowLayout, you can refer to https://developer.apple.com/documentation/uikit/uicollectionviewflowlayout.

The data displayed by a collection view is normally provided by a view controller. A view controller providing data for a collection view must conform to the UICollectionViewDataSource protocol. This protocol declares a list of methods that tells the collection view how many cells to display and what to display in each cell. It also covers the creation and configuration of supplementary views (such as the collection view section header).

To learn more about the `UICollectionViewDataSource` protocol, you can refer to https://developer.apple.com/documentation/ uikit/uicollectionviewdatasource.

To provide user interaction, a view controller for a collection view must also conform to the `UICollectionViewDelegate` protocol, which declares a list of methods which are triggered when a user interacts with the collection view.

 To learn more about the `UICollectionViewDelegate` protocol, you can refer to https://developer.apple.com/documentation/ uikit/uicollectionviewdelegate.

Let's see how this works by implementing a view controller for a collection view in a playground, which will display a collection view in the playground's live view, which acts as a display screen for the playground.

Understanding collection views

In the previous chapter, you implemented the view controllers for the collection views in the **Explore** and **Restaurant List** screens without learning how they work.

To understand how collection views work, you'll implement a `UIViewController` subclass that controls a collection view in your `CollectionViewBasics` playground. You will then compare this with the implementation for the collection views in the **Explore** and **Restaurant List** screens in the next section. As there is no storyboard in the playground, you can't add UI elements as you have done in previous chapters. Instead, you will do everything programmatically.

You'll start by creating `CollectionViewExampleController`, an implementation of a view controller that manages a collection view, similar to those used for the **Explore** and **Restaurant Detail** screens. After that, you'll create an instance of `CollectionViewExampleController` and make it display a collection view containing a single collection view cell in the playground's live view. Do the following steps:

1. Open your `CollectionViewBasics` playground that you have created at the beginning of this chapter. At the very top of the playground, remove the `var` statement and add an `import PlaygroundSupport` statement.

Your playground should now contain the following:

```
import UIKit
import PlaygroundSupport
```

The first `import` statement imports the API for creating iOS apps. The second statement enables the playground to display a live view, which you will use to display the collection view.

2. Press *Return* and then add the following code below the `import` statements:

```
class CollectionViewExampleController:UIViewController {

}
```

This is the declaration for the `CollectionViewExampleController` class. It is a subclass of `UIViewController`, that is, a class that Apple provides to manage views on the screen.

3. Add the following code inside the curly braces:

```
var collectionView:UICollectionView?
```

4. Check your code. The complete code should look like the following:

```
class CollectionViewExampleController:UIViewController {
    var collectionView:UICollectionView?
}
```

This adds an optional property `collectionView`, to the `CollectionViewExampleController` class, which is a reference to a collection view. As you know, a collection view displays a grid of collection view cells on the screen. However, before it can do this, it needs to know how many collection view cells to display, and what to put in each cell.

To provide this information to `collectionView`, you will designate `CollectionViewExampleController` as the data source for the `collectionView` instance, and make it adopt the `UICollectionViewDataSource` protocol.

This protocol has two required methods:

- `collectionView(_:numberOfItemsInSection:)` tells `collectionView` how many cells to display.
- `collectionView(_:cellForItemAt:)` tells `collectionView` how to configure each cell.

5. To make `CollectionViewExampleController` adopt the `UICollectionViewDataSource` protocol, type a comma after the superclass declaration and then type `UICollectionViewDataSource`. When you are done, you should have the following:

```
class CollectionViewExampleController: UIViewController,
    UICollectionViewDataSource {
      var collectionView:UICollectionView?
}
```

6. An error will appear because you have not yet implemented the two required methods. Click on the error icon:

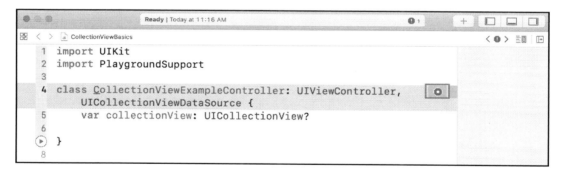

The error message states that the required methods for the `UICollectionViewDataSource` protocol are missing.

7. Click on the **Fix** button to add the required methods:

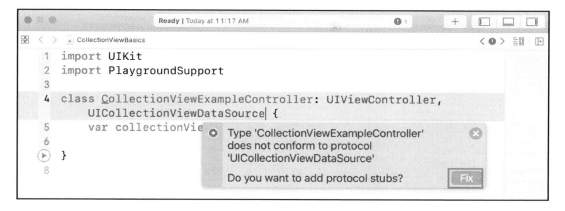

8. Check your code. The complete code should look like the following:

```
class CollectionViewExampleController: UIViewController,
    UICollectionViewDataSource {

    func collectionView(_ collectionView: UICollectionView,
        numberOfItemsInSection section: Int) -> Int {
        code
    }

    func collectionView(_ collectionView: UICollectionView,
        cellForItemAt indexPath: IndexPath) ->
UICollectionViewCell{
        code
    }

    var collectionView:UICollectionView?
}
```

9. Rearrange the code so that the `collectionView` property declaration is at the top. It should look like this:

```
class CollectionViewExampleController: UIViewController,
UICollectionViewDataSource {

    var collectionView:UICollectionView?

    func collectionView(_ collectionView: UICollectionView,
        numberOfItemsInSection section: Int) -> Int {
        code
```

```
        }

        func collectionView(_ collectionView: UICollectionView,
            cellForItemAt indexPath: IndexPath) ->
UICollectionViewCell{
            code
        }
    }
```

10. In `collectionView(_:numberOfItemsInSection:)`, click on the word code and type `return 1`. The completed method should look like this:

```
func collectionView(_ collectionView: UICollectionView,
  numberOfItemsInSection section: Int) -> Int {
    return 1
}
```

This will make the `collectionView` instance display a single collection view cell. Typically, the number of cells to be displayed will be provided by a model object. However, for the purpose of this example, we will just set it to 1 for now.

11. In `collectionView(_:cellForItemAt:)`, click on the word code and type the following:

```
let cell =
collectionView.dequeueReusableCell(withReuseIdentifier:
        "BoxCell", for: indexPath)
cell.backgroundColor = .red
return cell
```

12. Check your code. The completed method should look like this:

```
        func collectionView(_ collectionView: UICollectionView,
            cellForItemAt indexPath: IndexPath) ->
UICollectionViewCell{
            let cell =
collectionView.dequeueReusableCell(withReuseIdentifier:
                "BoxCell", for: indexPath)
            cell.backgroundColor = .red
            return cell
        }
```

Here is how this method works: imagine you have 1,000 items to display in a collection view. You don't need 1,000 collection view cells, you only need just enough to fill the screen. Collection view cells that scroll off the top of the screen can be reused to display items that appear at the bottom of the screen. To make sure you are using the right type of cell, you can use a **reuse identifier** to identify a cell type. The **reuse identifier** needs to be registered with the collection view, which you will do later. The next line of code sets the cell's background color to red, and the line after that returns the cell, which is then displayed on the screen. The process is repeated for the number of cells given in the first method, which, in this case, is 1.

13. Check your code. Your `CollectionViewExampleController` class should look like the following:

```
class CollectionViewExampleController: UIViewController,
UICollectionViewDataSource {

    var collectionView:UICollectionView?

    func collectionView(_ collectionView: UICollectionView,
      numberOfItemsInSection section: Int) -> Int {
        return 1
    }

    func collectionView(_ collectionView: UICollectionView,
      cellForItemAt indexPath: IndexPath) ->
UICollectionViewCell{
        let cell =
collectionView.dequeueReusableCell(withReuseIdentifier:
                "BoxCell", for: indexPath)
        cell.backgroundColor = .red
        return cell
    }
}
```

You have completed the implementation of the `CollectionViewExampleController` class. Now you will write a method to create an instance of it. Do the following steps:

1. Type in the following code after the variable declaration:

```
func createCollectionView(){

}
```

This declares a new method, `createCollectionView()`.

2. Type in the following code after the opening curly brace:

```
self.collectionView = UICollectionView(frame: CGRect(x:0, y:0,
    width:self.view.frame.width, height:
self.view.frame.height),
collectionViewLayout:UICollectionViewFlowLayout())
```

This creates a new collection view instance and assigns it to `collectionView`. The dimensions of this collection view is exactly the same size as its enclosing view, with the default flow layout. The flow layout dictates the order the collection view cells are displayed.

3. Type *Return* to go to the next line, and then type in the following code:

```
self.collectionView?.dataSource = self
```

This tells the collection view instance that its data source is `CollecionViewExampleController`.

4. Type *Return* to go to the next line, and then type in the following code:

```
self.collectionView?.backgroundColor = .white
```

This sets the background color of the collection view instance to `white`.

5. Type *Return* to go to the next line, and then type in the following code:

```
self.collectionView?.register(UICollectionViewCell.self,
forCellWithReuseIdentifier:"BoxCell")
```

Remember the reuse identifier used in the `collectionView(_:cellForItemAt:)` method to identify the cells to be reused? This registers `BoxCell` as the reuse identifier for the collection view cells for this collection view instance.

6. Type *Return* to go to the next line, and then type in the following code:

```
self.view.addSubview(self.collectionView!)
```

This adds the collection view instance as a subview to the view of the `CollectionViewExampleController` instance.

7. Check your code. The completed method should look like this:

```
func createCollectionView() {
    self.collectionView = UICollectionView(frame: CGRect(x:0,
y:0,
        width:self.view.frame.width,
height:self.view.frame.height),
        collectionViewLayout: UICollectionViewFlowLayout())
    self.collectionView?.dataSource = self
    self.collectionView?.backgroundColor = .white
    self.collectionView?.register(UICollectionViewCell.self,
        forCellWithReuseIdentifier: "BoxCell")
    self.view.addSubview(self.collectionView!)
}
```

Now you need to call this method. `UIViewController` has a method called `viewDidLoad()`, which is called when its view is loaded, and this is the perfect time to call `createCollectionView`. You will override this method in your class:

1. Type in the following code just above the `createCollectionView()` method:

```
override func viewDidLoad(){
    super.viewDidLoad()
    createCollectionView()
}
```

This creates a collection view instance, assigns it to `collectionView` and adds it as a subview to the view of the `CollectionViewExampleController` instance. The data source methods are then used to determine how many collection view cells to display, and how each collection view cell is configured. `collectionView(_:numberOfItemsInSection:)` returns 1, so a single collection view cell is displayed. `collectionView(_:cellForItemAt:)` sets the background color of the cell to `red`.

2. Check your code. Your completed playground should look like this:

```
import UIKit
import PlaygroundSupport

class CollectionViewExampleController: UIViewController,
    UICollectionViewDataSource{

    var collectionView:UICollectionView?

    override func viewDidLoad(){
        super.viewDidLoad()
        createCollectionView()
    }

    func createCollectionView() {
        self.collectionView = UICollectionView(frame:
        CGRect(x:0, y:0, width:self.view.frame.width,
        height:self.view.frame.height), collectionViewLayout:
        UICollectionViewFlowLayout())
        self.collectionView?.dataSource = self
        self.collectionView?.backgroundColor = .white
self.collectionView?.register(UICollectionViewCell.self,
        forCellWithReuseIdentifier: "BoxCell")
        self.view.addSubview(self.collectionView!)
    }

    func collectionView(_ collectionView: UICollectionView,
     numberOfItemsInSection section: Int) -> Int {
        return 1
    }

    func collectionView(_ collectionView: UICollectionView,
        cellForItemAt indexPath: IndexPath) ->
UICollectionViewCell {
        let cell =
collectionView.dequeueReusableCell(withReuseIdentifier:
                "BoxCell", for: indexPath)
        cell.backgroundColor = .red
         return cell
    }
}
```

3. Now it's time to see what it does. Type the following after all the other code in the playground:

```
PlaygroundPage.current.liveView =
CollectionViewExampleController()
```

This command creates the instance of
`CollectionViewExampleController` and displays its view in the
playground's live view. Since you added a collection view to the view of the
`CollectionViewExampleController` instance, it should appear on the
screen.

4. Run the playground. If you don't see a representation of the collection
view on your screen, you will need to turn on live view. Click on the
Adjust Editor Options button:

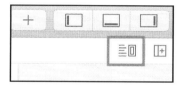

5. Make sure that **Live View** is selected:

6. You will see the collection view displaying one red collection view cell in the live view:

This concludes the section on collection view controllers.

Next, you'll revisit how collection view controllers are used in the **Explore** and **Restaurant List** screens, which you implemented in Chapter 10, *Building Your App Structure in Storyboard,* and Chapter 11, *Finishing Up Your App Structure in Storyboard,* of this book. Using what you have learned in this section as a reference, you should be able to understand how they work.

Revisiting the Explore and Restaurant List screens

Remember `ExploreViewController` that you added in Chapter 10, *Building Your App Structure in Storyboard*, and `RestaurantListViewController` that you added in Chapter 11, *Finishing Up Your App Structure in Storyboard*? Both of these are examples of view controllers that manage a collection view. Note that the code in both of them is very similar to that in your playground. The differences are as follows:

- You set the cell background color programmatically in `collectionView(_:cellForItemAt:)`, instead of setting it in the Attributes inspector.
- You created and assigned the collection view to the `collectionView` property in `CollectionViewExampleController` programmatically.
- You set the dimensions of the collection view programmatically in `UICollectionView(frame: collectionViewLayout:)`, instead of using the Size inspector.
- You connected the data source outlet to the view controller programmatically, instead of using the Connections inspector.
- You set the background color of the collection view programmatically, instead of using the Attributes inspector.
- You set the reuse identifier for the collection view cell programmatically, instead of using the Attributes inspector.
- You added the collection view as a subview of the view for `CollectionViewExampleController` programmatically, instead of dragging in a **Collection View** object from the Object library.

Open the `LetsEat` project. Review Chapter 10, *Building Your App Structure in Storyboard* and Chapter 11, *Finishing Up Your App Structure in Storyboard*, once more, in order to compare and contrast the implementation of the collection view using the storyboard, and by doing the implementation programmatically as you have done in this chapter.

Summary

In this chapter, you learned about the MVC design pattern and collection view controllers in detail. You then revisited the collection views used in the **Explore** and **Restaurant List** screens and learned how they work.

You should now understand the MVC design pattern, how to create a collection view controller, and how to use the collection view delegate and data source protocols. This will enable to you implement collection view controllers for your own apps.

Up to this point, you have set up the views and view controllers for the **Explore** and **Restaurant List** screens, but the **Explore** screen just displays a grid of cells, and the **Restaurant List** screen displays a single cell with a placeholder image.

In the next chapter, you're going to implement the model objects for the **Explore** screen so it can display a list of cuisines. To do this, you will read data from a file stored on your iOS device, create structures to store that data, and finally, provide it to `ExploreViewController` so that it may be displayed by the collection view in the **Explore** screen.

14

Getting Data into Collection Views

In the previous chapter, you learned about the **Model-View-Controller (MVC)** design pattern and about collection views. You've also revisited the **Explore** and **Restaurant List** screens, and now you understand how the collection views in both screens work. At this point, though, both screens just display cells that do not contain any data. As shown in the app tour in `Chapter 9`, *Setting Up the Basic Structure*, the **Explore** screen should display a list of cuisines, and the **Restaurant List** screen should display a list of restaurants.

In this chapter, you're going to implement the model objects for the **Explore** screen so it will display a list of cuisines.

You'll start by learning about model objects that you will use. Next, you'll learn about property lists, and see how they are used to store cuisine data, and you'll create a Swift structure that can store cuisine instances. After that, you'll create a data manager class that reads data from the property list and populates an array of structures. This array of structures will then be used as the data source for the collection view in the **Explore** screen.

By the end of this chapter, you'll learn how property lists are used to store data, how to create model objects, how to create a data manager class that can load data from a property list into an array of model objects, how to configure view controllers to provide model objects to collection view, and how to configure collection views to display data on screen.

The following topics will be covered:

- Understanding model objects
- Understanding `.plist` files
- Creating a structure to represent a cuisine
- Implementing a data manager class to read data from a `.plist` file
- Displaying data in a collection view

Technical requirements

You will continue working on the `LetsEat` project that you modified in `Chapter 12`, *Modifying and Configuring Cells*.

The resource files and completed Xcode project for this chapter are in the `Chapter14` folder of the code bundle for this book, which can be downloaded here:

`https://github.com/PacktPublishing/iOS-13-Programming-for-Beginners`.

Let's start by looking at the different model objects that are required to hold the initial data, load the data into the app, and store the data within the app.

Check out the following video to see the code in action:

`http://bit.ly/37m7dBQ`

Understanding model objects

As you learned in `Chapter 13`, *Getting Started with MVC and Collection Views*, a common design pattern for iOS Apps is MVC. To recap, MVC divides an app into three different parts:

- **Model**: This handles data storage, representation, and data processing tasks.
- **View**: This is anything that is on the screen that the user can interact with.
- **Controller**: This manages the flow of information between model and view.

Let's look at the design of the **Explore** screen that you saw during the app tour:

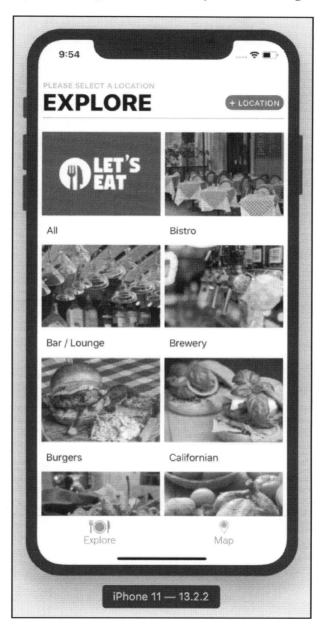

Now, build and run your app, and the **EXPLORE** screen will look like the following:

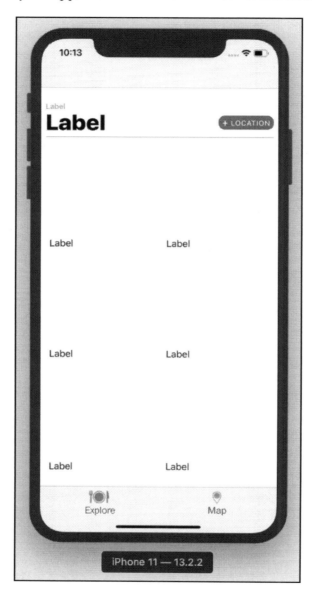

As you can see, all of the cells are currently empty. Based on the MVC design pattern, you have completed the implementation of the views (collection view section header and collection view) and the controller (ExploreViewController). Now, you will add model objects that will provide the data to be displayed.

In this section, you will add a property list, ExploreData.plist, to your project, which contains the name and the image filename for each cuisine.

Next, you will create a model object, ExploreItem, which will be a structure with two properties. One property will be used to store image filenames, and the other will be used to store cuisine names. After that, you will create a data manager class, ExploreDataManager, which will load the data from ExploreData.plist, put it into an array of ExploreItem instances and provide the array to ExploreViewController. Finally, you will modify ExploreViewController so it can provide data for the collection view to display.

Let's add ExploreData.plist to your project now and see how it stores cuisine data.

Understanding .plist files

Property lists were developed by Apple to store data structures or object states so that they may be transmitted or reconstituted later. They are commonly used to store preferences for applications. Property list files use the .plist filename extension, and hence are often referred to as .plist files. You will be using a .plist file containing cuisine data, ExploreData.plist, in your project.

You will need to download the code bundle for this book to get the ExploreData.plist file. After that you can use Xcode to view its contents. Do the following steps:

1. If you have not yet done so, download the resource files and completed Xcode project for this from this link: https://github.com/PacktPublishing/iOS-13-Programming-for-Beginners

2. Open the Chapter14 folder and look inside the resources folder to find ExploreData.plist. This file stores cuisine names and image filenames.

3. Open the LetsEat project, right-click on the Explore folder in the Project navigator, and choose **New Group**.

4. Rename the new group that you just added `Model`.
5. Drag `ExploreData.plist` into this group.
6. Make sure **Copy items if needed** is ticked and click **Finish**.

When you click on `ExploreData.plist` in the Project navigator, you'll see an array that contains dictionaries. This can be seen in the following screenshot:

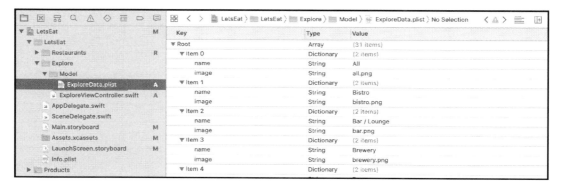

Each dictionary has two elements. The first element has a key, `name`, and a value describing a type of cuisine. The second element has a key, `image`, and a value containing the filename of a cuisine image. All of the cuisine images are stored in the `Assets.xcassets` file in your project.

To use the data contained in `ExploreData.plist`, you'll need to create a structure to hold it in the app, and accessed later by `ExploreViewController`. You will make one in the next section.

Creating a structure to represent a cuisine

You need a model object that can represent a cuisine in your app. For this, you will create a new file, `ExploreItem.swift`, and declare an `ExploreItem` structure that has properties for a cuisine's name and image.

> Structures are covered in Chapter 7, *Classes, Structures, and Enumerations*.

Follow these steps:

1. Right-click on the `Model` folder and select **New File**.
2. **iOS** should already be selected. Choose **Swift File**, then click **Next**.
3. Name the file `ExploreItem.swift` and then click **Create**. It appears in the Project navigator.

    The only thing in this file is an `import` statement.

 The `import` statement allows you to import other code libraries into your project, giving you the ability to use classes, properties, and methods from them. Foundation is one of Apple's core frameworks.

4. Add the following code to the file:

    ```
    struct ExploreItem {

    }
    ```

5. This declares a new structure named `ExploreItem`. Add the following code before the last curly brace:

    ```
    var name: String
    var image: String
    ```

This adds two `String` properties to the `ExploreItem` structure. The `name` property will store the cuisine name, and the `image` property will store the filename of an image that's already in your `Assets.xcassets` file. Your structure should look like the following code:

```
struct ExploreItem {
    var name: String
    var image: String
}
```

Unlike a class, structures automatically get a default initializer. You can create an instance of `ExploreItem` by using the following code:

```
let myExploreItem = ExploreItem(name:"name", image:"image")
```

However, the name and image filename in `ExploreData.plist` are stored as elements in a dictionary, as shown in the following example:

```
["name": "All", "image": "all.png"]
```

Dictionaries are covered in Chapter 5, *Collection Types.*

You will need to create a custom initializer that takes a dictionary as a parameter and assigns the values obtained from the dictionary elements to the properties in ExploreItem. You'll use an extension to add this custom initializer to the ExploreItem structure.

Extensions are covered in Chapter 8, *Protocols, Extensions, and Error Handling.*

6. Type the following after the ExploreItem structure declaration:

```
extension ExploreItem {

}
```

This creates an extension that allows you to add new capabilities to ExploreItem.

7. Add the following between the curly braces of the extension:

```
init(dict:[String:AnyObject]){
}
```

Ignore the error that appears, as you will fix it shortly. Here, you declare an initializer that takes a dictionary as an argument. Note that dict is of the [String:AnyObject] type, which means that the keys are of the String type and values are of the AnyObject type. This means you can use any valid Swift class as a value.

8. Now add the following code between the curly braces of the initializer:

```
self.name = dict["name"] as! String
self.image = dict["image"] as! String
```

This assigns the value of the dictionary item with the key `name` to the `name` property, and the value of the dictionary item with the key `image` to the `image` property. Since the dictionary values are of the `AnyObject` type, you use `as! String` to cast the value as `String`. The completed extension should look as follows:

```
extension ExploreItem {
    init(dict:[String:AnyObject]){
        self.name = dict["name"] as! String
        self.image = dict["image"] as! String
    }
}
```

So, at this point, you have a structure, `ExploreItem`, with two `String` properties, `name` and `image`, that can be initialized by a dictionary containing elements with a key of the `String` type and a value of the `AnyObject` type.

Now, you need to implement a data manager class. This will read the array of dictionaries from the `.plist` file and assign the values of the dictionary elements to `ExploreItem` instances.

Implementing a data manager class to read data from a .plist

You have added a `.plist` file, `ExploreData.plist`, to your project containing the cuisine data, and you have created a structure, `ExploreItem`, that can store details of each cuisine. Now, you need to create a class that can read the data in the `.plist` file and store it in an array of `ExploreItem` instances. This will be known as the data manager class. You will create a new class, `ExploreDataManager`, to do this. Follow the steps given here:

1. Right-click on the `Model` folder and select **New File**.
2. **iOS** should already be selected. Choose **Swift File**, then click **Next**.
3. Name the file `ExploreDataManager.swift` and then click **Create**.
4. Type the following code in the file to declare the `ExploreDataManager` class:

   ```
   class ExploreDataManager {

   }
   ```

5. Next, type in the following code between the curly braces:

```
fileprivate func loadData() -> [[String: AnyObject]] {
    guard let path = Bundle.main.path(forResource:
"ExploreData",
      ofType: "plist"), let items = NSArray(contentsOfFile:
path)
      else {
          return [[:]]
      }
      return items as! [[String:AnyObject]]
}
```

This implements a method, `loadData()`. Let's break down this method:

- `fileprivate`: The `fileprivate` keyword means that the method may only be used within this class.
- `func loadData() -> [[String: AnyObject]]`: The `loadData()` method declaration has no arguments and returns an array of dictionaries, and each dictionary contains elements with a key of the `String` type and a value of the `AnyObject` type.
- `guard`: The `guard` statement attempts to perform two statements, `let path = Bundle.main.path(forResource: "ExploreData", ofType: "plist")` and `let items = NSArray(contentsOfFile: path)` (explained in detail next). If either statement is unsuccessful, an empty array of dictionaries is returned.
- `let path = Bundle.main.path(forResource: "ExploreData", ofType: "plist")`: When you build your app, the result is a folder with all of the app resources inside it, called the application bundle. `ExploreData.plist` is inside this bundle. This statement gets the path to the `ExploreData.plist` file and assigns it to a constant, `path`.
- `let items = NSArray(contentsOfFile: path)`: If you click `ExploreData.plist` in your project, note that the root level object is an array, and each item in the array is a dictionary:

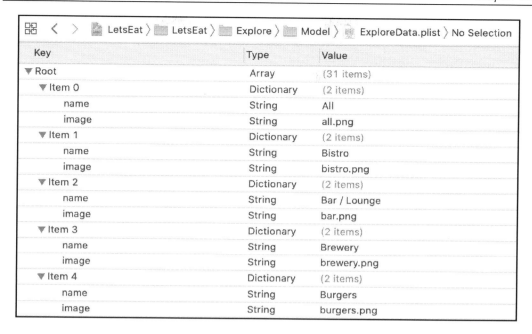

This statement attempts to create an array from the contents of the ExploreData.plist file and assign it to a constant, items.

- return items as! [[String:AnyObject]]: The final statement returns items as an array of dictionaries, and each dictionary is of the [String:AnyObject] type.

At this point, you have a data manager class, ExploreDataManager, containing a method that loads data from a .plist file and assigns it to an array, items. Next, you will look at how to use this array to initialize ExploreItem instances, which can then be accessed within the app.

Using the data manager to initialize ExploreItem instances

Currently, you have a data manager class, `ExploreDataManager`. This class contains a method, `loadData()`, which reads data from `ExploreData.plist` and returns an array of dictionaries. Next, you'll add a method that creates and initializes `ExploreItem` instances with that array. Follow the steps given here:

1. In the `ExploreDataManager` class, add the following code above the `loadData()` method:

   ```
   func fetch() {
       for data in loadData() {
           print(data)
       }
   }
   ```

   This method will call `loadData()`, which returns an array of dictionaries. The `for` loop is then used to print the contents of each dictionary in the array to the Debug area to ensure that this method is working.

2. Click `ExploreViewController.swift` in the Project navigator. Add the following to the `viewDidLoad()` method:

   ```
   let manager = ExploreDataManager()
   manager.fetch()
   ```

   This creates an instance of `ExploreDataManager` in your app and calls its `fetch()` method when the app is run. Your `viewDidLoad()` method should look like the code given here:

   ```
   override func viewDidLoad() {
       super.viewDidLoad()
       let manager = ExploreDataManager()
       manager.fetch()
   }
   ```

3. Let's build and run your app. The contents of the `ExploreData.plist` file are read and printed in the Debug area. This is what the Debug area should look like:

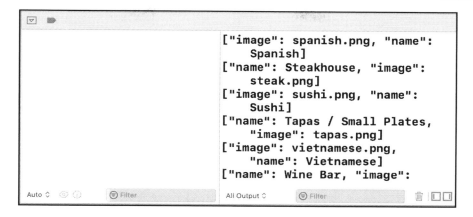

```
["image": spanish.png, "name":
    Spanish]
["name": Steakhouse, "image":
    steak.png]
["image": sushi.png, "name":
    Sushi]
["name": Tapas / Small Plates,
    "image": tapas.png]
["image": vietnamese.png,
    "name": Vietnamese]
["name": Wine Bar, "image":
```

Now, you'll assign the name and image strings from each dictionary to an ExploreItem instance.

4. Click ExploreDataManager.swift. Add the following code just above the fetch() method:

```
fileprivate var items:[ExploreItem] = []
```

This adds a property, items, which is an array of ExploreItem instances, to ExploreDataManager and assigns an empty array to it.

5. Inside the fetch() method, replace the print() statement with the following:

```
items.append(ExploreItem(dict: data))
```

This assigns the name and image strings in each dictionary read from ExploreData.plist to the name and image properties of an ExploreData instance, and adds that instance to the items array.

Our completed ExploreDataManager class should look like this:

```
import Foundation

class ExploreDataManager {
    fileprivate var items:[ExploreItem] = []

    func fetch() {
        for data in loadData() {
            items.append(ExploreItem(dict: data))
        }
```

```
    }

    fileprivate func loadData() -> [[String: AnyObject]] {
        guard let path = Bundle.main.path(forResource:
"ExploreData",
                            ofType: "plist"),
        let items = NSArray(contentsOfFile: path) else {
            return [[:]]
        }
        return items as! [[String:AnyObject]]
    }
}
```

At this point, you have an `ExploreDataManager` class that reads data from `ExploreData.plist` and stores it in `items`, an array of `ExploreItem` instances. The next step is to provide that data to the collection view managed by `ExploreViewController` so it will be visible on the screen.

Displaying data in a collection view

You've implemented a data manager class, `ExploreDataManager`, that reads cuisine data from a `.plist` file and stores it in an array of `ExploreItem` instances. Now, you will use that array as the data source for the collection view in the **Explore** screen.

At present, the collection view in the **Explore** screen displays 20 collection view cells, with each cell containing an empty image view and a label. You need a way to set the values for the image view and the label in the cells, so you will create a view controller, `ExploreCell`, for this purpose. Then, you can configure the view controller for the collection view, `ExploreViewController`, to get cuisine details from `ExploreDataManager` and provide it to the collection view for display.

To create `ExploreCell`, perform the following steps:

1. Right-click on the `Explore` folder in the Project navigator and choose **New Group**.
2. Rename the new group `View`.
3. Right-click on the `View` folder and select **New File**.
4. **iOS** should already be selected. Choose **Cocoa Touch Class**, then click **Next**.

5. Configure the class as shown here:

- **Class**: ExploreCell
- **Subclass**: UICollectionViewCell
- **Also create XIB**: Unchecked
- **Language**: Swift
- Click **Next**

6. Click **Create**.

7. A new file, ExploreCell, will be added to your project. Click it and you will see the following:

```
import UIKit
class ExploreCell: UICollectionViewCell {
}
```

8. Open Main.storyboard and click exploreCell inside the **Explore View Controller Scene** in the document outline. Click the Identity inspector:

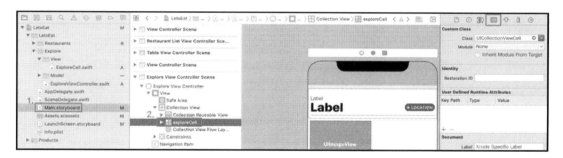

9. Set the **Custom Class** to ExploreCell. This sets ExploreCell as the view controller for exploreCell. Press *Return* when done:

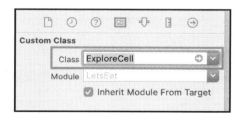

Now, you'll create outlets in ExploreCell that will be connected to the image view and the label in exploreCell, so you can control what exploreCell displays.

Connecting the outlets in exploreCell

You need to connect the image view and label in `exploreCell` to outlets in the
`ExploreCell` class. You'll be using the assistant editor to do this. Follow the steps
given here:

1. Click the Navigator and Inspector buttons to hide the Navigator and
   Inspector areas:

2. Click the Adjust Editor Options button:

3. Choose **Assistant** from the menu:

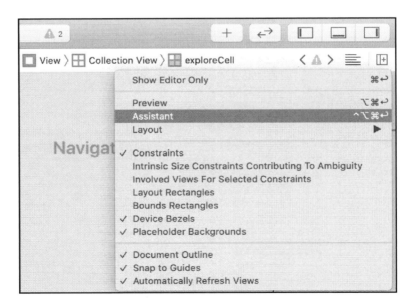

4. The assistant editor path should be set to **Automatic | ExploreCell.swift**. If you don't see ExploreCell.swift in the path, select the label of exploreCell in the storyboard and select ExploreCell.swift from the assistant editor's path drop-down menu:

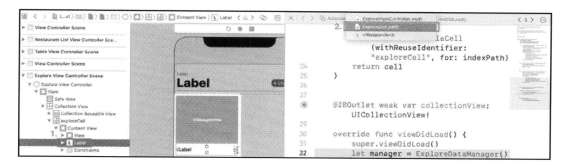

5. Ctrl + Drag from the **Label** in the document outline to the space between the curly braces as shown in the following screenshot:

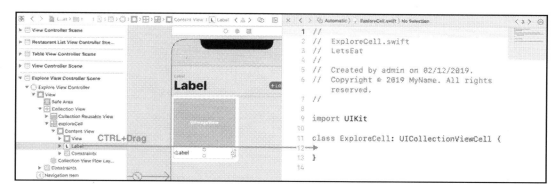

6. In the pop-up dialog, enter lblname in the **Name** field:

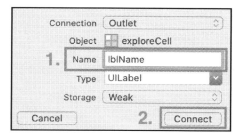

7. Ctrl + Drag from the **Image View** in the document outline to space just after the lblName property:

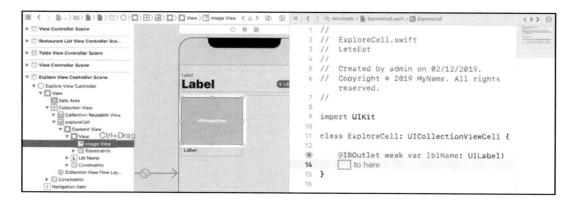

8. In the pop-up dialog, enter imgExplore in the **Name** field:

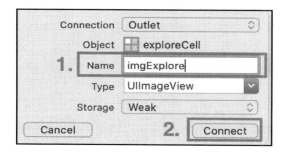

9. The lblName and imgExplore outlets have been added to ExploreCell and connected to the exploreCell image view and label in the storyboard. This is what it should look like:

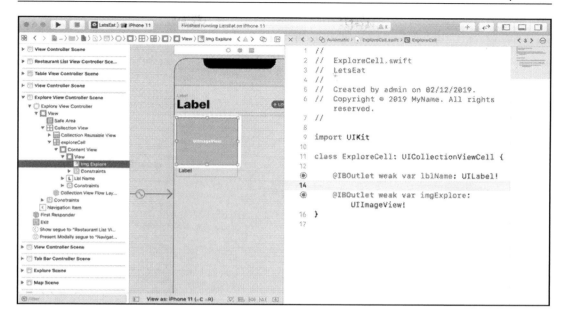

10. Click the **x** button to close the assistant editor:

exploreCell in Main.storyboard has now been set up with a view
controller, ExploreCell. Now, you can set the lblName and
imgExplore outlets in ExploreCell to display a cuisine image and name
in each cell when the app is run.

 You can check whether the outlets are connected properly in the
Connections inspector.

Next, you will add code to ExploreDataManager to provide the number of cells to
be displayed by collectionView, and provide an ExploreItem instance whose
properties will be used to determine what image and label the cell will display.

Implementing additional data manager methods

As you learned in Chapter 13, *Getting started with MVC and Collection Views*, a
collection view needs to know how many cells to display and what to put in each cell.
You will add two methods to ExploreDataManager that will provide the number of
ExploreItem instances in the items array and return an ExploreItem instance at a
specified array index. Click ExploreDataManager.swift in the Project navigator
and add these two methods above the loadData() method:

```
func numberOfItems() -> Int {
    return items.count
}

func explore(at index: IndexPath) -> ExploreItem {
    return items[index.item]
}
```

The first method, numberOfItems(), will determine the number of cells to be
displayed by the collection view.

The second method, `explore(at:)`, will return `ExploreItem` that corresponds to a cell's position in the collection view.

Now, you need to update the data source methods in `ExploreViewController` to display the correct number of `exploreCell` collection view cells in the collection view and to provide the cuisine name and image for each cell.

Updating the data source methods in ExploreViewController

The data source methods in `ExploreViewController` are currently set to display 20 cells with an empty image view and label. You'll need to update them so that they can get the number of cells to display and the data to put in each cell from `ExploreDataManager`. Click `ExploreViewController.swift` and find the `viewDidLoad()` method. It should look like this:

```
override func viewDidLoad() {
    super.viewDidLoad()

    let manager = ExploreDataManager()
    manager.fetch()
}
```

This means the `ExploreDataManager` instance is only accessible within `viewDidLoad()`. You need to make it available to the entire class.

Move the `let manager = ExploreDataManager()` line to just below the `collectionView` property declaration. It should look like this:

```
@IBOutlet var collectionView: UICollectionView!
let manager = ExploreDataManager()
```

This makes the `ExploreDataManager` instance assigned to `manager` available to all methods within the `ExploreViewController` class.

Update `collectionView(_:numberOfItemsInSection:)` as follows:

```
func collectionView(_ collectionView: UICollectionView,
  numberOfItemsInSection section: Int) -> Int {
    return manager.numberOfItems()
}
```

This will make `collectionView` display a cell for every item in the `items` array.

Update `collectionView(_:cellForItemAt:)` as follows:

```
func collectionView(_ collectionView: UICollectionView,
    cellForItemAt indexPath: IndexPath) -> UICollectionViewCell {
    let cell = collectionView.dequeueReusableCell(withReuseIdentifier:
            "exploreCell", for: indexPath) as! ExploreCell
    let item = manager.explore(at: indexPath)
    cell.lblName.text = item.name
    cell.imgExplore.image = UIImage(named: item.image)
    return cell
}
```

Let's break this down:

- `let cell = collectionView.dequeueReusableCell(withReuseIdentifier:"exploreCell", for: indexPath) as! ExploreCell`: This is to specify the cell that is dequeued is of type `ExploreCell`.

- `let item = manager.explore(at: indexPath)`: This statement gets the `ExploreItem` instance that corresponds to the current cell in `collectionView`. In other words, the first cell in `collectionView` corresponds to the first `ExploreItem` instance in the `items` array, the second cell corresponds to the second `ExploreItem` instance, and so on.

- `cell.lblName.text = item.name`: This statement sets the `text` property of the cell's `lblName` to the `name` of `ExploreItem` instance.

- `cell.imgExplore.image = UIImage(named: item.image)`: This statement gets the `image` string from `ExploreItem`instance, gets the corresponding image from the `Assets.xcassets` file, and assigns in to the `image` of the cell's `imgExplore` property.

Build and run the app. We should now see that the collection view in the **Explore** screen displays images and text of different cuisines:

Tapping a cell will display a single restaurant in the Restaurant List screen's collection view:

In Chapter 17, *Getting Started with JSON Files*, you will modify RestaurantListViewController to display a list of restaurants offering the selected cuisine. But before you can do that, you'll need to set a location in the **Locations** screen, which will provide a list of all available restaurants at that location.

Summary

In this chapter, you added a .plist file, ExploreData.plist, to your project. You implemented ExploreItem, the model objects for the **Explore** screen. You created a data manager, ExploreDataManager, to read data from ExploreData.plist, put the data into an array of ExploreItem instances, and provide it to ExploreViewController.

Finally, you created a view controller for exploreCell and configured the data source methods in ExploreViewController to set the values to be displayed by exploreCell in the collection view for the **Explore** screen. The **Explore** screen now displays a list of cuisines. Great job!

You should now know how to provide data to an app using .plist files, create model objects, create data manager classes that load .plist files into model objects, configure collection views to display data that has been loaded, and configure view controllers for collection views. This will be useful should you wish to create your own apps that use collection views.

In the next chapter, you will look at table views, which are similar in some ways to collection views, and configure the **Locations** screen display a list of locations in a table view when you tap the **LOCATION** button in the **Locations** screen.

15
Getting Started with Table Views

In the previous chapter, you added a `.plist` file, `ExploreData.plist`, to your project. You implemented `ExploreItem`, the model object for the **Explore** screen. Then, you created a data manager, `ExploreDataManager`, to read data from `ExploreData.plist`, put the data into an array of `ExploreItems`, and provided it to `ExploreViewController`.

Finally, you created a view controller for `exploreCell` and configured the data source methods in `ExploreViewController` to set the values to be displayed by `exploreCell` in the collection view for the **Explore** screen.

In this chapter, you will start by learning about table views and table view controllers. You'll implement a table view programmatically (which means implementing it using code instead of storyboards) using a playground, to understand how table views work.

Next, you will implement a table view controller for the **Locations** screen, create a `.plist` file from scratch to hold a list of locations, create a data manager class to read data from the `.plist` file, and configure the table view controller to get data from the data manager and provide it to the table view. The **Locations** screen will then display a list of restaurant locations.

Finally, you'll clean up the user interface for the **Explore** and **Locations** screens so that they match the screens shown in the app tour.

By the end of this chapter, you'll have learned how to create `.plist` files to store data, and how to implement a view controller that will be used to manage a table view. You should then be able to implement table views in your own apps.

The following topics will be covered in this chapter:

- Understanding table views
- Creating `LocationViewController`
- Adding location data for the table view
- Creating `LocationDataManager`
- Cleaning up the user interface

Technical requirements

You will continue working on the `LetsEat` project that you modified in the previous chapter.

The resource files and completed Xcode project for this chapter are in the `Chapter15` folder of the code bundle for this book, which can be downloaded here:

`https://github.com/PacktPublishing/iOS-13-Programming-for-Beginners`.

Let's begin by learning more about how a table view works by implementing a view controller that manages a table view in a playground. Create a new playground and name it `TableViewBasics`. You can type in and run all the code shown in the upcoming sections as you go along.

Check out the following video to see the code in action:

`http://bit.ly/371RMd9`

Understanding table views

The *Let's Eat* app uses a table view in the **Locations** screen to display a list of restaurant locations. A table view presents table view cells using rows arranged in a single column.

 To learn more about table views, visit `https://developer.apple.com/documentation/uikit/uitableview`.

To provide data to be displayed by a table view, view controllers for a table view must conform to the `UITableViewDataSource` protocol and implement the required methods.

 To learn more about the `UITableViewDataSource` protocol, visit https://developer.apple.com/documentation/uikit/ uitableviewdatasource.

To allow users to interact with a table view, view controllers for a table view must conform to the `UITableViewDelegate` protocol and implement the desired methods.

 To learn more about the `UITableViewDelegate` protocol, visit https://developer.apple.com/documentation/uikit/ uitableviewdelegate.

To learn how table views work, you'll implement a view controller subclass that controls a table view in your `TableViewBasics` playground. Since there is no storyboard in the playground, you can't add the UI elements using the Object library, as you did in the previous chapters. Instead, you will do everything programmatically. Do the following steps:

1. Remove all the existing code from the playground. Then, at the very top of the playground, add the following `import` statements:

   ```
   import UIKit
   import PlaygroundSupport
   ```

   The first `import` statement imports the API for creating iOS applications. The second allows the playground to display a live view, which you will use to display the table view.

2. Type *Return* and then add the following code:

   ```
   class TableViewExampleController: UIViewController {

   }
   ```

   This is the declaration for the `TableViewExampleController` class. It is a subclass of `UIViewController`, which is a class that Apple provides to manage views on the screen.

3. Add the following code inside the curly braces:

```
var tableView:UITableView?
var names:[String] = ["Kajal","Akhil","Divij"]
```

4. The complete code should look as follows:

```
class TableViewExampleController: UIViewController {
    var tableView:UITableView?
    var names:[String] = ["Kajal","Akhil","Divij"]
}
```

The first line adds an optional property to the tableView class, which is of the UITableView type. A UITableView instance, or table view, displays a single column of rows on the screen, and each row contains a UITableViewCell. Before it can do so, it needs to know how many rows to display and what to put in each row.

The second line creates an array called names. This is the model object that will be used to provide data to the table view. To do so, you will designate TableViewExampleController as the data source for the table view and make it adopt the UITableViewDataSource protocol.

5. To make TableViewExampleController adopt the UITableViewDataSource protocol, type a comma after the superclass name, UIViewController, and type UITableViewDataSource. When you are done, you should have the following code:

```
class TableViewExampleController: UIViewController,
UITableViewDataSource {
    var tableView:UITableView?
    var names:[String] = ["Kajal","Akhil","Divij"]
}
```

This protocol has two required methods. The first one, tableview(_:numberOfRowsInSection:), tells the table view how many rows to display, while the second one, tableView(_:cellForRowAt:), tells the table view what to put in each row.

An error will appear because you haven't implemented the two required methods yet:

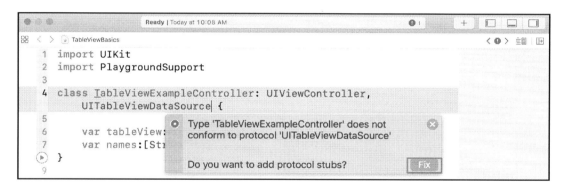

6. Click the error icon. You should see the following error message:

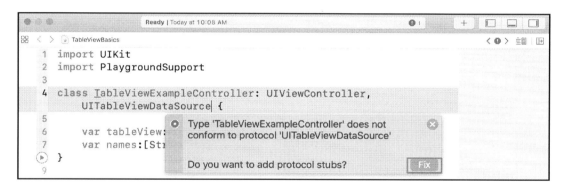

7. Click the **Fix** button to add the required methods to the class. Your code should look as follows:

```
class TableViewExampleController: UIViewController,
  UITableViewDataSource {

    func tableView(_ tableView: UITableView,
numberOfRowsInSection
      section: Int) -> Int {
        code
    }

    func tableView(_ tableView: UITableView, cellForRowAt
      indexPath: IndexPath) -> UITableViewCell {
```

```
             code
      }

      var tableView:UITableView?
      var names:[String] = ["Kajal","Akhil","Divij"]
}
```

8. Rearrange the code so that the property declarations are at the top. It should look like this:

```
class TableViewExampleController: UIViewController,
   UITableViewDataSource {

   var tableView:UITableView?
   var names:[String] = ["Kajal","Akhil","Divij"]

   func tableView(_ tableView: UITableView,
numberOfRowsInSection
      section: Int) -> Int {
      code
   }

   func tableView(_ tableView: UITableView, cellForRowAt
      indexPath: IndexPath) -> UITableViewCell {
      code
   }
}
```

9. Inside `tableView(_:numberOfRowsInSection:)`, click the word `code` and type in `return names.count`. The modified method should look like this:

```
func tableView(_ tableView: UITableView, numberOfRowsInSection
   section: Int) -> Int {
   return names.count
}
```

`names.count` returns the number of items inside the `names` array. Since there are three names in the `names` array, this will make the table view display three rows.

10. Inside `tableView(_:cellForRowAt:)`, click the word `code` and type the following:

```
let cell = tableView.dequeueReusableCell(withIdentifier:
            "Cell", for:indexPath) as UITableViewCell
let name = names[indexPath.row]
```

```
cell.textLabel?.text = name
return cell
```

11. The completed method should look as follows:

```
func tableView(_ tableView: UITableView, cellForRowAt
indexPath:
    IndexPath) -> UITableViewCell {
    let cell = tableView.dequeueReusableCell(withIdentifier:
            "Cell", for:indexPath) as UITableViewCell
    let name = names[indexPath.row]
    cell.textLabel?.text = name
    return cell
}
```

Let's go over how this method works, bit by bit:

- `let cell = tableView.dequeueReusableCell(withIdentifier: "Cell", for:indexPath) as UITableViewCell`: This creates a new table view cell or reuses an existing table view cell and assigns it to `cell`. Imagine you have 1,000 items to display in a table view. You don't need 1,000 rows containing 1,000 table view cells—you only need just enough to fill the screen. Table view cells that scroll off the top of the screen can be reused to display items that appear at the bottom of the screen. To make sure you are using the right type of cell, you need to use a reuse identifier, which is set to `Cell`. The reuse identifier needs to be registered with the table view, and you will do that later.

- `let name = names[indexPath.row]`: The `indexPath` returns the section and row number of a particular row in a table view. The first row has an `indexPath` containing section 0 and row 0. `indexPath.row` returns 0 for the first row, so we get the first item in the `names` array and assign it to the `name` constant.

- `cell.textLabel?.text = name`: This assigns `name` to the `text` property of the table view cell's `textLabel`.

- `return cell`: This returns the cell, which is then displayed on the screen.

This process is repeated for the number of cells given in the first method, which, in this case, is 3.

12. Your file should look as follows:

```
class TableViewExampleController: UIViewController,
    UITableViewDataSource {

    var tableView:UITableView?
    var names:[String] = ["Kajal","Akhil","Divij"]

    func tableView(_ tableView: UITableView,
numberOfRowsInSection
        section: Int) -> Int {
            return names.count
    }

    func tableView(_ tableView: UITableView, cellForRowAt
indexPath:
        IndexPath) -> UITableViewCell {
            let cell =
tableView.dequeueReusableCell(withIdentifier:
                    "Cell", for:indexPath) as UITableViewCell
let name = names[indexPath.row]
            cell.textLabel?.text = name
            return cell
    }
}
```

Now that you have completed the declaration of `TableViewExampleController`, you will write a method to create an instance of it. Follow these steps to do so:

1. Type in the following code after the property declarations:

```
func createTableView() {
    self.tableView = UITableView(frame:CGRect(x: 0, y: 0,
width:
                        self.view.frame.width, height:
                        self.view.frame.height))
    self.tableView?.dataSource = self
    self.tableView?.backgroundColor = .white
    self.tableView?.register(UITableViewCell.self,
        forCellReuseIdentifier: "Cell")
    self.view.addSubview(self.tableView!)
}
```

This declares a new method, `createTableView()`. Here's how it works:

- `self.tableView = UITableView(frame:CGRect(x: 0, y: 0, width: self.view.frame.width, height: self.view.frame.height))`: This creates a new instance of `UITableView` that is exactly the same size as its enclosing view, and assigns it to `tableView`.
- `self.tableView?.dataSource = self`: This tells the table view that its data source is `TableViewExampleController`.
- `self.tableView?.backgroundColor = .white`: This sets the table view's background color to `white`.
- `self.tableView?.register(UITableViewCell.self, forCellReuseIdentifier: "Cell")`: This sets the reuse identifier for the table view cells to `"Cell"`. This reuse identifier will be used in the `tableView(_:cellForRowAt:)` method to identify the cells that can be reused.
- `self.view.addSubview(self.tableView!)`: This adds the table view as a subview to the `view` of `TableViewExampleController`.

Now, you need to call this method. `UIViewController` has a method, `viewDidLoad()`, that is called when its view is loaded, and this is the perfect method to override to call `createTableView()`.

2. Type in the following code, just above the `createTableView()` method:

```
override func viewDidLoad() {
    super.viewDidLoad()
    createTableView()
}
```

This creates a table view and adds it as a subview to the view of the `TableViewExampleController` instance. The data source methods are then used to determine how many table view cells to display, as well as what to put in each table view cell.
`tableView(_:numberOfRowsInSection:)` returns 3, so three rows are displayed. `tableView(_:cellForRowAt:)` sets the text of each cell to the corresponding name in the `names` array.

3. Your completed code should look like this:

```
import UIKit
import PlaygroundSupport

class TableViewExampleController: UIViewController,
    UITableViewDataSource {

    var tableView:UITableView?
    var names:[String] = ["Kajal","Akhil","Divij"]

    override func viewDidLoad() {
        super.viewDidLoad()
        createTableView()
    }

    func createTableView() {
        self.tableView = UITableView(frame:CGRect(x: 0, y: 0,
                        width: self.view.frame.width, height:
                        self.view.frame.height))
        self.tableView?.dataSource = self
        self.tableView?.backgroundColor = .white
        self.tableView?.register(UITableViewCell.self,
            forCellReuseIdentifier: "Cell")
        self.view.addSubview(self.tableView!)
    }

    func tableView(_ tableView: UITableView,
numberOfRowsInSection
            section: Int) -> Int {
          return names.count
      }

    func tableView(_ tableView: UITableView, cellForRowAt
        indexPath: IndexPath) -> UITableViewCell {
        let cell =
tableView.dequeueReusableCell(withIdentifier:
                    "Cell", for:indexPath) as UITableViewCell
        let name = names[indexPath.row]
        cell.textLabel?.text = name
        return cell
    }
}
```

4. Now, it's time to see what it does. Type the following after all the other code in the playground:

```
PlaygroundPage.current.liveView = TableViewExampleController()
```

This command creates an instance of `TableViewExampleController` and displays its view in the playground's live view.

5. Run the playground. If you don't see the table view, click the Adjust Editor Options button shown in the following screenshot:

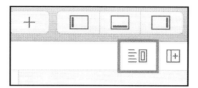

6. Make sure **Live View** is selected from the pop-up menu:

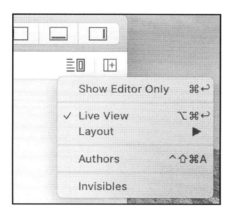

7. You will see the table view displaying a table with three rows containing names, as shown in the following screenshot:

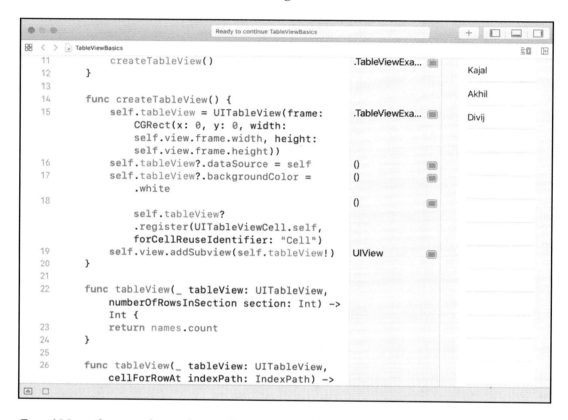

Great! Now that you know how table views work, let's complete the implementation for the **Locations** screen. You'll start by creating a view controller for this screen so that it can manage what the table view will display.

Creating LocationViewController

As shown in the app tour in Chapter 9, *Setting Up the Basic Structure*, the **Locations** screen displays a list of locations in a table view. At the end of Chapter 12, *Modifying and Configuring Cells*, you configured the **Locations** screen to display a table view and set the identifier of the table view cells to locationCell. Referring to the **Model-View-Controller (MVC)** design pattern, you have completed the views that are needed, but you haven't completed the controller or the model yet.

In this section, you will create `LocationViewController` as the view controller for the table view in the **Locations** screen, add an outlet for the table view to it, and configure it as the table view's data source and delegate.

At the moment, when you click the **LOCATION** button in the **Explore** screen, an empty table view is displayed, as shown in the following screenshot:

Now, you will create `LocationViewController`, a view controller class that's used to manage this table view. Do the following steps.

1. Open your `LetsEat` Xcode project from the previous chapter. Create a new folder, `Location`, inside your `LetsEat` project by right-clicking the `LetsEat` folder and choosing **New Group**. Create two more folders, `View` and `Model`, inside the `Location` folder. When you're done, you will see the following folder structure:

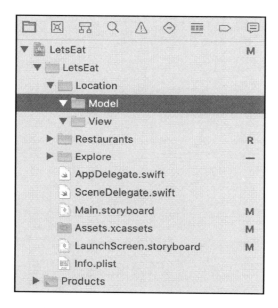

2. Right-click on the `Location` folder and select **New File**.
3. **iOS** should already be selected. Choose **Cocoa Touch Class** and click **Next**.
4. Configure the class with the following details:

   - **Class**: `LocationViewController`
   - **Subclass**: `UIViewController`
   - **Also create XIB**: Unchecked
   - **Language**: `Swift`
   - Click **Next**

5. Click **Create**.

Now, you need to set the identity of the view controller scene that's presented when you tap the **LOCATION** button to `LocationViewController`. Follow these steps to do so:

1. Open `Main.storyboard`.
2. Choose the **View Controller Scene** that's presented when you click on the **LOCATION** button. Click the Identity inspector and, under **Custom Class**, set **Class** to `LocationViewController`.

Cool! Now, let's connect the table view to `LocationViewController`. By doing this, `LocationViewController` will be able to manage the table view.

Connecting the table view to LocationViewController

Currently, `LocationViewController` has no way of communicating with the table view. In this section, you will create a new outlet in `LocationViewController` and assign the table view to it. Follow these steps to do so:

1. Click the Navigator and Inspector buttons to hide the Navigator and Inspector areas, as shown in the following screenshot:

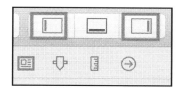

2. Click the Adjust Editor Options button, as shown in the following screenshot:

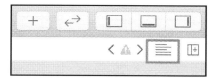

3. Choose **Assistant** from the menu, as shown in the following screenshot:

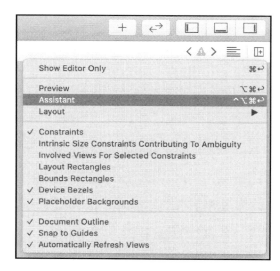

4. Click the table view in the document outline. The assistant editor should be set to **Automatic > LocationViewController.swift**:

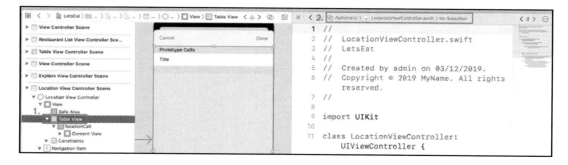

5. *Ctrl + Drag* from the table view to the space just above `viewDidLoad()`:

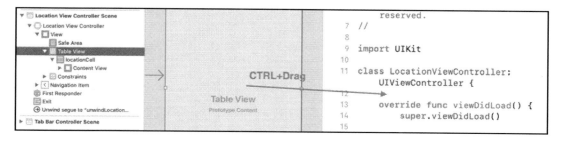

6. In the pop-up menu, enter `tableView` in the **Name** field and click **Connect**:

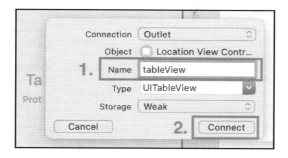

7. The `tableView` outlet has been added to `LocationViewController` and connected to the table view in the storyboard:

```
 9   import UIKit
10
11   class LocationViewController:
         UIViewController {
12
         @IBOutlet weak var tableView:
             UITableView!
14       override func viewDidLoad() {
15           super.viewDidLoad()
```

8. Click the **x** button to close the assistant editor:

```
1   //
2   //   LocationViewController.swift
3   //   LetsEat
4   //
5   //   Created by admin on 03/12/2019.
6   //   Copyright © 2019 MyName. All rights
         reserved.
7   //
8
9   import UIKit
10
11  class LocationViewController:
        UIViewController {
```

As you saw in the playground, in order for a table view to display data and respond to user interaction, a view controller for a table view needs to adopt the table view data source and delegate protocols and implement the required methods. You will do that next.

Adding the data source and delegate methods

A view controller for a table view needs to adopt the table view data source and delegate protocols, as well as implement the required methods to allow data display and user interaction. In this section, you'll connect `LocationViewController` to the data source and delegate outlets for the table view, configure the attributes for the table view cells, and implement the required data source methods. You will implement delegate methods in `Chapter 17`, *Getting Started with JSON Files*. Do the following steps:

1. Click the Navigator and Inspector buttons to show the Navigator and Inspector areas:

2. In `Main.storyboard`, make sure you have the table view selected in the document outline. Click the Connections inspector:

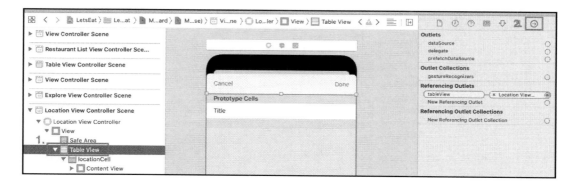

3. Click and drag from the **dataSource** and **delegate** outlets to the `LocationViewController` icon. The data source and delegate outlets for the table view are now connected to `LocationViewController`:

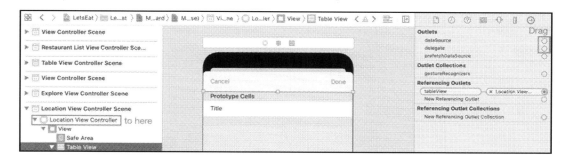

4. You need to update the attributes for the table view cell. Click `locationCell` in the document outline:

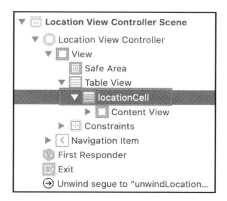

5. Click the Attributes inspector and set the following values for `locationCell`:

- **Style**: Basic
- **Identifier**: locationCell
- **Selection**: Gray
- **Accessory**: Disclosure indicator

This can be seen in the following screenshot:

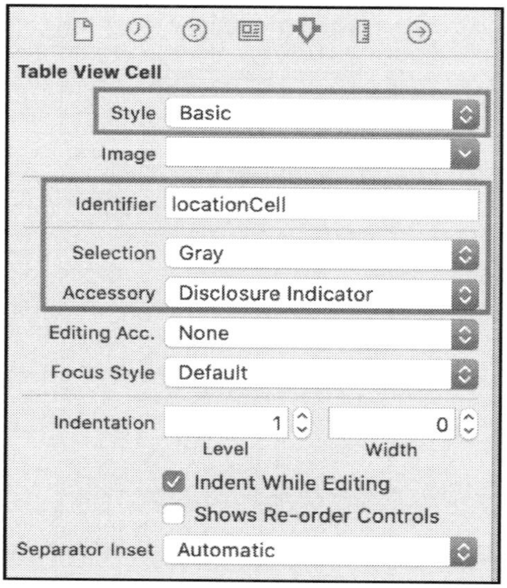

Next, to display data in the table view, you need to make
`LocationViewController` conform to the `UITableViewDataSource`
protocol and implement the required methods for this protocol.

6. Click `LocationViewController.swift` in the Project navigator and
   remove all the boilerplate code so that only the following is left:

```
class LocationViewController: UIViewController {

    @IBOutlet weak var tableView: UITableView!

    override func viewDidLoad()
        super.viewDidLoad()
    }
}
```

To make `LocationViewController` adopt the `UITableViewDataSource`
protocol, type a comma after the superclass name, `UIViewController`, and
type in `UITableViewDataSource`. When you are done, you should have
the following:

```
class LocationViewController: UIViewController,
UITableViewDataSource {
```

```
@IBOutlet weak var tableView: UITableView!

override func viewDidLoad() {
    super.viewDidLoad()
}
}
```

An error will appear because you haven't implemented the two required methods yet.

7. Click the error icon to see the error message:

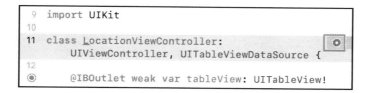

8. Click the **Fix** button to add the required methods to the class:

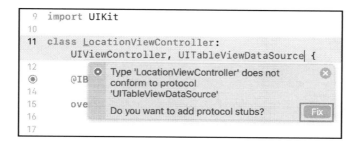

Rearrange the code so that the property declarations and `viewDidLoad()` are at the top. It should look like this:

```
class LocationViewController: UIViewController,
    UITableViewDataSource {

    @IBOutlet weak var tableView: UITableView!

    override func viewDidLoad() {
        super.viewDidLoad()
    }

    func tableView(_ tableView: UITableView,
     numberOfRowsInSection section: Int) -> Int {
        code
```

```
        }

        func tableView(_ tableView: UITableView, cellForRowAt
            indexPath: IndexPath) -> UITableViewCell {
              code
        }
    }
```

9. Inside the first required method, click the word `code` and type `return 10`. The complete method should look like this:

```
    func tableView(_ tableView: UITableView, numberOfRowsInSection
        section: Int) -> Int {
          return 10
    }
```

This will make the table view display 10 rows.

10. Inside the second required method, click the word `code` and type the following:

```
    let cell = tableView.dequeueReusableCell(withIdentifier:
               "locationCell", for: indexPath) as UITableViewCell
    cell.textLabel?.text =  "A Cell"
    return cell
```

The completed method should look like this:

```
    func tableView(_ tableView: UITableView, cellForRowAt
    indexPath:
        IndexPath) -> UITableViewCell {
        let cell = tableView.dequeueReusableCell(withIdentifier:
                   "locationCell", for: indexPath) as
    UITableViewCell
        cell.textLabel?.text = "A Cell"
        return cell
    }
```

Here's how this method works:

- `let cell = tableView.dequeueReusableCell(withIdentifier: "locationCell", for: indexPath) as UITableViewCell`: This creates a new table view cell or reuses an existing table view cell with the `locationCell` identifier and assigns it to `cell`. You set this identifier in the **Location View Controller Scene** in `Main.storyboard` in `Chapter 12`, *Modifying and Configuring Cells*.

- `cell.textLabel?.text = "A Cell"`: This assigns a string, `A Cell` to the `text` property of the table view cell's `textLabel`.

- `return cell`: This returns the cell, which is then displayed on the screen. This process is repeated for the number of cells that are given in the first method, which, in this case, is 10.

11. Build and run your project. Click the **LOCATION** button in the **Explore** screen to see the table view display 10 rows, with each row containing **A Cell**. This can be seen in the following screenshot:

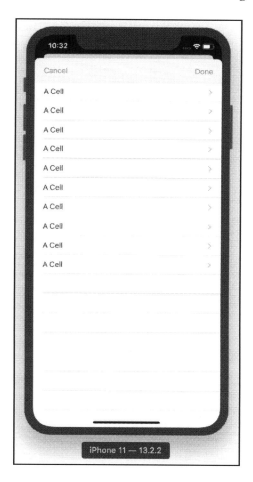

Great! Now that your table view's view controller has been set up, let's create some model objects so that we can provide data for it.

Adding location data for the table view

At this point, you have created and configured `LocationViewController`, which acts as the view controller for this table view. Now, you'll need to create model objects to make the table view display a list of actual locations. Just like you did in the previous chapter, you'll use a `.plist` file that contains location data, but instead of using an existing `.plist` file, you'll create one from scratch and add location data to it.

Before you create the `.plist` file, you'll create an array containing a list of cities and configure `LocationViewController` to display them in the table view to make sure `LocationViewController` is working properly. Follow these steps to do so:

1. Directly under the `tableView` property declaration, add the following:

```
let locations = ["Aspen", "Boston", "Charleston", "Chicago",
                 "Houston", "Las Vegas", "Los Angeles",
                 "Miami", "New Orleans", "New York",
                 "Philadelphia", "Portland", "San Antonio",
                 "San Francisco",
                 "Washington District of Columbia"]
```

   This creates `locations`, an array of strings that contains all the locations.

2. Modify `tableView(_:numberOfRowsInSection:)`, as shown in the following code snippet:

```
func tableView(_ tableView: UITableView, numberOfRowsInSection
  section: Int) -> Int {
    return locations.count
}
```

   This will display the same number of rows as there are strings in the `locations` array.

3. Modify `tableView(_:cellForRowAt:)`, as shown in the following code snippet:

```
func tableView(_ tableView: UITableView, cellForRowAt
indexPath:
  IndexPath) -> UITableViewCell {
    let cell = tableView.dequeueReusableCell(withIdentifier:
             "locationCell", for: indexPath) as
UITableViewCell
    cell.textLabel?.text = locations[indexPath.row]
```

```
        return cell
    }
```

This will assign a location corresponding to the row position in the table view. `LocationViewController` should now look as follows:

```
class LocationViewController: UIViewController,
UITableViewDataSource {
    @IBOutlet weak var tableView: UITableView!
    let locations = ["Aspen", "Boston", "Charleston",
"Chicago",
                     "Houston", "Las Vegas", "Los Angeles",
                     "Miami", "New Orleans", "New York",
                     "Philadelphia", "Portland", "San
Antonio",
                     "San Francisco",
                     "Washington District of Columbia"]

    override func viewDidLoad() {
        super.viewDidLoad()
    }

    func tableView(_ tableView: UITableView,
numberOfRowsInSection
        section: Int) -> Int {
            return locations.count
        }

    func tableView(_ tableView: UITableView, cellForRowAt
        indexPath: IndexPath) -> UITableViewCell {
        let cell = tableView.dequeueReusableCell(withIdentifier:
                "locationCell", for: indexPath) as
UITableViewCell
        cell.textLabel?.text = locations[indexPath.row]
            return cell
        }
    }
```

Build and run your project. Click the **LOCATION** button in the **Explore** screen to see the table view display all the locations stored in the `locations` array. This can be seen in the following screenshot:

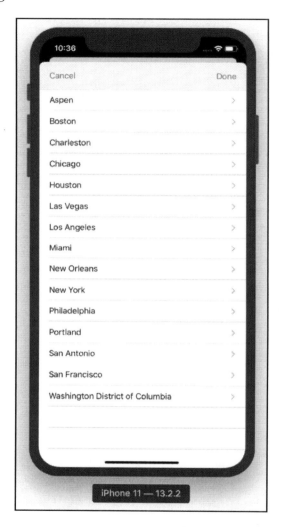

Awesome! However, hard coding a list of locations in this way is not recommended. It is better to use a `.plist` file, which will allow you to easily adapt your app so that it can obtain data from an online source if required. Instead of using an existing `.plist` file, like you did in the previous chapter, you will create a `.plist` file from scratch. We'll learn how to do this in the next section.

Creating a property list (.plist) file

In the previous chapter, you used `ExploreData.plist` to provide data for the list of cuisines in the **Explore** screen. You will do the same for the **Locations** screen, but create the .plist file from scratch instead. Follow these steps to do so:

1. Right-click the `Model` folder in the `Location` folder and choose **New File**.
2. **iOS** should already be selected. Type `proper` into the filter field; **Property List** will appear. Choose **Property List** and click **Next**.
3. Name the file `Locations`, and click **Create**.

The `Locations.plist` file has been added to the project. In the next section, you will learn how to configure and add data to your `.plist` file.

Adding data to the .plist file

As you saw in the previous chapter, `ExploreData.plist` stores data as an array of dictionaries. In this section, you will configure `Locations.plist` so that it stores data for the **Locations** screen in the same format and then add all the restaurant locations to it. Follow these steps to do so:

1. Click on **Dictionary** in the `.plist` file and change it to **Array**. Note that the disclosure triangle on the left should be pointing down. Click the + button:

2. A new item, **Item 0**, will be added to the array. Change the type to **Dictionary**. Click the disclosure triangle to make it point down. Click the + button, as shown in the following screenshot:

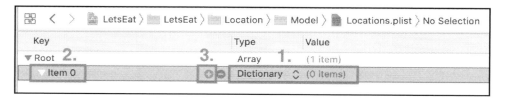

3. A new item, **New Item**, will be added to the **Item 0** dictionary. Click the **+** button, as shown in the following screenshot:

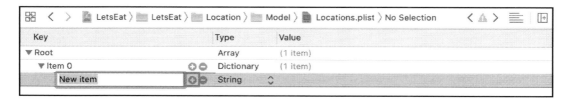

4. A second item will be added to the **Item 0** dictionary. For the first item, change the key to `city` and the value to `Aspen`. For the second item, change the key to `state` and the value to `CO`:

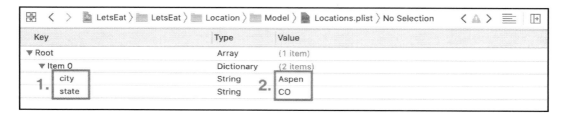

5. Click the disclosure triangle next to the **Item 0** dictionary to collapse it:

6. Select **Item 0** and press *command* + *C* on the keyboard to copy it and *command* + *V* to paste. You will see a new item, **Item 1**:

7. Click the disclosure triangle next to the **Item 1** dictionary to expand it. Update the city to `Boston` and the state to `MA`:

8. Continue with the same process by adding the following cities and states:

Item	City	State
Item 2	Charleston	NC
Item 3	Chicago	IL
Item 4	Houston	TX
Item 5	Las Vegas	NV
Item 6	Los Angeles	CA
Item 7	Miami	FL
Item 8	New Orleans	LA
Item 9	New York	NY
Item 10	Philadelphia	PA
Item 11	Portland	OR
Item 12	San Antonio	TX
Item 13	San Francisco	CA

The completed `.plist` file should look like this:

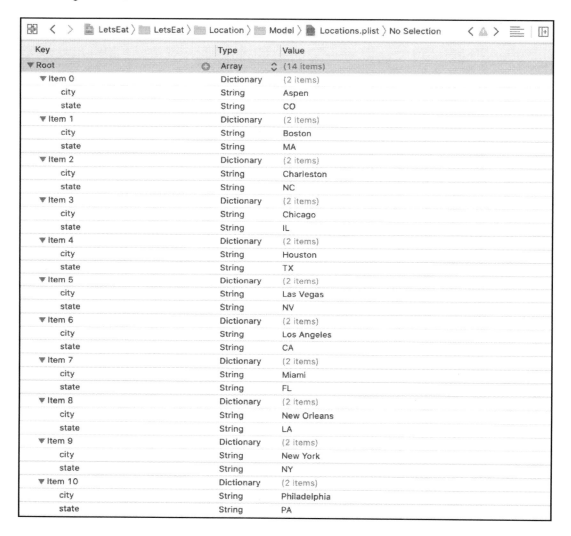

The `Locations.plist` file is complete. Now, you will create a data manager class, similar to the one you made in the previous chapter, which will read the `Locations.plist` file and provide it to `LocationViewController`.

Creating LocationDataManager

Like you did in the previous chapter, you will create a data manager class to load the location data from `Locations.plist` and provide it to `LocationsViewController`. To create the data manager class, follow these steps:

1. Right-click the `Model` folder in the `Location` folder and select **New File**.
2. **iOS** should already be selected. Choose **Swift File** and click **Next**.
3. Name this file `LocationDataManager` and click **Create**.
4. After the import statement, type in the following to declare the `LocationDataManager` class:

   ```
   class LocationDataManager {
   }
   ```

5. Inside the curly braces, add the following property to hold the list of locations:

   ```
   private var locations:[String] = []
   ```

   The `private` keyword means that the `locations` property may only be accessed by methods in this class.

6. Now, add the following methods after the property declaration:

   ```
   func fetch() {
       for location in loadData() {
           if let city = location["city"] as? String,
             let state = location["state"] as? String {
               locations.append("\(city), \(state)")
           }
       }
   }

   func numberOfItems() -> Int {
       return locations.count
   }

   func locationItem(at index:IndexPath) -> String {
       return locations[index.item]
   }

   private func loadData() -> [[String: AnyObject]] {
       guard let path = Bundle.main.path(forResource:
   "Locations",
   ```

```
                            ofType: "plist"),
        let items = NSArray(contentsOfFile: path) else {
            return [[:]]
        }
        return items as! [[String : AnyObject]]
    }
```

These methods are similar to those in ExploreDataManager, but, instead of an array of ExploreData instances, LocationDataManager has an array of strings.

Now that LocationDataManager is complete, let's configure LocationViewController so that it can get data from LocationDataManager and provide it to the table view. You will learn how to do this in the next section.

Displaying data in a table view using LocationDataManager

Currently, LocationViewController gets a list of locations from the locations array. In this section, you will update LocationViewController so that it uses LocationDataManager instead. Follow these steps to do so:

1. You won't need the locations array anymore, so delete the following code:

   ```
   let locations = ["Aspen", "Boston", "Charleston", "Chicago",
                    "Houston", "Las Vegas", "Los Angeles",
                    "Miami", "New Orleans", "New York",
                    "Philadelphia", "Portland", "San Antonio",
                    "San Francisco",
                    "Washington District of Columbia"]
   ```

2. Next, create an instance of LocationDataManager by typing the following property declaration before the viewDidLoad() method:

   ```
   let manager = LocationDataManager()
   ```

3. Inside viewDidLoad(), fetch the data for the table view by adding the following under super.viewDidLoad():

   ```
   manager.fetch()
   ```

viewDidLoad() **should look as follows:**

```
override func viewDidLoad() {
    super.viewDidLoad()
    manager.fetch()
}
```

4. Modify tableView(_:numberOfRowsInSection:) like so:

```
func tableView(_ tableView: UITableView, numberOfRowsInSection
  section: Int) -> Int{
    manager.numberOfItems()
}
```

5. Modify tableView(_:cellForRowAt:) like so:

```
func tableView(_ tableView: UITableView, cellForRowAt
indexPath:
  IndexPath) -> UITableViewCell {
    let cell = tableView.dequeueReusableCell(withIdentifier:
              "locationCell", for: indexPath) as
UITableViewCell
    cell.textLabel?.text = manager.locationItem(at:indexPath)
    return cell
}
```

Build and run your app. You should still see the locations in table view, but now they should be coming from ExploreData.plist. Great!

If you compare your app's **Explore** and **Locations** screens to the screens shown in the app tour, you'll notice some user interface issues. The text in the **Locations** screens is too small, and the labels at the top of the **Explore** screen just say **Label**. You need to make the table view text larger so that it will be easier to read, and modify the labels at the top of the **Explore** screen so that the subtitle displays **PLEASE SELECT A LOCATION** and the title displays **EXPLORE**, as shown in the app tour. You'll do this in the next section.

Cleaning up the user interface

Currently, your app's **Explore** and **Locations** screens have minor issues and don't match the screens shown in the app tour. The table view text in the **Locations** screen is too small, and the labels at the top of the **Explore** screen just say **Label**.

In this section, you will make the table view text larger so that it will be easier to read and modify the labels at the top of the **Explore** screen so that the subtitle displays **PLEASE SELECT A LOCATION** and the title displays **EXPLORE**. Follow these steps to do so:

1. Click `Main.storyboard`. Click the **Title** of `locationCell` in the document outline. In the Attributes inspector, change the **Font** size to `20`:

2. Click on the large black **Label** in the **Explore View Controller Scene** and change the text to `EXPLORE`:

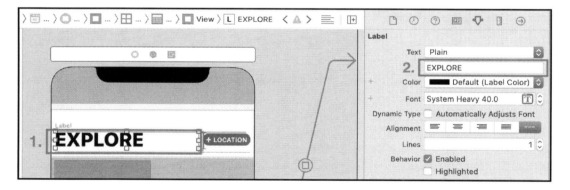

3. Click on the smaller grey **Label** in the **Explore View Controller Scene** and change the text to `PLEASE SELECT A LOCATION`:

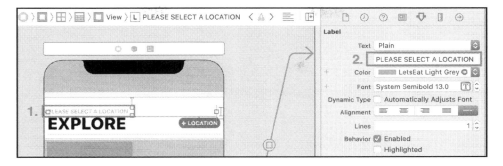

Build and run your app. The **Explore** screen should now look like the one in the app tour. Click the **LOCATION** button:

The **Locations** screen now displays a list of locations, and the text size also matches the screen shown during the app tour:

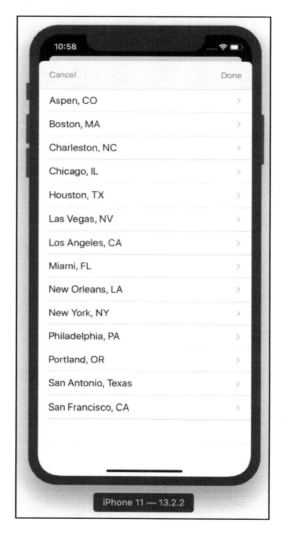

You've completed the implementation of the **Explore** and **Locations** screens. Good job!

Summary

In this chapter, you learned about table views and table view controllers, and you implemented a view controller for a table view in a playground.

Next, you implemented `LocationsViewController`, a table view controller for the **Locations** screen, and created a `.plist` file from scratch called `Locations.plist` to hold a list of locations. You created a data manager, `LocationsDataManager`, to read data from the `.plist` file. Finally, you configured `LocationsViewController` in order to get data from `LocationsDataManager` and provide it to the table view so that the **Locations** screen displays a list of restaurant locations. Awesome!

Now that you've completed this chapter, you know how to create a table view controller and link it to a table view, as well as how to create a `.plist` file and use the table view to display its data. You should now be able to implement table views for your own apps.

In the next chapter, you will add a map view to the **Map** screen and configure it to display restaurant locations. You'll also set up custom annotations for the **Map** screen and set up the **Restaurant Detail** screen, which will be displayed when a button in the annotation callout is tapped.

Getting Started with MapKit 16

In the last chapter, you learned about table views and table view controllers, and completed the implementation of the **Locations** screen so it now displays a list of restaurant locations.

In this chapter, you'll display restaurant locations on the **Map** screen using custom pins. When users tap on a pin, they'll see a screen that shows details of a particular restaurant.

To do this, you'll create a new class, `RestaurantItem`, that conforms to the `MKAnnotation` protocol. Next, you'll create `MapDataManager`, a data manager that loads restaurant data from a `.plist` file and puts it into an array of `RestaurantItem` instances. You'll make changes to both `MapDataManager` and `ExploreDataManager` to avoid redundant code (refactoring).

After that, you'll create `MapViewController`, a view controller for the **Map** screen, and configure it to display custom annotations.

Next, you'll configure callout buttons in the custom annotations to display the **Restaurant Detail** screen. You'll create `RestaurantDetailViewController`, a view controller for the **Restaurant Detail** screen, and pass data to it from `MapViewController`.

Finally, you'll clean up and organize your code to make it easier to read and maintain.

By the end of this chapter, you'll have learned how to create custom map annotations and add them to a map, how to use **storyboard references** to link storyboards together, and how to use extensions to organize your code, making it easier to read.

The following topics will be covered:

- Understanding and creating annotations
- Adding annotations to a map view
- Going from the map view to the **Restaurant Detail** screen
- Organizing your code

Technical requirements

You will continue working on the `LetsEat` project that you modified in the previous chapter.

The resource files and completed Xcode project for this chapter are in the `Chapter16` folder of the code bundle for this book, which can be downloaded here:

`https://github.com/PacktPublishing/iOS-13-Programming-for-Beginners`.

Now, let's learn about map annotations, which are used to mark restaurant locations on the **Map** screen.

Check out the following video to see the code in action:

`http://bit.ly/2NSXfQL`

Understanding and creating annotations

In `Chapter 11`, *Finishing Up Your App Structure in Storyboard*, you added a map view to the **Map** screen. A map view is an instance of the `MKMapView` class and is similar to the one in the Apple *Maps* app.

> To learn more about `MKMapView`, see `https://developer.apple.com/documentation/mapkit/mkmapview`.

When you build and run your app, you will see a map on the screen. The part of the map that is visible onscreen can be specified by setting the `region` property of the map.

To learn more about regions and how to make them, see `https://developer.apple.com/documentation/mapkit/mkmapview/1452709-region`.

Pins on the **Map** screen are used to mark specific locations. To add a pin to a map view, you need an object that conforms to the `MKAnnotation` protocol.

To learn more about `MKAnnotation`, see `https://developer.apple.com/documentation/mapkit/mkannotation`.

When an object conforming to the `MKAnnotation` protocol is added to a map view, an associated object named `MKAnnotationView` becomes a subview of the map view and is displayed on the screen. An `MKAnnotationView` can be customized to display custom icons, which can display callout bubbles when tapped. Callout bubbles can have buttons that perform actions, such as displaying a screen.

To learn more about `MKAnnotationView`, see `https://developer.apple.com/documentation/mapkit/mkannotationview`.

Let's learn more about what `MKAnnotation` is and how it works in the next section.

Introducing MKAnnotation

`MKAnnotation` is an interface for associating your content with a specific map location. Any object can conform to `MKAnnotation`. To conform to `MKAnnotation`, an object must implement a `coordinate` property, which contains a map location. Optional `MKAnnotation` properties are `title`, a string containing the annotation's title; and `subtitle`, a string containing the annotation's subtitle.

When an object conforming to `MKAnnotation` has its `coordinate` in the area of the map that is visible onscreen, the map view asks its delegate (usually a view controller) to provide a corresponding object of the `MKAnnotationView` type. If the user scrolls the map and `MKAnnotationView` goes off screen, it will be put into a reuse queue and recycled later, similar to the way table view cells and collection view cells are recycled.

For your app, you will create a new class, `RestaurantItem`, that conforms to `MKAnnotation`. This class will implement a `coordinate` property to store the restaurant's location. You will use `title` to store the restaurant name, and `subtitle` to store the cuisines it offers. Let's see how to create `RestaurantItem` in the next section.

Creating the RestaurantItem class

To represent restaurant locations on the **Map** screen, you will create a class, `RestaurantItem`, that conforms to `MKAnnotation`. When `RestaurantItem` objects are added to a map view, the delegate object (usually a view controller) of the map view will automatically provide `MKAnnotationView`, which appears as a pin, on the map view.

You need the location of the restaurant so that you can set the coordinate property of the `RestaurantItem` instance. The restaurant location data will be provided as a `.plist` file. Before you create the `RestaurantItem` class, you need to import the `.plist` file containing the restaurant details into your app. Do the following steps:

1. Open the `LetsEat` project. In the Project navigator, right-click the `LetsEat` folder and create a new group called `Map`.
2. Right-click the `Map` folder and create a new group called `Model`.
3. If you have not yet done so, download the completed project and project resources from `https://github.com/PacktPublishing/iOS-13-Programming-for-Beginners` and find the `Maplocations.plist` file inside the `resources` folder in the `Chapter16` folder.
4. Drag the `Maplocations.plist` file to the `Model` folder in your project, and click it to view its contents. You'll see that it is an array of dictionaries, with each dictionary representing a restaurant's details (including its location). You'll need to create properties for the data that you will use, which will be assigned to `RestaurantItem` and eventually be displayed on the **Restaurant Detail** screen:

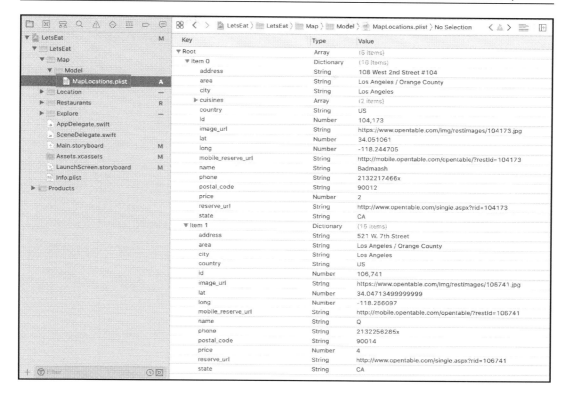

Next, you'll create the `RestaurantItem` class. Perform the following steps:

1. Right-click the `Model` folder and select **New File**.
2. **iOS** should already be selected. Choose **Cocoa Touch Class** and then click **Next**.
3. Configure the file as follows:

   - **Class**: `RestaurantItem`
   - **Subclass**: `NSObject`
   - **Also create XIB**: Greyed out
   - **Language**: `Swift`
   - Click **Next**

4. Click **Create**. `RestaurantItem.swift` appears in the Project navigator.

5. In `RestaurantItem.swift`, **under** `import UIKit`, **add** `import MapKit`. This tells Xcode you will be using the `MapKit` framework and gives you access to protocols such as `MKAnnotation` and `MKMapViewDelegate`.

6. Modify the class declaration as follows:

```
import UIKit
import MapKit

class RestaurantItem: NSObject, MKAnnotation {

}
```

This means `RestaurantItem` conforms to `MKAnnotation`. You'll see an error. This is because you have not yet implemented the `coordinate` property, which is a required property to conform to `MKAnnotation`. You will do so shortly.

7. Type the following inside the curly braces:

```
var name: String?
var cuisines:[String] = []
var lat: Double?
var long: Double?
var address: String?
var postalCode: String?
var state: String?
var imageURL: String?
```

These are the properties that will hold the data you get from `Maplocations.plist`. Note that you haven't created properties to store every detail of a restaurant stored in `Maplocations.plist`, and that's fine. You only need to create properties for the details relevant to the app.

8. You'll use a custom initializer to get the data from the `.plist` file into instances of `RestaurantItem`. Type the following after the last property declaration:

```
init(dict:[String:AnyObject]){
    if let lat = dict["lat"] as? Double { self.lat = lat }
    if let long = dict["long"] as? Double { self.long = long }
    if let name = dict["name"] as? String { self.name = name }
    if let cuisines = dict["cuisines"] as? [String]
                    { self.cuisines = cuisines }
    if let address = dict["address"] as? String
```

```
                          { self.address = address }
        if let postalCode = dict["postalCode"] as? String
                            { self.postalCode = postalCode }
        if let state = dict["state"] as? String
                      { self.state = state }
        if let image = dict["image_url"] as? String
                      { self.imageURL = image }
    }
```

Even though this initializer looks complicated, it's actually quite straightforward. Each line looks for a specific dictionary item key and assigns its value to the corresponding property. For example, the first line looks for the dictionary item with a key containing lat and assigns the associated value to the lat property. Note the lat and long properties, which will be used to create the value for the coordinate property.

9. Type the following after the init(dict:) method to implement the coordinate property:

```
var coordinate: CLLocationCoordinate2D {
    guard let lat = lat, let long = long else
                    { return CLLocationCoordinate2D() }
    return CLLocationCoordinate2D(latitude: lat, longitude: long)
}
```

The coordinate property is a required property for the MKAnnotation protocol. It is of the CLLocationCoordinate2D type, and it holds a geographical location.

Note that the coordinate property's value is not assigned directly, but is derived from the lat and long properties. The guard statement gets the latitude and longitude values from the lat and long properties, which are then used to create the value for the coordinate property. Such properties are called **computed properties**.

10. Add the following above the coordinate property to implement the subtitle property:

```
var subtitle: String? {
    if cuisines.isEmpty { return "" }
    else if cuisines.count == 1 { return cuisines.first }
    else { return cuisines.joined(separator: ", ") }
}
```

subtitle is also a computed property. The first line checks to see whether the cuisines property is empty, and if so, returns an empty string. If the cuisines property contains a single item, that item will be returned. If the cuisines property has more than a single item, each item is added to a string, with a comma in between items. For example, if cuisines contained the ["American", "Bistro", "Burgers"] array, the generated string would be American, Bistro, Burgers.

11. Finally, implement the title property by adding the following above the subtitle property:

```
var title: String? {
    return name
}
```

This just returns the contents of the name property.

Your RestaurantItem class is now complete and free of errors and should look as follows:

```
import UIKit
import MapKit

class RestaurantItem: NSObject, MKAnnotation {
    var name: String?
    var cuisines:[String] = []
    var lat: Double?
    var long: Double?
    var address: String?
    var postalCode: String?
    var state: String?
    var imageURL: String?

    init(dict:[String:AnyObject]){
        if let lat = dict["lat"] as? Double { self.lat = lat }
        if let long = dict["long"] as? Double { self.long = long }
        if let name = dict["name"] as? String { self.name = name }
        if let cuisines = dict["cuisines"] as? [String]
                        { self.cuisines = cuisines }
        if let address = dict["address"] as? String
                        { self.address = address }
        if let postalCode = dict["postalCode"] as? String
                            { self.postalCode = postalCode }
        if let state = dict["state"] as? String { self.state = state }
        if let image = dict["image_url"] as? String { self.imageURL =
image }
```

```
    }

        var title: String? {
            return name
        }

        var subtitle: String? {
            if cuisines.isEmpty { return "" }
            else if cuisines.count == 1 { return cuisines.first }
            else { return cuisines.joined(separator: ", ") }
        }

        var coordinate: CLLocationCoordinate2D {
            guard let lat = lat, let long = long else {
            return CLLocationCoordinate2D() }
            return CLLocationCoordinate2D(latitude: lat, longitude: long)
        }
    }
```

You have added `Maplocations.plist` to your app, and you have created the `RestaurantItem` class. Next, let's create a data manager class that reads restaurant data from `Maplocations.plist` and puts it into `RestaurantItem` instances, so they can be used by your app.

Creating MapDataManager

As you have done in previous chapters, you'll create a data manager class, `MapDataManager`, that will load restaurant data from `Maplocations.plist` and put the data into `RestaurantItem` instances. Perform the following steps:

1. Right-click on the `Model` folder inside the `Map` folder and select **New File**.
2. **iOS** should already be selected. Choose **Swift File** and then click **Next**.
3. Name this file `MapDataManager`. Click **Create**.
4. Add the following under the `import` statement to declare the `MapDataManager` class:

   ```
   class MapDataManager {

   }
   ```

5. Add the following properties between the curly braces:

```
fileprivate var items:[RestaurantItem] = []

var annotations:[RestaurantItem] {
    return items
}
```

The `items` array will contain `RestaurantItem` instances. `fileprivate` makes the `items` array only accessible inside the `MapDataManager` class, and `annotations` is a computed property that returns a copy of `items` when accessed.

6. Add the following methods after the property declarations:

```
func fetch(completion:(_ annotations:[RestaurantItem]) -> ()){
    if items.count > 0 { items.removeAll() }
    for data in loadData() {
        items.append(RestaurantItem(dict: data))
    }
    completion(items)
}

fileprivate func loadData() -> [[String:AnyObject]] {
    guard let path = Bundle.main.path(forResource:
                    "MapLocations", ofType: "plist"),
    let items = NSArray(contentsOfFile: path) else {
        return [[:]]
    }
    return items as! [[String:AnyObject]]
}
```

The `fetch()` and `loadData()` methods work the same way as those in `ExploreDataManager`. However, the `fetch()` method here has a completion closure as a parameter, which looks like this:

```
completion:(_ annotations:[RestaurantItem]) -> ()
```

Sometimes, you don't know when an operation will be finished. For example, you need to do an action after you've downloaded a file from the internet, but you don't know how long it would take to download. The completion closure here, in effect, is saying when all of the data from the `.plist` file has been processed, return the `annotations` array. The `annotations` array will later be used when adding `RestaurantItem` instances to the **Map** screen.

Now consider the `MapLocations.plist` file once more:

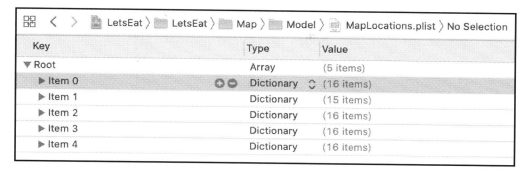

This file has the same structure as `ExploreData.plist`. The `Root` item is an array and contains dictionary items. Since both `ExploreData.plist` and `MapLocations.plist` have an array of dictionary objects, it would be more efficient if you could create a single method that will load `.plist` files and use it wherever it was needed. You will do this in the next section.

Creating the DataManager protocol

Instead of creating a method in each class to load a `.plist` file, you will create a new protocol, `DataManager`, to handle `.plist` file loading. This protocol will implement the necessary code to handle `.plist` file loading in an extension.

 You may wish to re-read Chapter 8, *Protocols, Extensions, and Error Handling,* which covers protocols and extensions.

Perform the following steps:

1. Right-click the `LetsEat` folder and create a new group called `Misc`.
2. Right-click on the `Misc` folder and choose **New File**.
3. **iOS** should already be selected. Choose **Swift File** and then click **Next**.
4. Name this file `DataManager`. Click **Create**.
5. Declare a new `protocol`, `DataManager`, inside this file, as follows:

```
protocol DataManager {

}
```

6. Add the following method requirement between the curly braces:

```
func load(file name:String) -> [[String:AnyObject]]
```

This requires any conforming object to have a method named `load` that takes a string as a parameter and returns an array of dictionaries. The string will hold the name of the `.plist` file to be loaded.

7. Add an extension below the protocol declaration:

```
extension DataManager {

}
```

8. Add the following method between the curly braces (what it does will be explained later):

```
func load(file name:String) -> [[String:AnyObject]] {
    guard let path = Bundle.main.path(forResource:
        name, ofType: "plist"),
        let items = NSArray(contentsOfFile: path)

else {
        return [[:]]
    }
    return items as! [[String:AnyObject]]
}
```

9. The completed file should look like this:

```
import Foundation

protocol DataManager {
    func load(file name:String) -> [[String:AnyObject]]
}

extension DataManager {
    func load(file name:String) -> [[String:AnyObject]] {
        guard let path = Bundle.main.path(forResource: name,
            ofType: "plist"), let items = NSArray
                                        (contentsOfFile: path)
            else {
               return [[:]]
           }
           return items as! [[String:AnyObject]]
    }
}
```

Any object that adopts this protocol will also gain the `load(file:)` method. This method looks for a `.plist` file specified in the `file` parameter inside the application bundle. If successful, the contents of the `.plist` file are loaded into an array of dictionaries and returned. If the file is not found, an empty array of dictionaries is returned.

Now that you have this protocol, you will modify `MapDataManager` and `ExploreDataManager` to adopt it. When you take existing code and modify it to accomplish the same thing more efficiently, this process is called **refactoring**.

You will start with refactoring `MapDataManager` to conform to the `DataManager` protocol in the next section.

Refactoring MapDataManager

`MapDataManager` already has a `loadData()` method, which is hardcoded to read `Maplocations.plist`. Now that you have created the `DataManager` protocol, you will modify `MapDataManager` to use it instead. Perform the following steps:

1. With `MapDataManager` selected in the Project navigator, find and delete the `loadData()` method. You'll see an error because the `fetch()` method calls the `loadData()` function, which you just removed. You'll fix this shortly.

2. Add the `DataManager` protocol to the class declaration as follows:

   ```
   class MapDataManager: DataManager
   ```

   This makes the `load(file:)` method available to `MapDataManager`.

3. Modify the `for data in loadData()` line in the `fetch()` method as follows to fix the error:

   ```
   for data in load(file: "MapLocations")
   ```

   Your updated `MapDataManager` class should look like the following:

   ```
   import Foundation

   class MapDataManager: DataManager {

       fileprivate var items:[RestaurantItem] = []

       var annotations:[RestaurantItem] {
   ```

```
            return items
        }

        func fetch(completion:(_ annotations:[RestaurantItem]) ->
()){
            if items.count > 0 { items.removeAll() }
            for data in load(file: "MapLocations") {
                items.append(RestaurantItem(dict: data))
            }
            completion(items)
        }
}
```

The error should be gone. Now, you will refactor ExploreDataManager as well to make it adopt the DataManager protocol in the next section.

Refactoring ExploreDataManager

Like MapDataManager, ExploreDataManager has a loadData() method, which is hardcoded to read ExploreData.plist.

 You may wish to re-read Chapter 14, *Getting Data into Collections Views*, to refresh your memory on ExploreDataManager.

You need to make the same changes to ExploreDataManager that you made to MapDataManager. Click ExploreDataManager and do the following:

1. Delete the private loadData() function because you won't need it anymore. Ignore the error because it will be fixed shortly.
2. Add the DataManager protocol to the class declaration as follows:

   ```
   class ExploreDataManager: DataManager
   ```

   This makes the load(file:) method available to ExploreDataManager.

3. Modify the `for data in loadData()` line in the `fetch()` method as follows:

```
for data in load(file: "ExploreData")
```

This will load the data from `ExploreData.plist`

Your updated `ExploreDataManager` class should look like the following:

```
import Foundation
class ExploreDataManager: DataManager {

    fileprivate var items:[ExploreItem] = []

    func fetch() {
        for data in load(file: "ExploreData") {
            items.append(ExploreItem(dict: data))
        }
    }

    func numberOfItems() -> Int {
        return items.count
    }

    func explore(at index:IndexPath) -> ExploreItem {
        return items[index.item]
    }
}
```

You can now make any class that needs to load a `.plist` file containing an array of dictionaries adopt the `Data Manager` protocol, as you did here with `MapDataManager` and `ExploreDataManager`. It's not always clear when you should refactor, but the more experience you have, the easier it becomes. The most prominent indicator that you need to refactor is when you are writing the same code in more than one class.

You have completed the implementation of `MapDataManager`, which can load data from the `MapLocations.plist` file and return an array of `RestaurantItem` instances. Now, let's see how to use this array to add annotations to a map view, which will be displayed as pins when the user selects the **Map** screen.

Adding annotations to a map view

At this point, you have created the `RestaurantItem` class, which conforms to `MKAnnotation`, and `MapDataManager`, which loads data from `MapLocations.plist` and returns an array of `RestaurantItem` instances. Now, you need to create `MapViewController`, a view controller for the map view. `MapViewController` will add the array of `RestaurantItem` instances to the map view, and provide an `MKAnnotationView` object for any `RestaurantItem` object that is visible onscreen. After that, you will customize the `MKAnnotationView` instances so they look like the ones in the app tour.

In the next section, you'll start by implementing `MapViewController`, which is the view controller for the map view and is responsible for providing an `MKAnnotationView` instance for each `MKAnnotation` instance on the **Map** screen.

Creating MapViewController

In `Chapter 11`, *Finishing Up Your App Structure in Storyboard*, you added a map view to the **Map** screen. In the previous sections, you added `MapLocations.plist` to your project and created a new class, `RestaurantItem`, and a data manager class, `MapDataManager`. Remember the MVC design pattern? At this point, you have created the views and models for the **Map** screen, and now you will create the controller.

A view controller managing a map view can provide objects conforming to `MKAnnotation` for it. It is also usually the delegate for the map view and will provide `MKAnnotationView` objects for `MKAnnotation` objects visible onscreen. You will now implement a view controller for the map view named `MapViewController`. Perform the following steps:

1. Right-click the `Map` folder and select **New File**.
2. **iOS** should already be selected. Choose **Cocoa Touch Class** and then click **Next**.
3. Configure the file as follows:

   - **Class**: `MapViewController`
   - **Subclass**: `UIViewController`

- **Also create XIB**: Unchecked
- **Language**: Swift
- Click **Next**

4. Click **Create**. MapViewController.swift appears in the Project navigator.

5. In MapViewController.swift, under import UIKit, add import MapKit. This tells Xcode you will be using the MapKit framework.

6. Modify the class declaration as follows:

```
class MapViewController: UIViewController, MKMapViewDelegate {
```

This makes MapViewController conform to the MKMapViewDelegate protocol. Now that you have the MapViewController class, you need to assign it to the view controller in the view controller scene for the **Map** screen and create an outlet for the map view. You will do this in the next section.

Connecting the outlets for the map view to MapViewController

The view controller scene for the **Map** screen displays a map, but there is currently no way to set the map region to be displayed and no way to display annotations. Let's assign MapViewController to the view controller for the **Map** screen in Main.storyboard and add an outlet for the map view to it. Do the following steps:

1. Click Main.storyboard. Click the **View Controller** icon in the **View Controller Scene** for the **Map** screen. In the Identity inspector, under **Custom Class**, select MapViewController in the **Class** drop-down menu:

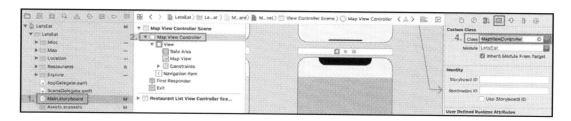

2. Select the **Map View** in the document outline:

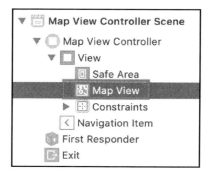

3. Click the Adjust Editor Options button:

4. Choose **Assistant** in the pop-up menu:

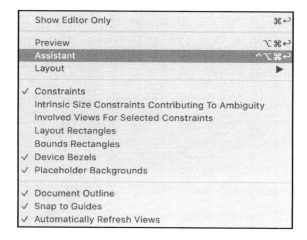

5. The assistant editor appears, showing the contents of `MapViewController`. *Ctrl* + Drag from the **Map View** to the space just under the class declaration:

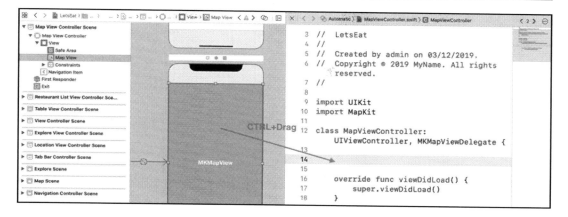

6. Type `mapView` in the **Name** field and click **Connect**:

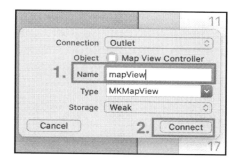

7. The **Map View** has been connected to the `mapView` outlet in `MapViewController`. Click the **x** button to close the assistant editor:

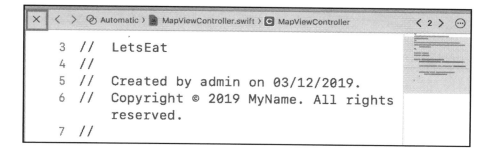

MapViewController now has an outlet, mapView, that is linked to the map view in the **Map** screen. Next, you'll modify MapDataManager so it can provide a map region for the map view to display, by adding a method to generate a new region based on the restaurant's location.

Setting the map view region to be displayed

In a map view, the portion of the map that is displayed on the screen is referred to as a **region**. To specify a region, you need to know the coordinates for the region's center point and the horizontal and vertical **span** representing the amount of map to display.

MapDataManager returns an array of RestaurantItem instances. You will implement a method, currentRegion, to get the first RestaurantItem instance from this array. From this RestaurantItem instance, you can get coordinates. You will then set the region's center point using these coordinates and specify a **span** for this region. Perform the following steps:

1. Click MapDataManager.swift in the Project navigator. Below the import Foundation statement, add import MapKit.

2. Just before the closing curly brace, implement currentRegion, as follows:

```
func currentRegion(latDelta:CLLocationDegrees,
longDelta:CLLocationDegrees) -> MKCoordinateRegion {
    guard let item = items.first else {
        return MKCoordinateRegion()
}
    let span = MKCoordinateSpan(latitudeDelta: latDelta,
             longitudeDelta: longDelta)
    return MKCoordinateRegion(center:item.coordinate,
span:span)
}
```

Let's see what this method does:

- func currentRegion(latDelta:CLLocationDegrees, longDelta:CLLocationDegrees) -> MKCoordinateRegion: The method takes two parameters and returns MKCoordinateRegion. latDelta specifies the north-to-south distance (measured in degrees) to display for the map region. One degree is approximately 69 miles. longDelta specifies the amount of east-to-west distance (measured in degrees) to display for the map region. MKCoordinateRegion determines the region that will appear onscreen.

- `guard let item = items.first else { return MKCoordinateRegion() }`: The `guard` statement gets the first item in the array of `RestaurantItem` instances and assigns it to `item`. If the array is empty, an empty `MKCoordinateRegion` is returned.
- `let span = MKCoordinateSpan(latitudeDelta: latDelta, longitudeDelta: longDelta)`: `latDelta` and `longDelta` are used to make `MKCoordinateSpan`, which is the horizontal and vertical span representing the amount of map to display.
- `return MKCoordinateRegion(center: item.coordinate, span: span)`: `MKCoordinateRegion` is created using the `coordinate` property of `item` and `MKCoordinateSpan` in `span`. `MKCoordinateRegion` is then returned.

Now that the map region has been determined, you can determine which restaurants are in a particular region based on the `RestaurantItem` instance's `coordinate` property. Remember that `RestaurantItem` conforms to `MKAnnotation`. As the view controller for the map view, `MapViewController` is responsible for providing `MKAnnotationView` instances for any `RestaurantItem` located within the region. Let's modify `MapViewController` to do so now by getting an array of `RestaurantItem` instances from `MapDataManager` and adding it to the map view. You will do this in the next section.

Displaying annotations on the map view

At this point, you have implemented `MapViewController` to manage the map view on the **Map** screen, and you can set the map region. You will now modify `MapViewController` to get an array of `RestaurantItem` instances from `MapDataManager` and add it to the map view. Remember that `RestaurantItem` conforms to the `MKAnnotation` protocol. When objects conforming to the `MKAnnotation` protocol are added to a map view, the view controller for the map view, `MapViewController`, is responsible for providing the necessary `MKAnnotationView` instances, which will appear as pins in the map view. Do the following steps:

1. Click `MapViewController.swift` in the Project navigator and remove the boilerplate code.

2. Just below the `mapView` property declaration, add the following:

```
let manager = MapDataManager()
```

This creates an instance of `MapDataManager` and assigns it to `manager`.

3. Add the following method after `viewDidLoad()`:

```
func addMap(_ annotations: [RestaurantItem]) {
    mapView.setRegion(manager.currentRegion(latDelta: 0.5,
        longDelta: 0.5), animated: true)
    mapView.addAnnotations(manager.annotations)
}
```

This method takes a parameter, `annotations`, which is an array of `RestaurantItem` instances. It then sets the region of the map to be displayed in the map view using the `currentRegion` method of `MapDataManager`, then adds each `RestaurantItem` in the `annotations` array to the map view. The map view's delegate (`MapViewController` in this case) then automatically provides a pin for every `RestaurantItem` whose coordinates are visible on the screen.

4. You need to have `MapDataManager` fetch the `annotations` array, so add the following method above the `addMap(_:)` method:

```
func initialize() {
    manager.fetch { (annotations) in
    addMap(annotations)
    }
}
```

This calls the `fetch()` method in `MapDataManager` that you implemented earlier, which loads `MapLocations.plist` and creates and assigns the array of `RestaurantItem` instances to `annotations`.

5. Add `initialize()` inside `viewDidLoad()` so it will be called when the map view is loaded:

```
override func viewDidLoad() {
    super.viewDidLoad()
    initialize()
}
```

Build and run the application. You should see the following on the **Map** screen:

You now have pins showing restaurant locations on your map, but you need to update your code to use custom pins that look like the ones in the app tour. You will do that in the next section.

Creating custom annotations

Currently, the **Map** screen can display standard annotations views. An annotation view can have a custom image. There is a custom image in the `Assets.xcassets` file that you will use to make the pins onscreen match the ones in the app tour. You will now configure `MapViewController` to use these custom images:

1. Click `MapViewController.swift` in the Project navigator.

2. Add the following code inside the `initialize()` method:

   ```
   mapView.delegate = self
   ```

   This makes `MapViewController` the delegate for the map view.

3. Add the following directly under the `addMap(_:)` method:

   ```
   func mapView(_ mapView: MKMapView, viewFor
   annotation:MKAnnotation) -> MKAnnotationView? {
       let identifier = "custompin"
       guard !annotation.isKind(of: MKUserLocation.self) else {
   return nil }
       var annotationView: MKAnnotationView?
       if let customAnnotationView =
   mapView.dequeueReusableAnnotationView(withIdentifier:
   identifier) {
           annotationView = customAnnotationView
           annotationView?.annotation = annotation
       } else {
           let av = MKAnnotationView(annotation: annotation,
   reuseIdentifier: identifier)
           av.rightCalloutAccessoryView =
   UIButton(type: .detailDisclosure)
           annotationView = av
       }
       if let annotationView = annotationView {
           annotationView.canShowCallout = true
           annotationView.image = UIImage(named: "custom-
   annotation")
       }
       return annotationView
   }
   ```

This method returns a custom `MKAnnotationView` for every `MKAnnotation` on the map view. Let's break this down:

- `func mapView(_ mapView: MKMapView, viewFor annotation:MKAnnotation) -> MKAnnotationView`: This is one of the delegate methods specified in the `MKMapViewDelegate` protocol. It's triggered when `MKAnnotation` is placed on a map, and it returns `MKAnnotationView`, which the user will see on the screen. You use this method to replace the default pins with custom pins.

- `let identifier = "custompin"`: A constant, `identifier`, is assigned the `"custompin"` string. This will be the reuse identifier.

- `guard !annotation.isKind(of: MKUserLocation.self) else { return nil }`: This `guard` statement checks to see whether the annotation is the user location. If it is, `nil` is returned, as the user location is not a restaurant location. Otherwise, it goes to the next statement.

- `var annotationView: MKAnnotationView?`: `annotationView` is an optional variable of the `MKAnnotationView` type. `MKAnnotationView` is the class for the pins that you see onscreen. You create this so that you can configure and return it later.

- `if let customAnnotationView = mapView.dequeueReusableAnnotationView (withIdentifier: identifier) { annotationView = customAnnotationView annotationView?.annotation = annotation }`

  The if statement checks to see whether there are any existing annotations that were initially visible but have been scrolled off the screen. If yes, the `MKAnnotationView` instance for that annotation can be reused and is assigned to the `annotationView` variable. The `annotation` parameter is assigned to the `annotation` property of `annotationView`.

- `else {`
  `let av = MKAnnotationView(annotation: annotation,`
  `reuseIdentifier: identifier)`
  `av.rightCalloutAccessoryView =`
  `UIButton(type: .detailDisclosure)`
  `annotationView = av`
  `}`

  The else clause is executed if there are no existing `MKAnnotationView` instances that can be reused. A new `MKAnnotationView` instance is created with the reuse identifier specified earlier (`custompin`). `MKAnnotationView` is configured with a callout. When you tap `MKAnnotationView`, a callout bubble will appear showing the title (restaurant name), subtitle (cuisines), and a button. You'll program the button later to take the user to the **Restaurant Detail** screen.

- `if let annotationView = annotationView {`
  `annotationView.canShowCallout = true`
  `annotationView.image = UIImage(named: "custom-annotation")`
  `}`

  This indicates that the `MKAnnotationView` instance that you just created can display extra information in a callout bubble and sets the custom image to the `custom-annotation` image stored in `Assets.xcassets`.

- `return annotationView`: The custom annotation is returned.

Build and run the project. You can see the custom annotations on your map:

Tapping a pin displays a callout bubble showing the restaurant name and the cuisines it offers. Tapping the button in the callout bubble does not take you to the **Restaurant Detail** screen yet. Let's set that up in the next section.

Going from the Map screen to the Restaurant Detail screen

The **Map** screen now displays your custom annotations, and tapping one displays a callout bubble showing restaurant details. The callout button doesn't work yet, though. To go to the **Restaurant Detail** screen from the callout button, you will add a storyboard reference to your project. For your convenience, inside the `resources` folder that you downloaded earlier, you'll find the completed storyboards named `RestaurantDetail.Storyboard`, `PhotoFilter.Storyboard`, and `ReviewForm.Storyboard`. You will link the storyboard reference you added to `RestaurantDetail.storyboard` instead of using the **Restaurant Detail** screen you made earlier.

Creating and configuring a storyboard reference

If you look at `Main.storyboard`, you'll see that there are a lot of scenes in it. As your project grows, you'll find it more challenging to keep track of all the scenes in your app. One way to manage this is to create additional storyboards, and use storyboard references to link them. You will link the map view controller scene inside `Main.storyboard` to a restaurant detail scene inside `RestaurantDetail.storyboard` using a storyboard reference. Do the following steps to add a storyboard reference to your project:

1. Open `Main.storyboard`, and click the **Object library** button.
2. Type `story` in the filter field. **Storyboard Reference** will appear in the results.
3. Drag the **Storyboard Reference** into `Main.storyboard` next to the **Map View Controller Scene**:

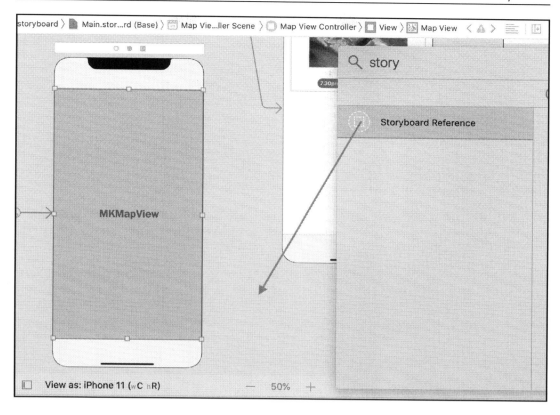

4. Open the `resources` folder that you downloaded earlier, and locate the three storyboard files in it (`RestaurantDetail.Storyboard`, `PhotoFilter.Storyboard`, and `ReviewForm.Storyboard`):

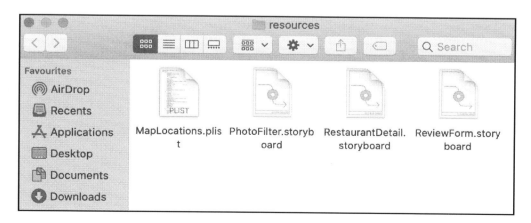

5. Create a new folder inside your `LetsEat` folder named `RestaurantDetail` and copy `RestaurantDetail.Storyboard` into it:

6. Create a new folder inside your `LetsEat` folder named `ReviewForm` and copy `ReviewForm.Storyboard` into it, and create a new folder inside your `LetsEat` folder named `PhotoFilter` and copy `PhotoFilter.Storyboard` into it:

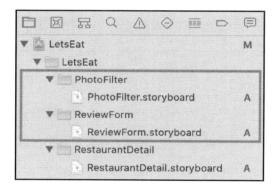

7. Click `Main.storyboard`, select the **Storyboard Reference** you added earlier, and click the Attributes inspector. Under **Storyboard Reference**, set **Storyboard** to `RestaurantDetail.Storyboard`:

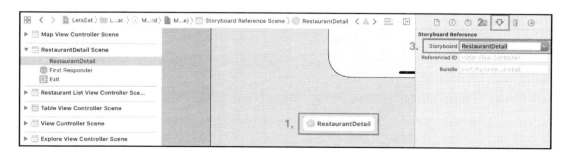

8. Hold *Ctrl + drag* from the **Map View Controller** icon to the **Storyboard Reference** and choose **Show** from the pop-up menu:

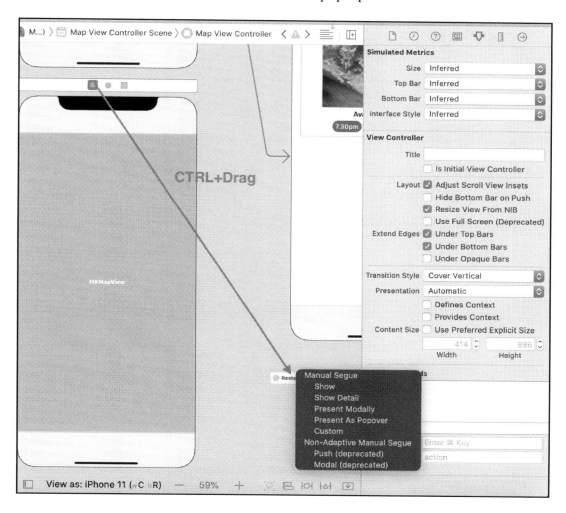

9. Select the segue connecting the **Map View Controller** to the **Storyboard Reference**:

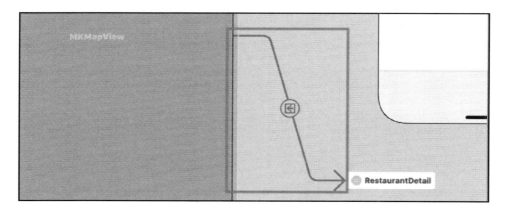

10. In the Attributes inspector, under **Storyboard Segue**, set **Identifier** to showDetail. In the next section, you will add a method that performs the segue with the showDetail identifier when the callout button is tapped, which displays the **Restaurant Detail** screen:

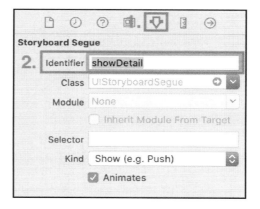

You have now linked the map view controller scene inside Main.storyboard to a restaurant detail scene inside RestaurantDetail.storyboard using a storyboard reference. Let's implement a method to display the **Restaurant Detail** screen when the callout button is tapped in the next section.

Performing the showDetail segue

You have linked the map view controller scene inside `Main.storyboard` to a restaurant detail scene inside `RestaurantDetail.storyboard` using a storyboard reference and you have set the segue identifier to `showDetail`. You now need to implement a method to perform that segue and assign it to the callout button. Before you do so, you'll use an enumeration (discussed in *Chapter 7, Classes, Structures, and Enumerations*) to hold all of the segue identifiers for this project. This reduces the chances of making a mistake by enabling autocompletion when you type the segue identifiers later in your code:

1. Right-click on the `Misc` folder inside the `LetsEat` folder and choose **New File**.
2. **iOS** should already be selected. Choose **Swift File** and then click **Next**.
3. Name this file `Segue`. Click **Create**.
4. Add the following under the `import` statement to declare the `Segue` enumeration:

```swift
enum Segue:String {
    case showDetail
    case showRating
    case showReview
    case showAllReviews
    case restaurantList
    case locationList
    case showPhotoReview
    case showPhotoFilter
}
```

Eventually, you will need all these segue identifiers, so you add them now. Note that `Segue` is of type `String`, so the raw values for each case are strings. For example, the raw value for `case showDetail` is `"showDetail"`.

Now you can add the method to perform the `showDetail` segue when the callout button is tapped.

5. Click `MapViewController.swift` in the Project navigator.
6. Add the following method under the `addMap(_:)` method:

```swift
func mapView(_ mapView: MKMapView, annotationView view:
    MKAnnotationView, calloutAccessoryControlTapped control:
    UIControl){
```

```
                 self.performSegue(withIdentifier:
        Segue.showDetail.rawValue,
             sender: self)
        }
```

`mapView(_:annotationView:calloutAccessoryControlTapped:)` is another method specified in the `MKMapViewDelegate` protocol. It is triggered when the user taps the callout button. `self.performSegue(withIdentifier: Segue.showDetail.rawValue, sender: self)` performs the segue with the `"showDetail"` identifier, which makes the **Restaurant Detail** screen appear.

Build and run your project. On the **Map** screen, tap an annotation:

Tap the callout button inside the annotation:

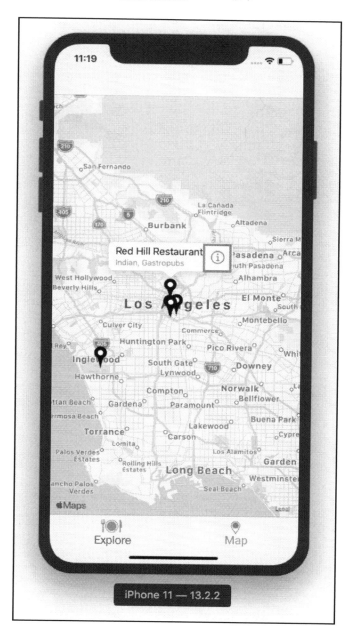

The new **Restaurant Detail** screen appears, but it does not contain any details about the restaurant:

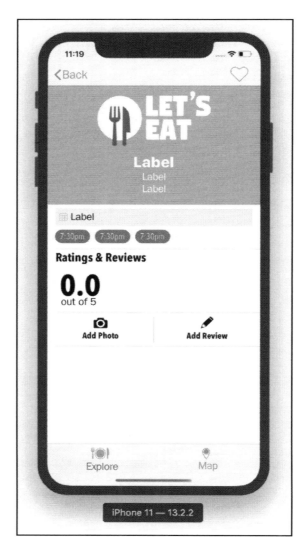

You will make the **Restaurant Detail** screen display the details of a restaurant in the next chapter, but for now, let's just pass the data about the selected restaurant to the **Restaurant Detail** screen's view controller and print it to the Debug area. You will do this in the next section.

Passing data to the Restaurant Detail screen

The **Map** screen now displays restaurant annotations. When you tap an annotation's callout button, the **Restaurant Detail** screen appears, but it does not contain any data about the restaurant. To pass restaurant data to the **Restaurant Detail** screen, you need to get the data from a `RestaurantItem` instance to the view controller in charge of the **Restaurant Detail** screen, which has not been created yet. Let's create it now:

1. Right-click the `RestaurantDetail` folder and select **New File**.
2. **iOS** should already be selected. Choose **Cocoa Touch Class** and then click **Next**.
3. Configure the file as follows:

    - **Class**: `RestaurantDetailViewController`
    - **Subclass**: `UITableViewController`
    - **Also create XIB**: Unchecked
    - **Language:** `Swift`
    - Click **Next**

4. Click **Create**. `RestaurantDetailViewController.swift` appears in the Project navigator.
5. Delete all of the code after the `viewDidLoad()` method. Your file should look as follows:

    ```
    import UIKit
    class RestaurantDetailViewController: UITableViewController {
        override func viewDidLoad() {
            super.viewDidLoad()
        }
    }
    ```

6. Add the following just before the `viewDidLoad()` method:

    ```
    var selectedRestaurant: RestaurantItem?
    ```

    This holds the `RestaurantItem` instance that will be passed to `RestaurantDetailViewController` from `MapViewController`.

7. Add the following code inside the `viewDidLoad()` method:

    ```
    dump(selectedRestaurant as Any)
    ```

This will print the `RestaurantItem` contents to the Debug area. This is just to show that `MapViewController` has successfully passed `RestaurantItem` to `RestaurantDetailViewController`.

8. Your file should now look like the following:

```
import UIKit
class RestaurantDetailViewController: UITableViewController {

    var selectedRestaurant: RestaurantItem?

    override func viewDidLoad() {
        super.viewDidLoad()
        dump(selectedRestaurant as Any)
    }
}
```

9. Click `RestaurantDetail.storyboard` inside the `RestaurantDetail` folder. Select the **Table View Controller Scene** in the Storyboard. Click the Identity inspector. Under **Custom Class**, set **Class** to `RestaurantDetailViewController`:

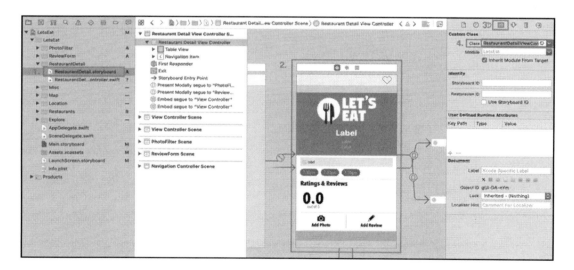

10. Click `MapViewController.swift` in the Project navigator.

11. Add the following code just after `let manager = MapDataManager()`:

```
var selectedRestaurant:RestaurantItem?
```

This adds a property to hold the `RestaurantItem` instance.

12. Add the following code into the `func mapView(_:annotationView:calloutAccessoryControlTapped:)` method, above `self.performSegue(withIdentifier:sender:)`:

```
guard let annotation = mapView.selectedAnnotations.first else
{ return }
selectedRestaurant = annotation as? RestaurantItem
```

This gets the `RestaurantItem` instance associated with `MKAnnotationView` that was tapped and assigns it to `selectedRestaurant`.

The `func mapView(_:annotationView:calloutAccessoryControlTapped:)` method should look as follows:

```
func mapView(_ mapView: MKMapView, annotationView view:
MKAnnotationView, calloutAccessoryControlTapped control:
UIControl){
    guard let annotation = mapView.selectedAnnotations.first
else { return }
    selectedRestaurant = annotation as? RestaurantItem
    self.performSegue(withIdentifier:
Segue.showDetail.rawValue, sender: self)
}
```

13. Add the following code after `viewDidLoad()`:

```
override func prepare(for segue: UIStoryboardSegue, sender:
Any?){
    switch segue.identifier! {
        case Segue.showDetail.rawValue:
            showRestaurantDetail(segue: segue)
        default:
            print("Segue not added")
    }
}
```

This method is called before the **Map** screen transitions to the **Restaurant Detail** screen. If the segue has the `showDetail` identifier (which it does in this case), the `showRestaurantDetail(segue:)` method is called. You'll see an error because `showRestaurantDetail(segue:)` has not been created yet.

14. Add the following code after the `addMap(_:)` method to implement `showRestaurantDetail(segue:)`:

```
func showRestaurantDetail(segue:UIStoryboardSegue){
    if let viewController = segue.destination as?
        RestaurantDetailViewController,
        let restaurant = selectedRestaurant {
            viewController.selectedRestaurant = restaurant
    }
}
```

This checks to make sure the segue destination is `RestaurantDetailViewController`, and if it is, it sets a temporary constant, `restaurant`, to the `selectedRestaurant` property in `MapViewController`. The `selectedRestaurant` property in `RestaurantDetailViewController` is then set to `restaurant`. In other words, the details of the restaurant that you get from the map view annotation are passed to `RestaurantDetailViewController`.

Build and run your project. In the **Map** screen, tap a pin and then tap the callout button. The **Restaurant Detail** screen will appear. Click the Report navigator and click the first line as shown. You should see the following:

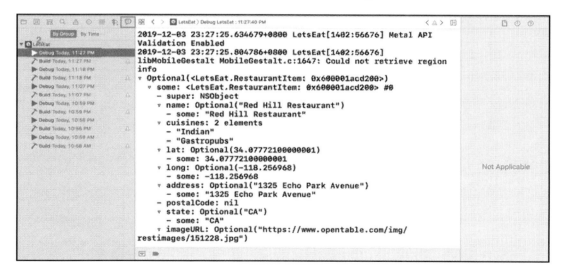

This shows that `RestaurantDetailViewController` now has the data from the `RestaurantItem` that was selected on the **Map** screen. Great!

As stated earlier, you will configure the **Restaurant Detail** screen to display that data in the next chapter.

You have done a lot of work in this chapter, so before you go on to the next chapter, let's organize the code that you have written to make it easier to understand. You will use extensions to do so.

Organizing your code

As your programs become more complex, you will use extensions (covered in `Chapter 8`, *Protocols, Extensions, and Error Handling*) to organize your code. Extensions can help you to make code more legible and avoid clutter. They also enable you to extend the functionality of a class.

You will update four classes: `ExploreViewController`, `RestaurantListViewController`, `LocationViewController`, and `MapViewController`. You will segregate blocks of related code using extensions. Let's begin with `ExploreViewController` in the next section.

Refactoring ExploreViewController

You will divide the code in `ExploreViewController` into distinct sections using the `// MARK:` syntax. Perform the following steps:

1. Click `ExploreViewController.swift` in the Project navigator. After the final curly brace, press *Return* a few times and add the following:

```
// MARK: Private Extension
private extension ExploreViewController {
    // code goes here
}
// MARK: UICollectionViewDataSource
extension ExploreViewController: UICollectionViewDataSource {
    // code goes here
}
```

Here, you are creating two extensions. The first one will be private, which means the contents of this extension are only accessible to `ExploreViewController`. You'll put all of the private methods for `ExploreViewController` here. The second one will contain all of the collection view data source methods.

2. You'll get an error because `UICollectionViewDataSource` appears in two places. Delete `UICollectionViewDataSource` from the class declaration at the top of the file. Your class declaration should look like this when done:

```
class ExploreViewController: UIViewController,
UICollectionViewDelegate {
```

3. Move all of the collection view data source methods into the second extension. It should look like this when done:

```
// MARK: UICollectionViewDataSource
extension ExploreViewController: UICollectionViewDataSource {

    func collectionView(_ collectionView: UICollectionView,
        viewForSupplementaryElementOfKind kind: String,
        at indexPath: IndexPath) -> UICollectionReusableView {
            let headerView =
collectionView.dequeueReusableSupplementaryView
            (ofKind: kind, withReuseIdentifier: "header", for:
indexPath)
        return headerView
    }

    func collectionView(_ collectionView: UICollectionView,
        numberOfItemsInSection section: Int) -> Int {
        return manager.numberOfItems()
    }

    func collectionView(_ collectionView: UICollectionView,
        cellForItemAt indexPath: IndexPath) ->
UICollectionViewCell {
            let cell =
collectionView.dequeueReusableCell(withReuseIdentifier:
                    "exploreCell", for: indexPath) as!
ExploreCell
let item = manager.explore(at: indexPath)
            cell.lblName.text = item.name
            cell.imgExplore.image = UIImage(named: item.image)
            return cell
    }
}
```

4. To keep `viewDidLoad()` as clean as possible, you will create an `initialize()` function inside the first extension, and put inside it everything you need to initialize the view controller there. After that, you will call this `initialize()` function inside `viewDidLoad()`. Add the following inside the first extension:

```
func initialize() {
    manager.fetch()
}
```

5. Move `@IBAction` inside the first extension as well:

```
@IBAction func unwindLocationCancel(segue:UIStoryboardSegue){
}
```

The first extension should look like this when done:

```
// MARK: Private Extension
private extension ExploreViewController {
    func initialize() {
        manager.fetch()
    }

    @IBAction func
unwindLocationCancel(segue:UIStoryboardSegue){
    }
}
```

6. Finally, modify `viewDidLoad()` as follows:

```
override func viewDidLoad() {
    super.viewDidLoad()
    initialize()
}
```

The benefits of segregating your code in this way may not seem obvious now, but as your classes become more complex, you will find it is easier to look for a specific method and to maintain your code. Before you do the same to the other files, let's see how the `// MARK:` syntax makes it easier to navigate your code.

Using the // MARK: syntax

The //MARK: syntax is used to navigate easily between different parts of your code. Let's see what it does:

1. Look at the path that is visible just under the Tool Bar and click on the last part as shown:

2. A menu is displayed, and you will see both `Private Extension` and `UICollectionViewDataSource` in it, generated by the //MARK: syntax. This enables you to easily jump to these sections:

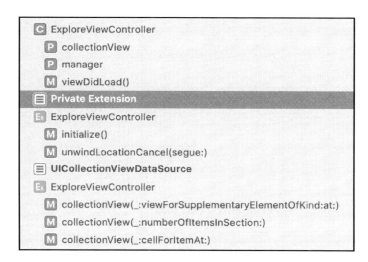

You are done cleaning up `ExploreViewController`, so let's do `RestaurantListViewController` next by refactoring it and adding extensions.

Refactoring RestaurantListViewController

You will add two extensions to `RestaurantListViewController`, similar to those you added to `ExploreViewController`. Perform the following steps:

1. Click `RestaurantListViewController.swift` in the Project navigator. After the final curly brace, press *Return* a few times and add the following:

```
// MARK: Private Extension
private extension RestaurantListViewController {
    // code goes here
}
// MARK: UICollectionViewDataSource
extension RestaurantListViewController:
UICollectionViewDataSource {
    // code goes here
}
```

As before, you'll put `private` methods for `RestaurantListViewController` in the first extension, and all of the collection view data source methods in the second extension.

2. Delete `UICollectionViewDataSource` from the class declaration at the top of the file. Your class declaration should look like this when done. As before, don't worry about any errors, as they will be fixed in the next step:

```
class RestaurantListViewController: UIViewController,
    UICollectionViewDelegate {
```

3. Move all of the collection view data source methods into the second extension. It should look like this when done:

```
// MARK: UICollectionViewDataSource
extension RestaurantListViewController:
UICollectionViewDataSource {
    func collectionView(_ collectionView: UICollectionView,
      numberOfItemsInSection section: Int) -> Int {
        return 1
    }

    func collectionView(_ collectionView: UICollectionView,
      cellForItemAt indexPath: IndexPath) ->
UICollectionViewCell {
        return
collectionView.dequeueReusableCell(withReuseIdentifier:
            "restaurantCell", for: indexPath)
```

```
        }
    }
```

You are done cleaning up `RestaurantListViewController`, so let's do `LocationViewController` next by refactoring it and adding extensions.

Refactoring LocationViewController

As you did before, you will add two extensions to `LocationViewController`. Perform the following steps:

1. Click `LocationViewController.swift` in the Project Navigator. After the final curly brace, press *Return* a few times and add the following:

   ```
   // MARK: Private Extension
   private extension LocationViewController {
       // code goes here
   }
   // MARK: UITableViewDataSource
   extension LocationViewController: UITableViewDataSource {
       // code goes here
   }
   ```

   The first one will be `private`. You'll put private methods for `LocationViewController` here. The second one will contain all of the table view data source methods.

2. Delete `UITableViewDataSource` from the class declaration at the top of the file. Your class declaration should look like this when done. As before, don't worry about any errors, as they will be fixed in the next step:

   ```
   class LocationViewController: UIViewController {
   ```

3. Move all of the table view data source methods into the second extension. It should look like this when done:

   ```
   // MARK: UITableViewDataSource
   extension LocationViewController: UITableViewDataSource {
       func tableView(_ tableView: UITableView,
         numberOfRowsInSection section: Int) -> Int {
           return manager.numberOfItems()
       }

       func tableView(_ tableView: UITableView, cellForRowAt
         indexPath: IndexPath) -> UITableViewCell {
   ```

```
        let cell =
tableView.dequeueReusableCell(withIdentifier:
                "locationCell", for: indexPath) as
UITableViewCell
        cell.textLabel?.text =
manager.locationItem(at:indexPath)
        return cell
    }
}
```

4. Just like you did in `ExploreViewController`, you will create an `initialize()` method inside the first extension, and put in it everything you need to initialize `LocationViewController` there. After that, you will call this `initialize()` function inside the `viewDidLoad()` method. Add the following inside the first extension:

```
func initialize() {
    manager.fetch()
}
```

The first extension should look like this when done:

```
// MARK: Private Extension
private extension LocationViewController {
    func initialize() {
        manager.fetch()
    }
}
```

Finally, modify `viewDidLoad()` as follows:

```
override func viewDidLoad() {
    super.viewDidLoad()
    initialize()
}
```

You are done cleaning up `LocationViewController`, so let's do `MapViewController` next by refactoring it and adding extensions.

Refactoring MapViewController

As you did before, you will add two extensions to `MapViewController`. Do the following:

1. Click `MapViewController.swift` in the Project Navigator. After the final curly brace, press *Return* a few times and add the following:

```
// MARK: Private Extension
private extension MapViewController {
    // code goes here
}
// MARK: MKMapViewDelegate
extension MapViewController: MKMapViewDelegate {
    // code goes here
}
```

The first one will be `private`. You'll put `private` methods for `MapViewController` here. The second one will contain all of the `MKMapViewDelegate` methods.

2. Delete `MKMapViewDelegate` from the class declaration at the top of the file. Your class definition should look like this when done:

```
class MapViewController: UIViewController {
```

3. Move all of the `MKMapViewDelegate` methods into the second extension. It should look like this when done:

```
// MARK: MKMapViewDelegate

extension MapViewController: MKMapViewDelegate {

    func mapView(_ mapView: MKMapView, annotationView view:
      MKAnnotationView, calloutAccessoryControlTapped control:
UIControl){
        guard let annotation =
mapView.selectedAnnotations.first else { return }
        selectedRestaurant = annotation as? RestaurantItem
        self.performSegue(withIdentifier:
Segue.showDetail.rawValue, sender: self)
    }

    func mapView(_ mapView: MKMapView, viewFor
annotation:MKAnnotation)
        -> MKAnnotationView? {
        let identifier = "custompin"
```

```
        guard !annotation.isKind(of: MKUserLocation.self)
            else { return nil }
        var annotationView: MKAnnotationView?
        if let customAnnotationView =
mapView.dequeueReusableAnnotationView
            (withIdentifier: identifier) {
            annotationView = customAnnotationView
            annotationView?.annotation = annotation
        } else {
            let av = MKAnnotationView(annotation: annotation,
                    reuseIdentifier: identifier)
            av.rightCalloutAccessoryView =
UIButton(type:.detailDisclosure)
            annotationView = av
        }
        if let annotationView = annotationView {
            annotationView.canShowCallout = true
            annotationView.image = UIImage(named: "custom-
annotation")
        }
        return annotationView
    }
}
```

4. **Move the following inside the first extension:**

```
func initialize() {
    mapView.delegate = self
    manager.fetch { (annotations) in
addMap(annotations)
    }
}

func addMap(_ annotations:[RestaurantItem]) {
mapView.setRegion(manager.currentRegion(latDelta: 0.5,
    longDelta: 0.5), animated: true)
    mapView.addAnnotations(manager.annotations)
}

func showRestaurantDetail(segue:UIStoryboardSegue){
    if let viewController = segue.destination as?
      RestaurantDetailViewController,
      let restaurant = selectedRestaurant {
      viewController.selectedRestaurant = restaurant
    }
}
```

The first extension should look like this when done:

```
// MARK: Private Extension
private extension MapViewController {

    func initialize() {
        mapView.delegate = self
        manager.fetch { (annotations) in
            addMap(annotations)
        }
    }

    func addMap(_ annotations:[RestaurantItem]) {
mapView.setRegion(manager.currentRegion(latDelta: 0.5,
    longDelta: 0.5), animated: true)
        mapView.addAnnotations(manager.annotations)
    }

    func showRestaurantDetail(segue:UIStoryboardSegue){
        if let viewController = segue.destination as?
            RestaurantDetailViewController,
            let restaurant = selectedRestaurant {
                viewController.selectedRestaurant = restaurant
        }
    }
}
```

You are done cleaning up all four view controllers (ExploreViewController, RestaurantListViewController, LocationViewController, and MapViewController). Great job!

Summary

In this chapter, you created a new class, `RestaurantItem`, that conforms to the `MKAnnotation` protocol. Next, you created `MapDataManager`, a data manager that loads restaurant data from a `.plist` file and puts it into an array of `RestaurantItem` instances. You refactored both `MapDataManager` and `ExploreDataManager` to avoid redundant code. After that, you created `MapViewController`, a view controller for the **Map** screen, and configured it to display custom annotations. Next, you configured callout buttons in the custom annotations to display a **Restaurant Detail** screen. You created `RestaurantDetailViewController`, a view controller for the **Restaurant Detail** screen, and passed data to it from `MapViewController`. Finally, you cleaned up and organized your code to make it easier to read and maintain.

You now know how to create custom map annotations and add them to a map, how to use storyboard references to link storyboards together, and how to use extensions to organize your code, making it easier to read. This will enable you to add maps to your own apps, and help you organize storyboards and code for large projects.

In the next chapter, you'll learn about JSON files, and how to load data from them so the **Restaurant List** and **Map** screens can display details about a particular restaurant.

Getting Started with JSON Files

17

In the last chapter, you configured the **Map** screen to display a list of restaurants using data from a `.plist` file. You configured custom annotations for each restaurant location and callout buttons in the custom annotations to display restaurant details when tapped. You also cleaned up and organized your code to make it easier to read and maintain.

In this chapter, you will use data in **JavaScript Object Notation (JSON)** format. Many apps get data from an online source using an **Application Programming Interface (API)** and JSON is a popular format for data hosted online.

You'll start by learning about APIs and the JSON format, and you'll create a data manager class that can load data from JSON files for use in the *Lets Eat* app. Next, you'll configure `LocationViewController` to store the location selected by the user and pass it to `ExploreViewController` when the **Done** button is tapped. After that, you'll configure `ExploreViewController` to pass the selected location and cuisine to `RestaurantListViewController` when a type of cuisine is selected. `RestaurantListViewController` will then be modified to get a list of restaurants from a JSON file corresponding to the selected location and cuisine and display them in the **Restaurant List** screen. You'll also modify `MapViewController` to display a list of restaurants from a JSON file based on the user's location.

By the end of this chapter, you'll know how to parse JSON data and load data from JSON files for use in your own apps. You'll also learn about `UITableViewDelegate` methods and ways to pass data from one view controller to another.

The following topics will be covered:

- Getting data from JSON files
- Using data from JSON files in your app

Technical requirements

You will continue working on the `LetsEat` project that you modified in the previous chapter.

The resource files and completed Xcode project for this chapter are in the `Chapter17` folder of the code bundle for this book, which can be downloaded here:

`https://github.com/PacktPublishing/iOS-13-Programming-for-Beginners`.

Let's start by creating a data manager class, which you will use to load data from JSON files.

Check out the following video to see the code in action:

`http://bit.ly/2Rl2ivF`

Getting data from JSON files

Similar to what you did in previous chapters, you will create a data manager class to load a file, read the data inside, and put it into objects in your app. The difference is that you will be reading a JSON file and not a `.plist` file. This will simulate reading data from an API, where JSON is a commonly used format. Let's start by learning more about APIs and how they work.

What is an API?

An API, in the context of this book, is a publicly available web-based service that returns data, likely in JSON or XML formats. Many iOS apps work with APIs to access JSON files, which are then used to provide the app with data. You will not be learning about how to connect to an API at this point. Instead, you will use JSON files downloaded from `http://opentable.herokuapp.com`, which have been updated by Craig Clayton for this book. As you will see, working with a JSON file is similar to working with `.plist` files.

Let's study the JSON format next to see how it stores data.

Understanding the JSON format

JavaScript Object Notation (JSON) is a way to structure data in a file so that it is easily readable by both people and computers. To help you to understand the JSON format, you will look at the structure of a sample JSON file.

Create a new group inside the `Misc` folder and name it `JSON`. If you have not yet downloaded the project files for this chapter, go ahead and download them from this link:

`https://github.com/PacktPublishing/iOS-13-Programming-for-Beginners`.

Unzip the folder and open the `resources` folder in the `Chapter17` folder. You should see several JSON files inside. Drag all of the JSON files there into the `JSON` folder you just created. Click **Finish** on the screen that appears. Finally, click `Charleston.json` and you should see the following:

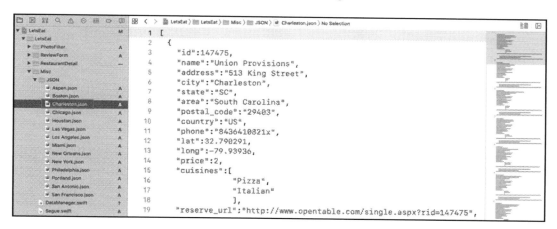

Each JSON file contains restaurant details for a particular city—**Charleston**, **SC**, in this case.

As you can see, the file starts with an opening square bracket, and each item inside consists of key-value pairs containing restaurant information, enclosed by curly braces and separated by commas. At the very end of the file, you can see a closing square bracket.

The square brackets denote arrays, and the curly braces denote dictionaries. In other words, the JSON file contains an array of dictionaries, exactly the same as the `.plist` files you have been using earlier.

Let's create a data manager class to load data from JSON files into your app in the next section.

Creating RestaurantAPIManager

You have learned how to create a data manager class to load data from a `.plist` file in earlier chapters. Loading data from JSON files will be similar. You will now create `RestaurantAPIManager`, a data manager class that loads data from JSON files that you have just added to your project.

 You can learn more about `JSONSerialization` at `https://developer.apple.com/documentation/foundation/jsonserialization`.

Perform the following steps:

1. Right-click on the `Misc` folder and choose **New File**.
2. **iOS** should already be selected. Choose **Swift File** and then click **Next**.
3. Name this file `RestaurantAPIManager`. Click **Create**.
4. Add the following under the `import` statement to declare the `RestaurantAPIManager` structure:

```
struct RestaurantAPIManager {

}
```

5. Implement the `loadJSON(file:)` method between the curly braces. This method takes the filename of a JSON file and returns an array of dictionaries containing the file data:

```
static func loadJSON(file name:String) ->
[[String:AnyObject]]{
    var items = [[String:AnyObject]]()
    guard let path = Bundle.main.path(forResource: name,
        ofType: "json"),let data = NSData(contentsOfFile: path)
else {
        return [[:]]
    }
```

```
        do {
            let json = try JSONSerialization.jsonObject(with: data
as
                     Data, options: .allowFragments) as
AnyObject
            if let restaurants = json as? [[String:AnyObject]] {
                items = restaurants as [[String:AnyObject]]
            }
        }
        catch {
            print("error serializing JSON: \(error)")
            items = [[:]]
        }
        return items
    }
```

Let's see how this method works:

- `static func loadJSON(file name:String) -> [[String:AnyObject]]`
  The `static` keyword indicates that this is a type method. Type methods are called on the type, and not on instances of the type. The method, `loadJSON(file:)`, takes a string, `name`, as a parameter and returns an array of dictionaries.

- `var items = [[String:AnyObject]]()`
  The `items` variable is assigned an empty array of dictionaries.

- `static func loadJSON(file name:String) -> [[String:AnyObject]]`
  This line looks for the file named `name` in the application bundle, and if found, loads the file into an `NSData` object, `data`. If the file is not found, an empty array of dictionaries is returned.

- ```
  do {
  let json = try JSONSerialization.jsonObject(with: data as
  Data, options:
  .allowFragments) as AnyObject
  if let restaurants = json as? [[String:AnyObject]] {
  items = restaurants as [[String:AnyObject]]
  }
  }
  catch {
  print("error serializing JSON: \(error)")
  items = [[:]]
  }
  ```
  ```

This part uses the `do-catch` block that you learned about in `Chapter 8`, *Protocols, Extensions, and Error Handling*. `JSONSerialization.jsonObject(with:options:)` tries to parse the JSON file and assigns it to a constant, `json`. The next line tries to cast `json` as an array of dictionaries, and if successful, assigns it to `items`. Otherwise, an error message is written to the Debug area and an empty array of dictionaries is assigned to `items`.

- `return items`
  If all goes well, `items` is returned as an array of dictionary objects containing restaurant data.

`RestaurantAPIManager` has been created, but before you can use it, you'll need to modify your project quite a bit. Let's see what's required to display restaurant information in the **Restaurant List** and **Map** screens next.

Using data from JSON files in your app

Let's review how the app works. In the **Explore** screen, the user will tap the **LOCATION** button and select a location such as **Charleston, NC** on the **Locations** screen. After a location has been selected, the user taps **Done** and will be returned to the **Explore** screen. The user will then select a cuisine in the **Explore** screen, and a list of restaurants in that location that offer that cuisine will be displayed in **Restaurant List** screen. Tapping a restaurant will display the details of said restaurant in the **Restaurant Detail** screen.

In the **Map** screen, the user will see all the restaurants near the user's location. Tapping a restaurant will display a callout bubble, and tapping the button in the callout button will display the details of said restaurant in the **Restaurant Detail** screen.

So, you will do the following:

- Configure `LocationViewController` to store the location selected by the user.
- Pass the selected location to `ExploreViewController`.

- Configure `ExploreViewController` to pass the selected location and cuisine to `RestaurantListViewController`.
- Configure `RestaurantListViewController` to get a list of restaurants from a JSON file corresponding to the selected location.
- Configure `MapViewController` to get a list of restaurants from a JSON file based on the user's location.
- Configure `RestaurantListViewController` to display a list of restaurants based on the location and cuisine selected.

This may seem daunting, so you'll do things step by step. To start, you'll configure `LocationViewController` so it can store the location selected by the user.

Storing a user-selected location in LocationViewController

At present, `LocationDataManager` loads data from `Locations.plist` and stores location information in an array of strings. You will create a new structure, `LocationItem`, and configure `LocationDataManager` to use it to store a location. After that, you'll modify `LocationViewController` so that it can store a `LocationItem` instance containing the location selected by the user. You can then pass this `LocationItem` instance to the other view controllers in your project. Perform the following steps:

1. Right-click on the `Model` folder inside the `Location` folder and select **New File**.
2. **iOS** should already be selected. Choose **Swift File** and then click **Next**.
3. Name this file `LocationItem`. Click **Create**.
4. Click the `LocationItem.swift` file in the Project navigator.
5. Add the following under the `import` statement to declare and define the `LocationItem` structure:

```
struct LocationItem {
    var state: String?
    var city: String?
}

extension LocationItem {
    init(dict: [String:AnyObject]) {
        self.state = dict["state"] as? String
```

```
        self.city = dict["city"] as? String
    }

    var full: String {
        guard let city = self.city, let state = self.state
    else { return "" }
        return "\(city), \(state)"
    }
}
```

As you can see, `LocationItem` has two properties, `city` and `state`, which are both strings.

The `init()` method in the extension takes a dictionary, `dict`, as a parameter and assigns the value of the `state` and `city` keys to the `state` and `city` properties.

The `full` computed property returns a string made from combining the `state` and `city` values.

Next, you will update `LocationDataManager` so that it can store city and state information in an array of `LocationItem` instances instead of strings.

6. Click `LocationDataManager.swift` in the Project navigator and modify the `locations` property declaration, as shown:

   ```
   private var locations:[LocationItem] = []
   ```

   So, `locations` now stores `LocationItem` instances instead of strings.

7. The `fetch()` method will now show an error. Modify the `fetch()` method as shown:

   ```
   func fetch() {
       for location in loadData() {
           locations.append(LocationItem(dict: location))
       }
   }
   ```

The `fetch()` method now gets each dictionary provided in the `loadData()` method and uses it to initialize `LocationItem` instances, which are appended to the `locations` array. Note that `loadData()` still uses the same `Locations.plist` file that you added in an earlier chapter.

8. The `locationItem(at:)` method now shows an error. Modify it as follows:

```
func locationItem(at index:IndexPath) -> LocationItem {
    return locations[index.item]
}
```

Now, this method returns a `LocationItem` instance instead of a string. You are done with `LocationDataManager` at this point. Next, you need to update `LocationViewController`:

1. Click `LocationViewController.swift` in the Project navigator.
2. You will see an error in the `tableView(_:cellForRowAtIndexPath:)` method. This error is because you can't assign a `LocationItem` instance to the cell's `textLabel`, which is a string.
   Modify `tableView(_:cellForRowAtIndexPath:)` as follows:

```
func tableView(_ tableView: UITableView, cellForRowAt
indexPath:
        IndexPath) -> UITableViewCell {
    let cell = tableView.dequeueReusableCell(withIdentifier:
                "locationCell", for: indexPath) as
UITableViewCell
    cell.textLabel?.text =
manager.locationItem(at:indexPath).full
    return cell
}
```

The `full` property of `LocationItem` returns a string that combines a location's city and state strings, so this fixes the error.

3. Now, you need a property to keep track of the user's selection. Add the following property declaration just below the `manager` declaration:

```
var selectedCity:LocationItem?
```

Next, you need to adopt the `UITableViewDelegate` protocol. You learned about this in Chapter 15, *Getting Started with Table Views*. This protocol specifies the messages that a table view will send to its delegate when the user interacts with the rows in it.

4. Add the following after the `UITableViewDataSource` extension to adopt `UITableViewDelegate protocol`:

```
//MARK: UITableViewDelegate
 extension LocationViewController: UITableViewDelegate {

 }
```

The `//MARK:` syntax makes this extension easy to find in the Editing area, and the extension helps to organize code within this class.

5. The `UITableViewDelegate` method is triggered when a user taps a row in the table view is `tableView(_:didSelectRowAt:)`. Add this method between the extension's curly braces. It should look like the following:

```
//MARK: UITableViewDelegate
extension LocationViewController: UITableViewDelegate {
    func tableView(_ tableView: UITableView, didSelectRowAt
    indexPath:IndexPath) {
        if let cell = tableView.cellForRow(at: indexPath) {
            cell.accessoryType = .checkmark
            selectedCity = manager.locationItem(at:indexPath)
            tableView.reloadData()
        }
    }
}
```

You are done with `LocationDataManager` at this point. Now you need to modify `locationCell`.

When the user taps a row in the **Locations** screen, a checkmark will appear in that row, and the `selectedCity` property is assigned the corresponding `LocationItem` instance in the locations array of `LocationDataManager`. For example, if you tap the third row, the `LocationItem` instance containing the string `Charleston, NC` is assigned to `selectedCity`.

For the checkmark to be visible, you need to update the attributes of `locationCell` in `Main.storyboard`. Do the following:

1. Click `Main.storyboard` in the Project navigator.
2. In the document outline, select `locationCell` in the **Location View Controller Scene**.

3. In the Attributes inspector, under **Table View Cell**, set **Selection** and **Accessory** to None:

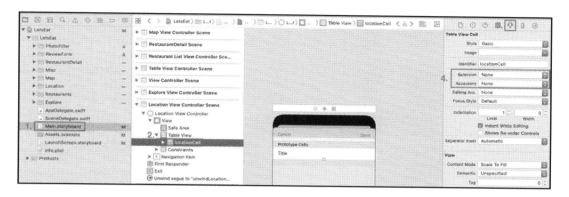

`LocationViewController` can now store the location selected by the user, but when the user selects a location in the **Locations** screen and taps **Done**, nothing happens. You will need to create an unwind action in `ExploreViewController` and assign it to the **Done** button to go back to the **Explore** screen. Before you do that, you'll add a view controller for the collection view section header in the next section, so you can display the user-selected location in the collection view section header's label.

Adding a view controller for the section header in the Explore screen

The **Explore** screen's collection view has a collection view section header, which contains a subtitle label, a title label, and the **LOCATION** button. There is currently no way to set the text for the labels. To do that, you need to create a view controller for it and set up the outlets for the labels. Perform the following steps:

1. Right-click the `View` folder inside the `Explore` folder and select **New File**.
2. **iOS** should already be selected. Choose **Cocoa Touch Class** and then click **Next**.
3. Configure the file as follows:

    - **Class**: `ExploreHeaderView`
    - **Subclass**: `UICollectionReusableView`
    - **Also create XIB**: Unchecked
    - **Language**: `Swift`

Click **Next**

4. Click **Create**. `ExploreHeaderView.swift` appears in the Project navigator. It contains the following:

```
class ExploreHeaderView: UICollectionReusableView {

}
```

5. Click `Main.storyboard` in the Project navigator. Select the **Collection Reusable View** in the **Explore View Controller Scene**. Click the Identity inspector and, under **Custom Class**, set **Class** to `ExploreHeaderView`. Note that **Collection Reusable View** will change to **Explore Header View** in the document outline:

`ExploreHeaderView` is now the view controller for the collection view section header. In the next section, you will link the labels in the collection view section header to outlets in `ExploreHeaderView` and add a property for `ExploreHeaderView` to `ExploreViewController`, so you can change the label text from `ExploreViewController`.

Connecting the section header's label to ExploreViewController

To be able to display the selected city in `ExploreHeaderView`, you need to connect the outlet of the subtitle label to a property in `ExploreHeaderView`. Perform the following steps:

1. In the document outline, click the label for the **Explore Header View** that has the text **PLEASE SELECT A LOCATION**:

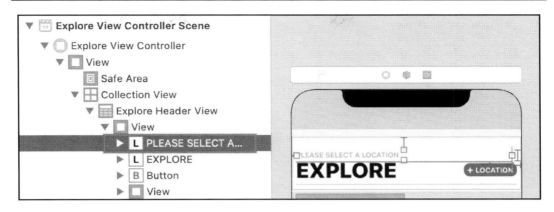

2. Click the Adjust Editor Options button and choose **Assistant**. An assistant editor appears on the right side of the screen. Make sure that it's showing the contents of `ExploreHeaderView.swift`.

3. *Ctrl + Drag* from the label to the space between the curly braces:

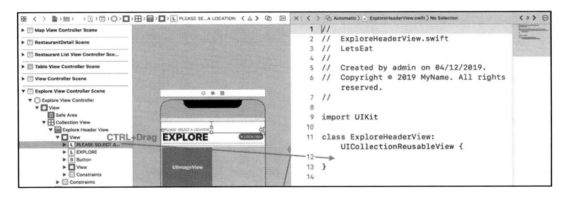

4. In the box that appears, set the name to `lblLocation` and click **Connect**.

5. The `lblLocation` outlet has been created in `ExploreHeaderView`. Close the assistant editor by clicking the **x** button.

6. Click `ExploreViewController.swift` in the Project navigator. Add the following property declaration just below the `manager` declaration to store the location passed to `ExploreViewController` by `LocationViewController`:

```
var selectedCity:LocationItem?
```

7. Just after the `selectedCity` property declaration, type the following:

```
var headerView:ExploreHeaderView!
```

This property will contain a link to `ExploreHeaderView` and allow `ExploreViewController` to set the value for `lblLocation`.

Next, let's configure the **Done** button in the **Locations** screen so that, when it is tapped, the **Explore** screen will appear with the selected city displayed in the collection view section header. You will do this in the next section.

Adding an unwind action method to the Done button

In `Chapter 10`, *Building Your App Structure in Storyboard*, you added an unwind action method for the **Cancel** button in `ExploreViewController`, which dismisses the **Locations** screen when it is tapped. Now, you'll add an unwind action method for the **Done** button, which dismisses the **Locations** screen and sets the `selectedCity` property in `ExploreViewController` to the location selected by the user. Perform the following steps:

1. Add the following just below the `unwindLocationCancel(segue:)` method:

```
@IBAction func unwindLocationDone(segue:UIStoryboardSegue){
    if let viewController = segue.source as?
LocationViewController {
        selectedCity = viewController.selectedCity
        if let location = selectedCity {
            headerView.lblLocation.text = location.full
        }
    }
}
```

This is the unwind action method that will be assigned later to the **Done** button in the **Locations** screen. The source view controller in this case is `LocationViewController` and the destination view controller is `ExploreViewController`. Let's see how it works.

The first line of this method checks whether the source view controller is
LocationViewController. If true, the selectedCity property of
ExploreViewController is set to the LocationItem instance stored in
the selectedCity property of LocationViewController.

The next line assigns selectedCity to a temporary constant, location,
and if successful, the full property of the LocationItem instance (a string
containing the name of the city and the state) is assigned to the text
property of the lblLocation property of headerView.

2. Modify the
   collectionView(_:viewForSupplementaryElementOfKind:at:)
   method as follows:

```
func collectionView(_ collectionView: UICollectionView,
    viewForSupplementaryElementOfKind kind: String, at
indexPath:
    IndexPath) -> UICollectionReusableView {
    let header =
collectionView.dequeueReusableSupplementaryView
        (ofKind: kind, withReuseIdentifier: "header", for:
indexPath)
    headerView = header as? ExploreHeaderView
    return headerView
}
```

This method is one of the data source methods declared in
the UICollectionViewDataSource protocol. It returns the view that will
be used in the collection view section header. Here, the collection view
section header in the **Explore** screen is set to ExploreHeaderView.

You can learn more about this at https://developer.apple.com/
documentation/uikit/uicollectionviewdatasource/1618037-
collectionview.

3. Click `Main.storyboard`. Look for the **Location View Controller Scene**. *Ctrl + Drag* from the **Done** button to the **Exit** icon in the **Scene Dock**:

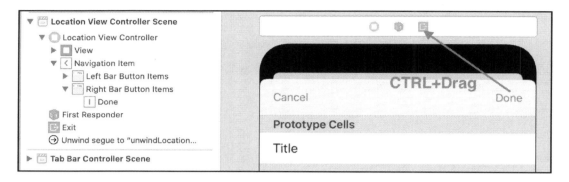

4. Choose `unwindLocationDoneWithSegue:` from the pop-up menu. This links the **Done** button with the `unwindLocationDone(segue:)` unwind action in `ExploreViewController`:

Build and run your app and tap the **LOCATION** button. Tap a city and a tick will appear in the row. Tap **Done**:

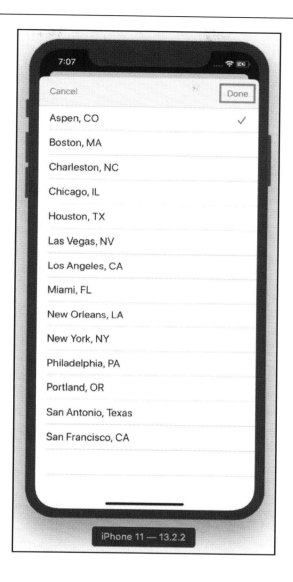

The selected city name and state will replace the **PLEASE SELECT A LOCATION** text in the subtitle label inside the collection view section header:

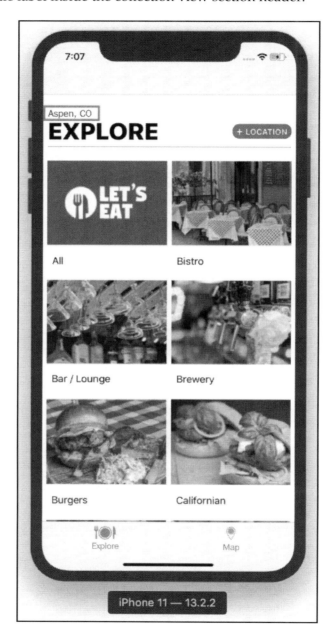

Although this works, there are two issues that you need to fix when selecting a location. The first issue is that you can select multiple locations:

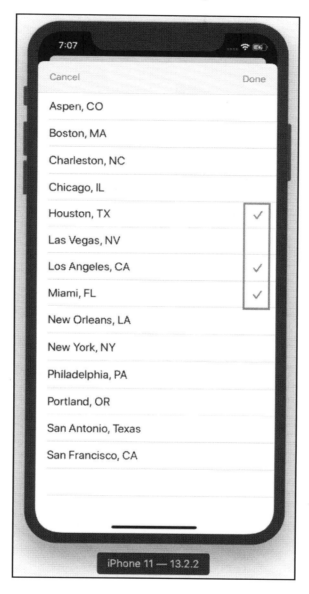

You want the user to only select one location, and if another is selected, the location selected earlier should be deselected.

The second issue is that the checkmark next to the user-selected location disappears if you click **Done** in the **Locations** screen and click the **LOCATION** button in the **Explore** screen again:

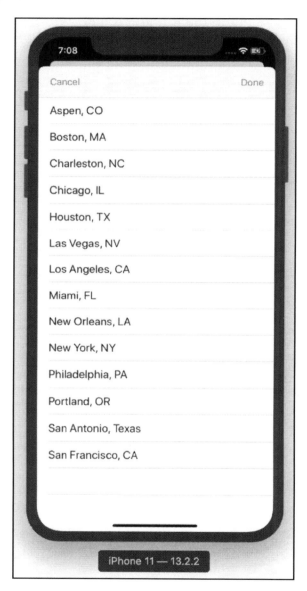

The last selected location should have a checkmark when you go back to the **Locations** screen.

Let's fix the first issue in the next section, which is to make sure only one location can be selected at a time.

Selecting only one location in the Location screen

You want the user to only select one location, and if another is selected, the location selected earlier should be deselected. Let's modify `LocationDataManager` to do this now. Perform the following steps:

1. Click `LocationDataManager.swift`. Implement this method before the closing curly brace:

   ```
   func findLocation (by name: String) -> (isFound:Bool,
   position:Int) {
       guard let index = locations.firstIndex ( where: { $0.city
   == name} )
       else {
           return (isFound:false, position:0)
       }
       return (isFound: true, position: index)
   }
   ```

   This method takes a city name as a parameter. It then searches the `locations` array for a matching city, and if found, returns `true` and the index where that array item is stored as a single value. Such values are called **tuples**, and you can access each component of a tuple using its label (`isFound` and `position`, respectively).

   You can learn more about tuples at `https://docs.swift.org/ swift-book/ReferenceManual/Types.html`.

2. Click `LocationViewController.swift`. Create the following method after the `viewDidLoad()` method:

   ```
   func set(selected cell:UITableViewCell, at indexPath:
   IndexPath) {
       if let city = selectedCity?.city {
   ```

```
            let data = manager.findLocation(by: city)
            if data.isFound {
                if indexPath.row == data.position {
                    cell.accessoryType = .checkmark
                }
                else { cell.accessoryType = .none }
            }
        }
        else {
            cell.accessoryType = .none
        }
    }
```

Let's break this method down:

- `set(selected cell:UITableViewCell, at indexPath: IndexPath)`
  This function takes `cell`, a table view cell, and the cell's index path as arguments.

- `if let city = selectedCity?.city {`
  `let data = manager.findLocation(by: city)`
  This checks to see whether the `selectedCity` property is set. If it is, the `findLocation(by:)` method in `LocationDataManager` is called. If a city is found, the tuple that is returned will have `isFound` set to `true` and `position` set to the index of the city in the `locations` array.

- `if data.isFound {`
  `if indexPath.row == data.position {`
  `cell.accessoryType = .checkmark`
  `}`
  `else { cell.accessoryType = .none }`
  `}`
  If `isFound` is `true`, the cell's row is compared with `position`. If they are the same, the checkmark for that row is set. Otherwise, the checkmark is not set.

- `else {`
  `cell.accessoryType = .none`
  If no data is found, the checkmark is not set.

3. In the `tableView(_:cellForRowAt:)` method, call `set(selected:at:)` after the line that sets the text for the cell's `textLabel` property. The `tableView(_:cellForRowAt:)` method should look like this:

```
func tableView(_ tableView: UITableView, cellForRowAt
indexPath: IndexPath)
    -> UITableViewCell {
    let cell = tableView.dequeueReusableCell(withIdentifier:
            "locationCell", for: indexPath) as
UITableViewCell
    cell.textLabel?.text =
manager.locationItem(at:indexPath).full
    set(selected: cell, at: indexPath)
    return cell
}
```

This means `set(selected:at:)` will be called for each row in the table view, and the checkmark will only be set on the row containing the selected location.

Build and run your project. You should only be able to set one location now, and if you choose another location, the location you chose earlier will be deselected.

You'll fix the second issue in the next section so that, once a location is selected, it will be persistent when you go back to the **Locations** screen. You'll also work on passing location and cuisine information to `RestaurantListViewController`, so it can eventually display a list of restaurants at a particular location matching the cuisine selected by the user.

Passing location and cuisine information to RestaurantListViewController

At present, you're able to set a location in the **Locations** screen and have that location appear in the collection view section header of the **Explore** screen. Now, you will add code so you can pass the location and cuisine values to `RestaurantListViewController`, which will then display the restaurants at the selected location filtered by the selected cuisine. You'll also make the checkmark next to your selected location reappear if you have selected a location in the **Locations** screen earlier.

Perform the following steps:

1. Open `Main.storyboard` and find the **Explore View Controller Scene**. Select the segue between **Explore View Controller Scene** and the **Location View Controller Scene**:

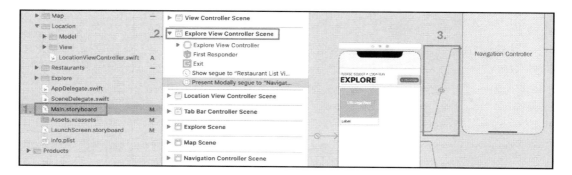

2. Click the Attributes inspector. Under **Storyboard Segue**, set **Identifier** to `locationList`:

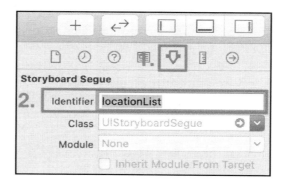

3. Select the segue between **Explore View Controller Scene** and the **Restaurant List View Controller Scene**. Click the Attributes inspector. Under **Storyboard Segue**, set **Identifier** to `restaurantList`:

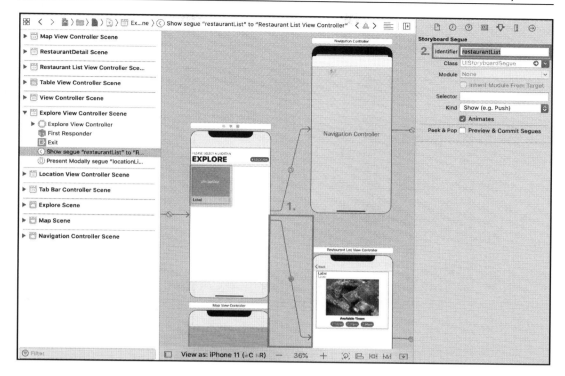

This is so you can identify which segue is occurring later.

4. Click `ExploreViewController.swift` in the Project navigator. Inside the `private` extension, add the following method above the `unwindLocationCancel()` method:

```
func showLocationList(segue:UIStoryboardSegue){
    guard let navController = segue.destination as?
UINavigationController,
        let viewController = navController.topViewController as?
                            LocationViewController else {
        return
    }
    guard let city = selectedCity else { return }
    viewController.selectedCity = city
}
```

You will call this method before `ExploreViewController` transitions to `LocationViewController`. Let's see how it works.

If you look in `Main.storyboard`, you can see that the location view controller scene is embedded in a navigation controller. A navigation controller has a `viewControllers` property that holds an array of view controllers, and the last view controller in the array has its view visible onscreen. You can access the last view controller in the array using the `topViewController` property of the navigation controller.

The `guard` statement checks whether the segue destination is `UINavigationController` and whether `topViewController` is `LocationViewController`. If it is, the `selectedCity` property of `ExploreViewController` is checked to see whether it contains a value. If it does, that value is assigned to the `selectedCity` property of `LocationViewController`. Remember that the `set(selected:at:)` method of `LocationViewController` will be called for each row in the table view, and this sets a checkmark on the row containing the selected city.

This fixes the second issue with the **Locations** screen. Now, let's add code to pass the location and cuisine to `RestaurantListViewController`. Perform the following steps:

1. Click `RestaurantListViewController.swift` in the Project navigator. Add the following properties inside the `RestaurantListViewController` class just above the `@IBOutlet` declaration:

   ```
   var selectedRestaurant:RestaurantItem?
   var selectedCity:LocationItem?
   var selectedType:String?
   ```

2. Add the following code under the `viewDidLoad()` method:

   ```
   override func viewDidAppear(_ animated: Bool) {
       super.viewDidAppear(animated)
       print("selected city \(selectedCity as Any)")
       print("selected type \(selectedType as Any)")
   }
   ```

`viewDidAppear()` is called every time a view controller's view appears onscreen, while `viewDidLoad()` is only called once when a view controller loads its view during app launch. `viewDidAppear()` is used here because depending on what location and cuisine the user picks, `RestaurantListViewController` will need to show a different list of restaurants each time its view appears onscreen. At the moment, the code just prints the selected location and cuisine to the Debug area, so you can see that these values are being set correctly.

3. Click `ExploreViewController.swift` in the Project navigator. Add the following below the `showLocationList()` method:

```
func showRestaurantListing(segue:UIStoryboardSegue) {
    if let viewController = segue.destination as?
RestaurantListViewController,
        let city = selectedCity, let index =
collectionView.indexPathsForSelectedItems?.first {
        viewController.selectedType = manager.explore(at:
index).name
        viewController.selectedCity = city
    }
}
```

You will call this method before `ExploreViewController` transitions to `RestaurantListViewController`. Let's see how it works.

The `if-let` statement checks to see whether the destination view controller is `RestaurantListViewController`, sets `city` to the `selectedCity` value of `ExploreViewController` if it is, and gets the index of the collection view cell the user tapped.

If successful, `ExploreDataManager` will return the `name` of the `ExploreItem` instance in the `items` array located at the same index as the tapped collection view cell. This `ExploreItem` instance will be assigned to the `selectedType` property of `RestaurantListViewController`.

In the next line, the `selectedCity` property of `RestaurantListViewController` will be assigned the value stored in `city`.

For this method to work, the `selectedCity` property of `ExploreViewController` has to be set first. You will alert the user to set the city first before choosing a cuisine. Perform the following steps:

1. Click `ExploreViewController` in the Project navigator. Add the following code before `unwindLocationCancel()`:

```
func showAlert() {
    let alertController = UIAlertController(title: "Location
Needed",
        message: "Please select a location.", preferredStyle:
.alert)
    let okAction = UIAlertAction(title: "OK", style: .default,
handler: nil)
    alertController.addAction(okAction)
    present(alertController, animated: true, completion: nil)
}
```

This function, `showAlert()`, creates a `UIAlertController` instance with the `"LocationNeeded"` title and a message, `"Please select a location."`. An **OK** button is then added to the `UIAlertController` instance. Finally, the alert is presented to the user, and clicking the **OK** button dismisses it.

2. Next, you need to show the user this alert if the city is not set. Add the following code after `viewDidLoad()`:

```
override func shouldPerformSegue(withIdentifier identifier:
String,
    sender: Any?) -> Bool {
    if identifier == Segue.restaurantList.rawValue {
        guard selectedCity != nil else {
            showAlert()
            return false
        }
        return true
    }
    return true
}
```

First, you check whether the segue identifier for the segue matches `restaurantList`. If it does, you check whether `selectedCity` is set; if not, the `showAlert()` method is called.

3. Finally, you implement `prepare(for:sender:)` to call `showLocationList()` or `showRestaurantListing()`, depending on the segue that will be executed. Add the following after `viewDidLoad()` and before `shouldPerformSegue(withIdentifier:)`:

```
override func prepare(for segue: UIStoryboardSegue, sender:
Any?) {
    switch segue.identifier! {
        case Segue.locationList.rawValue:
            showLocationList(segue: segue)
        case Segue.restaurantList.rawValue:
            showRestaurantListing(segue: segue)
        default:
        print("Segue not added")
    }
}
```

When the user clicks the **LOCATION** button, the segue identifier is `locationList`, so the `showLocationList(segue:)` method is executed before the transition to the **Locations** screen, which sets the checkmark for the selected city in the table view. When the user clicks a cell in the **Explore** screen, the segue identifier is `restaurantList`, so the `showRestaurantListing(segue:)` method is executed before the transition to the **Restaurant List** screen. This sets the `selectedType` and `selectedCity` properties in `RestaurantListViewController`, which will be printed to the Debug area.

Build and run your project. If you try to select a cuisine, you should see this alert, stating you need to select a location:

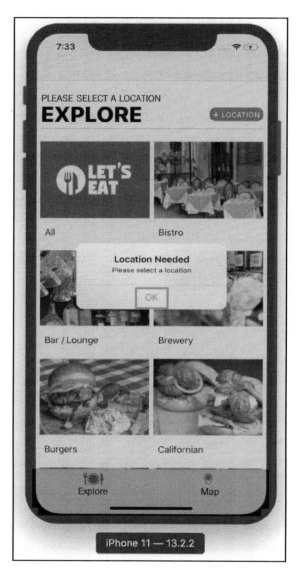

If you pick a location, tap **Done**, and tap the **LOCATION** button again; the location you selected earlier should still be selected:

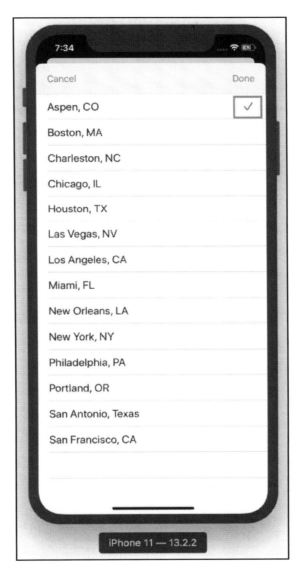

If you pick a cuisine, you should see the **Restaurant List** screen:

The location and cuisine you picked appear in the Debug Area:

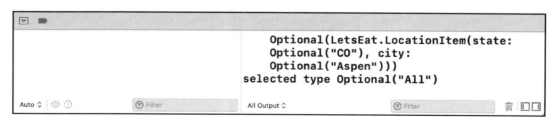

Now that `RestaurantListViewController` has a location, you can get the restaurant data for that location from `RestaurantAPIManager`. Click `RestaurantListViewController.swift` in the Project navigator and update `viewDidAppear()` as follows:

```
override func viewDidAppear(_ animated: Bool) {
    super.viewDidAppear(animated)
    guard let location = selectedCity?.city, let type = selectedType
        else { return }
    print("type \(type)")
    print(RestaurantAPIManager.loadJSON(file: location))
}
```

This prints the contents of the JSON file whose name matches that in the Debug area.

Build and run your project, select a city, and tap a cuisine. Click the Report navigator and select the first entry as shown:

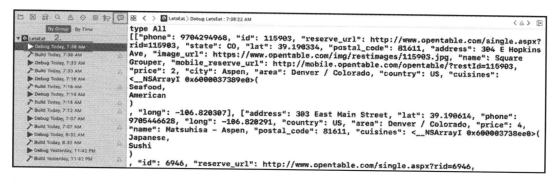

You'll see the contents of the JSON file.

So, at this point, `RestaurantListViewController` is successfully getting the data that it needs to display the list of restaurants. Now that you have this data, you need to configure the collection view to display it to the user. To do that, you will need to create a view controller for the collection view cells, and configure `RestaurantListViewController` to populate them. You will do this in the next section.

Creating a view controller for the cells on the Restaurant List screen

To create the view controller class for the cells on the **Restaurant List** screen, perform the following steps:

1. Right-click the `Restaurants` folder and choose **New Group**. Name it `View`.
2. Right-click the `View` folder and select **New File**.
3. **iOS** should already be selected. Choose **Cocoa Touch Class** and then click **Next**.
4. Configure the file as follows:

   - **Class**: `RestaurantCell`
   - **Subclass**: `UICollectionViewCell`
   - **Also create XIB**: Unchecked
   - **Language**: `Swift`
   - Click **Next**

5. Click **Create**. `RestaurantCell.swift` appears in the Project navigator. It should contain the implementation of the `RestaurantCell` class:

   ```
   import UIKit
       class RestaurantCell: UICollectionViewCell {
   }
   ```

Now, let's create the outlets for the collection view cell in the **Restaurant List** screen so their contents can be managed by `RestaurantCell`. You will do this in the next section.

Connecting the outlets for RestaurantCell

Now that you've created `RestaurantCell`, you'll need to create outlets in `RestaurantCell` and link them to the UI elements inside the collection view cells for the **Restaurant List** screen. This will allow `RestaurantCell` to manage what is displayed by the collection view cell.

Perform the following steps:

1. Click `Main.storyboard`. Click `restaurantCell` in the **Restaurant List View Controller Scene**. In the Identity inspector, under **Custom Class**, set **Class** to `RestaurantCell`:

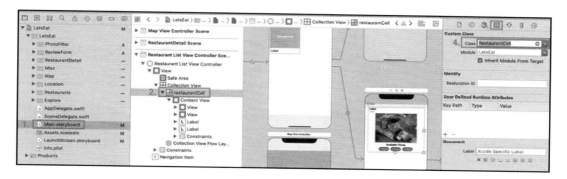

2. In **Restaurant List View Controller Scene**, click on the label with the text **Available Times**. Click on the **Adjust Editor Options** button:

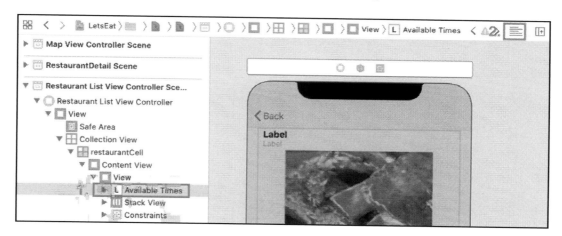

3. Choose **Assistant** from the menu:

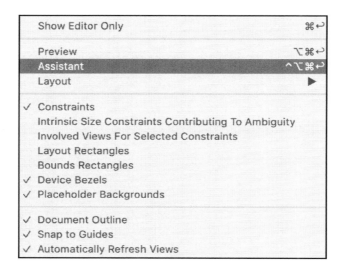

4. The assistant editor appears. The path bar at the top should show
`Automatic > RestaurantCell.swift`. *Ctrl + Drag* from the title **Label** to
the space between the curly braces in `RestaurantCell.swift`:

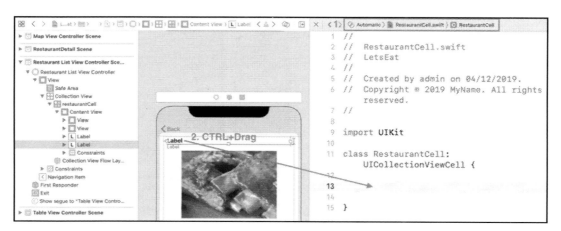

5. Type `lblTitle` in the **Name** field and click **Connect**:

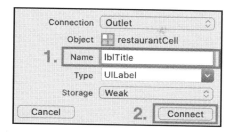

6. *Ctrl + Drag* from the subtitle **Label** to just after the `lblTitle` property you just created. Type `lblCuisine` in the **Name** field and click **Connect**:

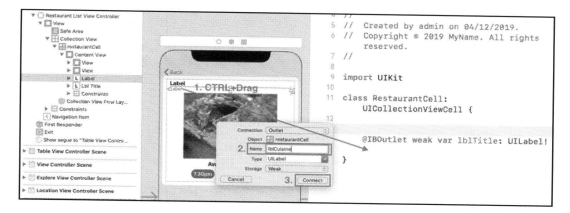

7. *Ctrl + Drag* from the **american** image view to just after the other properties you just created. Type `imgRestaurant` in the **Name** field and click **Connect**:

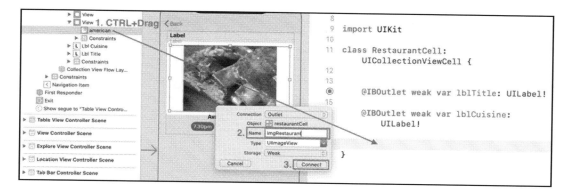

8. Click the **x** button to close the assistant editor.

The outlets for `RestaurantCell` are now connected. You will use an array of `RestaurantItem` instances as a data source for this collection view, and you will create a new data manager class to load the data from the JSON files and put them into this array in the next section.

Creating RestaurantDataManager

During WWDC 2017, Apple introduced a new way to parse JSON files, which is much simpler than the previous way of doing it. You implemented the old way of parsing JSON files earlier in `RestaurantAPIManager`. Now, you will see the new way of doing it, and this will be useful when you need to convert older projects. This also shows you that it is relatively easy to change the data manager class without making a lot of changes to the rest of your project.

 To learn more about the new way of parsing JSON files, watch the video available here: `https://developer.apple.com/videos/play/wwdc2017/212/`.

You will start by modifying `RestaurantItem` so it conforms to the `Decodable` protocol:

1. In the Project navigator, click `RestaurantItem.swift` inside the `Model` folder in the `Map` folder. Modify the class declaration for `RestaurantItem` as shown:

   ```
   class RestaurantItem: NSObject, MKAnnotation, Decodable {
   ```

2. Remove the `init()` method and add the following code:

   ```
   enum CodingKeys: String, CodingKey {
       case name
       case cuisines
       case lat
       case long
       case address
       case postalCode = "postal_code"
       case state
       case imageURL = "image_url"
   }
   ```

The `CodingKeys` enumeration matches the `RestaurantItem` properties to the keys in the JSON file. If the key name does not match the property name, you can map the key name to the property name using the = sign, as shown in the preceding code block for `postalCode` and `imageURL`.

Next, you will write a new data manager named `RestaurantDataManager` that uses the new way of getting data from JSON files. It then puts the data into an array of `RestaurantItems` instances. Perform the following steps:

1. Right-click on the `Restaurants` folder and create a new group named `Model`. Then, right-click on the `Model` folder and choose **New File**.

2. **iOS** should already be selected. Choose **Swift File** and then click **Next**.

3. Name this file `RestaurantDataManager`. Click **Create**.

4. Add the following under the `import` statement to declare the `RestaurantDataManager` class:

```
class RestaurantDataManager {

}
```

5. Add the following property between the curly braces to hold an array of `RestaurantItem` instances:

```
private var items:[RestaurantItem] = []
```

Here, `items` is `private`, which means it is only accessible from within this class.

6. Add the following method to the class:

```
func fetch(by location:String, with filter:String = "All",
    completionHandler:(_ items:[RestaurantItem]) -> Void) {
    if let file = Bundle.main.url(forResource: location,
        withExtension: "json") {
        do {
            let data = try Data(contentsOf: file)
            let restaurants = try
JSONDecoder().decode([RestaurantItem].self,
                from: data)
            if filter != "All" {
                items = restaurants.filter({
($0.cuisines.contains(filter))})
            }
            else { items = restaurants }
        }
```

```
        catch {
            print("there was an error \(error)")
        }
    }
    completionHandler(items)
}
```

Let's break this down:

- `func fetch(by location:String, with filter:String = "All", completionHandler:(_ items:[RestaurantItem]) -> Void)`
  This function takes two parameters: `location`, a string containing the restaurant location, and `filter`, a string containing cuisines. If you do not provide a value for `filter`, it will default to `"All"`. A completion handler is used to assign the result of this method to the `items` property when it has finished execution.

- `if let file = Bundle.main.url(forResource: location, withExtension: "json")`
  This gets the path of the JSON file in the app bundle and assigns it to `file`.

- `do {`
  `let data = try Data(contentsOf: file)`
  `let restaurants = try`
  `JSONDecoder().decode([RestaurantItem].self,`
  `from: data)`
  `if filter != "All" {`
  `items = restaurants.filter({`
  `($0.cuisines.contains(filter))})`
  `}`
  `else { items = restaurants }`

  The first line attempts to assign the contents of `file` to `data`. The next line attempts to parse `data` and decode it as an array of `RestaurantItem` instances, which is assigned to `restaurants`. In the next line, if `filter` is not `All`, the `filter` method is applied to the `restaurants` array using the `{ ($0.cuisines.contains(filter))}` closure. This results in an array of `RestaurantItem` instances where the `cuisines` property contains the `filter` value, and this array is assigned to `items`. Otherwise, the entire `restaurants` array is assigned to `items`.

- `catch {`
  `print("there was an error \(error)")`
  `}`
  This prints an error message to the Debug area if the `do` block fails.

- `completionHandler(items)`
  The result of this method is assigned to the `items` property.
  Note that when you type this method in Xcode, the autocomplete feature gives you two possible choices; one that includes the `with:` parameter (that takes a filter string) and one that doesn't (filter is set to `All`).

7. Add the following method to the class just after the previous method:

```
func numberOfItems() -> Int {
    return items.count
}
```

This method returns the number of items in the `items` array:

8. Add the following method to the class just after the previous method:

```
func restaurantItem(at index:IndexPath) -> RestaurantItem {
    return items[index.item]
}
```

This method returns the `RestaurantItem` from the `items` array located at the `index` given:

Now you have `RestaurantDataManager`, you can use it not only to provide restaurant data to the **Restaurant List** screen but also the **Map** screen. Let's see how to do this in the next section.

Configuring MapDataManager to use RestaurantDataManager

Currently, the **Map** screen only shows sample data from the `MapLocations.plist` file. You will now update `MapDataManager` to use `RestaurantDataManager`. Click `MapDataManager.swift` (inside the `Model` folder in the `Map` folder) in the Project navigator and update the `fetch()` method as follows:

```
func fetch(completion:(_ annotations:[RestaurantItem]) -> ()){
    let manager = RestaurantDataManager()
    manager.fetch(by: "Boston", completionHandler: { (items) in
        self.items = items
        completion(items)
    })
}
```

Let's break this down:

- `func fetch(completion:(_ annotations:[RestaurantItem]) -> ())`
  A completion handler is used to assign the result of this method to the `annotations` property when it has finished execution.
- `let manager = RestaurantDataManager()`
  This creates an instance of `RestaurantDataManager`
- `manager.fetch(by: "Boston", completionHandler: { (items) in self.items = items completion(items)`
  This calls the `fetch()` method of `RestaurantDataManager` to get a list of restaurants from `Boston.json`. This is hardcoded for now as the iOS Simulator does not have a functional GPS:

To see restaurants at a different location, change the name of the **JSON** file used.

To learn more about how to determine your location, visit `https://developer.apple.com/documentation/mapkit/mkmapview/converting_a_user_s_location_to_a_descriptive_placemark`.

If you run your app now and select the **Map** screen, you should see pins for restaurants in Boston.

You are now done with the **Map** screen, but before you can display data in the **Restaurant List** screen, there is a possibility to consider. The user's choices for location and cuisine may not return any results, so you will implement a screen that informs the user when there is no data to be displayed in the next section.

Displaying a custom UIView to indicate no data available

When there is no data to be displayed in the **Restaurant List** screen, you will display a custom `UIView` to inform the user there is no data to be displayed. To do this, you will create a `UIView` subclass and an accompanying **XIB** file. **Xcode Interface Builder (XIB)** term is used interchangeably with **NextStep Interface Builder (NIB)**. It was used to create the user interface before storyboards were implemented and is still used today. Let's create both files now:

1. Right-click on the `Misc` folder and select **New Group**. Name it `No Data`.
2. Right-click on the `No Data` folder and choose **New File**.
3. **iOS** should already be selected. Choose **Cocoa Touch Class** and then click **Next**.
4. Configure the file as follows:

   - **Class**: `NoDataView`
   - **Subclass**: `UIView`
   - **Also create XIB**: Grayed out
   - **Language**: `Swift`
   - Click **Next**.

5. Click **Create**. The `NoDataView.swift` file appears in the Project navigator.
6. Right-click on the `No Data` folder and create a new file.
7. **iOS** should already be selected. Choose **View** and then click **Next**.
8. Name this file `NoDataView`. Click **Create**. The `NoDataView.xib` file appears in the Project navigator.

9. Click `NoDataView.swift` in the Project navigator and add the following code to the file:

```
class NoDataView: UIView {
    var view: UIView!
    @IBOutlet var lblTitle: UILabel!
    @IBOutlet var lblDesc: UILabel!

    override init(frame: CGRect) {
        super.init(frame:frame)
        setupView()
    }

    required init?(coder aDecoder: NSCoder) {
        super.init(coder: aDecoder)!
        setupView()
    }

    func loadViewFromNib() -> UIView {
        let nib = UINib(nibName: "NoDataView", bundle:
Bundle.main)
        let view = nib.instantiate(withOwner: self, options:
nil) [0] as! UIView
        return view
    }

    func setupView() {
        view = loadViewFromNib()
        view.frame = bounds
        view.autoresizingMask = [.flexibleWidth,
.flexibleHeight]
        addSubview(view)
    }

    func set(title: String) {
        lblTitle.text = title
    }

    func set(desc: String) {
        lblDesc.text = desc
    }
}
```

This code declares and defines the `NoDataView` class, a subclass of `UIView`, which will be the view controller for the XIB file. Let's break this down.

- You'll start with the property declarations:

```
var view: UIView!
@IBOutlet var lblTitle: UILabel!
@IBOutlet var lblDesc: UILabel!
```

`view` will be assigned the `NoDataView.xib` during initialization. `lblTitle` and `lblDesc` will be assigned to two `UILabel` instances that will be placed in `NoDataView.xib` when you build the user interface in the next section.

- After that you have the class initializers:

```
override init(frame: CGRect) {
    super.init(frame:frame)
    setupView()
}
required init?(coder aDecoder: NSCoder) {
    super.init(coder: aDecoder)!
    setupView()
}
```

The `NoDataView` class is a subclass of `UIView`. A `UIView` object has two `init` methods: the first handles creation programmatically, and the second handles the loading of **XIB** files from the **App Bundle** stored on the device. Here, both `init` methods will call `setupView()`.

- Next, you have the `loadViewFromNib()` method:

```
func loadViewFromNib() -> UIView {
    let nib = UINib(nibName: "NoDataView", bundle:
Bundle.main)
    let view = nib.instantiate(withOwner: self, options: nil)
[0] as! UIView
    return view
}
```

This method finds and loads the `NoDataView.xib` file from the App Bundle and returns a `UIView` instance stored inside it.

- Next, you have the `setupView()` method:

```
func setupView() {
view = loadViewFromNib()
view.frame = bounds
view.autoresizingMask = [.flexibleWidth, .flexibleHeight]
addSubview(view)
}
```

This method calls `loadViewFromNib()`, configures the view so it is the same size as the device screen, makes the width and height of the view flexible to adapt to size and orientation changes, and adds it to the device view hierarchy so it is visible onscreen.

- Next, you have the `set(title:)` and `set(desc:)` methods:

```
func set(title: String) {
    lblTitle.text = title
}
func set(desc: String) {
    lblDesc.text = desc
}
```

These methods that allow the `title` and `description` properties to be set.

Now, let's set up `NoDataView.xib`. You may want to refer to Chapter 12, *Modifying and Configuring Cells*, which covers using the Size inspector and the Auto Layout constraint menus in more detail.

1. Click `NoDataView.xib` in the Project navigator.
2. Select **File's Owner** in the document outline. In the Identity inspector, under **Custom Class**, set **Class** to `NoDataView` and press *Return*.
3. Click the **Library** button to display the Object library. Type `label` in the filter field. A **Label** object appears in the results.
4. Drag two **Label** objects into the **View.**
5. Select one **Label** to represent the title. In the Attributes inspector, update the following values:

    - **Text**: Add `TITLE GOES HERE` to the text field under the **Text** setting
    - **Color**: `Default (Label Color)`
    - **Alignment**: `Center`
    - **Font**: `System Bold 26.0`

6. With the same **Label** selected, update the following values in the Size inspector:

   - **Width**: 374
   - **Height**: 36

7. Select the other **Label**. This will represent the description. In the Attributes inspector, update the following values:

   - **Text**: Add Description goes here to the text field under the **Text** setting
   - **Color**: Default (Label Color)
   - **Alignment**: Center
   - **Font**: System Thin 17.0

8. In the Size inspector, update the following values:

   - **Width**: 374
   - **Height**: 21

9. Select both **Labels**. Click the **Add New Constraints** button. Tick the **Height** constraint. Click **Add 2 constraints**.

10. With both **Labels** still selected, click the Editor menu and choose **Embed In | Stack View**.

11. Select the **Stack View** in the document outline, and then click the **Add New Constraints** button. Set the following values:

    - **Right**: 10
    - **Left**: 10
    - Click **Add 2 constraints**.

12. With the **Stack View** still selected, click the **Align** button. Set the following values:

    - **Horizontally in Container** (ticked)
    - **Vertically in Container** (ticked)
    - Click **Add 2 constraints.**

13. Click the Attributes inspector. Under **Stack View**, set **Spacing** to 8 and **Alignment** to Center.

14. Select **File's Owner** in the document outline.

15. Open the Connections inspector and connect `lblTitle` to the **Label** that says `TITLE GOES HERE`.

16. Connect `lblDesc` to the other **Label**.

When you are done, you should see the following:

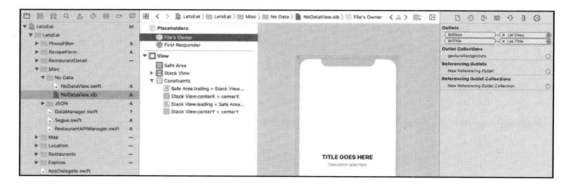

You have completed configuring `NoDataView.xib`. Now, let's put it all together so that the **Restaurant List** screen will display a list of restaurants based on the selected location and cuisine, or display the `NoDataView` if there aren't any restaurants offering the selected cuisine at a particular location. You will do this in the next section.

Displaying a list of restaurants on the Restaurant List screen

You now have everything you need to display a list of restaurants based on the selected location and cuisine on the **Restaurant List** screen. So, now it's time to put it all together. Perform the following steps:

1. Click `RestaurantListViewController.swift` in the Project navigator. Above the `selectedRestaurant` property, add the following:

```
var manager = RestaurantDataManager()
```

This creates an instance of `RestaurantDataManager` and assigns it to `manager`.

2. Add the following method inside the private extension:

```
func createData() {
    guard let location = selectedCity?.city,
        let filter = selectedType else { return }
    manager.fetch(by: location, with: filter) { _ in
        if manager.numberOfItems() > 0 {
            collectionView.backgroundView = nil
        } else {
            let view = NoDataView(frame: CGRect(x: 0, y: 0,
width:
                collectionView.frame.width, height:
collectionView.frame.height))
            view.set(title: "Restaurants")
            view.set(desc: "No restaurants found.")
            collectionView.backgroundView = view
        }
        collectionView.reloadData()
    }
}
```

Let's break this down:

- `guard let location = selectedCity?.city, let filter = selectedType else { return }` Checks to see whether the `selectedCity` and `selectedType` properties are set; if they are, assign `selectedCity` to `location` and `selectedType` to `filter`. Otherwise, exit the method.

- `manager.fetch(by: location, with: filter)` Calls the `fetch(by:with:)` method of `RestaurantDataManager`, which loads the appropriate `RestaurantItem` instances into its `items` array

- ```
  { _ in
  if manager.numberOfItems() > 0 {
  collectionView.backgroundView = nil
  } else {
  let view = NoDataView(frame: CGRect(x: 0, y: 0,
  width: collectionView.frame.width, height:
  collectionView.frame.height))
  view.set(title: "Restaurants")
  view.set(desc: "No restaurants found.")
  collectionView.backgroundView = view
  }
  ```
  ```

If the `items` array of `RestaurantDataManager` is not empty, set `backgroundView` of `collectionView` to nil. Otherwise, create an instance of `NoDataView`, set `title` and `description`, and set it as the `backgroundView` of `collectionView`.

- `collectionView.reloadData()`
  Tells `collectionView` to refresh its view.

3. Update `collectionView(_:cellForItemAt:)` as follows:

```
func collectionView(_ collectionView: UICollectionView,
        cellForItemAt indexPath: IndexPath) ->
UICollectionViewCell {
    let cell =
collectionView.dequeueReusableCell(withReuseIdentifier:
                "restaurantCell", for: indexPath) as!
RestaurantCell
    let item = manager.restaurantItem(at: indexPath)
    if let name = item.name { cell.lblTitle.text = name }
    if let cuisine = item.subtitle { cell.lblCuisine.text =
cuisine}
    if let image = item.imageURL {
        if let url = URL(string: image) {
            let data = try? Data(contentsOf: url)
            if let imageData = data {
                DispatchQueue.main.async {
                    cell.imgRestaurant.image = UIImage(data:
imageData)
                }
            }
        }
    }
    return cell
}
```

Let's break this down:

- `let item = manager.restaurantItem(at: indexPath)`
  Gets `RestaurantItem` from the `items` array of `RestaurantDataManager` corresponding to the `restaurantCell` position.`if let name = item.name { cell.lblTitle.text = name }`
- This sets the `name` of `restaurantCell` using the `name` of `item`.

- `if let cuisine = item.subtitle { cell.lblCuisine.text = cuisine}`
  This sets the `cuisine` of `restaurantCell` using the `subtitle` of `item`.

- `if let image = item.imageURL {`
  `if let url = URL(string: image) {`
  `let data = try? Data(contentsOf: url)`
  `if let imageData = data {`
  `DispatchQueue.main.async {`
  `cell.imgRestaurant.image = UIImage(data: imageData)`
  `}`
  `}`
  `}`
  `}`
  This goes to the URL specified in `item.imageURL`, downloads the picture of the restaurant, and assigns it to the `image` property of the `imgRestaurant` property of `restaurantCell`.

4. Update `collectionView(_:numberOfItemsInSection:)` as follows.

```
func collectionView(_ collectionView: UICollectionView,
numberOfItemsInSection section: Int) -> Int {
    return manager.numberOfItems()
}
```

This will return the number of items in the `items` array of `RestaurantDataManager` so the `collectionView` knows how many rows to create:

5. Update `viewDidAppear()` as follows:

```
override func viewDidAppear(_ animated: Bool) {
super.viewDidAppear(animated)
createData()
}
```

This kicks off the `createData()` process when the `collectionView` appears onscreen.

Build and run the project. Set a location and click a cuisine. If there are items in the items array of RestaurantDataManager, you will see the following screen:

If the array is empty, `NoDataView` will be displayed:

There is just one more thing. You don't see the selected city in the **Restaurant List** screen. Let's add code to display it at the top of **Restaurant List** screen's navigation bar using large titles.

1. In `RestaurantListViewController.swift`, add the following method into the `private` extension after `createData()`:

```
func setupTitle() {
    navigationController?.setNavigationBarHidden(false,
animated: false)
    if let city = selectedCity?.city, let state =
selectedCity?.state {
        title = "\(city.uppercased()), \(state.uppercased())"
    }
    navigationController?.navigationBar.prefersLargeTitles =
true
}
```

Every `UIViewController` instance has a `title` property, and if the navigation bar is visible, `title` will be visible as well. This method unhides the navigation bar and sets the `title` property of `RestaurantListViewController` with a string containing the city and state names in uppercase.

2. Call `setupTitle()` after `createData()` in the `viewDidAppear()` method:

```
override func viewDidAppear(_ animated: Bool){
super.viewDidAppear(animated)
    createData()
    setupTitle()
}
```

This calls the `setupTitle()` method when the **Restaurant List** screen appears.

Build and run the project. Select a location and cuisine. You should see the city and state in uppercase letters at the top of the **Restaurant List** screen:

You have finally reached the end of this chapter. Good job!

Summary

You have accomplished a lot in this chapter. You started by learning about APIs and the JSON format, and you created `RestaurantAPIManager`, a data manager that can load data from JSON files for use in the `LetsEat` app. Next, you configured `LocationViewController` to store the location selected by the user and pass it to `ExploreViewController` when the **Done** button is tapped. After that, you configured `ExploreViewController` to pass the selected location and cuisine to `RestaurantListViewController` when a type of cuisine is selected. Then, you created a second data manager called `RestaurantDataManager`, which uses the latest methods to get data from JSON files. You configured `MapViewController` to get data from `RestaurantDataManager` to display a list of restaurants on the **Map** screen.

Finally, you configured `RestaurantListViewController` to get a list of restaurants from `RestaurantDataManager`, and display them in the **Restaurant List** screen, filtered by the selected cuisine. You also created `NoDataView`, which is displayed if there are no restaurants at a particular location offering the selected cuisine.

You now know how to parse JSON data, and how to use both the old and new ways to load data from JSON files. This means you will be able to write apps that can read JSON files, and also be able to update any apps that you have that still use the older way of parsing JSON files. You also learned about `UITableViewDelegate` methods and ways of passing data from one view controller to another, enabling you to write apps that allow the user to interact with a table view and pass data between different screens.

In the next chapter, you'll implement the **Restaurant Detail** screen, which displays details of a specific restaurant using a table view containing static cells.

18
Displaying Data in a Static Table View

You've come a long way. At this point, your app has data in all its screens, except for the **Restaurant Detail** screen. This screen is accessed either by tapping a restaurant in the **Restaurant List** screen or by tapping the restaurant annotation's callout bubble button in the **Map** screen.

In this chapter, you'll set up outlets for the user interface elements in the **Restaurant Detail** screen and configure RestaurantDetailViewController to manage them. Next, you'll add methods to viewDidLoad() to populate the table view when the **Restaurant Detail** screen is displayed. Finally, you will pass the appropriate RestaurantItem instance from RestaurantListViewController and MapViewController to RestaurantDetailViewController. RestaurantDetailViewController will then be able to display the data from that RestaurantItem instance on the **Restaurant Detail** screen.

By the end of this chapter, you'll have learned how to make table views with static cells display data and how to create a custom map image. By doing so, you'll be able to implement this in your own apps.

The following topics will be covered in this chapter:

- Setting up outlets for RestaurantDetailViewController
- Displaying data in the static table view
- Passing data from RestaurantListViewController to RestaurantDetailViewController

Technical requirements

You will continue working on the `LetsEat` project that you modified in the previous chapter.

The completed Xcode project for this chapter is in the `Chapter18` folder of the code bundle for this book, which can be downloaded here:

`https://github.com/PacktPublishing/iOS-13-Programming-for-Beginners`.

Let's start by creating the outlets for the **Restaurant Detail** screen in `RestaurantDetailViewController`.

Check out the following video to see the code in action:

`http://bit.ly/38yWogc`

Setting up outlets for RestaurantDetailViewController

Your app has data in all its screens, except for the **Restaurant Detail** screen. This screen is accessed either by tapping a restaurant in the **Restaurant List** screen or by tapping the restaurant annotation's callout bubble button in the **Map** screen. If you build and run your app, tapping a restaurant in the **Restaurant List** screen shows the placeholder **Restaurant Detail** screen, as follows:

Tapping a restaurant annotation's callout bubble button in the **Map** screen shows the actual **Restaurant Detail** screen, but it does not contain any restaurant data, as can be seen in the following screenshot:

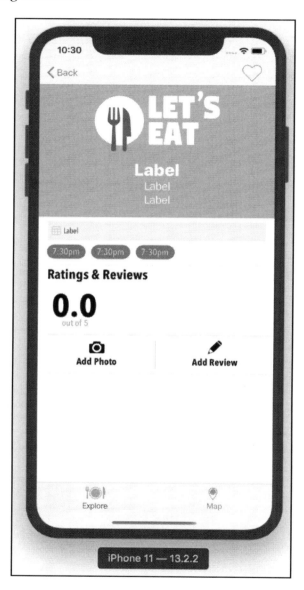

To fix this, let's start by setting up the outlets for `RestaurantDetailViewController`. Click `RestaurantDetailViewController` in the Project navigator. Add the following outlets after the `class` declaration and before the `selectedRestaurant` property declaration:

```
// Nav Bar
@IBOutlet weak var btnHeart:UIBarButtonItem!

// Cell One
@IBOutlet weak var lblName: UILabel!
@IBOutlet weak var lblCuisine: UILabel!
@IBOutlet weak var lblHeaderAddress: UILabel!

// Cell Two
@IBOutlet weak var lblTableDetails: UILabel!

// Cell Three
@IBOutlet weak var lblOverallRating: UILabel!

// Cell Eight
@IBOutlet weak var lblAddress: UILabel!

// Cell Nine
@IBOutlet weak var imgMap: UIImageView!
```

The outlets that you just set up are as follows:

- `btnHeart` is the outlet for the heart-shaped button in the navigation bar. You won't be implementing it in this book, but it's something that you can work on later on your own.
- `lblName` is the outlet for the label that displays the name of the restaurant in the first cell.
- `lblCuisine` is the outlet for the label that displays the cuisines offered by the restaurant in the first cell.
- `lblHeaderAddress` is the outlet for the label that displays the address of the restaurant in the first cell.
- `lblTableDetails` is the outlet for the label that displays the table details of the restaurant in the second cell.
- `lblOverallRating` is the outlet for the label that displays the overall rating for the restaurant in the third cell. You will calculate and set this value in `Chapter 22`, *Saving and Loading from Core Data*.

- lblAddress is the outlet for the label that displays the address of the restaurant in the eighth cell.
- imgMap is the outlet for the image view that displays a location map for the restaurant in the ninth cell. You will write methods to generate this map later in this chapter.

Now that you've created the outlets, you need to connect them to the UI elements in the **Restaurant Detail View Controller Scene** in RestaurantDetail.storyboard, as follows:

1. Open the RestaurantDetail folder in the Project navigator. Click RestaurantDetail.storyboard. Then, click the **View Controller** icon in the **Restaurant Detail View Controller Scene**. Next, click the Identity inspector. Under **Custom Class**, confirm that the **Class** has been set to RestaurantDetailViewController, as shown in the following screenshot:

Note that the name of the **View Controller** will change to **Restaurant Detail View Controller** once the **Custom Class** is set. Unlike the table view that is in the **Location View Controller Scene**, the table view of **Restaurant Detail View Controller Scene** has static cells, meaning the number of cells is not dynamically generated based on data from a model object. As can be seen in the document outline, there are nine cells, and each cell has already been configured with the appropriate view objects. Clicking on each table view cell in the document outline will display that cell in the Editing area.

2. Click the Connections inspector. You'll see all the outlets you added earlier in RestaurantDetailViewController, as follows:

3. Click and drag from the `btnHeart` outlet to the heart in the **Navigation Bar**, as shown in the following screenshot:

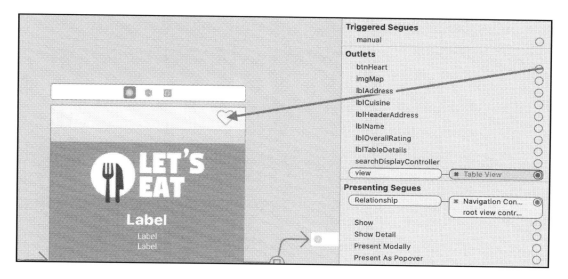

4. Note that the description of the view will change to `Btn Heart` in the document outline, as follows:

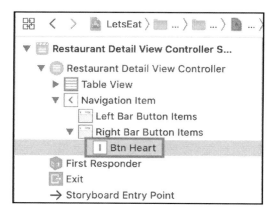

5. Click on the last **Table View Cell** in the document outline to see the bottom of the **Table View**. Click and drag from the `imgMap` outlet to the **Image View** in the last cell, as shown in the following screenshot. Note that the description of the **Image View** will change to `Img Map` in the document outline, as can be seen here:

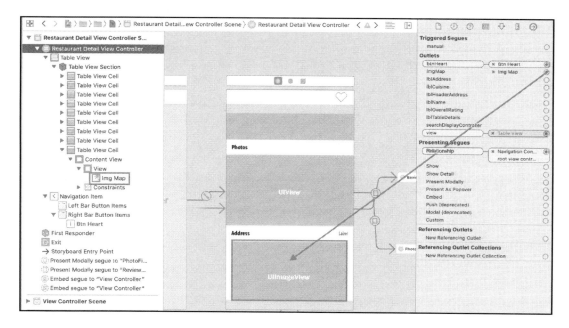

6. Click on the eighth **Table View Cell** in the document outline. Click and drag from the `lblAddress` outlet to the **Label** in the eighth cell, as shown in the following screenshot. Note that the description of the **Label** will change to `Lbl Address` in the document outline, as can be seen here:

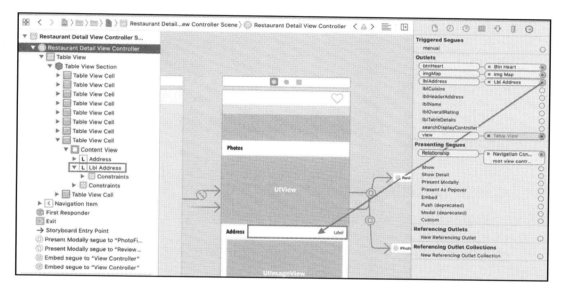

7. Click on the first **Table View Cell** in the document outline. Click and drag from the `lblCuisine` outlet to the second **Label** in the first cell, as shown in the following screenshot. Note that the description of the **Label** will change to `Lbl Cuisine` in the document outline, as can be seen here:

8. Click and drag from the `lblHeaderAddress` outlet to the third **Label** in the first cell, as shown in the following screenshot. Note that the description of the **Label** will change to `Lbl Header Address` in the document outline, as can be seen here:

9. Click and drag from the `lblName` outlet to the first **Label** in the first cell, as shown in the following screenshot. Note that the description of the **Label** will change to `Lbl Name` in the document outline, as can be seen here:

10. Click on the third **Table View Cell** in the document outline. Click and drag from the `lblOverallRating` outlet to the **Label** with the big black `0.0` inside it, as shown in the following screenshot. Note that the description of the **Label** will change to `Lbl Overall Rating` in the document outline, as can be seen here:

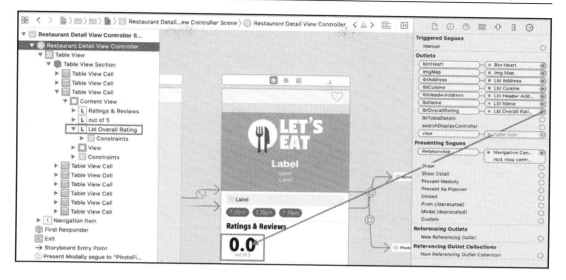

11. Click on the second **Table View Cell** in the document outline. Click and drag from the `lblTableDetails` outlet to the **Label** just above the three red buttons in the second cell, as shown in the following screenshot. Note that the description of the **Label** will change to `Lbl Table Details` in the document outline, as can be seen here:

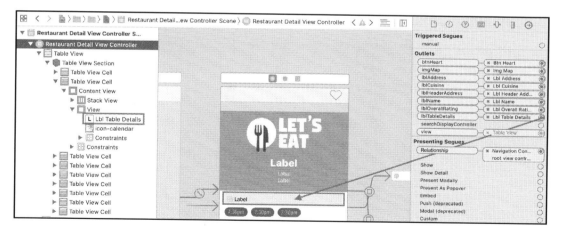

Now that all the outlets are connected, let's add some code to `RestaurantDetailViewController` so that it can populate the outlets, thus displaying the restaurant data in the **Restaurant Detail** screen. You will do this in the next section.

Displaying data in the static table view

You have successfully connected all the outlets in
`RestaurantDetailViewController` to the user interface elements in the table
view for the **Restaurant Detail** screen. Since this is a static table view, you won't be
using the methods that have been declared in the `UITableViewDataSource` protocol
to populate the outlets. Instead, you will write custom methods to do so. Do the
following steps:

1. Click `RestaurantDetailViewController.swift` in the Project
   navigator.
2. Add the following code after the existing `import` statement:

   ```
   import MapKit
   ```

   This is required since you will be using MapKit's properties and methods to
   generate an image of a map for the image view in the last cell.

3. Add the following code after the last curly brace:

   ```
   private extension RestaurantDetailViewController {

       func setupLabels() {
           guard let restaurant = selectedRestaurant else {
   return }
           if let name = restaurant.name {
               lblName.text = name
               title = name
           }
           if let cuisine = restaurant.subtitle {
               lblCuisine.text = cuisine
           }
           if let address = restaurant.address {
               lblAddress.text = address
               lblHeaderAddress.text = address
           }
           lblTableDetails.text = "Table for 7, tonight at 10:00
   PM"
       }
   }
   ```

As before, you will use a private extension to organize your code. The setupLabels() method is quite straightforward; it gets values from a RestaurantItem instance and puts them into the outlets in RestaurantDetailViewController, with the exception of lblTableDetails, which is just assigned a string.

In the last cell, you will display a map. It is possible to display an actual map view in the last cell, but that would take up a lot of system resources. What you will do instead is generate an image from a map region and set the imgMap outlet to display that image. This image will also display the same custom annotation image you used in the **Map** screen.

4. Add the following method under setupLabels() and before the last curly brace:

```
func createMap() {
    guard let annotation = selectedRestaurant,
        let long = annotation.long,
        let lat = annotation.lat else { return }
    let location = CLLocationCoordinate2D(latitude: lat,
longitude: long)
    takeSnapShot(with: location)
}
```

This method assigns selectedRestaurant to annotation and creates location using the lat and long properties of selectedRestaurant. Then, it calls takeSnapShot(with:), passing location as a parameter.

5. You'll see an error since takeSnapShot(with:) hasn't been implemented yet, so add the following code after the createMap() function:

```
func takeSnapShot(with location: CLLocationCoordinate2D){

    let mapSnapshotOptions = MKMapSnapshotter.Options()
    var loc = location
    let polyline = MKPolyline(coordinates: &loc, count: 1 )
    let region = MKCoordinateRegion(polyline.boundingMapRect)

    mapSnapshotOptions.region = region
    mapSnapshotOptions.scale = UIScreen.main.scale
    mapSnapshotOptions.size = CGSize(width: 340, height: 208)
    mapSnapshotOptions.showsBuildings = true
    mapSnapshotOptions.pointOfInterestFilter = .includingAll

    let snapShotter = MKMapSnapshotter(options:
```

```
mapSnapshotOptions)
    snapShotter.start() { snapshot, error in guard
            let snapshot = snapshot else { return }
UIGraphicsBeginImageContextWithOptions(mapSnapshotOptions.size
,
                true, 0)
            snapshot.image.draw(at: .zero)

        let identifier = "custompin"
        let annotation = MKPointAnnotation()
        annotation.coordinate = location

        let pinView = MKPinAnnotationView(annotation:
annotation,
                    reuseIdentifier: identifier)
        pinView.image = UIImage(named: "custom-annotation")!
        let pinImage = pinView.image
        var point = snapshot.point(for:location)

        let rect = self.imgMap.bounds
        if rect.contains(point) {
            let pinCenterOffset = pinView.centerOffset
            point.x -= pinView.bounds.size.width/2
            point.y -= pinView.bounds.size.height/2
            point.x += pinCenterOffset.x
            point.y += pinCenterOffset.y
            pinImage?.draw(at: point)
        }
        if let image =
UIGraphicsGetImageFromCurrentImageContext() {
            UIGraphicsEndImageContext()
            DispatchQueue.main.async {
                self.imgMap.image = image
            }
        }
    }
}
```

A full description of this method is beyond the scope of this book, but let's go over a simple explanation of what it does. Given a location, it takes a snapshot of the map at that location, adds the custom annotation you used earlier in the **Map** screen, converts it into an image, and assigns it to the `imgMap` outlet in `RestaurantDetailViewController`.

You have written all the methods that are required for
`RestaurantDetailViewController` to display the desired
`RestaurantItem` details in the **Restaurant Detail** screen. Now, you need to
call them, as follows:

6. In the `private extension`, add the following method, just above
`setupLabels()`:

```
func initialize() {
    setupLabels()
    createMap()
}
```

This method calls `setupLabels()` and `createMap()`.

7. The `initialize()` method needs to be called inside `viewDidLoad()` so
that it will be executed when `RestaurantDetailViewController` loads
its view. Modify `viewDidLoad()`, as follows:

```
override func viewDidLoad() {
    super.viewDidLoad()
    initialize()
}
```

Now, you have finished with `RestaurantDetailViewController`, but you still
need to pass the selected `RestaurantItem` instance from
`RestaurantListViewController` to `RestaurantDetailViewController`. You
will write the code to do this in the next section.

Passing data from RestaurantListViewController to RestaurantDetailViewController

So far, you have added and connected the outlets for the **Restaurant Detail** screen
inside `RestaurantDetailViewController`. You've also added code to get
restaurant data from a `RestaurantItem` instance and used it to populate the outlets.
The last thing you need to do is pass the selected `RestaurantItem` instance from
`RestaurantListViewController` to `RestaurantDetailViewController`.

To do this, do the following steps:

1. Click `RestaurantListViewController.swift` in the Project navigator.

2. Add the following code under `viewDidLoad()`:

```
override func prepare(for segue:UIStoryboardSegue,
sender:Any?) {
    if let identifier = segue.identifier {
        switch identifier {
        case Segue.showDetail.rawValue:
            showRestaurantDetail(segue:segue)
        default:
            print("Segue not added")
        }
    }
}
```

Recall that you added a segue between the **Restaurant List View Controller Scene** and the **Restaurant Detail View Controller Scene** in the storyboard. Before `RestaurantListViewController` transitions to another view controller, the segue identifier is checked. If the segue identifier is `showDetail`, then the `showRestaurantDetail` method is executed. Only the segue between the **Restaurant List View Controller Scene** and the **Restaurant Detail View Controller Scene** has the `showDetail` identifier, so the destination view controller must be `RestaurantDetailViewController`.

3. You'll see an error because `showRestaurantDetail(segue:)` hasn't been implemented. Add the following method to the `private` extension in `RestaurantListViewController`:

```
func showRestaurantDetail(segue:UIStoryboardSegue){
    if let viewController = segue.destination as?
        RestaurantDetailViewController,
        let index = collectionView.indexPathsForSelectedItems?
                    .first {
        selectedRestaurant = manager.restaurantItem(at: index)
        viewController.selectedRestaurant = selectedRestaurant
    }
}
```

This method passes `RestaurantListViewController`'s `selectedRestaurant` to `RestaurantDetailViewController`.

Build and run the project and go to the **Map** screen. Click on one of the restaurants to display a callout bubble. By clicking the button in the callout bubble, you should see the restaurant details appear in the **Restaurant Detail** screen, as follows:

If you scroll down, you will see the map image in the last cell, as follows:

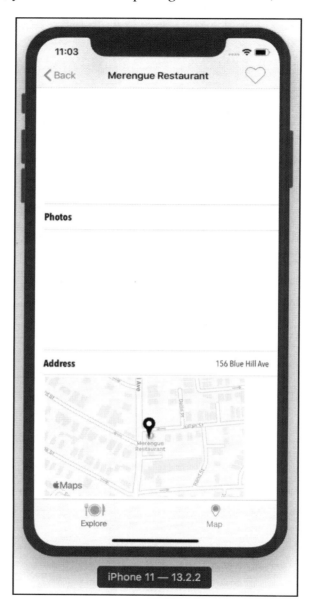

Now, let's take a look at the **Restaurant List View Controller Scene** in `Main.storyboard`. It is currently connected to a placeholder **View Controller Scene**. You'll need to update `Main.storyboard` to remove the placeholder and connect the **Restaurant List View Controller Scene** to the **Restaurant Detail View Controller Scene** in `RestaurantDetail.storyboard`. To do this, take the following steps:

1. Click `Main.storyboard`. Locate `restaurantCell` in the document outline. Then, *Ctrl + Drag* from `restaurantCell` to the `RestaurantDetail` storyboard reference (you added this storyboard reference in `Chapter 16`, *Getting Started with MapKit*), as shown in the following screenshot:

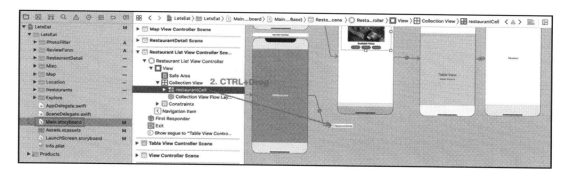

2. Choose **Show** from the popup menu, as follows:

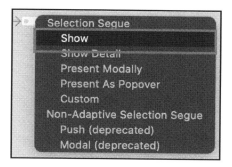

3. Remove the placeholder scenes from the storyboard by selecting them and pressing *Delete* on your keyboard, as follows:

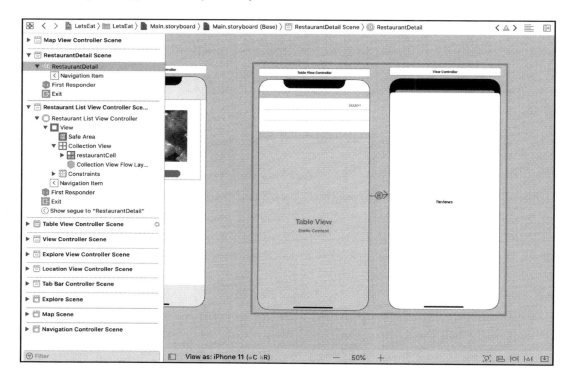

4. Select the segue you just added, as follows:

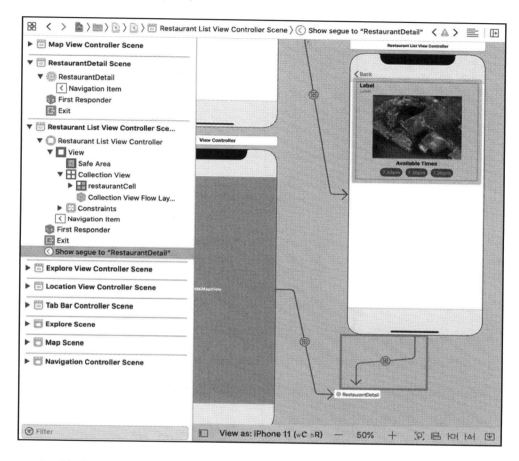

5. Click the Attributes inspector. Under **Storyboard Segue**, set **Identifier** to
   showDetail, as follows:

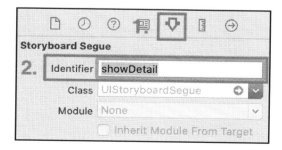

6. Build and run your project. Select a city and a type of cuisine. Click on one of the restaurants in the **Restaurant List** screen. The details of that restaurant will appear in the **Restaurant Detail** screen, as follows:

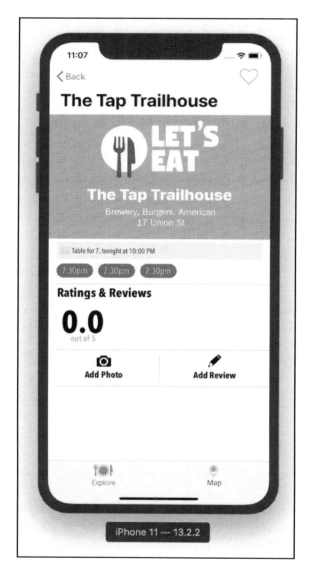

The implementation for the **Map** and **Restaurant Detail** screens is now complete. Awesome!

Summary

In this chapter, you set up the outlets for the **Restaurant Detail** screen in `RestaurantDetailViewController`. Next, you added methods to `viewDidLoad()` to populate the table view when the **Restaurant Detail** screen is displayed. Finally, you passed the appropriate `RestaurantItem` instance from `RestaurantListViewController` and `MapViewController` to `RestaurantDetailViewController`. `RestaurantDetailViewController` now displays data from that `RestaurantItem` on the **Restaurant Detail** screen.

By doing this, you have learned how to make table views with static cells display data, as well as how to create a custom map image, which you can now implement in your own apps.

Congratulations! All the screens in your app now display data. However, if you look at the **Restaurant Detail** screen, there are no ratings, reviews, or photos for the restaurant, and no way to add them. You will update all of this in the upcoming chapters.

In the next chapter, you'll create a custom control that allows you to add star ratings for a restaurant for the **Restaurant Detail** and **Review Form** screens.

19

Getting Started with Custom UIControls

In the previous chapter, you set up the outlets for the **Restaurant Detail** screen and configured `RestaurantDetailViewController` so that it manages them. Next, you added methods to `viewDidLoad()` to populate the table view when the **Restaurant Detail** screen is displayed. Finally, you passed the appropriate `RestaurantItem` instance from `RestaurantListViewController` and `MapViewController` to `RestaurantDetailViewController`. `RestaurantDetailViewController` now displays data from that `RestaurantItem` on the **Restaurant Detail** screen.

At this point, the app has data in all of its screens, but the **Restaurant Detail** screen is incomplete. You can't set a star rating for a restaurant, and you can't save photos and reviews.

So far, you have been using Apple's standard UI objects. In this chapter, you will learn how to build a custom user interface object of the `UIControl` type that displays restaurant ratings in the form of stars. You'll also learn about using **literals** in your code and responding to touch events. Finally, you'll implement a review form that users can use to write restaurant reviews.

By the end of this chapter, you'll have a good grasp of how to create custom `UIControl` objects for your own apps. You'll also learn how to implement a review form.

The following topics will be covered in this chapter:

- Creating a custom `UIControl` object
- Displaying stars in your custom `UIControl` object
- Adding support for touch events
- Implementing an unwind method for the **Cancel** button
- Creating `ReviewFormViewController`

Technical requirements

You will continue working on the `LetsEat` project that you modified in the previous chapter.

The completed Xcode project for this chapter is in the `Chapter19` folder of the code bundle for this book, which can be downloaded here:

`https://github.com/PacktPublishing/iOS-13-Programming-for-Beginners.`

Let's start by learning how to create a custom `UIControl` object that will display a star rating on the screen.

Check out the following video to see the code in action:

`http://bit.ly/3aBdSug`

Creating a custom UIControl object

So far, you have been using the user interface objects provided by Apple, such as labels and buttons. All you need to do is click the Object library button, search for the object you want, and drag it into the storyboard. However, there will be cases where the objects provided by Apple are either not suitable or don't exist. In such cases, you will need to build your own. Let's review the **Restaurant Detail** screen that you saw in the app tour, which can be seen in the following screenshot:

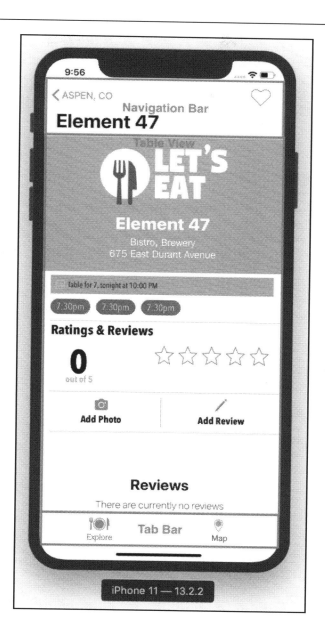

Here, you can see a group of five stars, just above the **Add Review** button. At the moment, the **Restaurant Detail View Controller Scene** in RestaurantDetail.storyboard and the **Table View Controller Scene** in ReviewForm.storyboard have blank view objects where the stars should be. You will build RatingsView, a custom subclass of a UIControl object, that you will use in both scenes. UIControl is a subclass of UIView, and it is used here instead of UIView because you require an object that can respond to user interactions.

 You can learn more about UIControl at https://developer. apple.com/documentation/uikit/uicontrol.

A RatingsView instance will display ratings in the form of stars. The user will also be able to select half-stars. Let's begin by creating a subclass of UIControl. Do the following steps:

1. Right-click the Review Form folder and select **New File**.
2. **iOS** should already be selected. Choose **Cocoa Touch Class** and then click **Next**.
3. Configure the file as follows:

    - **Class**: RatingsView
    - **Subclass**: UIControl
    - **Language**: Swift
    - Click **Next**

4. Click **Create**. RatingsView.swift will appear in the Project navigator.

Now, you need to set the identity of the view object next to the **0.0** label in the **Restaurant Detail View Controller Scene** to RatingsView. To do this, follow these steps:

1. Expand the RestaurantDetail folder in the Project navigator. Click RestaurantDetail.storyboard and select the **View** object next to the **0.0 Label**, as shown in the following screenshot:

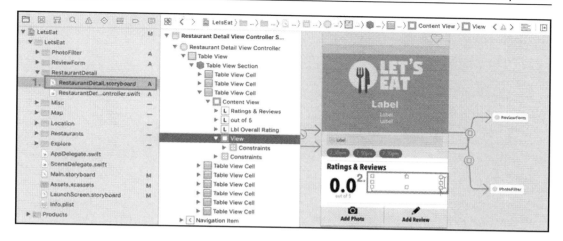

2. Click the Identity inspector. Under **Custom Class**, set **Class** to `RatingsView`, as shown in the following screenshot:

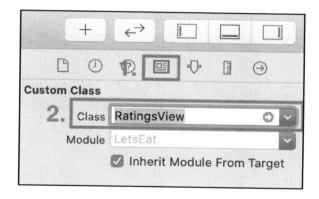

Now, let's add some code to the `RatingsView` class to make it display stars by using the graphic assets inside the `Assets.xcassets` folder. You will do this in the next section.

Displaying stars in your custom UIControl object

So far, you have created a new UIControl subclass named RatingsView in your project. You have also assigned the class of the view object next to the **0.0** label in the **Restaurant Detail** screen to RatingsView. Henceforth, an instance of the RatingsView class will be known as a **ratings view**. In this section, you will add some code to the RatingsView class to make a ratings view display stars. Do the following steps:

1. Click RatingsView.swift in the Project navigator.
2. Type the following text under the RatingsView class declaration:

   ```
   let imgFilledStar = Imag
   ```

3. The autocomplete menu will appear. Choose Image Literal, as shown in the following screenshot:

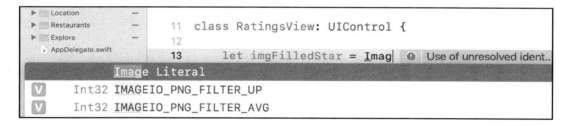

4. You'll see a placeholder graphic. Double-click it, as shown in the following screenshot:

```
10
11   class RatingsView: UIControl {
12
13       let imgFilledStar = [🖼]
14
15   }
```

5. All the custom graphics in `Assets.xcassets` should appear, as can be seen in the following screenshot:

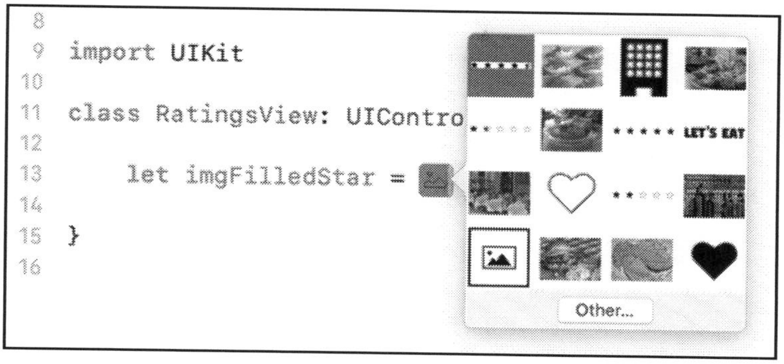

6. Search for and select the red star. This is what the completed line of code should look like:

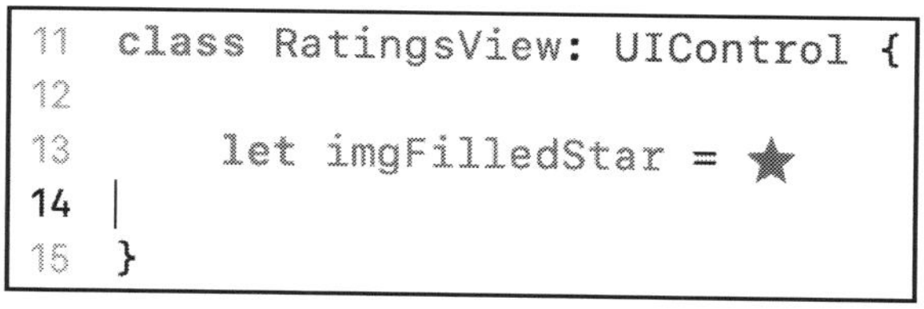

7. Type in the following, using `Image Literal` to assign the graphics for `imgHalfStar` and `imgEmptyStar`:

```
let imgFilledStar = (picture of a filled star)
let imgHalfStar = (picture of a half-filled star)
let imgEmptyStar = (picture of an empty star)
let shouldBecomeFirstResponder = true
var rating:CGFloat = 0.0
var totalStars = 5
```

8. This is what your code should look like:

```
11   class RatingsView: UIControl {
12
13       let imgFilledStar = ★
14       let imgHalfStar = ★
15       let imgEmptyStar = ☆
16       let shouldBecomeFirstResponder = true
17       var rating:CGFloat = 0.0
18       var totalStars = 5
19
20   }
21
```

The first three properties, imgFilledStar, imgHalfStar, and imgEmptyStar, are used to store the star images.

shouldBecomeFirstResponder is a Boolean value that is set to true. Later, you will use it in a method that determines whether a ratings view can accept touch events.

rating is used to keep track of the current rating. The number of stars that's drawn will be determined by the value of rating.

totalStars determines the total number of stars to be drawn.

9. Now, you need to add initializers for this class. Type the following code after the property declarations:

```
override init(frame: CGRect) {
super.init(frame: frame)
}

required init?(coder: NSCoder) {
super.init(coder: coder)
}
```

These are the standard initializers for UIView. Remember that UIControl is a subclass of UIView.

You may wish to re-read Chapter 7, *Classes, Structures, and Enumerations*, if you need help understanding this chapter.

You can learn more about UIView at https://developer.apple.com/documentation/uikit/uiview.

The first initializer, init(frame:) is used if a UIView instance is added using code. It creates a UIView instance at a specified CGRect.

A CGRect is a structure that contains the location and dimension of a rectangle. Location is expressed in *x*, *y* coordinates with the origin (0,0), located at the top-left corner of the screen, while dimension is the width and height of the rectangle in points.

You can learn more about CGRect at https://developer.apple.com/documentation/coregraphics/cgrect.

The second initializer, required init?(coder:) is used if a UIView instance is in a storyboard file. When you build your app, this is stored in the app bundle. The location and dimension are specified in the Size inspector.

Bear in mind that UIControl is a subclass of UIView. Generally, it is good practice to call the superclass initializers inside the subclass initializers, which is why you're doing so here.

Now, let's create some methods that will draw the stars on the screen. You'll need a method to draw a filled star, a half-filled star, and an empty star. To do this, proceed as follows:

10. Add the following extension after the last curly brace (outside of the class definition):

```
private extension RatingsView {
    func drawStar(with frame:CGRect, highlighted:Bool) {
        let image = highlighted ? imgFilledStar : imgEmptyStar
        draw(with: image, and: frame)
    }
```

```
        func drawHalfStar(with frame:CGRect) {
            draw(with: imgHalfStar, and: frame)
        }
        func draw(with image:UIImage, and frame:CGRect) {
            image.draw(in: frame)
        }
    }
```

The `drawStar(with:highlighted:)` method's parameters are `frame` (a
`CGRect`) and `highlighted` (a `Bool`). Depending on the value
of `highlighted`, you set `image` to a filled or an empty star and pass it to
the `draw(with:and:)` method, along with `frame`.

The `drawHalfstar(with:)` method passes `imgHalfStar` to
`draw(with:and:)`, along with `frame`.

The `draw(with:and:)` method uses the `UIImage`'s `draw(in:)` method
from `UIImage` to draw the appropriate star (filled, half-filled, or empty) in
the `CGRect` specified by `frame`.

Now, let's add code to make `RatingsView` draw a ratings view on the
screen. All the `UIView` subclasses have a `draw(_:)` method, which is
responsible for drawing their views on the screen. You need to override the
superclass implementation of this method for `RatingsView`:

11. Add the following code after the `init` methods:

```
override func draw(_ rect: CGRect){
    let context = UIGraphicsGetCurrentContext()
    context!.setFillColor(color literal showing a white
square)
    context!.fill(rect)

    let availWidth = rect.size.width
    let cellWidth = availWidth / CGFloat(totalStars)
    let starSide = (cellWidth <= rect.size.height) ?
                    cellWidth : rect.size.height

    for index in 0...totalStars {
        let value = cellWidth*CGFloat(index) + cellWidth/2
        let center = CGPoint(x: value+1, y:rect.size.height/2)
        let frame = CGRect(x: center.x - starSide/2,
                    y: center.y - starSide/2, width: starSide,
                    height: starSide)
        let highlighted = (Float(index+1) <=
ceilf(Float(self.rating)))
```

```
            if highlighted && (CGFloat(index+1) >
CGFloat(self.rating)) {
                drawHalfStar(with: frame)
            } else {
                drawStar(with: frame, highlighted: highlighted)
            }
        }
    }
```

Let's break this down, as follows:

- `let context = UIGraphicsGetCurrentContext()`
  You can think of `context` as a scratchpad, which you will use to draw something:

- `context!.setFillColor(color literal showing a white square)`
  When typing this line, type `Colo` inside the braces. The Autocomplete menu should show `Color Literal`, as follows:

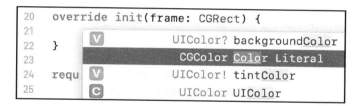

Choose `Color Literal`. A small box will appear between the braces, as follows:

```
28  override func draw(_ rect: CGRect) {
29      let context = UIGraphicsGetCurrentContext()
30      context!.setFillColor(   )
31      context!.fill(rect)
```

This box represents the color of the fill and is white by default. Double-clicking it should display a color picker, which allows you to select the color you want (white, in this case).

- `context!.fill(rect)`
  This line fills the rectangular area specified by `rect` with the fill color, which is white in this case.

- `let availWidth = rect.size.width`
  `let cellWidth = availWidth / CGFloat(totalStars)`
  `let starSide = (cellWidth <= rect.size.height) ? cellWidth`
  `: rect.size.height`
  These three lines get the dimension of the stars to be drawn by dividing the width of the ratings view by the number of stars that need to be drawn and assigning it to `cellWidth`. If `cellWidth` is less than or equal to the ratings view's `height`, `starSide` is set to `cellWidth`; otherwise, it's set to be the same as ratings view's `height`.

  For example, let's assume the ratings view is 200 points wide and 50 points high. `cellWidth` would be 200/5 = 40. Since 40 <= 50 evaluates to `true`, `starSide` will be set to 40.

- `for index in 0...totalStars {`
  Since `totalStars` is set to 5, this `for` loop repeats five times.

- `let value = cellWidth*CGFloat(index) + cellWidth/2`
  `let center = CGPoint(x: value+1, y:rect.size.height/2)`
  `let frame = CGRect(x: center.x - starSide/2, y: center.y -`
  `starSide/2,`
  `width: starSide, height: starSide)`
  These three lines calculate the location and size of the rectangle where each star should be drawn inside the ratings view. The location values are offset from the top-left corner of the ratings view, and the `width` and `height` are set to `starSide`.

  For example, for the first star, `value` is (40*0.0 + 40/2) = 20. `center` is a CGPoint where x is 20+1 = 21 and y is 50/2 = 25. `frame` would thus be a CGRect where x is 21 - 40/2 = 1, y is 25 - 20 = 5, `width` is 40, and `height` is 40.

- `let highlighted = (Float(index+1) <=`
  `ceilf(Float(self.rating)))`
  `if highlighted && (CGFloat(index+1) >`
  `CGFloat(self.rating)) {`
  `drawHalfStar(with: frame)`
  `} else {`
  `drawStar(with: frame, highlighted: highlighted)`
  `}`

Depending on the value of the ratings view's `rating` property, this code determines whether the star is filled, half-filled, or empty.

For example, let's assume `rating` is 3.5.

The first star has an `index` of 0. This means `highlighted` will be set to `Float(0 + 1) <= 3.5` rounded up to the next integer value, becoming `1.0 <= 4.0`, which evaluates to `true`. The next line evaluates `true &&` `1.0 > 3.5`, becoming `true && false`, which evaluates to false, so `drawStar(with:)` is passed the `frame` for the first star (x=1, y=5, width=40, height=40), with `highlighted` set to `true`. This means the first star that's drawn will be a filled star. The same is true for the second and third stars.

The fourth star has an `index` of 3. This means `highlighted` will be set to `Float(3 + 1) <= 3.5` rounded up to the next integer value, becoming `4.0 <= 4.0`, which evaluates to `true`. The next line evaluates `true &&` `4.0 > 3.5`, becoming true && true, which evaluates to true, so `drawHalfStar(with:)` is passed the frame for the fourth star. This means the fourth star drawn will be a half-filled star.

The fifth star has an `index` of 4. This means `highlighted` will be set to `Float(4 + 1) <= 3.5` rounded up to the next integer value, becoming `5.0 <= 4.0`, which evaluates to `false`. The next line evaluates `false &&` `5.0 > 3.5`, becoming false && true, which evaluates to false, so `drawStar(with:)` is passed the frame for the fifth star, with highlighted set to `false`. This means the fifth star that's drawn will be an empty star.

That's all the code that's needed for `RatingsView`. Now, let's add an outlet to `RestaurantDetailViewController` so that it can manage what the ratings view displays. To do this, follow these steps:

1. Click `RestaurantDetailViewController.swift` in the Project navigator.

2. Type in the following code after the `lblOverallRating` outlet:

```
@IBOutlet weak var ratingView: RatingsView!
```

This creates an outlet in `RestaurantDetailViewController` for the ratings view. You now have an outlet named `ratingView` of type `RatingsView` that you will connect to the ratings view in the storyboard later.

While you're still in `RestaurantDetailViewController`, let's add some code to assign a value of `3.5` to ratings view's `rating` property for testing:

3. Type the following in your `private` extension after the first curly brace to set the value of `rating` to `3.5`:

```
func createRating() {
    ratingView.rating = 3.5
}
```

4. Call this method in your `initialize()` method. It should look as follows:

```
func initialize() {
    setupLabels()
    createMap()
    createRating()
}
```

5. Open `RestaurantDetail.storyboard` and select **Restaurant Detail View Controller** in the document outline. Click the Connections inspector. Drag from the `ratingView` outlet to the ratings view object, as shown in the following screenshot:

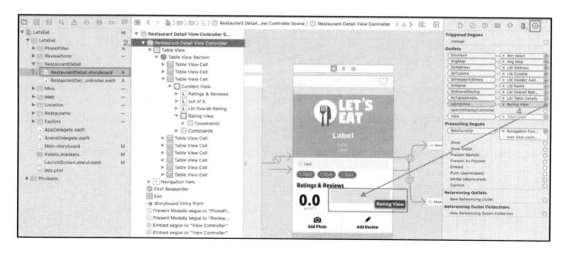

6. Build and run your project and go to `RestaurantDetailView` for any restaurant. The ratings view should display 3.5 stars, as shown in the following screenshot:

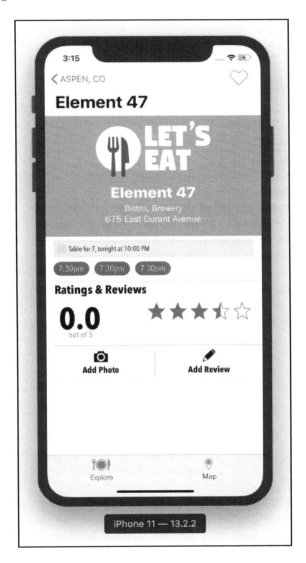

This looks great, but at the moment, the ratings view does not respond when you tap on it. You will enable it to respond to touch events in the next section so that the user can select a rating.

Adding support for touch events

Currently, `RestaurantDetailViewController` has an outlet, `ratingView` connected to a ratings view object in the **Restaurant Detail** screen. It displays a rating of 3.5 stars, but you can't change the rating. To make ratings view respond when touched so that the user can change the rating, you will need to support touch events.

 You can learn more about handling touches at `https://developer.apple.com/documentation/uikit/touches_presses_and_gestures/handling_touches_in_your_view`.

Perform the following steps:

1. Click `RatingsView.swift` in the Project navigator and add the following code after the `draw(_:)` method:

   ```
   override var canBecomeFirstResponder: Bool{
       return shouldBecomeFirstResponder
   }
   ```

   `canBecomeFirstResponder` is a `UIControl` property that determines whether an object can become the **first responder**. Ratings view needs to become first responder to respond to touch events. This method returns `false` by default, so you need to override this method and return `true` in order for ratings view to be able to become first responder.

2. Add the following code immediately after the `canBecomeFirstResponder` variable you just added:

   ```
   override func beginTracking(_ touch: UITouch, with event:
   UIEvent?) -> Bool {
       if self.isEnabled {
           super.beginTracking(touch, with: event)
           if (shouldBecomeFirstResponder &&
   self.isFirstResponder) {
               becomeFirstResponder()
           }
           handle(with:touch)
           return true
       } else {
           return false
       }
   }
   ```

This method is called when the user touches any part of the ratings view on the screen. This is known as a touch event. First, it checks to see if the isEnabled property is true. If it is, the superclass implementation is called. After that, the ratings view on the screen is set to be the first responder, so it will capture touch events when it is touched and the handle(with:) method will be executed for every touch event.

3. You'll see an error because you haven't implemented handle(with:) yet, so type the following code into the private extension:

```
func handle(with touch: UITouch){
    let cellWidth = self.bounds.size.width /
CGFloat(totalStars)
    let location = touch.location(in: self)
    var value = location.x / cellWidth

    if (value + 0.5 < CGFloat(ceilf(Float(value)))) {
        value = floor(value) + 0.5
    } else {
        value = CGFloat(ceilf(Float(value)))
    }
    updateRating(with: value)
}

func updateRating(with value:CGFloat) {
    if (self.rating != value && value >= 0 &&
      value <= CGFloat(totalStars)) {
        self.rating = value
        setNeedsDisplay()
    }
}
```

handle(with:) takes a touch event as a parameter. First, cellWidth is assigned the ratings view's width, divided by 5. Next, the touch event's location within the ratings view is assigned to location. Then, value is assigned the x position of location, divided by cellWidth. The if statement calculates the rating corresponding to the position of the touch and calls updateRating(with:), passing it the value.

For example, let's say the ratings view's `width` is 200. `cellWidth` would be set to 200/5 = 40. Let's assume the user touched the screen at position x = 130; y = 17. `value` would be assigned 130/40 = 3.25. So, the `if` statement would evaluate (3.25 + 0.5 < ceilf(3.25)), which becomes (3.75 < 4.0), which returns `true`, thus `value` would be set to floor(3.25) + 0.5, which becomes 3.0 + 0.5, which is 3.5. So, `updateRating(with:)` would be passed a `value` of 3.5.

`updateRating(with:)` checks to see if `value` is not equal to the current `rating` and between 0 and 5. If it is, `value` is assigned to `rating`, and the screen is redrawn.

Following on from the preceding example, since 3.5 is between 0 and 5, it will be assigned to `rating` if it's not equal to the current value of `rating`.

You've added all the code that's necessary for the ratings view to respond to touches. Now, you'll need to update `RestaurantDetailViewController` to set the `isEnabled` property for the ratings view, as follows:

1. Click `RestaurantDetailViewController.swift` in the Project navigator and modify the `createRating()` method, as follows:

```
func createRating() {
    ratingView.rating = 3.5
    ratingView.isEnabled = true
}
```

Setting the `isEnabled` property to `true` allows the ratings view to become the first responder and begin tracking touches, which will trigger `handle(with:)`, which in turn calls `updateRating(with:)`.

2. Build and run your project. Tapping on the ratings view now changes the rating, depending on where you tapped. Tap between the first and second stars, as follows:

3. The rating will change to 1.5. Now, let's take a look at the **Review Form** screen. The segue between the **Add Review** button and the **Review Form** screen has already been made for you. Tap the **Add Review** button, as shown in the following screenshot:

4. The **Review Form** screen is displayed, as shown in the following screenshot (note that it should have a ratings view in the top cell, which you will add later):

Once the **Review Form** screen appears on the screen, you can't dismiss it, as the button actions for the **Save** and **Cancel** buttons have not been configured. In the next section, you'll configure the **Cancel** button so that it returns the user to the previous screen when tapped.

Implementing an unwind method for the Cancel button

Eventually, you will calculate an overall rating by averaging the ratings that have been submitted by users via the **Review Form** screen, but at the moment, when you tap the **Add Review** button, the **Review Form** screen doesn't have a ratings view. Also, you can't dismiss the **Review Form** screen by tapping on the **Cancel** button. Let's fix that first. Just as you did with the **Locations** screen, you need to implement an unwind method to dismiss the **Review Form** screen. Take the following steps:

1. Click `RestaurantDetailViewController.swift` in the Project navigator.

2. Add the following code to the `private` extension, before the `createRating()` method:

   ```
   @IBAction func unwindReviewCancel(segue:UIStoryboardSegue) {}
   ```

   This method will dismiss the **Review Form** screen.

3. Open `ReviewForm.storyboard` and *Ctrl + Drag* from the **Cancel** button to the **Exit** icon in the **Scene Dock**, as shown in the following screenshot:

4. Choose `unwindReviewCancelWithSegue` in the popup menu, as shown in the following screenshot:

5. Build and run your project. You can now dismiss the **Review Form** screen by tapping the **Cancel** button.

Next, let's take a look at the **Save** button. You need to create a view controller for the **Table View Controller Scene** in the **Review Form** screen to get the data the user entered into the **Review Form** screen's fields when the **Save** button is tapped. You'll do this in the next section.

Creating ReviewFormViewController

To process user input, you'll create `ReviewFormViewController`, which will grab all the values from the **Review Form** screen's fields and print them in the Debug area. You will learn how to store reviews in `Chapter 22`, *Saving and Loading from Core Data*. Do the following steps:

1. Right-click the `ReviewForm` folder and select **New File**.
2. **iOS** should already be selected. Choose **Cocoa Touch Class** and then click **Next**.
3. Configure the file as follows:

    - **Class**: `ReviewFormViewController`
    - **Subclass**: `UITableViewController`
    - **Also create XIB**: Unchecked
    - **Language**: `Swift`
    - Click **Next**

4. Click **Create**. `ReviewFormViewController.swift` will appear in the Project navigator.

5. Delete everything after the `viewDidLoad()` method and add the following outlets after the class declaration. They correspond to the fields inside the **Review Form** screen:

```
@IBOutlet weak var ratingView: RatingsView!
@IBOutlet weak var tfTitle: UITextField!
@IBOutlet weak var tfName: UITextField!
@IBOutlet weak var tvReview: UITextView!
```

6. You also need to configure the action for the **Save** button. Add the following code after the outlet declarations:

```
@IBAction func onSaveTapped(_ sender: Any) {
    print(ratingView.rating)
    print(tfTitle.text as Any)
    print(tfName.text as Any)
    print(tvReview.text as Any)
    dismiss(animated: true, completion: nil)
}
```

As you can see, this method just prints the contents of the outlets to the Debug area and dismisses the **Review Form** screen.

Now, let's connect the outlets in `ReviewFormViewController` to the user interface elements in the **Table View Controller Scene** in `ReviewForm.storyboard`, as follows:

1. Click `ReviewForm.storyboard` in the Project navigator and find the **Table View Controller** icon inside the **Table View Controller Scene**. Click the Identity inspector. Then, under **Custom Class**, set **Class** to `ReviewFormViewController`, as shown in the following screenshot. Note that **Table View Controller Scene** will change to **Review Form View Controller Scene**:

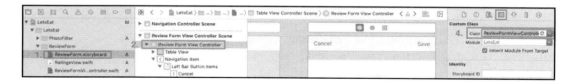

2. Click the view in the document outline as shown, click the Identity inspector, and under **Custom Class**, set **Class** to `RatingsView`. The view's name will change to **Ratings View**, as shown in the following screenshot:

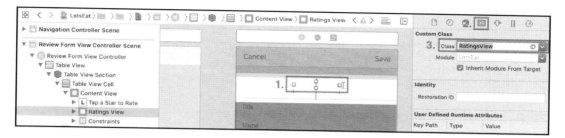

3. Next, you will connect the outlets. Click the **Review Form View Controller** icon in the document outline and click the Connections inspector, as shown in the following screenshot:

4. Connect the `ratingView` outlet to the **Ratings View**, as shown in the following screenshot:

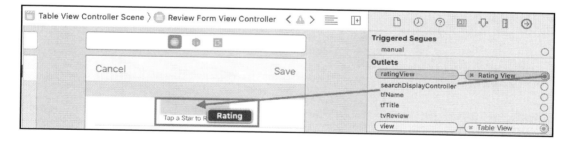

5. Connect the `tfTitle` outlet to the first **Text Field**, as shown in the following screenshot:

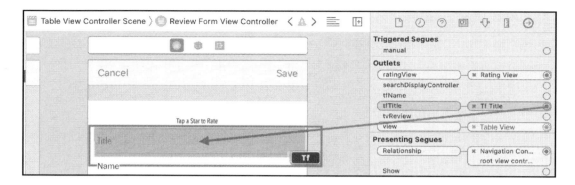

6. Connect the `tfName` outlet to the second **Text Field**, as shown in the following screenshot:

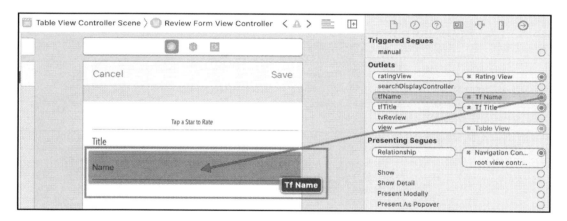

7. Connect the `tvReview` outlet to the **Text View**, as shown in the following screenshot:

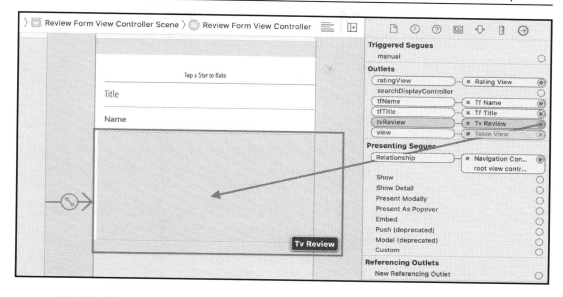

8. Finally, connect the `onSaveTapped:` action to the **Save** button, as shown in the following screenshot:

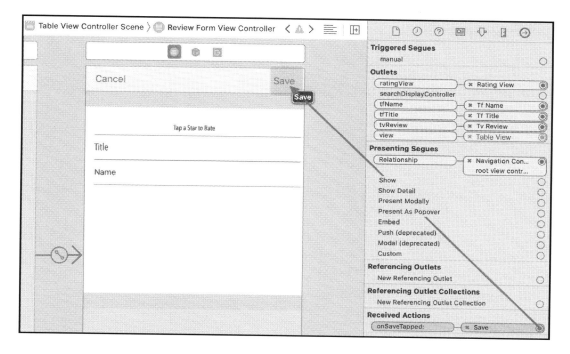

9. Build and run your app. Go to the **Review Form** screen, add some sample text to the fields, and tap the **Save** button, as shown in the following screenshot:

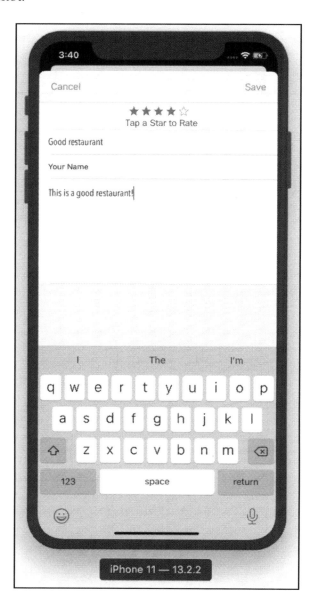

10. You'll see the data you entered appear in the Debug area, as follows:

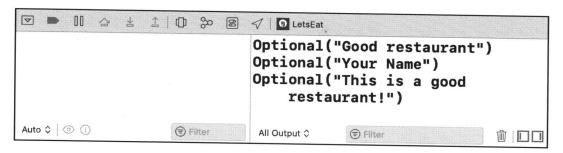

Congratulations! The **Review Form** screen is now able to accept user input. You'll learn how to save and present the review data in a `Chapter 22`, *Saving and Loading from Core Data*.

Summary

In this chapter, you created a new custom control class, ratings view, from scratch and added it to the **Restaurant Detail** screen. You also added it to the **Review Form** screen. You configured it to respond to touches so that a user can use it to set a rating. Finally, you implemented `ReviewFormViewController`, a view controller for the **Review Form** screen, and configured the **Cancel** and **Done** button actions so that the user can dismiss the **Review Form** screen or submit a review. The submitted review is just printed to the Debug area at the moment, but you'll learn how to save it in a later chapter.

You now have a good grasp of how to create custom `UIControl` objects, which you can use for your own apps. You also know how to implement a review form that can accept user input for your own apps.

In the next chapter, you'll learn how to work with photos from the camera or Photo Library, as well as how to apply photo filters to the photos that you have.

20
Getting Started with Cameras and Photo Libraries

In the previous chapter, you created the `RatingsView` class, a custom `UIControl` subclass that allows the user to set a star rating for a restaurant. Then, you added it to the **Restaurant Detail** and **Review Form** screens. You also implemented `ReviewFormViewController`, a view controller for the **Review Form** screen, and configured the **Cancel** and **Done** button actions so that the user can dismiss the **Review Form** screen or submit a review. The submitted review is only printed to the Debug area for now.

In this chapter, you will implement the **Photo Filter** screen to allow the user to select a photo and apply a filter to it. You'll start by importing a `.plist` file containing the filters you want to use and then create a data manager class to read the `.plist` file and populate an array of filter objects. Then, you'll create a protocol, along with a method to apply filters to images.

Next, you'll create view controllers for the views in the **Photo Filter** screen, implement the **image picker delegate protocol**, which allows you to get pictures from the camera or the photo library, and implement methods to apply a selected filter to a picture. Note that the selected picture will not be saved. You will learn how to implement Core Data and save reviews and pictures in the next two chapters.

By the end of this chapter, you'll have learned how to apply filters to photos, and how to import photos from the camera or photo library for use in your app.

The following topics will be covered in this chapter:

- Understanding filters
- Creating a scrolling list of filters
- Getting permission to use the camera or photo library

Technical requirements

You will continue working on the `LetsEat` project that you modified in the previous chapter.

The resource files and completed Xcode project for this chapter are in the `Chapter20` folder of the code bundle for this book, which can be downloaded here:

`https://github.com/PacktPublishing/iOS-13-Programming-for-Beginners`.

Let's start by learning about photo filters, and how to apply them to images.

Check out the following video to see the code in action:

`http://bit.ly/3aD6kak`

Understanding filters

iOS has a range of built-in filters that you can use to enhance photos that are available through the Core Image library. Core Image is an image processing and analysis technology that provides high-performance processing for still and video images. There are over 170 filters available, giving you the ability to apply a wide range of cool effects to your photos.

 You can learn more about Core Image at `https://developer.apple.com/documentation/coreimage`

For this app, you'll just be using 10 filters, which are provided in a `.plist` file. Import this file into your app by following these steps:

1. If you have not yet done so, download and unzip the code bundle for this book at this link: `https://github.com/PacktPublishing/iOS-13-Programming-for-Beginners`
   You will find the `FilterData.plist` inside the `resources` folder in the `Chapter20` folder.
2. In the Project navigator, create a new group inside the `PhotoFilter` folder and name it `Model`.
3. Drag `FilterData.plist` to the `Model` folder. Make sure **Copy items if needed** is ticked and click **Finish**.

4. Click `FilterData.plist` in the Project navigator to see what it contains, as shown in the screenshot:

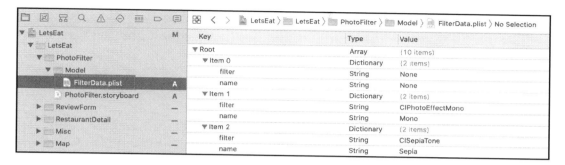

As you can see, `FilterData.plist` is an array of dictionaries. Each dictionary object contains the name of the filter and a descriptive label. Like you did in previous chapters, you will create a class, `FilterItem`, that can store details about a filter, and a data manager class, `FilterManager`, that will load `FilterData.plist` and create an array of `FilterItem` instances. Let's start by creating `FilterItem`. Follow these steps:

1. Right-click the `ReviewForm` folder and create a new group named `Model`.
2. Right-click the `Model` folder and select **New File.**
3. **iOS** should already be selected. Choose **Swift File** and click **Next.**
4. Name this file `FilterItem`. Click **Create.** `FilterItem.swift` will appear in the Project navigator.
5. Under the `import` statement, type the following code inside `FilterItem.swift` to declare and define `FilterItem`:

```
class FilterItem:NSObject {
    let filter:String
    let name:String

    init(dict:[String:AnyObject]){
        name = dict["name"] as! String
        filter = dict["filter"] as! String
    }
}
```

The `filter` property will store filter names, while the `name` property will store the brief filter description.

Now that you've created `FilterItem`, you need to create the data manager class, `FilterManager`. Follow these steps:

1. Right-click the `PhotoFilter` folder and select **New File.**
2. **iOS** should already be selected. Choose **Swift File** and click **Next.**
3. Name this file `FilterManager`. Click **Create.** `FilterManager.swift` will appear in the Project navigator.
4. Type in the following code under the `import` statement, to declare and define `FilterManager`:

```
class FilterManager: DataManager {
    func fetch(completionHandler:(_ items:[FilterItem]) ->
Swift.Void) {
        var items:[FilterItem] = []
        for data in load(file: "FilterData") {
            items.append(FilterItem(dict: data))
        }
        completionHandler(items)
    }
}
```

`FilterManager` conforms to the `DataManager` protocol you created earlier in `Chapter 16`, *Getting Started with MapKit.* Calling the `fetch()` method loads data from `FilterData.plist`, creates an array of `FilterItem` objects, and assigns it to `items`.

Now, you need a way to apply a filter to an image. You will create a protocol, `ImageFiltering`, to do this. Any class that adopts this protocol will have access to the `apply(filter:originalImage:)` method, which applies a specified filter to an image. Follow these steps:

1. Right-click the `PhotoFilter` folder and select **New File.**
2. **iOS** should already be selected. Choose **Swift File** and click **Next.**
3. Name this file `ImageFiltering`. Click **Create.** `ImageFiltering.swift` will appear in the Project navigator.
4. Modify this file, as follows:

```
import UIKit
import CoreImage

protocol ImageFiltering {
    func apply(filter:String, originalImage:UIImage) ->
UIImage
}
```

```
protocol ImageFilteringDelegate:class {
    func filterSelected(item:FilterItem)
}

extension ImageFiltering {
    func apply(filter:String, originalImage:UIImage) ->
UIImage {
        let initialCIImage = CIImage(image: originalImage,
                            options: nil)
        let originalOrientation =
originalImage.imageOrientation
        guard let ciFilter = CIFilter(name: filter) else {
            print("filter not found")
            return UIImage()
        }
        ciFilter.setValue(initialCIImage, forKey:
kCIInputImageKey)
        let context = CIContext()
        let filteredCIImage = (ciFilter.outputImage)!
        let filteredCGImage =
context.createCGImage(filteredCIImage,
                            from: filteredCIImage.extent)
        return UIImage(cgImage: filteredCGImage!, scale: 1.0,
            orientation: originalOrientation)
    }
}
```

Let's break this down, as follows:

- `import UIKit`
  The UIKit framework provides the required infrastructure for your iOS app. You import UIKit instead of Foundation because support for images is not available in Foundation.

- `import CoreImage`
  Core Image is an image processing and analysis technology that provides high-performance processing for still and video images. You import CoreImage as it is required to access the built-in photo filters.

- `protocol ImageFiltering {`
  `func apply(filter:String, originalImage:UIImage) ->`
  `UIImage`
  `}`

Here, you declare a protocol named `ImageFiltering`. This protocol specifies a method, `apply(filter:originalImage:)`, that takes a filter name and an image as parameters.

- ```
  protocol ImageFilteringDelegate:class {
  func filterSelected(item:FilterItem)
  }
  ```
  Here, you declare a protocol named `ImageFilteringDelegate`. The `class` keyword means this protocol may only be adopted by a class. It specifies a method, `filterSelected(item:)`, that takes a `FilterItem` as a parameter. It will be used later when you're passing data between view controllers.

- ```
  extension ImageFiltering {
  func apply(filter:String, originalImage:UIImage) ->
  UIImage {
  ```
  This extension of the `ImageFiltering` protocol contains the implementation of the `apply(filter:originalImage:)` method. This means that any class that adopts the `ImageFiltering` protocol will be able to execute this method.

- ```
  let initialCIImage = CIImage(image: originalImage,
  options: nil)
  ```
  This statement converts the original image into `CIImage` format so that you can apply filters to it, and assigns it to `initialCIImage`.

- ```
  let originalOrientation = originalImage.imageOrientation
  ```
  This statement stores the original image orientation in `originalOrientation`.

- ```
  guard let ciFilter = CIFilter(name: filter) else {
  print("filter not found")
  return UIImage()
  }
  ```
  This `guard` statement gets the filter with the same name as `filter` and assigns it to `ciFilter`, and returns an empty `UIImage` if the filter is not found.
  ```

- `ciFilter.setValue(initialCIImage, forKey: kCIInputImageKey)`
  `let context = CIContext()`
  `let filteredCIImage = (ciFilter.outputImage)!`
  These statements applies the selected filter to `initiaCIImage` and stores the result in `filteredCIImage`.

- `let filteredCGImage = context.createCGImage(filteredCIImage, from: filteredCIImage.extent)`
  `return UIImage(cgImage: filteredCGImage!, scale: 1.0, orientation: originalOrientation)`
  These statements converts the `CIImage` stored in `filteredCIImage` back into `UIImage` format and returns it.

At this point, you have the following:

- `FilterData.plist`, which contains photo filter data inside your app.
- `FilterItem`, a class that can hold a filter and a filter description.
- `FilterManager`, a data manager class that loads data from `FilterData.plist` and generates an array of `FilterItems` instances.
- `ImageFiltering`, a protocol that contains a method, `apply(filter:originalImage:)`, which applies a filter to an image

In the next section, you'll learn how to provide a UI that allows the user to select a filter from a scrolling list that can then be applied to an image.

Creating a scrolling list of filters

So far, you have imported `FilterData.plist` into your app and have created all the classes, protocols, and methods that are needed to apply a filter to an image. In this section, you'll set up a user interface that allows the user to apply a filter to an image.

Inside the `PhotoFilter` folder, you'll find `PhotoFilter.storyboard`. It contains a scene that consists of a large image view that will hold the photo and a collection view that will display filter previews. The following screenshot shows what this will look like when you have completed the implementation:

Let's learn how this screen is supposed to work. When the user taps on the **Add Photo** button in the **Restaurant Detail** screen and selects a photo, a **Photo Filter** screen will appear, showing the selected photo with a scrolling list of filters just under it. Tapping a filter in the scrolling list will apply the selected filter to the photo.

Each filter in the scrolling view is displayed in a collection view cell. You'll start by configuring the cells. Then, you will create a view controller for them and configure them so that they display a preview of a photo with the filter applied. You'll do this in the next section.

Creating a view controller for the filter cell

The **Photo Filter** screen provides the user interface that allows the user to select a filter to be applied to a photo. The filters will be displayed in a collection view. If you click `PhotoFilter.storyboard` in the Project navigator, you will see that the collection view is already present in the **View Controller Scene**, but there is no way to set the contents of the collection view cells. You will need to create a view controller for the collection view cells. To do so, follow these steps:

1. Right-click the `PhotoFilter` folder and select **New File**.
2. **iOS** should already be selected. Choose **Cocoa Touch Class** and click **Next**.
3. Configure the file, as follows:

   - **Class**: `FilterCell`
   - **Subclass**: `UICollectionViewCell`
   - **Also create XIB**: Unchecked
   - **Language**: `Swift`
   - Click **Next**

4. Click **Create**. `FilterCell.swift` will appear in the Project navigator.
5. Update the contents of the file, as follows:

```swift
import UIKit
class FilterCell: UICollectionViewCell {
    @IBOutlet var lblName: UILabel!
    @IBOutlet var imgThumb: UIImageView!
}

extension FilterCell: ImageFiltering {
    func set(image:UIImage, item:FilterItem) {
        if item.filter != "None" {
```

```
            let filteredImg = apply(filter: item.filter,
                           originalImage: image)
            imgThumb.image = filteredImg
        } else {
            imgThumb.image = image
        }
        lblName.text = item.name
        roundedCorners()
    }

    func roundedCorners() {
        imgThumb.layer.cornerRadius = 9
        imgThumb.layer.masksToBounds = true
    }
}
```

As you can see, the implementation of `FilterCell` is very straightforward. It has two properties: a label, `lblName`, and an image view, `imgThumb`. The label will display the filter name, while the image view will display a thumbnail picture, which has the filter applied to it.

`FilterCell` also contains two methods, `set(image:item:)` and `roundedCorners()`. `set(image:item:)` takes a `UIImage` and a `FilterItem` as parameters, applies the filter determined by `FilterItem` to the `UIImage`, and assigns the filtered image to `imgThumb`. The `name` of `FilterItem` is assigned to `lblName`.

`roundedCorners()` just rounds the corners of the collection view cell.

6. Click `PhotoFilter.storyboard` in the Project navigator.

7. In the document outline, select **Collection View Cell** which can be found in the **View Controller Scene**. Click the Identity inspector. Under **Custom Class**, set **Class** to `FilterCell`, as shown in the following screenshot:

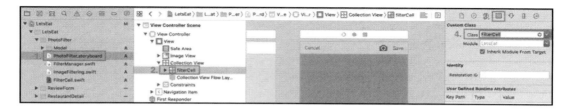

8. Click the Attributes inspector. Set **Identifier** to `filterCell`, as shown in the following screenshot:

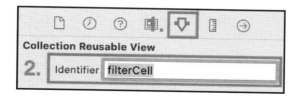

9. Click the Connections inspector. Connect the `lblName` and `imgThumb` outlets, as shown in the following screenshot:

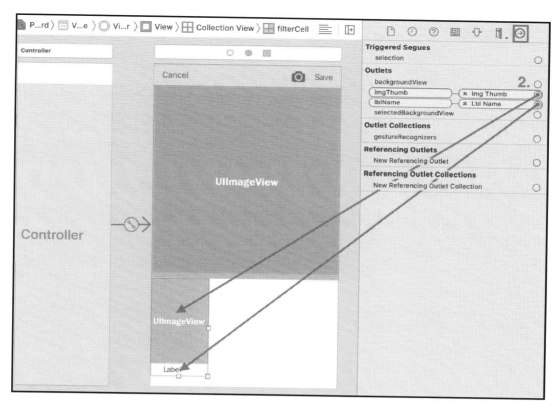

10. The **Cancel** button is used to exit this screen if the user does not wish to make a selection. To set this up, you'll connect the **Cancel** button to an existing unwind method that will dismiss this screen and return the user to the **Restaurant Detail** screen. *Ctrl + Drag* from the **Cancel** button to the **Exit** icon in the **Scene Dock**, as shown in the following screenshot:

11. Select `unwindReviewCancelWithSegue:` in the pop-up menu as shown in the following screenshot:

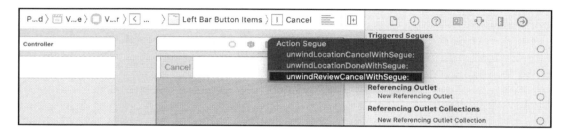

You implemented this method in the previous chapter to dismiss the **Review Form** screen, and the code in it will also work to dismiss the **Photo Filter** screen when the **Cancel** button is tapped.

You have now completed setting up `FilterCell`. Next, you'll create the view controller for the **Photo Filter** screen. This screen will allow the user to select a photo from the camera or photo library and apply a filter to it.

Creating a View Controller for the Photo Filter screen

So far, you've already set up `FilterCell` to manage the collection view cells and configured the **Cancel** button to dismiss the **Photo Filter** screen, but you haven't set up the view controller for the **Photo Filter** screen yet, which is required to manage the screen's contents. Let's create one now. Follow these steps:

1. Right-click the `PhotoFilter` folder and select **New File**.
2. **iOS** should already be selected. Choose **Cocoa Touch Class** and click **Next**.
3. Configure the file, as follows:

    - **Class**: `PhotoFilterViewController`
    - **Subclass**: `UIViewController`
    - **Also create XIB**: Unchecked
    - **Language**: `Swift`
    - Click **Next**

4. Click **Create**. `PhotoFilterViewController.swift` will appear in the Project navigator. Delete all the boilerplate code after the `viewDidLoad()` method.
5. Add the following code to the file:

```swift
import UIKit
import AVFoundation
import MobileCoreServices

class PhotoFilterViewController: UIViewController {
    var image: UIImage?
    var thumbnail: UIImage?
    let manager = FilterManager()
    var selectedRestaurantID:Int?
    var data:[FilterItem] = []

    @IBOutlet var collectionView: UICollectionView!
    @IBOutlet weak var imgExample: UIImageView!

    override func viewDidLoad() {
        super.viewDidLoad()
        initialize()
    }
}
```

The `AVFoundation` framework combines encompasses a wide range of tasks for capturing, processing, synthesizing, controlling, importing and exporting audiovisual media on Apple platforms. `MobileCoreServices` covers the programming interfaces for working with the system-declared uniform types. Both `AVFoundation` and `MobileCoreServices` are required if you wish to work with photos and videos, so it is necessary that you import them into this file.

After that is the `PhotoFilterViewController` class declaration. You'll set up the properties and outlets for this class in a storyboard later. You'll also update `viewDidLoad()` to call `initialize()`, which is used to set up the **Photo Filter** screen. Note that this will generate an error, since `initialize()` hasn't been implemented yet.

6. As usual, you will use extensions to organize your code. Add the following `private` extension:

```
//MARK: - Private Extension
private extension PhotoFilterViewController {

    func initialize() {
        requestAccess()
        setupCollectionView()
        checkSource()
    }

}
```

This extension contains the implementation of the `initialize()` method, which calls three other methods. Note that this will generate an error since the other methods haven't been implemented yet. `requestAccess()` asks for the user's permission to use the camera.

`setupCollectionView()` does a basic setup for the collection view, which will be used to display filters.

`checkSource()` checks the user authorization status for the use of the camera. You'll implement these methods next.

7. Add the following methods after the `initialize()` method:

```
func requestAccess() {
    AVCaptureDevice.requestAccess(for: AVMediaType.video)
      { granted in
        if granted {}
    }
```

```
}

func setupCollectionView() {
    let layout = UICollectionViewFlowLayout()
    layout.scrollDirection = .horizontal
    layout.sectionInset = UIEdgeInsets(top: 7,
                         left: 7, bottom: 7, right: 7)
    layout.minimumInteritemSpacing = 0
    layout.minimumLineSpacing = 7

    collectionView?.collectionViewLayout = layout
    collectionView?.delegate = self
    collectionView?.dataSource = self
}

func checkSource() {
    let cameraMediaType = AVMediaType.video
    let cameraAuthorizationStatus =
AVCaptureDevice.authorizationStatus
                              (for: cameraMediaType)
    switch cameraAuthorizationStatus {
        case .authorized:
        self.showCameraUserInterface()
        case .restricted, .denied:
        break
        case .notDetermined:
        AVCaptureDevice.requestAccess(for: cameraMediaType) {
            granted in
            if granted {
                self.showCameraUserInterface()
            }
        }
    }
}
```

Let's break this down, as follows:

- `requestAccess()` asks for the user's permission to use the camera. Later, you will need to provide an explanation for your app's use of capture devices by using the `NSCameraUsageDescription` or `NSMicrophoneUsageDescription` key in `Info.plist`.

- `setupCollectionView()` does a basic setup for the collection view that will be used to display filters. Here, you determine the flow layout, which determines the size of items, headers, and footers in each section and grid. Note that you're setting the `delegate` and `dataSource` in code rather than in the storyboard. There's no right or wrong way to do this; either approach is acceptable. Don't worry about the errors; they will be fixed later.
- `checkSource()` checks the user authorization status for the use of the camera. Possible cases are as follows. `.authorized` means the user has previously granted access to the camera. `.restricted` means the user can't be granted access due to restrictions that have been set on the device. `.denied` means the user has previously denied camera access to the app. `.notDetermined` means the user hasn't been asked for access to the camera. If the status is `.restricted` or `.denied`, the method exits. If the status is `.authorized`, the `showCameraUserInterface()` method is called. If the status is `.notDetermined`, the app will ask the user for permission and, if permission is given, the `showCameraUserInterface()` method is called. Note that this will generate an error because `showCameraUserInterface()` has not been implemented yet.

8. There are a few more helper methods required; let's add them now. Add the following code under the `checkSource()` method:

```
func showApplyFilter() {
    manager.fetch { (items) in
        if data.count > 0 { data.removeAll() }
        data = items
        if let image = self.image {
            imgExample.image = image
            collectionView.reloadData()
        }
    }
}

func filterItem(at indexPath: IndexPath) -> FilterItem {
    return data[indexPath.item]
}

@IBAction func onPhotoTapped(_ sender: Any) {
    checkSource()
}
```

Let's break this down, as follows:

- `showApplyFilter()` calls the data manager's `fetch()` method, which loads the `FilterData.plist` and puts its contents into an array of `FilterItems`. The resulting array is then assigned to `data`, which will later be used to populate the collection view. The next line assigns `image` to `imgExample`, which is the large image above the collection view. The final line just tells the collection view to redraw itself.
- `filterItem(at:)` will return the `FilterItem` located at the `indexPath.item` index inside the data array. The filter specified in this `FilterItem` will be applied to the large image above the collection view.
- `onPhotoTapped()` calls the `checkSource()` method you implemented earlier, which calls `showCameraUserInterface()` if authorization has been granted.

To learn more about requesting permission to use the camera, go to `https://developer.apple.com/documentation/avfoundation/ cameras_and_media_capture/requesting_authorization_for_ media_capture_on_ios`.

Collection views were covered in detail in Chapter 13, *Getting Started with MVC and Collection Views*.

9. You need to add data source methods to allow the collection view to display a list of filters. Add a new extension below the private extension, and implement the data source methods, as shown in the following screenshot:

```
extension PhotoFilterViewController:
UICollectionViewDataSource {

    func collectionView(_ collectionView: UICollectionView,
        numberOfItemsInSection section: Int) -> Int {
        return data.count
    }

    func collectionView(_ collectionView: UICollectionView,
        cellForItemAt indexPath: IndexPath) ->
UICollectionViewCell {
```

```
      let cell =
collectionView.dequeueReusableCell(withReuseIdentifier:
                "filterCell", for: indexPath) as!
FilterCell
      let item = self.data[indexPath.row]
      if let img = self.thumbnail {
          cell.set(image: img, item: item)
      }
      return cell
    }
}
```

 You can learn more about UICollectionViewDataSource at https://developer.apple.com/documentation/uikit/uicollectionviewdatasource.

The following should be familiar to you as you have done this before, but let's go over it again:

- collectionView(_:numberOfItemsInSection:) determines the number of items the collection view is supposed to display, which is the same number of FilterItems inside the data.

- collectionView(_:cellForItemAt:) determines what to put in each cell. Here, you get the FilterItem instance corresponding to the cell's position in the collection view and pass it, along with the thumbnail, to the set(image:item:) method, which sets the image and label for the FilterCell instance.

10. Next, you need to make sure the collection view is laid out correctly. Add the following extension below the extension containing the data source methods:

```
extension PhotoFilterViewController:
    UICollectionViewDelegateFlowLayout {
    func collectionView(_ collectionView: UICollectionView,
        layout collectionViewLayout: UICollectionViewLayout,
        sizeForItemAt indexPath: IndexPath) -> CGSize {
      let screenRect = collectionView.frame.size.height
      let screenHt = screenRect - 14
      return CGSize(width: 150, height: screenHt)
    }
}
```

`collectionView(_:layout:sizeForItemAt:)` returns the size each cell should be. Previously, you did this using the Size inspector in storyboard; now, you're doing it in code.

You can learn more about `UICollectionViewDelegateFlowLayout` at https://developer. apple.com/documentation/uikit/ uicollectionviewdelegateflowlayout.

Next, let's hook up the two outlets for the **Photo Filter** screen that you added earlier. `collectionView` is the outlet for the collection view that displays the list of filters, while `imgExample` is for the image view just above it, which shows the image the user selected. Follow these steps:

1. Click `PhotoFilter.storyboard` in the Project navigator. Select the **View Controller** icon of the **View Controller Scene** in the document outline. Click the Identity inspector. Under **Custom Class**, set **Class** to `PhotoFilterViewController` as shown in the screenshot below and press *Return*:

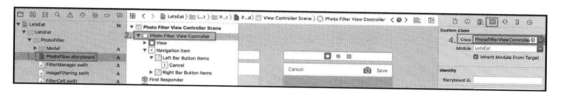

2. Select the Connections inspector. Click and drag from the **collectionView** outlet to the **Collection View** in the document outline, as shown in the screenshot below:

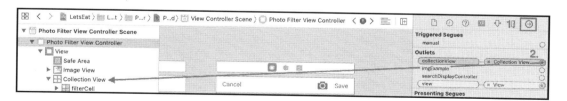

3. Click and drag from the **imgExample** outlet to the **Image View** in the document outline, as shown in the screenshot below:

4. Click and drag from the `onPhotoTapped:` action to the **Camera** icon, as follows:

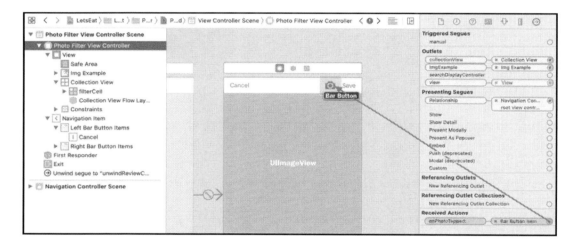

All the outlets and actions for `PhotoFilterViewController` have been added, but you still need to add some more code to `PhotoFilterViewController` to complete the implementation.

You'll implement `showCameraUserInterface()`, which will display either the view from the device camera or the photo library in an image picker interface and the two `UIImagePickerControllerDelegate` methods that will be called when the user chooses a picture in the image picker or cancels.

To learn more about `UIImagePickerController`, go to `https://developer.apple.com/documentation/uikit/uiimagepickercontroller`.

To learn more about the `UIImagePickerControllerDelegate`, go to https://developer.apple.com/documentation/uikit/ uiimagepickercontrollerdelegate

To implement the `showCameraUserInterface()` and `UIImagePickerControllerDelegate` methods, click `PhotoFilterViewController.swift` in the Project navigator and add the following extension after the `UICollectionViewDelegateFlowLayout` extension:

```swift
extension PhotoFilterViewController:
    UIImagePickerControllerDelegate,
    UINavigationControllerDelegate {

    func imagePickerControllerDidCancel(_ picker:
      UIImagePickerController) {
        picker.dismiss(animated: true, completion: nil)
    }

    func imagePickerController(_ picker:
UIImagePickerController,
        didFinishPickingMediaWithInfo info:
        [UIImagePickerController.InfoKey : Any]) {
        let image = info[UIImagePickerController.InfoKey.
                    editedImage] as? UIImage
        if let img = image {
            self.thumbnail = generate(image: img, ratio:
                        CGFloat(102))
            self.image = generate(image: img,
                        ratio: CGFloat(752))
        }
        picker.dismiss(animated: true, completion: {
            self.showApplyFilter()
        })
    }

    func showCameraUserInterface() {
        let imagePicker = UIImagePickerController()
        imagePicker.delegate = self
        #if targetEnvironment(simulator)
        imagePicker.sourceType = UIImagePickerController.
                        SourceType.photoLibrary
        #else
        imagePicker.sourceType = UIImagePickerController.
                        SourceType.camera
        imagePicker.showsCameraControls = true
        #endif
```

```
        imagePicker.mediaTypes = [kUTTypeImage as String]
        imagePicker.allowsEditing = true
        self.present(imagePicker, animated: true,
            completion: nil)
    }

    func generate(image: UIImage, ratio: CGFloat)
        -> UIImage {
        let size = image.size
        var croppedSize:CGSize?
        var offsetX:CGFloat = 0.0
        var offsetY:CGFloat = 0.0
        if size.width > size.height {
            offsetX = (size.height - size.width) / 2
            croppedSize = CGSize(width: size.height,
                        height: size.height)
        } else {
            offsetY = (size.width - size.height) / 2
            croppedSize = CGSize(width: size.width, height:
                        size.width)
        }
        guard let cropped = croppedSize,
          let cgImage = image.cgImage else {
            return UIImage()
        }
        let clippedRect = CGRect(x: offsetX * -1, y: offsetY *
-1,
                        width: cropped.width, height:
                        cropped.height)
        let imgRef = cgImage.cropping(to: clippedRect)
        let rect = CGRect(x: 0.0, y: 0.0, width: ratio,
                height: ratio)
        UIGraphicsBeginImageContext(rect.size)
        if let ref = imgRef {
            UIImage(cgImage: ref).draw(in: rect)
        }
        let thumbnail =
UIGraphicsGetImageFromCurrentImageContext()
        UIGraphicsEndImageContext()
        guard let thumb = thumbnail else {
            return UIImage()
        }
        return thumb
    }
}
```

Let's talk about `showCameraUserInterface()` first. This method is triggered when the **Camera** button is tapped, creating an instance of `UIImagePickerController`, which displays an image picker on the screen. This image picker is the standard iOS image picker that appears when you want to use an image—for instance, to add an image to a Facebook post or to a tweet. If you're running this app in the Simulator, the photo library is displayed; otherwise, the view from the camera is displayed.

When the image picker appears on screen, the user now has the option of selecting a picture or canceling. If they cancel, `imagePickerControllerDidCancel(_:)` is triggered and the image picker is dismissed.

If the user selects a picture, `imagePickerController(_:didFinishPickingMediaWithInfo:)` is triggered. This will either be the picture the user took using the camera or the picture the user picked from the photo library.

The `generate()` function will be used to create a large and a small image, which will be assigned to the `PhotoFilterViewController` image and thumbnail properties, respectively, and the image picker will be dismissed.

For example, let's assume an image has a width of 1,024, a height of 768, and the ratio is 102. The size will be assigned as `(1024,768)`. Since `size.width` is greater than `size.height`, `offset.x` is `(768-1024)/2 = -128` and `croppedSize` is `(768,768)`. `clippedRect` is assigned a `CGRect` `(128,0,768.768)`, while `imgRef` is image clipped to `clippedRect`. `rect` is assigned `(0,0,102,102)`. A new image context is opened and `imgRef` is drawn in `rect`. The result, an image with a width and height of 102, is then obtained from the image context and returned.

Next, you'll implement the `filterSelected(item:)` method specified by the `ImageFilteringDelegate` protocol. Add the following extension after the `UIImagePickerControllerDelegate` extension:

```
extension PhotoFilterViewController: ImageFiltering,
    ImageFilteringDelegate {
    func filterSelected(item: FilterItem) {
        let filteredImg = image
        if let img = filteredImg {
            if item.filter != "None" {
                imgExample.image = self.apply(filter:
item.filter,
                                    originalImage: img)
            } else {
                imgExample.image = img
            }
```

```
                    }
                 }
              }
```

This makes `PhotoFilterViewController` adopt the `ImageFiltering` and `ImageFilteringDelegate` protocols. Remember that any class that adopts `ImageFiltering` will be able to execute the `apply(filter:originalImage:)` method. `filterSelected(item:)` applies the filter the user selected for the image stored in the `PhotoFilterViewController` image property, and the result is assigned to the `imgExample` outlet so that it is visible on the screen.

You still need to know which filter the user picked, so you need to implement a method that identifies which cell in the collection view was tapped. Add the following extension after the `ImageFiltering` extension:

```
extension PhotoFilterViewController: UICollectionViewDelegate {
    func collectionView(_ collectionView: UICollectionView,
      \ didSelectItemAt indexPath: IndexPath) {
        let item = self.data[indexPath.row]
        filterSelected(item: item)
    }
}
```

This method is called whenever the user taps a cell in the collection view. The `FilterItem` corresponding to the cell that was tapped is then passed to `filterSelected(item:)`.

 You can learn more about `UICollectionViewDelegate` at `https:/ /developer.apple.com/documentation/uikit/ uicollectionviewdelegate`.

Remember that you have to ask for permission to use the camera or to access the photo library. You'll need to modify the `Info.plist` file in your app so that messages will be displayed to the user when your app attempts to access the camera or photo library.

Getting permission to use the camera or photo library

As we mentioned earlier, Apple stipulates that your app must inform the user if it wishes to access the camera or photo library. If you don't do this, your app will be rejected and will not be allowed on the app store.

> To learn more about requesting permission to use the camera, go to `https://developer.apple.com/documentation/avfoundation/ cameras_and_media_capture/requesting_authorization_for_ media_capture_on_ios`.

Follow these steps:

1. Click `Info.plist` in the Project navigator to display a list of keys. Move your mouse pointer over any existing key and click the **+** button, as follows:

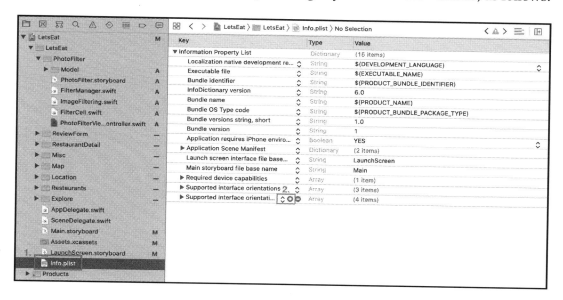

2. A field should appear, allowing you to enter an additional key, as follows:

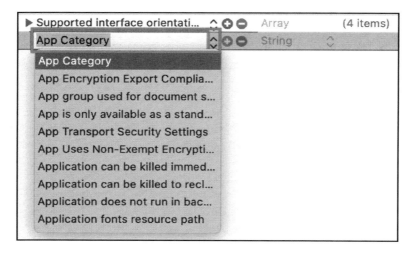

3. Enter the following keys:

```
NSPhotoLibraryUsageDescription
NSCameraUsageDescription
```

4. For each key's value, enter a string that explains to the user why you wish to use the camera or photo library, as shown in the following screenshot:

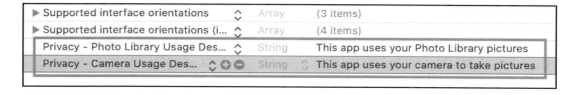

5. Build and run the project. Go to the **Restaurant Detail** screen and tap the **Add Photo** button. You should see the following alert:

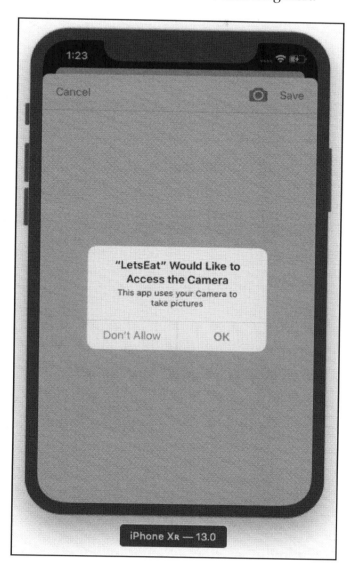

6. Tap **OK**. The image picker will appear, as follows:

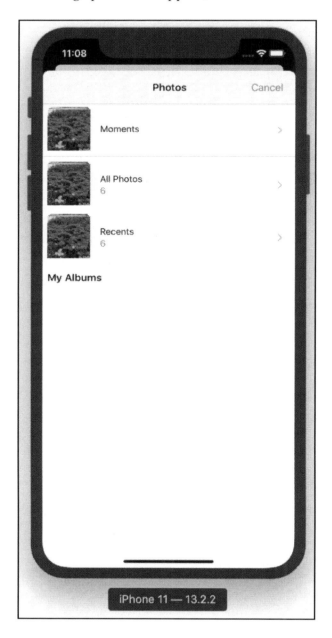

7. Select a picture. You will see the following output:

8. Tapping any filter in the collection view will apply its effect to the main picture. You can use the **Cancel** button to dismiss the **Photo Filter** screen and return to the **Restaurant Detail** screen. However, note that you can't use the **Save** button yet; you'll implement its functionality in the next two chapters.

The implementation of the **Photo Filter** screen is now complete. Awesome!

Summary

In this chapter, you completed the implementation of the **Photo Filter** screen.

You imported `FilterData.plist`, a `.plist` file containing the filters you want to use, and created `FilterManager`, a data manager, to read the `.plist` file and populate an array of `FilterItem` objects. You created a protocol, `ImageFiltering`, with a method to apply filters to images.

Then, you created `FilterCell` and `PhotoFilterViewController` in order to manage the collection view cells and the **Photo Filter** screen, and implemented the image picker delegate protocol, which allows you to get pictures from the camera or photo library. Finally, you added code to `PhotoFilterViewController` to apply a selected filter to a picture. Now, the user can tap the **Camera** button in the **Photo Filter** screen, select a photo and apply a filter to it.

Now, you know how to apply filters to photos, as well as how to import photos from your camera or photo library for use in your app.

Note that the selected picture cannot be saved. You will learn how to save reviews and pictures using Core Data in the next two chapters so that they will reappear after you quit and relaunch the app.

21
Understanding Core Data

Your app is almost complete at this point. Every screen works as shown in the app tour. However, there is one last thing that you need to do. In Chapter 19, *Getting Started with Custom UIControls*, you implemented a **Review Form** screen, which lets the user enter a review about a particular restaurant. In the previous chapter, you implemented a **Photo Filter** screen, which lets the user select pictures from the photo library and add filters to them. But, there is no way at present to save either reviews or photos.

In this chapter, you will use **Core Data** to save reviews and photos in your app. First, you'll learn about Core Data and its different components. Next, you'll create a data model for reviews and restaurant photos and create corresponding model objects for your app. After that, you'll set up Core Data components for your app. Finally, you'll create a data manager class that acts as the interface between Core Data and the rest of your app.

By the end of this chapter, you'll understand how Core Data works. You'll also be able to set up Core Data components for your own apps, and enable an interface between your app and Core Data components using a data manager class.

The following topics will be covered:

- Introducing Core Data
- Implementing Core Data components for your app
- Implementing a data manager for reviews and photos

Technical requirements

You will continue working on the LetsEat project that you modified in the previous chapter.

The completed Xcode project for this chapter is in the Chapter21 folder of the code bundle for this book, which can be downloaded here:

https://github.com/PacktPublishing/iOS-13-Programming-for-Beginners.

Let's start by learning about the components of Core Data and how it works.

Check out the following video to see the code in action:

http://bit.ly/2tzOuV6

Introducing Core Data

Core Data is Apple's mechanism for saving app data to your device. It provides persistence, undo/redo, background tasks, view synchronization, versioning, and migration. You can define your data types and relationships using Core Data's data model editor, and Core Data will generate class definitions automatically. Core Data can then create and manage object instances based on the class definitions.

 You can learn more about Core Data at https://developer.apple.com/documentation/coredata

Core Data provides a set of classes collectively known as the Core Data stack to manage and persist object instances, which are as follows:

- NSManagedObjectModel
  Describes your app's types, including their properties and relationships.
- NSManagedObject
  A class used to implement instances of your app's objects based on data from the NSManagedObjectModel.
- NSManagedObjectContext
  Tracks changes to instances of your app's types.

- NSPersistentStoreCoordinator
  Saves and fetches instances of your app's types from stores.
- NSPersistentContainer
  Sets up the model, context, and store coordinator simultaneously.

 You can learn more about the Core Data stack at `https://developer.apple.com/documentation/coredata/core_data_stack`

In the next section, you'll implement Core Data components so that your app is able to save reviews or photos.

Implementing Core Data components for your app

Before you implement Core Data components for your app, let's think about what you need to do to save reviews or photos.

Imagine you're saving a review or photo using Microsoft Word. You first create a new Word document template with the relevant fields for a review or photo. You then create new Word documents based on the templates and fill in the data. You make whatever changes are necessary, perhaps changing the text of the review, or changing the effect you're applying to the photo. At this point, you have not saved the file yet. When you are happy with your document, you save it to the hard disk of your computer. The next time you want to view your review or photo, you search your hard disk for the relevant document and double-click it to open it in Word so you can see it once more.

Now that you have an idea of what you need to do, let's review the steps required to implement it. First, you need to create a data model for a review or photo. You do this by creating **entities** in Xcode's data model editor, which are like Microsoft Word templates. Entities can have **attributes**, which are like fields in the Microsoft Word templates.

Xcode can then create an NSManagedObjectModel from this data model. Core Data will then use this NSManagedObjectModel to create NSManagedObject instances, similar to Microsoft Word templates being used to create Microsoft Word files.

These NSManagedObject instances are placed in an NSManagedObjectContext, where your app has access to them. Then, when you bring up the **Review Form** screen or **Photo Filter** screen, the details of the review or the photo with the filter will be written to NSManagedObject instances, and you can modify them as much as you like, similar to Microsoft Word documents being edited in Microsoft Word.

When you're done with the review or photo, the NSManagedObject instances in the NSManagedObjectContext are saved to a file in your iOS device, called the **persistent store**. This is similar to saving Word documents to your hard disk when you're done with them.

The NSPersistentStoreCoordinator manages the flow of information between the persistent store and the NSManagedObjectContext.

Prior to iOS 10, you had to create each object manually, but now you just use NSPersistentContainer to simplify the creation of NSManagedObjectModel, NSManagedObjectContext, and NSPersistentStoreCoordinator.

> You can learn more about how to set up the Core Data stack at https://developer.apple.com/documentation/coredata/setting_up_a_core_data_stack

Now, let's create entities and attributes to represent a review or photo using Xcode's data model editor in the next section.

Creating a data model

Currently, when you tap **Save** in the **Review Form** screen, the data you entered in the fields is just printed to the Debug area, and tapping **Save** in the **Photo Filter** screen doesn't do anything. The first step is to create objects to store data from the **Review Form** screen and the photo from the **Photo Filter** screen. You'll create entities for reviews and photos using Xcode's data model editor. Let's create the entity for reviews now:

1. Right-click the Misc folder in the Project navigator and create a **New Group**. Name this group Core Data.
2. Right-click the Core Data group and choose **New File**.
3. **iOS** should already be selected. Type data in the filter field, and select **Data Model**. Click **Next**:

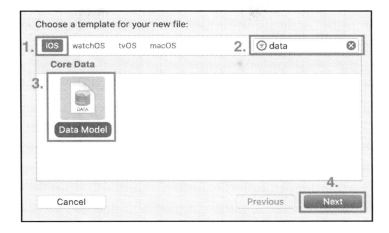

4. Name the file `LetsEatModel` and click **Create**. The data model editor appears in the Editing area:

5. Click the **Add Entity** button:

6. An **Entity** appears under the **ENTITIES** section. The **Attributes, Relationships,** and **Fetched Properties** appear to the right of the entity:

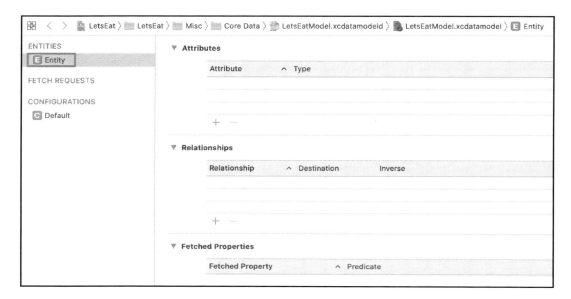

7. Click the **Entity** and rename it `Review`:

8. Click the **+** button in the **Attributes** section to create an attribute. Set the **Attribute** to `name` and the **Type** to `String`:

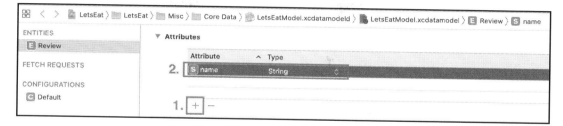

9. Add the following attributes and types:

Attribute	Type
customerReview	String
date	Date
rating	Float
restaurantID	Integer 32
title	String

10. Your Review entity's attributes should look like this when done:

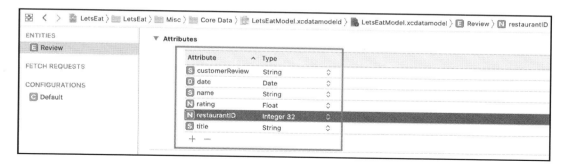

11. Add one more attribute, uuid, of type String. Click the Data Model inspector, and under **Attribute**, untick **Optional**:

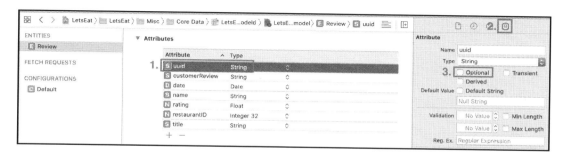

12. Add a second entity, called `RestaurantPhoto`, with the following attributes:

Attribute	Type
date	Date
photo	Binary Data
restaurantID	Integer 32
uuid	String

For `uuid`, uncheck **Optional** in the Data Model inspector:

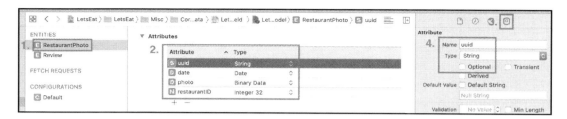

Core Data can't store `UIImage` objects, so the `photo` attribute's type is set to **Binary Data**. You will convert photos to binary data so that Core Data can store them, and convert them back to `UIImage` objects when you need them.

Note, however, that images can be large and quickly fill up the device's storage, and you're just doing it this way for learning purposes.

Build your app. Class files for the `Review` and `RestaurantPhoto` entities will be automatically created by Xcode, but will not be visible in the Project navigator. To make them easier to work with, you will create a model object for each entity, starting with `ReviewItem` in the next section.

Creating ReviewItem

You have created two entities to store reviews and photo data. After you have created the two entities, Xcode will automatically generate two `NSManagedObject` objects from the `NSManagedObjectModel`, `Review` and `RestaurantPhoto`, but you can't see them in the Project navigator.

You will create model objects, `ReviewItem` and `RestaurantPhotoItem`, that will work hand-in-hand with the `NSManagedObject` objects. Let's create `ReviewItem` now:

1. Right-click the `Model` inside the `ReviewForm` folder and select **New File**.
2. **iOS** should already be selected. Choose **Swift File** and then click **Next**.
3. Name this file `ReviewItem`. Click **Create**.
4. Modify the file as shown:

```swift
import UIKit
struct ReviewItem {
    var rating:Float?
    var name:String?
    var title:String?
    var customerReview:String?
    var date:Date?
    var restaurantID:Int?
    var uuid = UUID().uuidString

    var displayDate:String{
        let formatter = DateFormatter()
        formatter.dateFormat = "MMMM dd, yyyy"
        guard let reviewDate = date else { return ""}
        return formatter.string(from: reviewDate as Date)
    }
}

extension ReviewItem {
    init(data:Review) {
        if let reviewDate = data.date {
        self.date = reviewDate}
        self.customerReview = data.customerReview
        self.name = data.name
        self.title = data.title
        self.restaurantID = Int(data.restaurantID)
        self.rating = data.rating
        if let uuid = data.uuid { self.uuid = uuid }
    }
}
```

As you can see, the `ReviewItem` structure's properties are the same as the `Review` entity's attributes. The initializer creates a `ReviewItem` instance and maps the attributes from `Review` to the properties of the `ReviewItem` instance.

ReviewItem does have one additional property, displayDate. This is a computed property that formats the date as a string containing the month, day, and year.

 You can learn more about DateFormatter at https://developer. apple.com/documentation/foundation/dateformatter

Now, let's create a second model object, RestaurantPhotoItem, which will be the model object for the RestaurantPhoto entity, in the next section.

Creating RestaurantPhotoItem

The process for creating RestaurantPhotoItem is similar to creating ReviewItem, and you will do so now. Perform the following steps:

1. Right-click the LetsEat folder and choose **New Group**. Name the group PhotoReviews.
2. Right-click the PhotoReviews folder and select **New File**.
3. **iOS** should already be selected. Choose **Swift File** and then click **Next**.
4. Name this file RestaurantPhotoItem. Click **Create**.
5. Modify the file as shown:

```
import UIKit

struct RestaurantPhotoItem {
    var photo:UIImage?
    var date:Date?
    var restaurantID:Int?
    var uuid = UUID().uuidString
    var photoData:NSData {
        guard let image = photo else {
            return NSData()
        }
        return NSData(data: image.pngData()!)
    }
}

extension RestaurantPhotoItem {
    init(data:RestaurantPhoto) {
        self.restaurantID = Int(data.restaurantID)
        if let restaurantPhoto = data.photo {
            self.photo = UIImage(data:restaurantPhoto,
```

```
                        scale:1.0)}
      if let uuid = data.uuid { self.uuid = uuid }
      if let reviewDate = data.date { self.date =
                        reviewDate }
   }
}
```

Similar to ReviewItem, the properties of the RestaurantPhotoItem structure are the same as the RestaurantPhoto entity's attributes. There is one additional computed property, photoData, which is used to store the representation of photo in binary data format.

The initializer creates a RestaurantPhotoItem instance and maps the attributes from the RestaurantPhoto entity to properties in RestaurantPhotoItem instance. Note the conversion from binary data to UIImage when setting the value for photo.

Now that you have ReviewItem and RestaurantPhotoItem, let's set up the Core Data manager, which will be used to set up the Core Data components.

Creating a Core Data manager

You have created the Core Data entities required to save reviews and photos, and you have created the corresponding model objects. Now, you will create a CoreDataManager class that will set up the Core Data components for your app. Perform the following steps:

1. Right-click the Core Data folder inside the Misc folder and choose **New File**.
2. **iOS** should already be selected. Choose Cocoa Touch Class and then click **Next**.
3. Configure the file as follows:

   - **Class**: CoreDataManager
   - **Subclass**: NSObject
   - **Also create XIB**: Greyed out
   - **Language**: Swift
   - Then, click **Next**

4. Click **Create**. `CoreDataManager.swift` appears in the Project navigator.

5. Add the following code after the `import` statement:

```
import CoreData
```

This gives you access to the Core Data library.

6. Add the following code between the curly braces after the class declaration:

```
let container:NSPersistentContainer

override init() {
    container = NSPersistentContainer(name: "LetsEatModel")
    container.loadPersistentStores { (storeDesc, error) in
        guard error == nil else {
            print(error?.localizedDescription as Any)
            return
        }
    }
    super.init()
}
```

This creates and initializes `NSManagedObjectModel`, `NSPersistentStoreCoordinator`, and `NSManagedObjectContext`.

7. Add the following code after the initializer:

```
func addReview(_ item:ReviewItem) {
    let review = Review(context: container.viewContext)
    review.name = item.name
    review.title = item.title
    review.date = Date()
    if let rating = item.rating { review.rating = rating }
    review.customerReview = item.customerReview
    review.uuid = item.uuid

    if let id = item.restaurantID {
        review.restaurantID = Int32(id)
        print("restaurant id \(id)")
        save()
    }
}
```

This method takes a `ReviewItem` instance as a parameter and gets an empty `Review` object from the context. The properties of the `ReviewItem` instance are assigned to the attributes of `Review` object, and the `save()` method is called to save the context to the persistent store. Note that you will see an error as you have not yet implemented the `save()` method.

8. Add the following code after the `addReview(_:)` method:

```
func addPhoto(_ item:RestaurantPhotoItem) {
    let photo = RestaurantPhoto(context:
                container.viewContext)
    photo.date = Date()
    photo.photo = item.photoData as Data
    photo.uuid = item.uuid

    if let id = item.restaurantID {
        photo.restaurantID = Int32(id)
        print("restaurant id \(id)")
        save()
    }
}
```

This method is similar to `addReview(_:)`. It takes a `RestaurantPhotoItem` as a parameter and gets an empty `RestaurantPhoto` NSManagedObject from the context. The properties of `RestaurantPhotoItem` are assigned to the properties of `RestaurantPhoto`, and the `save()` method is called to save the context to the persistent store. Note that you will see an error as you have not yet implemented the `save()` method.

Later, when you want to retrieve reviews and photos from Core Data, you will use `restaurantID` as a unique identifier to get reviews and photos for a particular restaurant. Let's implement this now.

9. Add the following code after the `addPhoto(_:)` method:

```
func fetchReviews(by identifier:Int) -> [ReviewItem] {
    let moc = container.viewContext
    let request:NSFetchRequest<Review> = Review.fetchRequest()
    let predicate = NSPredicate(format:
                "restaurantID = %i", Int32(identifier))
    var items:[ReviewItem] = []
    request.sortDescriptors = [NSSortDescriptor(key:
                "date", ascending: false)]
```

```
            request.predicate = predicate
            do {
                for data in try moc.fetch(request) {
                    items.append(ReviewItem(data:data))
                }
                return items
            } catch {
                fatalError("Failed to fetch reviews: (error)")
            }
        }

    func fetchPhotos(by identifier:Int) -> [RestaurantPhotoItem] {
        let moc = container.viewContext
        let request:NSFetchRequest<RestaurantPhoto> =
            RestaurantPhoto.fetchRequest()
        let predicate = NSPredicate(format:
                        "restaurantID = %i", Int32(identifier))
        var items:[RestaurantPhotoItem] = []
        request.sortDescriptors = [NSSortDescriptor(key:
                                "date", ascending: false)]
        request.predicate = predicate
        do {
            for data in try moc.fetch(request) {
                items.append(RestaurantPhotoItem(data:data))
            }
            return items
        } catch {
            fatalError("Failed to fetch photos: (error)")
        }
    }
```

Let's break this down, starting with `fetchReview(by:)`:

- `let moc = container.viewContext`
  This gets a reference to `NSManagedObjectContext`.
- `let request:NSFetchRequest<Review> = Review.fetchRequest()`
  This creates a **fetch request** that gets `Review NSManagedObjects` from the persistent store.
- `let predicate = NSPredicate(format: "restaurantID = %i", Int32(identifier))`
  This creates a **fetch predicate** that only gets those `Review` objects with the specified `restaurantID`.
- `var items:[ReviewItem] = []`
  This creates an array, `items`, that you will use to store the results of the fetch request.

- `request.sortDescriptors = [NSSortDescriptor(key: "date", ascending: false)]`
  This sorts the results of the fetch request by date, with the most recent items first:

- `request.predicate = predicate`
  This sets the predicate for the fetch request:

- ```
  do {
  for data in try moc.fetch(request) {
  items.append(ReviewItem(data:data))
  }
  return items
  } catch {
  fatalError("Failed to fetch reviews: (error)")
  }
  ```
  This `do-catch` block performs the fetch request and places the results in the `items` array. If unsuccessful, an error returned.

`fetchPhotos(by:)` works the same way as `fetchReview(by:)`, but returns an array of `RestaurantPhotoItems` instead.

10. Implement the `save()` method by adding the following code before the final curly brace:

```
fileprivate func save() {
    do {
        if container.viewContext.hasChanges {
            try container.viewContext.save()
        }
    }
    catch let error {
        print(error.localizedDescription)
    }
}
```

This `do-catch` block saves the contents of `NSManagedObjectContext` to the persistent store. If the save was not successful, an error message is printed in the Debug area.

You've created a `CoreDataManager` class that adds data to and retrieves data from the persistent store. Now, you'll add another data manager class that will manage the data flow between `CoreDataManager` and the rest of your app. This is similar to the way `ExploreDataManager` manages the data flow between `ExploreData.plist` and the rest of your app. You will do this in the next section.
```

Creating ReviewDataManager

You have created the Core Data entities required to save reviews and photos, the corresponding model objects for those entities, and a `CoreDataManager` class that will set up the Core Data components for your app.

Now, you will create a `ReviewDataManager` class to interface between Core Data and the rest of your app. This is similar to the way `ExploreDataManager` acts as an interface between `ExploreData.plist` and the rest of your app. Perform the following steps:

1. Right-click the `Misc` folder and choose **New File**.
2. **iOS** should already be selected. Choose **Cocoa Touch Class** and then click **Next**.
3. Configure the file as follows:

   - **Class**: `ReviewDataManager`
   - **Subclass**: `NSObject`
   - **Also create XIB**: Unchecked
   - **Language**: `Swift`
   - Then, click **Next**

4. Click **Create**. `ReviewDataManager.swift` appears in the Project navigator.
5. Modify the file as shown:

```swift
import UIKit

class ReviewDataManager: NSObject {

    private var reviewItems:[ReviewItem] = []
    private var photoItems:[RestaurantPhotoItem] = []
    let manager = CoreDataManager()

    func fetchReview(by restaurantID:Int) {
        if reviewItems.count > 0 {
            reviewItems.removeAll()
        }
        for data in manager.fetchReviews(by: restaurantID) {
            reviewItems.append(data)
        }
    }
```

```
func fetchPhoto(by restaurantID:Int) {
    if photoItems.count > 0 {
        photoItems.removeAll()
    }
    for data in manager.fetchPhotos(by: restaurantID) {
        photoItems.append(data)
    }
}

func numberOfReviews() -> Int {
    return reviewItems.count
}

func numberOfPhotos() -> Int {
    return photoItems.count
}

func reviewItem(at index:IndexPath) -> ReviewItem {
    return reviewItems[index.item]
}

func photoItem(at index:IndexPath) -> RestaurantPhotoItem
{
        return photoItems[index.item]
    }
}
```

As you can see, this class is similar to the other **data manager** classes that you have created so far:

- fetchReview(by:) uses Core Data to fetch reviews for a particular restaurant, and stores them in the reviewItems array.
- fetchPhoto(by:) uses Core Data to fetch photos for a particular restaurant, and stores them in the photoItems array.
- numberOfReviews() returns the number of items in the reviewItems array.
- numberOfPhotos() returns the number of items in the photoItems array.
- reviewItem(at:) returns a ReviewItem at a specified index in the reviewItems array.
- photoItem(at:) returns a RestaurantPhotoItem at a specified index in the photoItems array.

Build and run your app to test for errors. It should work the same way as it did before.

You've implemented all the components of Core Data in your app. You'll configure `RestaurantDetailViewController` to use Core Data to display reviews and photos in the **Restaurant Detail** screen in the next chapter.

Summary

In this chapter, you learned about Core Data and its different components.

You created data models for your app named `Review` and `RestaurantPhoto`, and you created the corresponding model objects for your app named `ReviewItem` and `RestaurantPhotoItem`. After that, you implemented `CoreDataManager` to set up Core Data components for your app.

Finally, you created `ReviewDataManager`, a data manager class that acts as the interface between Core Data and the rest of your app.

You now have a basic understanding of how Core Data works. You're also able to set up Core Data components for your own apps, and enable an interface between your app and Core Data components using a data manager class.

In the next chapter, you'll implement saving reviews entered in the **Review Form** screen, and saving photos selected in the **Photo Filter** screen. You'll also implement loading saved reviews and photos for a particular restaurant, so that they appear in the **Restaurant Detail** screen.

22
Saving and Loading from Core Data

Your app is almost done! In the previous chapter, you implemented Core Data components for your app, but you can't use the **Review Form** and **Photo Filter** screens to save reviews and photos yet. Tapping the **Save** button in the **Review Form** screen just prints the contents of the fields to the Debug area, and tapping the **Save** button in the **Photo Filter** screen doesn't do anything.

In this chapter, you will complete the implementation of the **Save** buttons, and load saved reviews and photos for display in the **Restaurant Detail** screen. A lot of the setup has already been done and, mostly, you'll be using methods you created earlier.

You'll start by learning the mechanism used to save reviews and photos for a particular restaurant using the restaurant identifier.Next, you'll modify the `RestaurantItem` class with a property to hold the restaurant identifier. After that, you'll update `ReviewFormViewController` and `PhotoFilterViewController` to save reviews and photos for a particular restaurant, and modify `RestaurantDetailViewController` to load and display reviews for a particular restaurant. You'll also calculate and display the overall rating for that restaurant.

Finally, on your own, you'll modify `RestaurantDetailViewController` to load and display photos for a particular restaurant.

By the end of this chapter, you'll have learned to save and load reviews and photos using Core Data, which you will then be able to implement in your own apps.

The following topics will be covered in this chapter:

- Understanding how saving and loading works
- Updating `ReviewFormViewController` to save reviews

- Updating `PhotoFilterViewController` to save photos
- Displaying saved reviews and photos in the **Restaurant Detail** screen
- Calculating a restaurant's overall rating

Technical requirements

You will continue working on the `LetsEat` project that you modified in the previous chapter.

The resource files and completed Xcode project for this chapter are in the `Chapter22` folder of the code bundle for this book, which can be downloaded here:

`https://github.com/PacktPublishing/iOS-13-Programming-for-Beginners`.

Let's start by learning how to use a restaurant identifier to save and load reviews and photos.

Check out the following video to see the code in action:

`http://bit.ly/2GioxvI`

Understanding how saving and loading works

Open the `Misc` folder in your project, and open the `JSON` folder. If you click on any one of the JSON files inside, you'll see that each restaurant is uniquely identified by a numeric identifier. For example, the identifier for **The Tap Trailhouse** is 145237, as shown in the screenshot below:

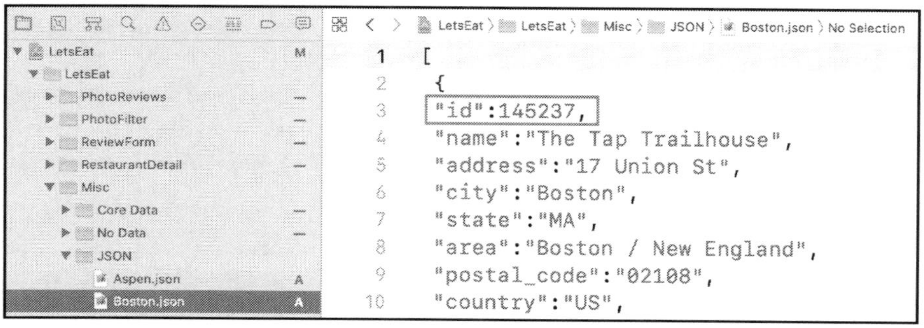

When you save photos and reviews to Core Data, you will save them together with this identifier. Then, when a particular restaurant is displayed in the **Restaurant Detail** screen, `RestaurantDetailViewController` will use the identifier to search for reviews and photos of that restaurant and display them in collection views, as shown in the screenshot:

If there are no reviews or photos, you'll use the `NoDataView` to inform the user there are no reviews or photos, as shown in the screenshot:

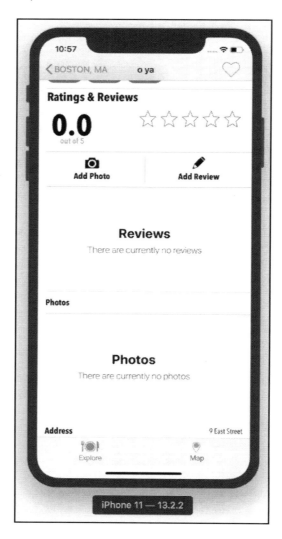

You'll need a way to store the restaurant identifier. To do so, you will modify `RestaurantItem` with an additional property to store restaurant identifiers, which can then be used to get reviews and photos for that particular restaurant.

Adding a restaurantID property to RestaurantItem

To uniquely identify reviews and photos for a particular restaurant, you need to save them with the restaurant identifier. This enables you to retrieve reviews and photos for that particular restaurant from Core Data later. You'll begin by updating `RestaurantItem` so that it can store identifiers obtained from the JSON files, which are stored inside the `JSON` folder, in the `Misc` folder. Do the following steps:

1. Open the `Model` folder inside the `Map` folder, and click `RestaurantItem.swift` in the Project navigator.

2. Add the following code after `var imageURL:String?`:

   ```
   var restaurantID:Int?
   ```

3. Inside the `CodingKeys:String` enumeration, add a new `case`, as follows:

   ```
   case restaurantID = "id"
   ```

Now, when `RestaurantDataManager` loads the JSON file and creates an array of `RestaurantItem` instances, the identifier for each restaurant will be stored in the `restaurantID` property.

Next, you'll update `ReviewFormViewController` to save a review with a restaurant identifier using Core Data.

Updating ReviewFormViewController to save reviews

The **Save** button in the **Review Form** screen currently just prints the review to the Debug area when tapped. You have updated `RestaurantItem` to store the restaurant identifier. To save reviews, you'll need to modify the `onSaveTapped(_:)` method to save a review using Core Data when the **Save** button is tapped. Do the following steps:

1. Click `ReviewFormViewController.swift`, and add the following property to `ReviewFormViewController`, above the outlets to store the restaurant identifier:

   ```
   var selectedRestaurantID:Int?
   ```

2. Create a `private` extension, move the `onSaveTapped(_:)` method into it, and modify it, as shown in the following code block:

```
private extension ReviewFormViewController {

    @IBAction func onSaveTapped(_ sender: Any) {

        var item = ReviewItem()
        item.name = tfName.text
        item.title = tfTitle.text
        item.customerReview = tvReview.text
        item.restaurantID = selectedRestaurantID
        item.rating = Float(ratingView.rating)

        let manager = CoreDataManager()
        manager.addReview(item)

        dismiss(animated: true, completion: nil)

    }
}
```

Instead of printing the review details to the Debug area, `onSaveTapped(_:)` will now create a `ReviewItem` instance, assign review data to its properties, and call `manager.addReview(item)` to save the review to the persistent store.

In the next section, you'll see how to pass a restaurant identifier to `ReviewFormViewController`.

Passing RestaurantID to ReviewFormViewController

The **Save** button in the **Review Form** screen can now save a review with a restaurant identifier, but where does `ReviewFormViewController` get that identifier from? You must pass the identifier value from `RestaurantDetailViewController` to `ReviewFormViewController` so that it can save reviews for that restaurant. Do the following steps:

1. Open `RestaurantDetail.storyboard` and select the segue used to go to the **ReviewForm** scene, as follows:

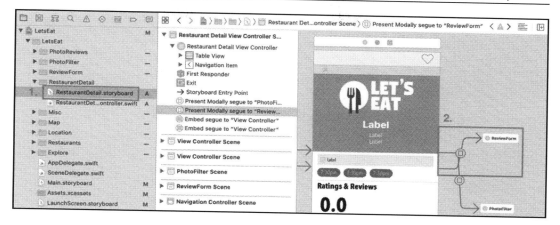

2. In the Attributes inspector, set **Identifier** under **Storyboard Segue** to
   showReview, as follows (hit *Return* when done):

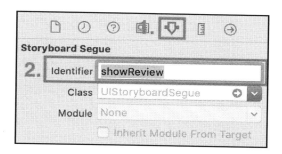

3. Click RestaurantDetailViewController.swift, and add the following
   after viewDidLoad():

```
override func prepare(for segue: UIStoryboardSegue, sender:
Any?){
    if let identifier = segue.identifier {
        switch identifier {
        case Segue.showReview.rawValue:
            showReview(segue: segue)
        default:
            print("Segue not added")
        }
    }
}
```

The `prepare(for:sender:)` method checks to see if the segue has the `showReview` segue identifier. If it does, the `showReview(segue:)` method is executed when transitioning from the **Restaurant Detail** screen to the **Review Form** screen. There will be an error because `showReview(segue:)` has not been implemented yet. You'll add that next.

4. Add the `showReview(segue:)` method inside the `private` extension, above the `createRating()` method:

```
func showReview(segue:UIStoryboardSegue) {
    guard let navController = segue.destination as?
                            UINavigationController,
        let viewController = navController.topViewController
                            as?
        ReviewFormViewController else {
          return
    }
    viewController.selectedRestaurantID =
selectedRestaurant?.restaurantID
    }
```

This sets the `restaurantID` property of `ReviewFormViewController` to the identifier of the selected restaurant.

5. Click `ReviewFormViewController.swift` in the Project navigator, and add the following code inside the `viewDidLoad()` method:

```
print(selectedRestaurantID as Any)
```

This will print the restaurant identifier to the Debug area so that you know you have successfully passed the identifier value to `ReviewFormViewController`.

6. Build and run your project, set a location, and tap **All**. Tap a restaurant, and tap the **Add Review** button. In the **Review Form** screen, enter a review and tap **Save**, as follows:

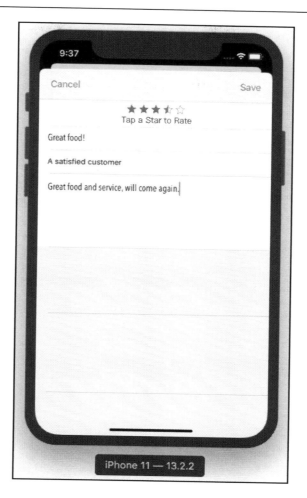

7. The restaurant identifier will appear in the Debug area, as follows:

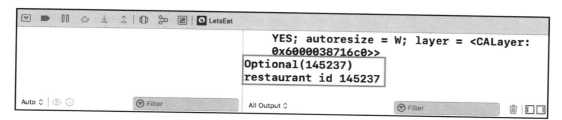

You've successfully passed the restaurant identifier from
`RestaurantDetailViewController` to `ReviewFormViewController`. Now, let's
work on saving photos. You'll update `PhotoFilterViewController` to save photos
with a restaurant identifier using Core Data when the **Save** button is tapped.

Updating PhotoFilterViewController to save photos

The code that enables `PhotoFilterViewController` to save photos is similar to the
code you implemented in `ReviewFormViewController` for saving reviews. You will
now update `PhotoFilterViewController` to save photos when the **Save** button is
tapped. Do the following steps:

1. Click `PhotoFilterViewController.swift` in the Project navigator, and
   add the following method inside the `private` extension:

   ```
   func checkSavedPhoto() {
       if let img = self.imgExample.image {
           var item = RestaurantPhotoItem()
           item.photo = generate(image: img, ratio: CGFloat(102))
           item.date = NSDate() as Date
           item.restaurantID = selectedRestaurantID
           let manager = CoreDataManager()
           manager.addPhoto(item)

           dismiss(animated: true, completion: nil)
       }
   }
   ```

   `checkSavedPhoto()` first checks to see if the `image` property of
   `imgExample` is set. If it is, a `RestaurantPhotoItem` instance with the data
   from that image will be saved to the persistent store.

2. You need to trigger this method when the **Save** button is tapped. Add the following method inside the `private` extension:

```
@IBAction func onSaveTapped(_ sender: AnyObject) {
    DispatchQueue.main.async {
        self.checkSavedPhoto()
    }
}
```

Note the use of `DispatchQueue.main.async` here. What this does is perform the `checkSavedPhoto()` operation in the background so that the user interface does not become unresponsive.

3. You need to assign this action to the **Save** button. Open `PhotoFilter.storyboard`, and click the **Photo Filter View Controller** icon in the **Photo Filter View Controller Scene.** Open the Connections inspector. Drag from the **onSaveTapped** action to the **Save** button, as follows:

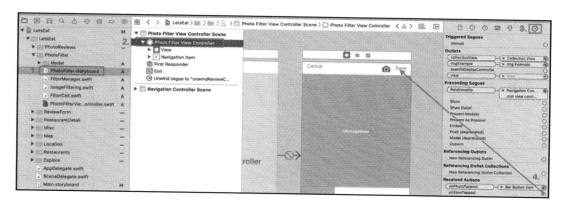

Before you can save, you need to pass the restaurant identifier to
`PhotoFilterViewController`. Do the following steps:

1. Click `RestaurantDetail.storyboard` in the Project navigator and select
   the segue used to go to the **Photo Filter** screen, as follows:

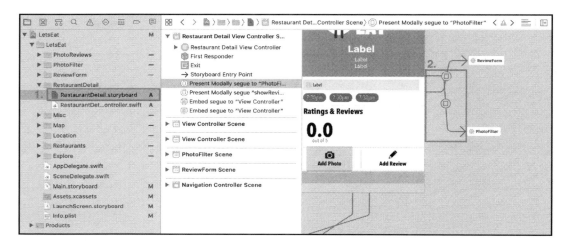

2. In the Attributes inspector, set **Identifier** under **Storyboard Segue** to
   `showPhotoFilter`, as follows (hit *Return* when done):

3. Click `RestaurantDetailViewController.swift` in the Project
   navigator.

4. Update the `prepare(for:sender:)` method, as follows:

```
override func prepare(for segue: UIStoryboardSegue, sender:
Any?){
    if let identifier = segue.identifier {
        switch identifier {
        case Segue.showReview.rawValue:
            showReview(segue: segue)
        case Segue.showPhotoFilter.rawValue:
            showPhotoFilter(segue: segue)
        default:
            print("Segue not added")
        }
    }
}
```

This makes the `prepare(for:sender:)` method check to see if the segue has the `showPhotoFilter` segue identifier. If it does, the `showPhotoFilter(segue:)` method is executed when transitioning from the **Restaurant Detail** screen to the **Photo Filter** screen. There will be an error because `showPhotoFilter(segue:)` has not been implemented yet.

5. Add the `showPhotoFilter(segue:)` method after the `showReview()` method inside your `private` extension:

```
func showPhotoFilter(segue:UIStoryboardSegue){
    guard let navController = segue.destination as?
                             UINavigationController,
        let viewController = navController.topViewController as?
        PhotoFilterViewController else {
            return
        }
    viewController.selectedRestaurantID =
    selectedRestaurant?.restaurantID
}
```

This sets the `PhotoFilterViewController`'s `restaurantID` property to the identifier of the selected restaurant.

6. Build and run your project, set a location, and tap **All**. Tap a restaurant, and tap the **Add Photo** button. Select a photo, apply a filter and tap **Save:**

The photo will be saved to the persistent storage, and you will be brought back to the **Restaurant Detail** screen.

At this point, you can save reviews and photos. Fantastic!

Next, you will add code to load the reviews and photos from the persistent store to be displayed on the **Restaurant Detail** screen. You will do this in the next section.

Displaying saved reviews and photos on the Restaurant Detail screen

The **Save** buttons inside the **Review Form** and **Photo Filter** screens now save reviews and photos with a restaurant identifier. Now, you need to configure the **Restaurant Detail** screen to display them. If you look in `RestaurantDetail.storyboard`, you'll see that collection views have already been set up to display photos and reviews in the static table view cells. All you need to do is to implement the respective view controllers for the view and collection view cells. You'll start with the view and collection view cells used to display reviews. Do the following steps:

1. Create a new folder called `Reviews` in your project.
2. Right-click the folder and select **New File**.
3. **iOS** should already be selected. Choose **Cocoa Touch Class**, and then click **Next**.
4. Configure the file as follows:

   - **Class**: `ReviewCell`
   - **Subclass**: `UICollectionViewCell`
   - **Also create XIB**: Unchecked
   - **Language**: `Swift`
   - Then, click **Next**

5. Click **Create**. `ReviewCell.swift` appears in the Project navigator. Enter the following code between the curly braces:

```
import UIKit
class ReviewCell: UICollectionViewCell {
    @IBOutlet weak var lblTitle: UILabel!
    @IBOutlet weak var lblDate: UILabel!
    @IBOutlet weak var lblName: UILabel!
    @IBOutlet weak var lblReview: UILabel!
    @IBOutlet weak var ratingView: RatingsView!
}
```

`ReviewCell` now has the properties of all the outlets in the collection view cell. Let's create `ReviewsViewController` next. Do the following steps:

1. Right-click the **Reviews** folder, and select **New File**.
2. **iOS** should already be selected. Choose **Cocoa Touch Class**, and then click **Next**.

3. Configure the file as follows:

- **Class**: ReviewsViewController
- **Subclass**: UIViewController
- **Also create XIB**: Unchecked
- **Language**: Swift
- Then, click **Next**

4. Click **Create**. ReviewsViewController.swift appears in the Project navigator. Replace everything in this file with the following code:

```swift
import UIKit

class ReviewsViewController: UIViewController {

    @IBOutlet weak var collectionView: UICollectionView!
    var selectedRestaurantID:Int?
    let manager = CoreDataManager()
    var data: [ReviewItem] = []

    override func viewDidLoad() {
        super.viewDidLoad()
        initialize()
    }

    override func viewDidAppear(_ animated: Bool) {
        super.viewDidAppear(animated)
        setupDefaults()
    }
}
```

As you can see, the implementation of ReviewsViewController is straightforward. You have an outlet for a collection view, collectionView. selectedRestaurantID stores the restaurant identifier. manager is an instance of CoreDataManager and data contains an array of ReviewItem instances. Don't worry about the errors, as you'll be typing in the implementation of the initialize() and setupDefaults() methods in the next step.

5. Add a private extension with the following code, as shown:

```swift
private extension ReviewsViewController {
    func initialize() {
        setupCollectionView()
    }
```

```
func setupDefaults() {
    checkReviews()
}

func setupCollectionView() {
    let flow = UICollectionViewFlowLayout()
    flow.sectionInset = UIEdgeInsets(top: 7, left: 7,
                           bottom: 7, right: 7)
    flow.minimumInteritemSpacing = 0
    flow.minimumLineSpacing = 7
    flow.scrollDirection = .horizontal
    collectionView?.collectionViewLayout = flow
}
}
```

The `private` extension contains the implementation for
`initialize()`, `setupDefaults()` and `setupCollectionView()`
methods. `initialize()` just calls `setupCollectionView()`.
`setupDefaults()` just calls `checkReviews()`. `setupCollectionView()`
is used to configure the flow and spacing of the collection views and is
similar to code you've written before.

6. Add the following method after `setupCollectionView()` to implement
   `checkReviews()`:

```
func checkReviews() {
    let viewController = self.parent as?
                          RestaurantDetailViewController
    if let id =
    viewController?.selectedRestaurant?.restaurantID {
        if data.count > 0 { data.removeAll() }
        data = manager.fetchReviews(by: id)
        if data.count > 0 {
            collectionView.backgroundView = nil
        } else {
            let view = NoDataView(frame: CGRect(x: 0, y: 0,
                        width: collectionView.frame.width,
                        height: collectionView.frame.height))
            view.set(title: "Reviews")
            view.set(desc: "There are currently no reviews")
            collectionView.backgroundView = view
        }
        collectionView.reloadData()
    }
}
```

This method will retrieve all restaurant reviews for the specified restaurant identifier. Let's break this down:

- `let viewController = self.parent as? RestaurantDetailViewController`
  This statement assigns `RestaurantDetailViewController` to a temporary constant, `viewController`.

- `if let id = viewController?.selectedRestaurant?.restaurantID {`
  This statement assigns the restaurant identifier of the restaurant shown in the **Restaurant Detail** screen to `id`.

- `if data.count > 0 { data.removeAll() }`
  This statement removes all items from the `data` array since you will need to populate this array with reviews for the selected restaurant only.

- `data = manager.fetchReviews(by: id)`
  This statement gets an array of reviews matching the given `id` via Core Data, and assigns it to `data`.

- ```
  if data.count > 0 {
  collectionView.backgroundView = nil
  } else {
  let view = NoDataView(frame: CGRect(x: 0, y: 0,
  width: collectionView.frame.width,
  height: collectionView.frame.height))
  view.set(title: "Reviews")
  view.set(desc: "There are currently no reviews")
  collectionView.backgroundView = view
  }
  ```
  If there are reviews for this restaurant, the collection view's background view is set to `nil`; otherwise, you create a `NoDataView` instance, set the `title` and `desc` to `Reviews` and `There are currently no reviews` respectively, and add it as a `backgroundView` for the collection view.

- `collectionView.reloadData()`
  This code tells the collection view to redraw itself.
  ```

7. Implement the data source methods for the collection view by adding the following extension:

```
extension ReviewsViewController:
    UICollectionViewDataSource {

    func collectionView(_ collectionView: UICollectionView,
        numberOfItemsInSection section: Int) -> Int {
        return data.count
    }

    func collectionView(_ collectionView: UICollectionView,
        cellForItemAt indexPath: IndexPath) ->
        UICollectionViewCell {
        let cell = collectionView.dequeueReusableCell
                    (withReuseIdentifier: "reviewCell",
                        for: indexPath) as! ReviewCell
        let item = data[indexPath.item]
        cell.lblName.text = item.name
        cell.lblTitle.text = item.title
        cell.lblReview.text = item.customerReview
        cell.lblDate.text = item.displayDate
        if let rating = item.rating {
            cell.ratingView.rating = CGFloat(rating)
        }
        return cell
    }
}
```

This is similar to what you've done before. The number of cells to be displayed in the collection view is the same as the number of items in `data`. You set each cell's contents using the properties of the corresponding `ReviewItem`.

8. Add the flow layout delegate methods for the collection view by adding the following extension:

```
extension ReviewsViewController:
UICollectionViewDelegateFlowLayout {

    func collectionView(_ collectionView: UICollectionView,
        layout collectionViewLayout: UICollectionViewLayout,
        sizeForItemAt indexPath:IndexPath) -> CGSize {
        if data.count == 1 {
            let width = collectionView.frame.size.width - 14
            return CGSize(width: width, height: 200)
        } else {
```

```
                            let width = collectionView.frame.size.width - 21
                            return CGSize(width: width, height: 200)
                    }
            }
    }
```

If there is only one item in the data array, the item's width is set to the width of the collection view—14 points, otherwise, it is set to the width of the collection view—21 points.

`ReviewsViewController` is now complete. Now, you'll finish the implementation of `RestaurantDetail.storyboard`, as follows:

1.   Click `RestaurantDetail.storyboard` in the Project navigator. Select the collection view for reviews. Click the Identity inspector, and set **Class** to `ReviewsViewController`, as shown in the following screenshot:

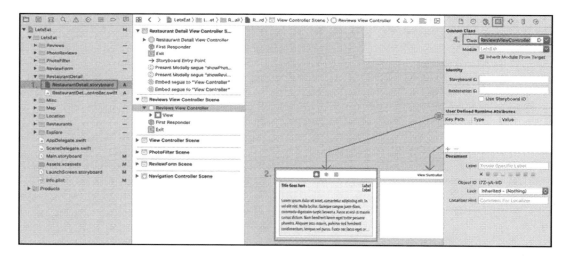

2.   Select the **Collection View Cell** in the document outline. Click the Identity inspector and set **Class** to `ReviewCell`, as shown in the following screenshot:

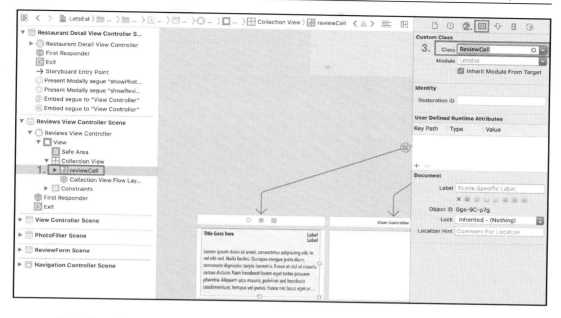

3. Select the **Rating View** in the document outline. Click the Identity inspector and set **Class** to RatingsView, as shown in the following screenshot:

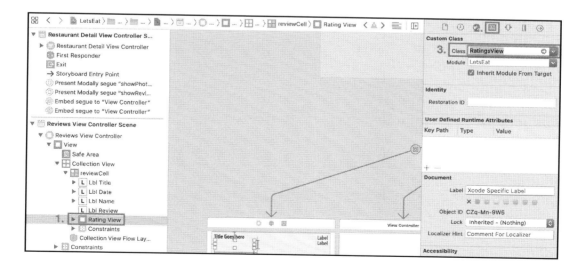

4. Select `reviewCell` in the document outline. Click the Attributes inspector. Set **Identifier** to `reviewCell` if it's not already set, as shown in the following screenshot:

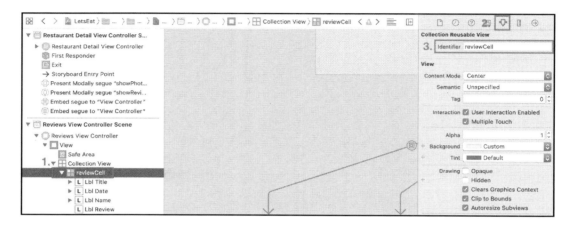

5. Click the Connections inspector. Drag from the **Lbl Date** outlet to the **Label** shown in the following screenshot, if it is not set already:

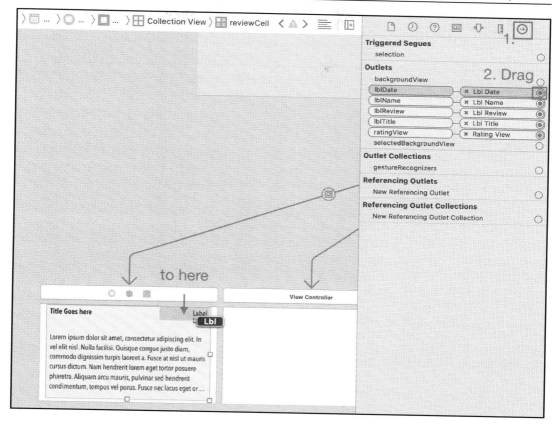

6. Drag from the **Lbl Name** outlet to the **Label** shown in the following screenshot, if it is not set already:

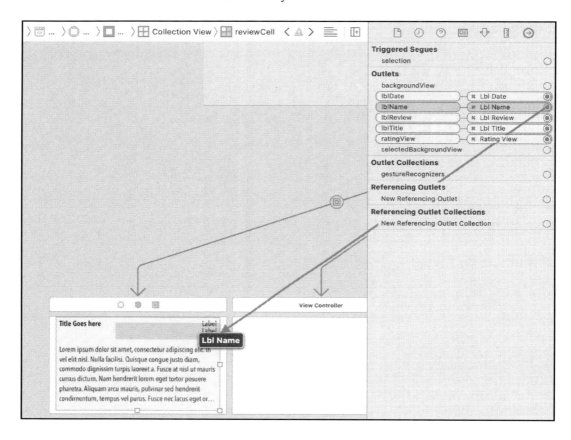

7. Drag from the **Lbl Review** outlet to the **Label** shown in the following screenshot, if it is not set already:

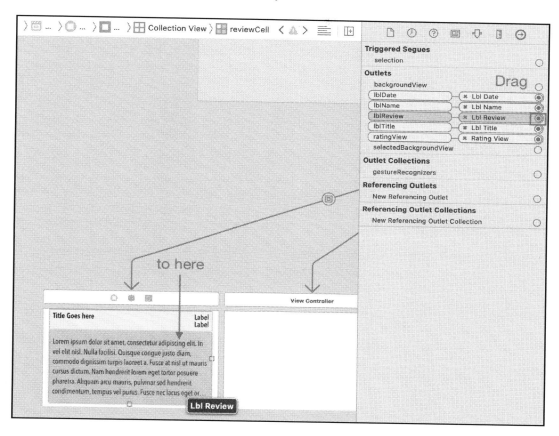

8. Drag from the **Lbl Title** outlet to the **Label** shown in the following screenshot, if it is not set already:

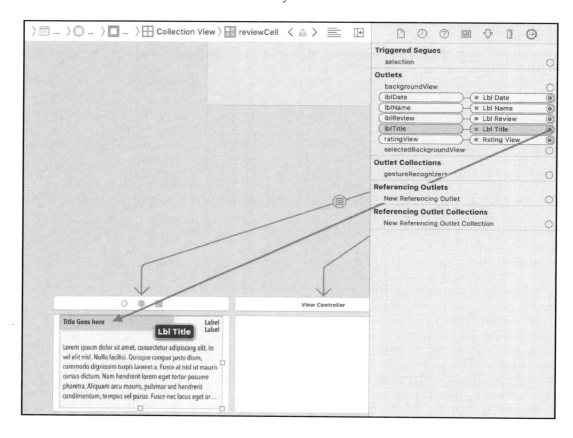

9. Drag from the **ratingView** outlet to the ratings view shown in the following screenshot, if it is not set already:

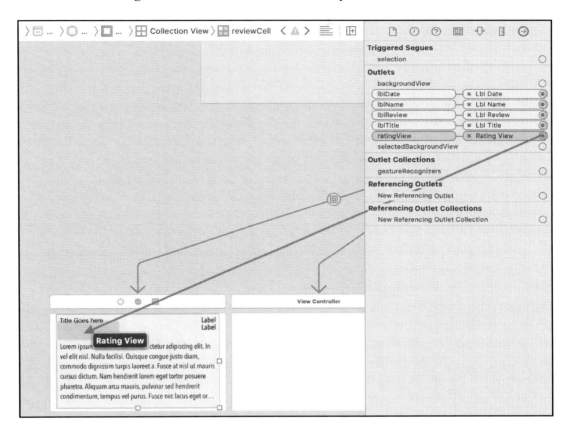

10. Select the **Reviews View Controller** icon for the **Reviews View Controller Scene** in the document outline. Drag from the **collectionView** outlet to the **Collection View**, as shown in the following screenshot, if it is not set already:

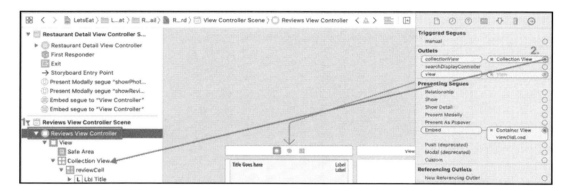

11. Select **Collection View** in the document outline. Drag from the **delegate** and **datasource** outlets to the **Reviews View Controller** icon, as shown in the following screenshot:

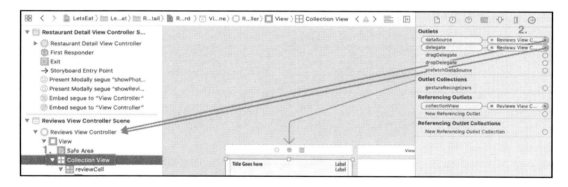

12. Build and run your app. You should see the reviews you added earlier appear:

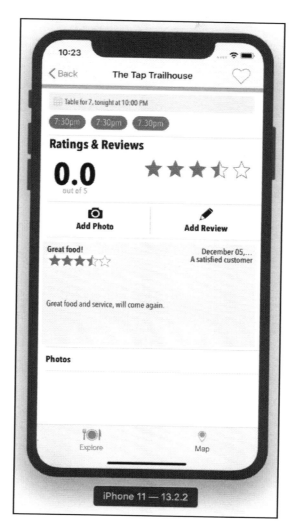

You can swipe to see each review if you have more than one review. Since each review has a rating, you can use them to calculate and add an overall rating for a restaurant. Let's modify the app to do this next.

Calculating a restaurant's overall rating

The **Restaurant Detail** screen's overall rating label displays **0.0**, and the ratings view displays 3.5 stars, regardless of the actual rating. To add an overall rating, you need to get the ratings from all the reviews and average them. Let's add a new method to `CoreDataManager` to do this. Do the following steps:

1. Click `CoreDataManager.swift` inside the Project navigator (inside the `Core Data` folder in the `Misc` folder), and add the following method before the `addReview(_:)` method:

```
func fetchRestaurantRating(by identifier:Int) -> Float {
    let reviews = fetchReviews(by: identifier).map({ $0 })
    let sum = reviews.reduce(0, {$0 + ($1.rating ?? 0)})
    return sum / Float(reviews.count)
}
```

In this method, all reviews for a particular restaurant are fetched from Core Data. The `reduce()` method takes a closure, which is used to add all the review ratings together, and calculate the average rating value.

2. Click `RestaurantDetailViewController.swift` inside the Project navigator (inside the `RestaurantDetail` folder), and add the following code under the `selectedRestaurant` property to create an instance of `CoreDataManager`:

```
let manager = CoreDataManager()
```

3. Update the `createRating()` method, as follows:

```
func createRating() {
    ratingView.isEnabled = false
    if let id = selectedRestaurant?.restaurantID {
        let value = manager.fetchRestaurantRating(by: id)
        ratingView.rating = CGFloat(value)
        if value.isNaN {
            lblOverallRating.text = "0.0"
        } else {
            let roundedValue = ((value * 10).rounded()/10)
            lblOverallRating.text = "\(roundedValue)"
        }
    }
}
```

The method first assigns the `selectedRestaurant` instance's `restaurantID` property to `id`. If successful, the `manager.fetchRestaurantRating()` method is called which gets all the reviews with `id`'s restaurant identifier value, and calculates the average rating. `value` is then set to the average rating and used to update the ratings view's `rating` property, which determines the number of stars displayed in the **Restaurant Detail** screen. `roundedValue` is then calculated from `value` to return a number with 1 decimal point, and is used to set the text property for `lblOverallRating`.

4. Build and run your project, and you should now see an overall rating for restaurants that have reviews, as well as a corresponding star rating as shown in the screenshot:

There's still one thing left to do, and that's adding photo reviews. Your challenge is to add photo reviews and to display them in the collection view just under the collection view used for reviews. The way to do this is very similar to the way you used to add reviews. This chapter covers all you need to know, and if you get stuck, feel free to use the completed project files for this chapter, which you will find in the `Chapter22` folder of the code bundle of this book downloadable from `https://github.com/PacktPublishing/iOS-13-Programming-for-Beginners`.

Summary

In this chapter, you modified `RestaurantItem` to hold the identifier of a restaurant in the `restaurantID` property.

You updated `ReviewFormViewController` and `PhotoFilterViewController` to save reviews and photos together with a restaurant identifier using Core Data.

You modified `RestaurantDetailViewController` to load reviews for a particular restaurant based on the restaurant identifier, and displayed them in a collection view. You also calculated and displayed the overall rating for that restaurant.

Finally, on your own, you modified `RestaurantDetailViewController` to load photos for a particular restaurant based on the restaurant identifier, and displayed them in a collection view.

You now know how to save and load reviews and photos using Core Data, which you will now be able to implement in your own apps.

You have come to the end of a long journey, and have now finished building your app's primary functionality. All the screens work, and reviews and photos are persistent. Fantastic job!

This concludes *Section 3* of this book. In the next part, you'll find out about the cool new features Apple will be introducing in iOS 13 and how to add them to your app, starting with Dark Mode in the next chapter.

Section 4: Features

4

Welcome to section four of this book. In this part, you will implement the latest iOS 13 features. You will make your app support Dark Mode, which gives your app a fresh and exciting UI. Next, you will modify your app, to work on both an iPhone and an iPad, and make it work on the Mac as well, using Mac Catalyst. After that, you will learn how to develop SwiftUI views, a great new way of specifying what the UI should look like. You'll modify your app to use Sign in with Apple, to further personalize the app to a user. Finally, you'll see how to test your app with internal and external testers, and, upload it into the App Store.

This part comprises the following chapters:

- Chapter 23, *Getting Started with Dark Mode*
- Chapter 24, *Getting Started with Mac Catalyst*
- Chapter 25, *Getting Started with SwiftUI*
- Chapter 26, *Getting Started with Sign In with Apple*
- Chapter 27, *Testing and Submitting Your App to the App Store*

By the end of this part, you'll be able to implement cool iOS 13 features in your own apps. You'll also be able to test and publish your own apps to the App Store. Let's get started!

23
Getting Started with Dark Mode

Welcome to *Section 4* of this book, where you will learn about the cool new features Apple introduced in iOS 13, and how to implement them in your app.

This chapter will focus on **Dark Mode**, a color scheme that works system-wide and across all native apps. Apple has made it really easy for third-party developers to integrate it into their apps. You will learn how to integrate Dark Mode into the `LetsEat` application. You'll update storyboard elements and modify your code to use adaptive colors, and learn about **SF Symbols**, a set of over 1,500 consistent, highly configurable symbols you can use in your app.

By the end of this chapter, you'll be able to update your existing apps to Dark Mode programmatically, or by choosing adaptive colors in the storyboard and take advantage of Apple's new SF Symbols set.

The following topics will be covered in this chapter:

- Turning on Dark Mode in the simulator
- Updating the **Launch** screen to work with Dark Mode
- Updating the **Explore** screen to work with Dark Mode
- Updating the **Restaurant List** screen to work with Dark Mode
- Updating the **Restaurant Detail** screen to work with Dark Mode

Technical requirements

You will continue working on the `LetsEat` project that you modified in the previous chapter.

The completed Xcode project for this chapter is in the `Chapter23` folder of the code bundle for this book, which can be downloaded here:

`https://github.com/PacktPublishing/iOS-13-Programming-for-Beginners`.

Let's start by learning about how to turn on Dark Mode in the simulator in the next section. You need to do this so that your app will use Dark Mode when it is launched.

Check out the following video to see the code in action:

`http://bit.ly/3aEqyQP`

Turning on Dark Mode in the simulator

In iOS 13.0 and later, you can configure your app to adopt a dark system-wide appearance, named Dark Mode. In Dark Mode, a darker color palette is used for all user interface elements, and colors are modified to make foreground content stand out against darker backgrounds.

 To watch a video of Apple's presentation on Dark Mode during WWDC 2019, see `https://developer.apple.com/videos/play/wwdc2019/214/`.

You have implemented all the screens and functionality required for your app in the previous parts of this book. Since you've been building the app in Xcode 11 and using iOS 13 in the Simulator, your app is already configured for Dark Mode. Let's turn it on in the Simulator. Do the following steps:

1. Build and run the app so that you can see how it looks in the default mode (Light Mode).
2. Stop the app. The Simulator reverts to the home screen. Tap the **Settings** app.
3. Tap **Developer.**
4. Turn on **Dark Appearance.**

5. Note the change in the user interface, as shown in the following screenshot:

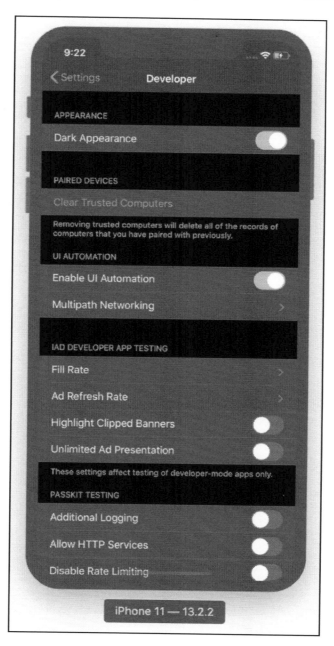

6. Build and run the app again. You'll notice that some parts look fine, but other parts don't, as shown in the following screenshot:

You'll be making changes so that everything works in Dark Mode. The first thing that you'll do is to update the **Launch** screen to make it use a different color when in Dark Mode by modifying the custom colors you made earlier. You will do this in the next section.

Updating the Launch screen to work with Dark Mode

The **Launch** screen currently looks the same in both Light Mode and Dark Mode when you run your app in the Simulator. You will update the custom color used for the **Launch** screen in `Launchscreen.storyboard`, so it looks different depending on the mode. Take the following steps:

1. Click `Assets.xcassets` in the Project navigator. Click `colors`, and click the Attributes inspector. Select `LetsEat Dark Grey`, if it is not already selected. Note that **Appearances** is set to **None**, as shown in the following screenshot:

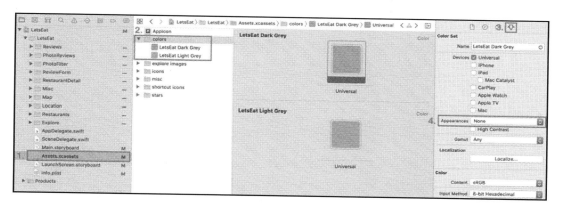

2. Set **Appearances** to **Any, Dark,** as shown in the following screenshot. Do the same for `LetsEat Light Grey`:

3. A new color appears for both `LetsEat Dark Grey` and `LetsEat Light Grey`, representing the color that will be used when Dark Mode is on. Select the **LetsEat Dark Grey Dark Appearance** color, and click the **Show Color Panel** button, as follows:

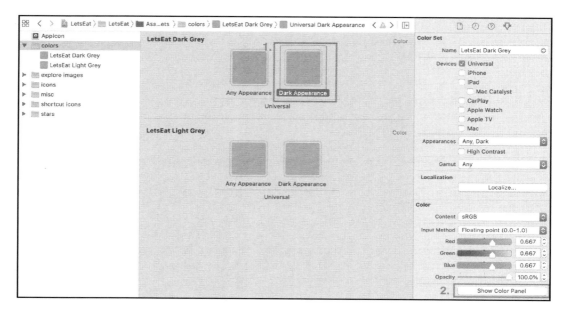

4. Click the **Sliders** tab, and choose **Grayscale Slider** from the pop-up menu. Set the value to `25%` by clicking the dark gray square, as shown in the following screenshot. Close the **Color Panel** when done:

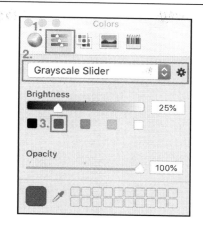

5. Select the **LetsEat Light Grey Dark Appearance** color, and click the **Show Color Panel** button.

6. Click the **Sliders** tab, and choose **Grayscale Slider** from the pop-up menu. Set the value to 100% by clicking the white square. Close the **Color Panel** when done.

7. Here's what the **Dark Appearance** colors for LetsEat Dark Grey and LetsEat Light Grey should look like:

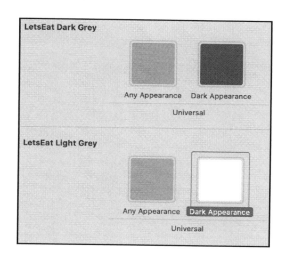

8. Click `Launchscreen.storyboard` in the Project navigator. Select **View** in the document outline and select the Attributes inspector, as follows:

9. Under **View**, set **Background** to **LetsEat Dark Grey**, as follows:

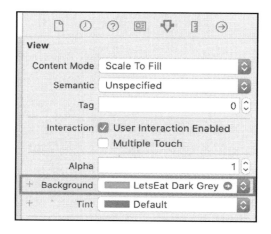

10. Turn off Dark Mode in the Simulator's **Settings** app, and build and run the app. You should see the **Launch** screen briefly.

11. Turn on Dark Mode in **Settings**, and build and run the app again, and you should see the following:

As you can see, the dark appearance colors are used in the background of the **Launch** screen automatically when Dark Mode is activated.

More information on Dark Mode colors can be found at `https://developer.apple.com/design/human-interface-guidelines/ios/visual-design/dark-mode/`
A good article about color and contrast can be found at `https://developer.apple.com/design/human-interface-guidelines/accessibility/overview/color-and-contrast/.`

Now, take a look at the **Explore** screen after your app has launched. Note that the cuisine labels in the **Explore** screen are missing. This is because the color of the labels is set to white, and is not changing automatically. You will modify the label colors for the collection view cells so that they change automatically when Dark Mode is enabled. You will do this in the next section.

Updating the Explore screen to work with Dark Mode

You have updated the **Launch** screen to make its color change when the app is launched in Dark Mode, but when the **Explore** screen appears, the cuisine names are missing, as shown in the following screenshot:

This is because the `exploreCell` label color is set to white. You will change the label color in the storyboard. Do the following steps:

1. Click `Main.storyboard` in the Project navigator. Choose **exploreCell** in the document outline and click the Attributes inspector. Note that the **Background** is **White Color**, so **exploreCell** will have a white background regardless of mode, as follows:

2. You'll need to change the color to a dynamic color, which changes automatically depending on mode. Set **Background** to **Default**, as follows:

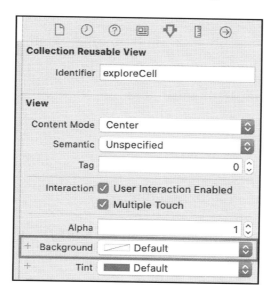

3. Build and run the app. Now, the cuisine names appear in the **Explore** Screen, as can be seen in the following screenshot:

4. Click the **Location** button. Since the table view uses default colors, it works fine in Dark Mode. Choose a location and click **Done.**

5. Tap a cuisine. When you go into the **Restaurant List** screen, note that the cell background is white, which does not suit the Dark Mode appearance, as can be seen in the following screenshot:

You'll make changes to the collection view cells in the **Restaurant List** screen to fix this in the next section. You will do this by changing the colors used by the collection view cell in the storyboard.

Updating the Restaurant List screen to work with Dark Mode

When you build and run your app in the Simulator in Dark Mode, the cell background is white in the **Restaurant List** screen. Let's fix that by modifying `restaurantCell`. Take the following steps:

1. Click `Main.storyboard` in the Project navigator. Choose **restaurantCell** in the document outline, and click the Attributes inspector. Note that the **Background** color is **White**, so **restaurantCell** will have a white background, regardless of mode, as can be seen in the following screenshot:

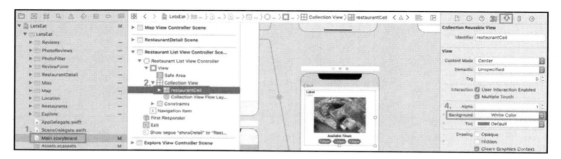

2. You'll need to change the color to a dynamic color, which changes automatically depending on mode. Set **Background** to **Default**, as follows:

3. Build and run the app. Now, the `restaurantCell` background switches color automatically when Dark Mode is on, as can be seen in the following screenshot:

4. When you tap a restaurant in the list, note that the **Restaurant Detail** screen doesn't look right, as can be seen in the following screenshot:

The first cell's color is too light, the label under it is blank, the ratings view has a white background, the buttons for the **Review Form** and **Photo Filter** screens are white with no labels, and the cells containing the reviews, photos, and map also don't look right.

In the next section, you will update the table view so that the **Restaurant Detail** screen will work properly in Dark Mode.

Updating the Restaurant Detail screen to work with Dark Mode

When you build and run your app, the **Explore**, **Locations**, and **Restaurant List** screens look fine, but when you go to the **Restaurant Detail** screen, it does not look right. You will need to modify the table view in the **Restaurant Detail** screen to make it work properly in Dark Mode. You will do this by changing the colors used by the user interface elements in the storyboard, and you will also replace the graphics with symbols from the SF Symbols library. Since the table view has multiple UI elements in each table view cell, you'll update each table view cell in turn. Do the following steps:

1. Click `RestaurantDetail.storyboard` in the Project navigator. Choose **Table View** for the **Restaurant Detail View Controller Scene** in the document outline, and click the Attributes inspector. Under the **View** section, set the **Background** to **Default**, as follows:

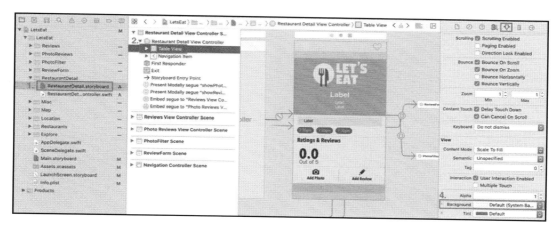

2. In the document outline, click the main **View** inside the first **Table View Cell**, as shown in the following screenshot. Set **Background** to **LetsEat Dark Grey**, as follows:

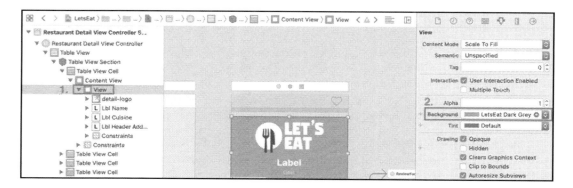

3. Build and run the app. The background of the first cell now changes automatically when in Dark Mode.

4. In the document outline, click **View** inside the second **Table View Cell**, as shown in the following screenshot. Under the **View** section, set the **Background** to **LetsEat Dark Grey**, as follows:

5. Click `RatingsView.swift` inside the `ReviewForm` folder in the Project navigator and modify the second line of the `draw(_:)` method, as shown in the following code block:

```
context!.setFillColor(UIColor.systemBackground.cgColor)
```

This will set the background color of `RatingsView` to the system's default background color.

6. Build and run the app, and note the `Label` below the restaurant details and the `RatingsView` background has been updated.

7. Click `RestaurantDetail.storyboard` in the Project navigator. Choose the first **View** in the fourth **Table View Cell** in the document outline, and click the Attributes inspector. Set the **Background** to **Default**, as follows:

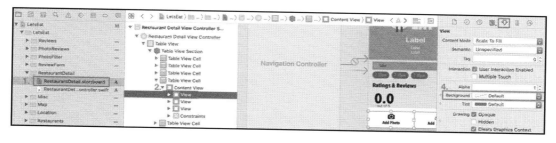

8. Choose the **View** containing the **Add Photo** button in the document outline. Set the **Background** to **Default**, as follows:

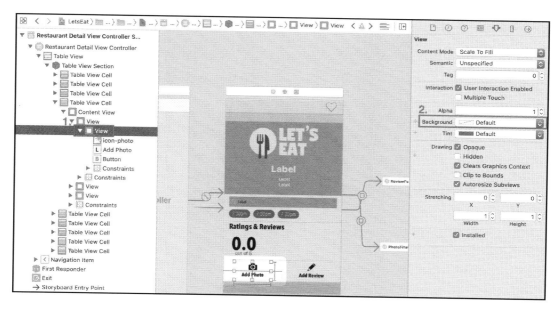

9. Click on the **Image View** in the **View**, which is currently set to **icon-photo**, as follows:

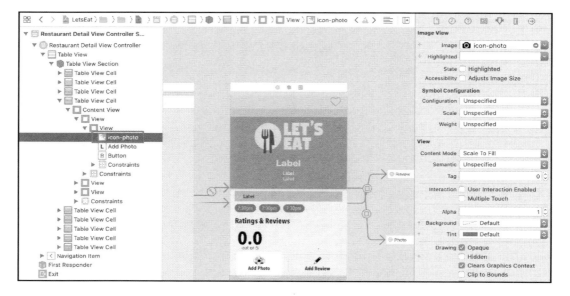

10. Set **Image** to **camera.fill**, as follows (this icon is part of Apple's new SF Symbols set, and is already configured to work in Dark Mode):

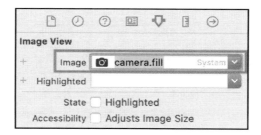

11. Build and run the app, and note that the **Add Photo** button has been updated.

12. Choose the third **View** in the fourth **Table View Cell** in the document outline. Set **Background** to **Default**, as follows:

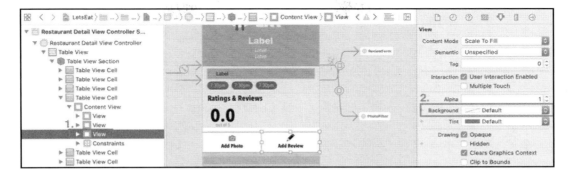

13. Choose the **View** containing the **Add Review** button in the document outline. Set **Background** to **Default**, as follows:

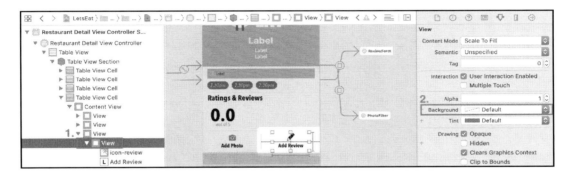

14. Click on the **Image View** in the **View**, which is currently set to **icon-review**, as follows:

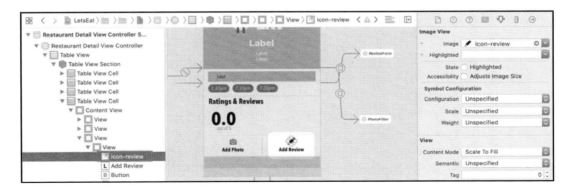

15. Set **Image** to **pencil**, as follows (this icon is also part of Apple's new SF Symbols set, and is already configured to work in Dark Mode):

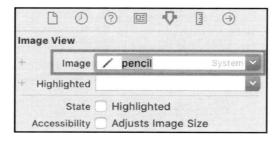

16. Build and run the app, and note the **Add Review** button has been updated.

17. Choose the **View** in the last **Table View Cell** in the document outline. Set **Background** to **Default**, as follows:

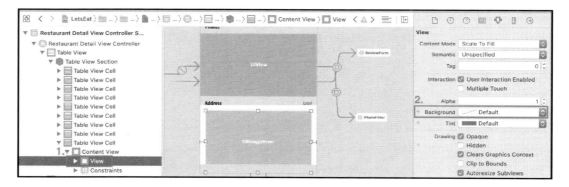

18. Build and run the app, and note the **Table View Cell** containing the map picture has been updated.

 You can learn more about SF Symbols at `https://developer.`
`apple.com/design/human-interface-guidelines/sf-symbols/`
`overview/`.

As you can see, the table view cell containing the map picture works properly in Dark Mode, but the collection views that are used to display reviews and photos do not. You'll modify them in the next section.

Updating the Reviews View Controller scene and NoDataView to work with Dark Mode

When you build and run your app and go to the **Restaurant Detail** screen, you'll see that the collection view used to display reviews is currently blank, as there are no reviews. You'll now modify the collection view to make it work properly in Dark Mode. You will do this by changing the colors used by the collection view in the storyboard. You'll also modify the NoDataView in the storyboard. Do the following steps:

1. Click RestaurantDetail.storyboard in the Project navigator. Choose the **View** for **Reviews View Controller Scene** in the document outline, and click the Attributes inspector. Set **Background** to **Default**, as follows:

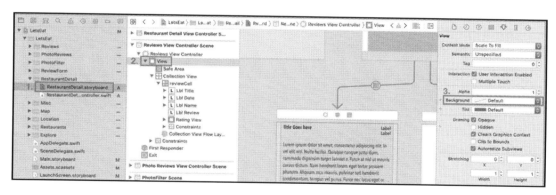

2. Choose the **Collection View** inside the **View** in the document outline, and click the Attributes inspector. Under the **View** section, set **Background** to **Default**, as follows:

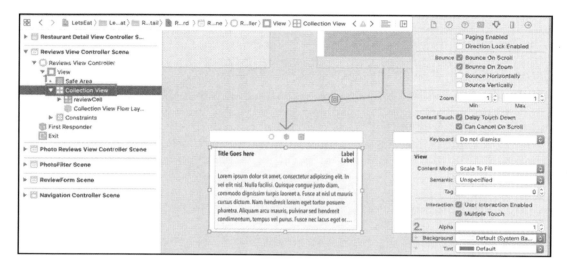

3. Choose **reviewCell** in the document outline, and click the Attributes inspector. Set **Background** to **Default**, as follows:

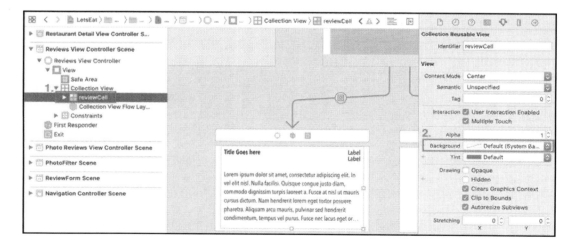

4. You'll need to modify `NoDataView` as well. Click `NoDataView.xib` in the Project navigator. Choose **View** in the document outline, and click the Attributes inspector. Set **Background** to **Default**, as follows:

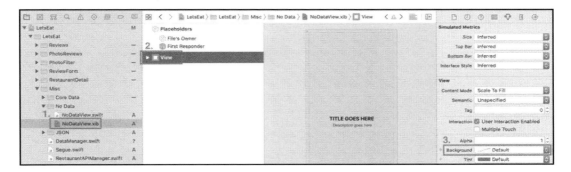

5. Build and run the app, and note that `NoDataView` is now displaying properly if there are no reviews.

You're almost done! Let's modify the collection view used to display photos to make it work properly with Dark Mode in the next section.

Updating the Photo Reviews View Controller Scene to work with Dark Mode

When you build and run your app and go to the **Restaurant Detail** screen, you'll see that the collection view used to display photos is currently blank, as there are no photos. You'll modify it in the same way you modified the collection view used to display reviews, by changing the colors used by the user interface elements in the storyboard.

Do the following steps:

1. Click `RestaurantDetail.storyboard` in the Project navigator. Choose the **View** for **Photo Reviews View Controller Scene** in the document outline, and click the Attributes inspector. Set **Background** to **Default**, as follows:

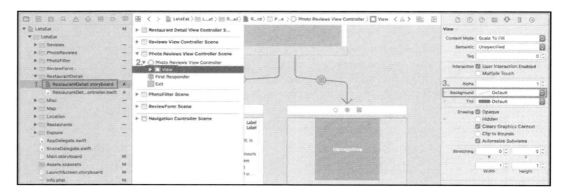

2. Choose the **Collection View** inside the **View** in the document outline. Under the **View** section, set **Background** to **Default**, as follows:

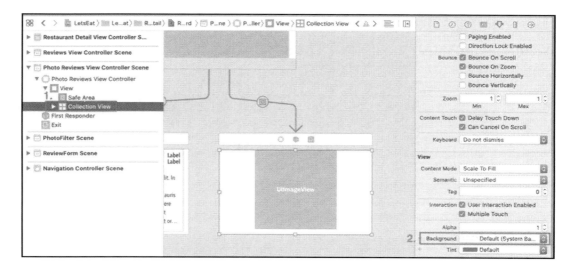

3. Build and run the app, and note that `NoDataView` is now displaying properly if there are no photos.

4. Add some reviews and photos, and the collection views should now work fine in Dark Mode as well, as can be seen in the following screenshot:

You've finished updating the **Restaurant Detail** screen to work with Dark Mode. Congratulations!

There are still two more storyboards to update, though: `ReviewForm.storyboard` and `PhotoFilter.storyboard`.

Try updating them on your own, and if you get stuck, you can refer to the completed project files downloadable from the link at `https://github.com/PacktPublishing/iOS-13-Programming-for-Beginners`.

Summary

You have successfully updated your app to use Dark Mode. In the process, you learned how to use dynamic colors in the storyboard and in code, and you also learned about the SF Symbols icons, and how to use them.

You are now able to update your existing apps to Dark Mode by choosing adaptive colors programmatically or in the storyboard and take advantage of Apple's new SF Symbols set.

In the next chapter, you'll modify your app so that it looks good on an iPad, then learn how to make your app work on a Mac, using Catalyst.

24
Getting Started with Mac Catalyst

This chapter will focus on **Mac Catalyst**, which makes it easy to build a Mac app from an existing iPad app. Your apps will share the same project and source code, so you can focus on adding Mac-specific features. By doing so, you will be able to reach an audience of over 100 million active Mac users.

In this chapter, you'll make a Mac version of the *Let's Eat* app from your existing iOS app. First, you'll refine the user interface of the app when running on the iPhone. Next, you'll learn how to make your app's user interface work on the iPad, taking advantage of the iPad's larger screen size to make it easier to use. After that, you'll use the iPad version of your app to create the Mac version.

By the end of this chapter, you'll be able to make your existing iPhone apps run well on iPad, and also be able to make Mac apps from your iPad apps.

The following topics will be covered:

- Cleaning up design elements
- Updating the app for iPad
- Updating the app for Mac

Technical requirements

You will continue working on the `LetsEat` project that you modified in the previous chapter.

The completed Xcode project for this chapter is in the `Chapter24` folder of the code bundle for this book, which can be downloaded here:

`https://github.com/PacktPublishing/iOS-13-Programming-for-Beginners`.

Let's start by making some changes to the user interface to make it look better and more closely match the design shown during the app tour.

Check out the following video to see the code in action:

`http://bit.ly/30QO4ph`

Cleaning up the design

One of the things that you will find is that an iOS app is never really done. You'll always find ways to improve and refine your app. Build and run the *Let's Eat* app, and compare it with the design shown in the app tour. You will notice upon close inspection that your app's screens have minor differences when compared to the screens shown in the app tour, and require minor changes.

Refer to the screenshot of your app's **Explore** screen shown here:

The changes required for the **Explore** screen are as follows. Refer to the numbers to see the parts that need to be changed:

- The grey navigation bar (**1**) is not present on the app tour and will need to be removed.
- The collection view cells (**2**) have sharp edges. You'll need to implement rounded corners for the cells to match the cells shown in the app tour.

- The color of the Tab Bar (**3**) is grey and the tab bar buttons are blue. You'll need to change the color of the tab bar to white, and the colors of the **Explore** and **Map** buttons on the tabs to red to match the app tour.

Now let's take a look at the **Locations** screen for your app. Again, refer to the numbers to see the parts that need to be changed:

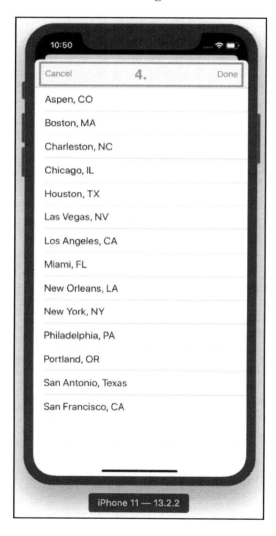

- The large title at the top of the **Locations** screen (**4**) shown in the app tour is missing, and you will need to add it.

Finally, let's modify the **Restaurant Detail** screen. As before, the number indicates the part that needs to be changed:

- For the **Restaurant Detail** screen, the icons for the **Add Photo** and **Add Review** buttons (**5**) are blue. You'll need to change the icon colors to red to match the app tour.

As you can see, there are only five minor changes that need to be made, and you'll find these changes easy to implement. You'll start by modifying the **Explore** screen. Do the following steps:

1. Click `ExploreViewController.swift` inside the `Explore` folder in the Project navigator.

2. Add a `viewWillAppear()` method after the `viewDidLoad()` method, as follows:

```
override func viewWillAppear(_ animated: Bool) {
    super.viewWillAppear(animated)
    navigationController?.setNavigationBarHidden(true,
animated: false)
}
```

This will hide the navigation controller's grey navigation bar.

3. Click `ExploreCell.swift` (inside the `View` folder in the `Explore` folder) in the Project navigator, and add the following `private` extension and the `roundedCorners()` method after the class definition:

```
private extension ExploreCell {
    func roundedCorners() {
        imgExplore.layer.cornerRadius = 9
        imgExplore.layer.masksToBounds = true
    }
}
```

This will round the corners of the collection view cells on the **Explore** screen.

4. Add a new method, `layoutSubviews()`, just after the `lblName` and `imgExplore` property declarations. Call `roundedCorners()` in `layoutSubviews()` as follows:

```
override func layoutSubviews() {
    super.layoutSubviews()
    roundedCorners()
}
```

This will execute `roundedCorners()` when the collection view is being drawn on the screen.

5. Click `AppDelegate.swift` in the Project navigator and add a `private` extension at the bottom of the file after the last curly brace:

```
private extension AppDelegate {

    func initialize() {
        setupDefaultColors()
    }

    func setupDefaultColors() {
        UITabBar.appearance().tintColor = .systemRed
        UITabBarItem.appearance().setTitleTextAttributes
            ([NSAttributedString.Key.foregroundColor:
        UIColor.systemRed],
            for: UIControl.State.selected)
        UINavigationBar.appearance().tintColor = .systemRed
        UITabBar.appearance().isTranslucent = false
    }
}
```

The `AppDelegate.swift` file contains the declaration and the definition of the `AppDelegate` class. This class handles application events, for example, what happens when an application is launched, sent to the background, terminated, and so on. You can add code here to configure your app as it is starting up. As before, you will use an `initialize()` method to call all other setup methods. The `setupDefaultColors()` method will change the tint colors for items in the tab bar and navigation bar to red, and make the tab bar not translucent.

6. You need to call `initialize()` as the app is starting up, so modify `application(_:didFinishLaunchingWithOptions:)` as follows:

```
func application(_ application: UIApplication,
    didFinishLaunchingWithOptions launchOptions:
    [UIApplication.LaunchOptionsKey: Any]?) -> Bool {
    // Override point for customization after application
launch.
    initialize()
    return true
}
```

7. Build and run the app. The **Explore** screen should look like the following screenshot:

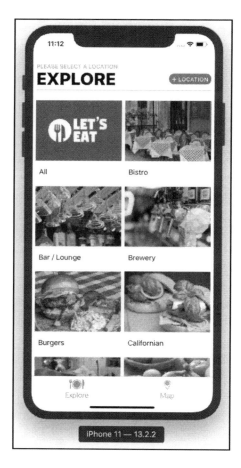

You'll see that the navigation bar is gone, the corners of each cell are rounded, and the **Explore** and **Map** buttons are now red when selected.

Next, you'll update `LocationViewController`.

8. Click `LocationViewController.swift` inside the `Location` folder in the Project navigator and modify the `initialize()` function inside the `private` extension as follows:

```
func initialize() {
    manager.fetch()
```

```
    title = "Select a location"
    navigationController?.navigationBar.prefersLargeTitles =
true
    }
```

Each view controller has a `title` property that can be displayed in the navigation bar. This sets `title` to `Select a location` and displays in large letters at the top of the screen.

9. Build and run the app, and tap the **LOCATION** button. The **Locations** screen should look like the following screenshot:

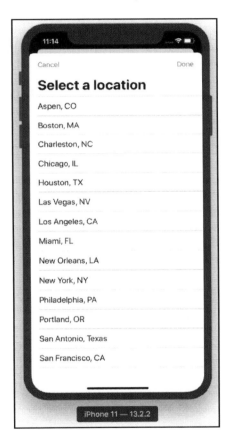

You'll see **Select a location** in large letters at the top of the screen, and the **Cancel** and **Done** buttons are now red.

Now let's fix the button colors on the **Restaurant Detail** screen. To do that, perform the following steps:

1. Click `RestaurantDetail.storyboard` inside the `RestaurantDetail` folder in the Project navigator.

2. Click the image view containing the **camera.fill** icon in the document outline. Click the Attributes inspector and under **View**, set **Tint** to **System Red Color**, as shown in the following screenshot:

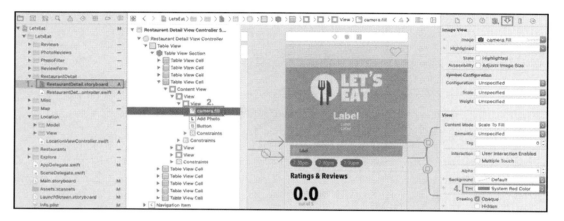

3. Do the same thing for the image view containing the **pencil** icon, as shown in the following screenshot:

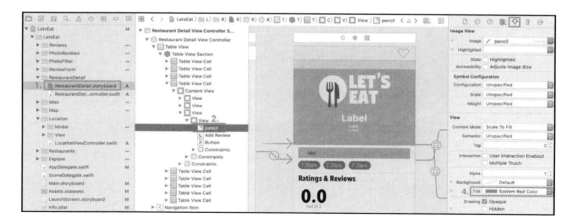

4. Build and run the app, and navigate to the **Restaurant Detail** screen, as shown in the following screenshot:

Now we can see that the **Add Review** and **Add Photo** icons are now red.

Great! You've finished cleaning up the design for the app on the iPhone. The five issues mentioned earlier have been addressed, and your app's screens now look exactly like the screen's shown in the app tour. As you can see, even minor changes can make your app more visually appealing.

So far, you've been running your app in the iPhone Simulator. In the next section, you'll run your app in the iPad Simulator to see what changes are required. You'll then modify your app so that the user interface will change based on the device it's running on, and adjust the user interface of your app to take advantage of the iPad's larger screen.

Updating the app to work on iPad

Before you can make a Mac app from your existing iOS app, you need to modify the user interface to take advantage of the iPad's larger screen. To see what changes will need to be made, you'll build and run your app on the iPad Simulator. To do that, perform the following steps:

1. Quit the Simulator if it is running. Choose **iPad Pro (9.7-inch)** from the list of Simulators, as shown, and build and run the app.
2. The iPad Simulator will launch and appear as shown in the following screenshot:

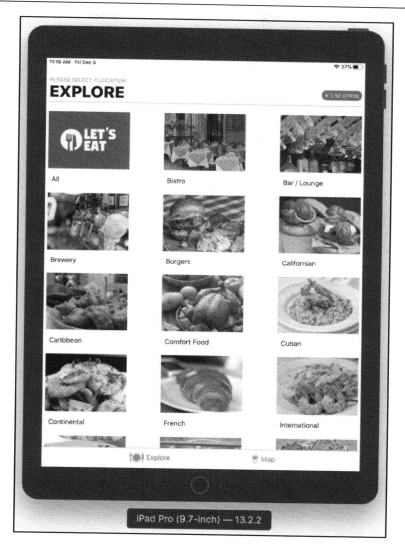

As you can see, the **Collection View** on the **Explore** screen takes up the whole width of the screen, but the spaces between the cells are a little too wide. Even though you can use exactly the same user interface for both iPhone and iPad, it would be better if you could customize it to suit each device. First, you'll add some code so your app can identify the device type. Next, you'll update your app's user interface to suit the iPad's larger screen and make your app automatically switch the user interface based on the device type.

Let's see how to make your app detect the type of device it is running on in the next section.

Checking device type

You need to add some code so your app knows the device it is running on. Perform the following steps:

1. Right-click the `Misc` folder and select **New File**.
2. **iOS** should already be selected. Choose **Swift File** and then click **Next**.
3. Name this file `Device.swift`. Click **Create**.
4. Modify the file as shown in the following code block:

```
import UIKit

struct Device {
    static var currentDevice: UIDevice {
        struct Singleton {
            static let device = UIDevice.current
        }
        return Singleton.device
    }

    static var isPhone: Bool {
        return currentDevice.userInterfaceIdiom == .phone
    }

    static var isPad: Bool {
        return currentDevice.userInterfaceIdiom == .pad
    }
}
```

Here, `UIDevice` represents the device the app is running on. Apple only provides two user interface idioms, `.phone` if the app is running on any iPhone, and `.pad` if the app is running on any iPad. So `isPhone` returns true when the app is running on the iPhone, and `isPad` returns true when the app is running on the iPad.

Now that you can tell what kind of device your app is running on, let's add some code to change the user interface depending on the device.

Updating ExploreViewController for iPad

Since you can now identify what kind of device your app is running on, let's modify `ExploreViewController` to change the way the **Explore** screen looks depending on the device. The app should display two columns on the iPhone and three columns on the iPad:

1. Click `ExploreViewController.swift` in the Project navigator and add the following property before `viewDidLoad()`:

   ```
   fileprivate let minItemSpacing: CGFloat = 7
   ```

   The `minItemSpacing` property will determine the spacing between cells.

2. Modify the `initialize()` method inside the `private` extension as follows:

   ```
   func initialize() {
       manager.fetch()
       setupCollectionView()
   }
   ```

   You'll see an error because `setupCollectionView()` is not declared or defined yet. You'll do that next.

3. Add the following just after the `initialize()` method:

   ```
   func setupCollectionView() {
       let flow = UICollectionViewFlowLayout()
       flow.sectionInset = UIEdgeInsets(top: 7, left: 7,
                           bottom: 7, right: 7)
       flow.minimumInteritemSpacing = 0
       flow.minimumLineSpacing = 7
       collectionView?.collectionViewLayout = flow
   }
   ```

   The `setupCollectionView()` method creates an instance of `UICollectionViewFlowLayout` and configures it to make sure you have seven pixels of spacing all the way around, and assigns it to the collection view.

4. Add an extension that will handle all the spacing programmatically, overriding the Storyboard settings:

```
extension ExploreViewController:
UICollectionViewDelegateFlowLayout {

    func collectionView(_ collectionView: UICollectionView,
        layout collectionViewLayout: UICollectionViewLayout,
        sizeForItemAt indexPath: IndexPath) -> CGSize {
        var factor = 0
        var delta = 0
        if Device.isPad {
            factor = 3
            delta = 50
        } else {
            factor = traitCollection.horizontalSizeClass ==
                    .compact ? 2:3
            delta = traitCollection.horizontalSizeClass ==
                    .compact ? 10:70
        }
        let screenRect = collectionView.frame.size.width
        let screenWidth = screenRect -
(CGFloat(minItemSpacing) *
                        CGFloat(factor + 1))
        let cellWidth = screenWidth / CGFloat(factor)
        let cellHeight = cellWidth - CGFloat(delta)
        return CGSize(width: cellWidth, height: cellHeight)
    }

    func collectionView(_ collectionView: UICollectionView,
        layout collectionViewLayout: UICollectionViewLayout,
        referenceSizeForHeaderInSection section: Int) ->
CGSize {
        return CGSize(width: self.collectionView.frame.width,
            height: 100)
    }
}
```

Let's break this down:

- ```
  func collectionView(_ collectionView: UICollectionView,
  layout collectionViewLayout: UICollectionViewLayout,
  sizeForItemAt indexPath: IndexPath) -> CGSize {
  ```
  This method returns a `CGSize` that the collection view cell size should be set to.

- ```
  var factor = 0
  var delta = 0
  ```
  The `factor` variable determines how many columns appear on screen and `delta` variable is used to adjust the cell height.

- ```
  if Device.isPad {
  ```
  Checks to see whether the app is running on the iPad.

- ```
  factor = 3
  delta = 50
  ```
  If the app is running on the iPad, sets `factor` to 3 and `delta` to 50.

- ```
  } else {
  factor = traitCollection.horizontalSizeClass ==
  .compact ? 2:3
  delta = traitCollection.horizontalSizeClass ==
  .compact ? 10:70
  }
  ```
  Here, `traitCollection` describes the properties, or traits, of the device the app is running on. The `horizontalSizeClass` property describes the width trait, and can be either `.compact` or `.regular`. An iPhone 11 in portrait mode has a `horizontalSizeClass` of `.compact` but when it is rotated, it has a `horizontalSizeClass` of `.regular`, so `factor` and `delta` will need to be adjusted accordingly to display two columns in portrait mode and three columns in landscape mode.

- ```
  let screenRect = collectionView.frame.size.width
  let screenWidth = screenRect - (CGFloat(minItemSpacing)
  * CGFloat(factor + 1))
  let cellWidth = screenWidth / CGFloat(factor)
  let cellHeight = cellWidth - CGFloat(delta)
  return CGSize(width: cellWidth, height: 195)
  }
  ```

- Assume you're running on iPhone in portrait mode. The factor variable is set to 2 and delta is set to 10. The screenRect would be assigned the width of the iPhone screen, which is 414 points. The screenWidth is 414 - (7 x 3) = 393. The cellWidth is screenWidth / factor = 196.5, and cellHeight is 196.5 - 10 = 186.5, so the CGSize returned would be (196.5, 186.5), enabling two cells to fit in a row.

When you rotate the iPhone to landscape mode, factor is set to 3 and delta is set to 70. The screenRect would be assigned the width of the iPhone screen, which is 896 points. The screenWidth is 896 - (7 x 4) = 868. The cellWidth is screenWidth / factor = 289.3, and cellHeight is 289.3 - 70 = 219.3, so the CGSize returned would be (289.3, 219.3), enabling three cells to fit in a row.

- func collectionView(_ collectionView: UICollectionView, layout collectionViewLayout: UICollectionViewLayout, referenceSizeForHeaderInSection section: Int) -> CGSize {
  This method returns the size the collection view section header should be set to.
- return CGSize(width: self.collectionView.frame.width, height: 100)
  The CGSize returned would be (768, 100) for the iPad and (320,100) for the iPhone.

5. Build and run the app on the iPad Simulator. You should see that the spaces between the cells are now nice and even, as shown in the following screenshot:

6. Build and run the app on the iPhone Simulator, and it should look like the following screenshot. Note that two columns are displayed:

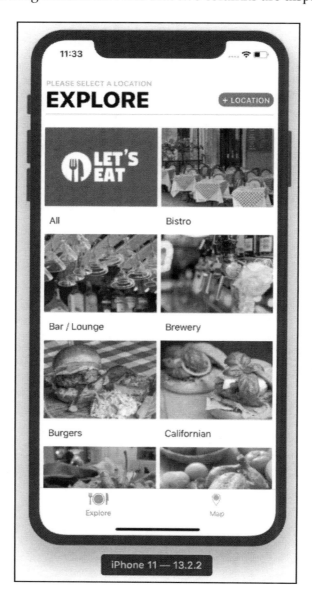

7. Choose **Hardware | Rotate Left** in the Simulator and it should look like the following screenshot. Note that three columns are displayed:

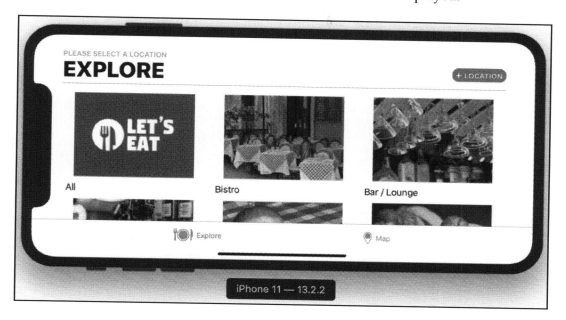

8. Choose **Hardware | Rotate Right** in the Simulator to return to a vertical orientation. Quit the Simulator.

When running on the iPhone Simulator, the **Explore** screen looks just as it did before you modified the code to make it work on the iPad. This shows the code you added to automatically detect the device the app is running on is working.

You have completed modifying `ExploreViewController`. Now, let's see how to make the **Restaurant List** screen change based on the device as well, by modifying `RestaurantListViewController` in the next section.

Updating RestaurantListViewController for iPad

You have already modified the **Explore** screen to automatically adapt to the device your app is running on. For the **Restaurant List** screen, you want a single column on the iPhone and three columns on the iPad. If you build and run on the iPad Simulator, the following screenshot shows what the **Restaurant List** screen looks like:

As you can see, there are only two columns, and there is a large white space between them. Let's fix this now. Do the following steps:

1. Click `RestaurantListViewController.swift` inside the `Restaurants` folder in the Project navigator and add the following property before `viewDidLoad()`:

   ```
   fileprivate let minItemSpacing: CGFloat = 7
   ```

   The `minItemSpacing` property will determine the spacing between cells.

2. Create an `initialize()` method inside the `private` extension before all other code already in the extension, as follows:

   ```
   func initialize() {
       createData()
       setupTitle()
       setupCollectionView()
   }
   ```

   The `createData()` and `setupTitle()` methods are both called in `viewDidAppear()`, but you'll modify `viewDidAppear()` to call `initialize()` instead later. You'll see an error because `setupCollectionView()` is not declared or defined yet.

3. Add the following inside the `private` extension after the `initialize()` method:

   ```
   func setupCollectionView() {
       let flow = UICollectionViewFlowLayout()
       flow.sectionInset = UIEdgeInsets(top: 7, left: 7,
                           bottom: 7, right: 7)
       flow.minimumInteritemSpacing = 0
       flow.minimumLineSpacing = 7
       collectionView?.collectionViewLayout = flow
   }
   ```

   Just like before, `setupCollectionView()` creates an instance of `UICollectionViewFlowLayout` and configures it to make sure you have seven pixels of spacing all the way around, and assigns it to the collection view.

4. Add a `UICollectionViewDelegateFlowLayout` extension that will handle all the spacing programmatically, overriding the Storyboard settings as follows:

```
extension RestaurantListViewController:
    UICollectionViewDelegateFlowLayout {

    func collectionView(_ collectionView: UICollectionView,
        layout collectionViewLayout: UICollectionViewLayout,
        sizeForItemAt indexPath: IndexPath) -> CGSize {
      var factor = 0
      var delta = 0
      if Device.isPad {
          factor = 3
          delta = -60
      } else {
          factor = traitCollection.horizontalSizeClass ==
                  .compact ? 1:2
          delta = 90
      }
      let screenRect = collectionView.frame.size.width
      let screenWidth = screenRect -
(CGFloat(minItemSpacing)
                          * CGFloat(factor + 1))
      let cellWidth = screenWidth / CGFloat(factor)
      let cellHeight = cellWidth - CGFloat(delta)
      return CGSize(width: cellWidth, height: cellHeight)
    }
}
```

The `collectionView(_:layout:sizeForItemAt:)`, as implemented here, works exactly the same as the implementation in `ExploreViewController`, just with different values for `factor` and `delta`.

5. Update `viewDidAppear()` by removing calls to `createData()` and `setupTitle()` and adding a call for `initialize()`:

```
override func viewDidAppear(_ animated: Bool) {
    super.viewDidAppear(animated)
    initialize()
}
```

6. Build and run the app on the iPad Simulator, as shown in the following screenshot:

7. There are three columns now, and the wide white gap is gone. Now build and run the app on the iPhone 11 Simulator. It should appear as shown in the following screenshot. Note that a single column is shown:

8. Choose **Hardware** | **Rotate Left** in the Simulator, and you should see a screen like the one shown in the following screenshot. Note that two columns are shown:

9. Choose **Hardware** | **Rotate Right** in the Simulator, and quit the Simulator.

When running on the iPhone Simulator, the **Restaurant List** screen looks just as it did in portrait orientation before you modified the code to make it work on the iPad. However, the layout changes to two columns when in landscape orientation. This shows the code you added to automatically detect the device the app is running on is working.

Now that you're done with the **Restaurant List** screen, let's modify the **Restaurant Detail** screen to work properly on both iPhone and iPad as well.

Updating the Restaurant Detail screen for iPad

You have already modified the **Explore** and **Restaurant List** screens to automatically adapt to the device your app is running on. Now you'll do the same for the **Restaurant Detail** screen. Build and run the app on the iPad Simulator, and navigate to the **Restaurant Detail** screen. You should see the screen shown in the following screenshot:

As you can see, the photos and map sections are misaligned. This isn't obvious while running on the iPhone Simulator. Let's fix this now. Perform the following steps:

1. Click `RestaurantDetail.storyboard` inside the `RestaurantDetail` folder in the Project navigator.

2. Click **Collection View** inside **Photo Reviews View Controller Scene** in the document outline. Click the **Add New Constraints** button, as shown in the following screenshot:

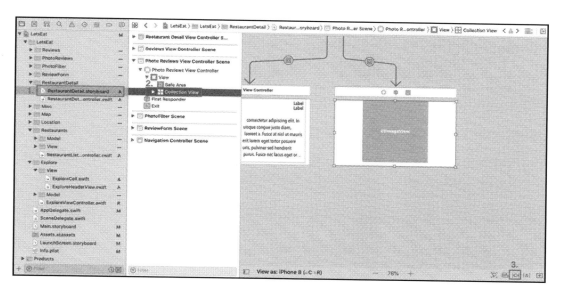

3. Add the following constraints:

- **Top**: 0
- **Left**: 0
- **Right**: 0
- **Bottom**: 0

4. Click the **Add 4 Constraints** button when done.

5. Click the **img Map** Image View inside **Restaurant Detail View Controller Scene** in the document outline. Click the **Add New Constraints** button:

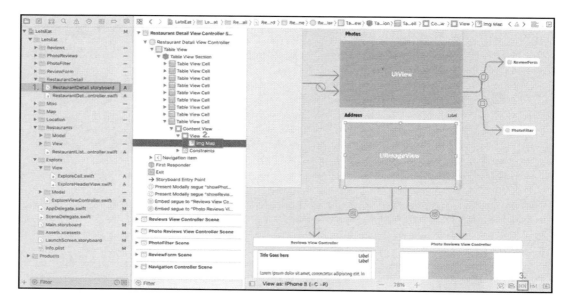

6. Add the following constraints:

   - **Top**: 0
   - **Left**: 0
   - **Right**: 0
   - **Bottom**: 0

7. Click the **Add 4 Constraints** button when done.

8. Build and run the app in the iPad Simulator, and you should see a screen like the one in the following screenshot:

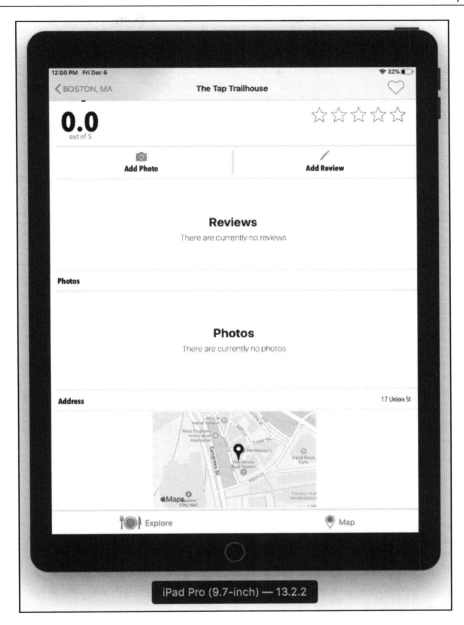

All the issues with the **Explore** screen, the **Restaurant List** screen, and the **Restaurant Detail** screen have been resolved and now the app looks good on the iPad. It's now a perfect candidate to be made into a Mac app. Let's see how you can build a Mac app from your existing iPad app in the next section.

Updating the app to work on macOS

You have modified your app's screens to work well on iPad, and you've also made your app switch its user interface based on the device it's running on. Now you'll learn how to make your app run on a Mac.

Apple announced Mac Catalyst during WWDC 2019, which makes it possible to build a Mac app from an existing iPad app and enables you to reach a whole new audience. As you will see, both your iPad and Mac apps will share the same project and source code.

 Watch the video at the following link to see the Mac Catalyst WWDC 2019 session: `https://developer.apple.com/videos/play/wwdc2019/205/`. More information about Mac Catalyst is available at `https://developer.apple.com/mac-catalyst/`.

Before you begin, note that this only works if you're using Xcode 11 and macOS 10.15 Catalina, and you'll need a free or paid Developer account. If you use the project files in the `Chapter24` folder downloaded from GitHub at `https://github.com/PacktPublishing/iOS-13-Programming-for-Beginners`, you need to set the development team by performing the following steps:

1. Select your project in the Project navigator:

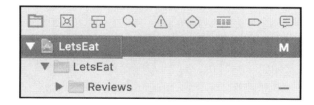

2. Tick the **Mac** checkbox and click **Enable**:

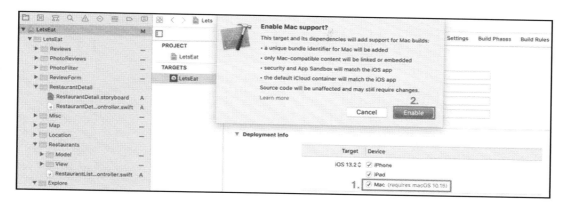

3. Note the build target has changed to your Mac. Build and run your app:

4. If your project fails to build, click the Issue navigator:

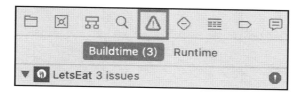

5. Check the error message. If you see the following one, it means you need to add a development team:

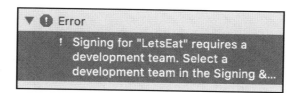

6. Check to see that your developer account has been added to Xcode in **Xcode | Preferences | Accounts.**

7. Close the **Preferences** window. Click **Signing & Capabilities**, as shown:

8. Select your paid or free developer account in the **Team** drop-down menu:

9. Build and run again, and you should see the app running on your Mac, as shown in the following screenshot:

Your app is now running on a Mac! Great!

You'll need to do some more work to make it a really nice Mac app, but that is beyond the scope of this book.

Summary

In this chapter, you learned how to build a Mac app from an existing iOS app.

We started by refining your app's user interface when running on the iPhone. Next, you added some code to make your app detect the device that it's running on, and modified your app's screens to suit the larger screen of an iPad. You also modified your code so that your app's user interface will automatically change based on the device it's running on. Finally, you used Mac Catalyst to build a Mac app from your iPad app. Your app now works great on iPhone, iPad, and Mac.

You're now able to make your existing iPhone apps run well on iPad, and also to make Mac apps from your iPad apps. As you have seen, once you have an iPhone app, you can make it work on iPad and Mac with relatively little effort.

In the next chapter, you'll learn a completely new way to build user interfaces using SwiftUI, a modern way to declare user interfaces for any Apple platform.

Getting Started with SwiftUI **25**

In previous chapters, you created the **User Interface (UI)** for the *Let's Eat* app using storyboards. The process involved dragging objects representing views to a storyboard, creating outlets in view controller files, and connecting the two together.

This chapter will focus on **SwiftUI**, an easy and innovative way to create a user interface across all Apple platforms. Instead of using storyboards, SwiftUI uses a declarative Swift syntax, and works with new Xcode design tools to keep your code and design in sync. Features such as Dynamic Type, Dark Mode, localization, and accessibility are automatically supported.

In this chapter, you will build a new version of the **Restaurant Detail** screen using SwiftUI. Since SwiftUI is very different from storyboards and is very early in its development, you will not be modifying the `LetsEat` app you have been working on. You will create a new SwiftUI Xcode project instead.

You'll start by adding and configuring text views to a screen. Next, you'll learn how to combine views using stacks. After that, you'll learn how to add an image view to the screen and configure its appearance, and learn how to use UIKit and SwiftUI views together by adding and configuring a map view to the screen. Finally, you'll create the **Restaurant Detail** screen by combining all the views you created earlier.

By the end of this chapter, you'll have learned how to use SwiftUI to create a screen containing text views, stacks, image views, and UIKit views, which you can then use for your own projects.

The following topics will be covered:

- Creating a SwiftUI Xcode project
- Working with text
- Combining views using stacks
- Working with images
- Using UIKit and SwiftUI views together
- Composing the **Restaurant Detail** screen

Technical requirements

You will create a new SwiftUI Xcode project for this chapter.

The resource files and completed Xcode project for this chapter are in the `Chapter25` folder of the code bundle for this book, which can be downloaded here:

`https://github.com/PacktPublishing/iOS-13-Programming-for-Beginners`.

Let's start by creating the new SwiftUI Xcode project, which eventually will be used to implement a **Restaurant Detail** screen in the next section.

Check out the following video to see the code in action:

`http://bit.ly/2Gfj2OD`

Creating a SwiftUI project

A SwiftUI Xcode project in created in the same way as a regular Xcode project, but with one difference: you configure it to use SwiftUI instead of storyboards. As you will see, the user interface is generated entirely in code, and you'll be able to see changes in the user interface immediately as you modify your code.

You can watch a video of Apple's SwiftUI presentation during WWDC 2019 at `https://developer.apple.com/videos/play/wwdc2019/204/`.
Apple's official SwiftUI tutorial can be found online at `https://developer.apple.com/tutorials/swiftui/tutorials`.

Let's begin by creating a new SwiftUI Xcode project. Perform the following steps:

1. Create a new Xcode project.
2. iOS should already be selected. Select the **Single View App** template, and then click **Next.**
3. Enter `LetsEatSwiftUI` as the **Product Name**, choose **SwiftUI** from the **User Interface** menu, and click **Next**:

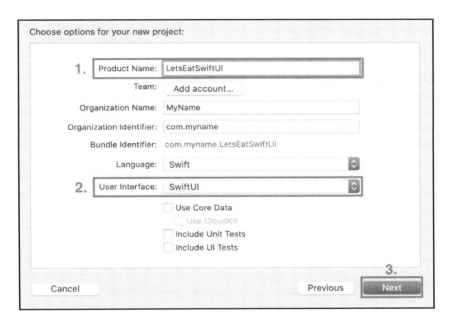

4. Choose a location to save the `LetsEatSwiftUI` project and click **Create.**

5. In the Project navigator, click `ContentView.swift`. You should see the content of the file on the left, and a preview canvas on the right. Click the **Scheme** menu:

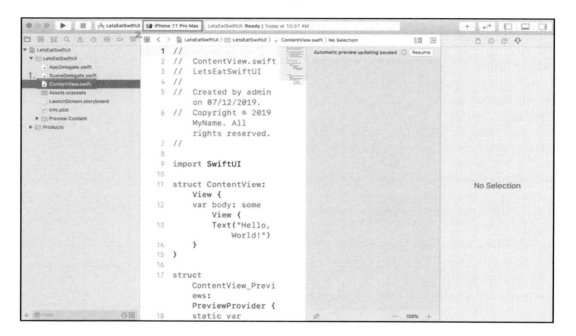

6. Choose **iPhone 11.**

7. In the **Preview** area, click the **Resume** button:

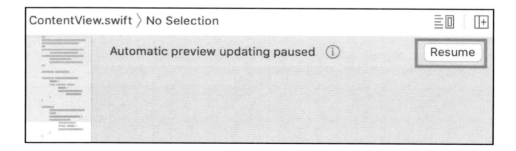

8. A preview of the user interface running on the iPhone 11 is displayed as shown in the following screenshot. If the canvas isn't visible, select **Canvas** from the **Adjust Editing Options** menu to show it. If you are using a MacBook, you can use the pinch gesture to resize the simulated image. You can also click the Navigator and Editor to hide the **Navigator** and **Editor** areas:

Now let's look at the `ContentView.swift` file. By default, SwiftUI view files declare two structures, `ContentView` and `ContentView_Previews`. `ContentView` describes the view's content and layout, and conforms to the `View` protocol. `ContentView_Previews` declares a preview for the `ContentView` that is displayed in the canvas.

9. Inside the `body` property, change the `Hello World` text to `Lets Eat` as shown:

```
struct ContentView: View {
    var body: some View {
        Text("Lets Eat")
    }
}
```

10. The preview updates to reflect your changes as shown in the following screenshot:

You have successfully created your first SwiftUI project. Now let's see how to modify text objects, properties using SwiftUI modifiers.

Working with text

When using Storyboards, you modify attributes of a view using the Attributes inspector. In SwiftUI, you can modify either your code or the preview. As you will see, changing the code in `ContentView.swift` will immediately update the preview, and modifying the preview will update the code.

Let's learn how you can modify the text view in your project. Perform the following steps:

1. In the preview, *command* + click the **Lets Eat** text on the screen. The structured editing popover will appear. Choose **Show SwiftUI Inspector...**:

2. **SwiftUI Inspector** appears on screen. Change the **Text** modifier to `The Tap Trailhouse`. This is the name of a restaurant in Boston, and can be found in the `Boston.json` file:

3. Change the **Font** modifier to **Title**:

4. The code in `ContentView.swift` will be automatically updated, as shown:

```
struct ContentView: View {
    var body: some View {
        Text("The Tap Trailhouse")
            .font(.title)
    }
}
```

Note the additional code added to the file. To customize a SwiftUI view, you call modifier methods. These are applied to a view to change its properties. As you can see here, the `.font` property is set to `.title`.

5. Modify the code as follows:

```
struct ContentView: View {
    var body: some View {
        Text("The Tap Trailhouse")
            .font(.title)
            .foregroundColor(.green)
    }
}
```

Modifiers can be chained together. The `.foregroundColor` modifier changes the text's color to green.

6. Hold *command* + click on the `Text` declaration, and choose **Show SwiftUI Inspector...**:

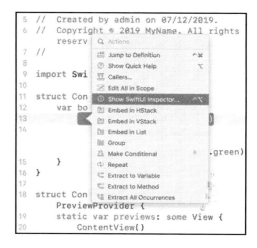

7. Note the **Color** is set to **Green**:

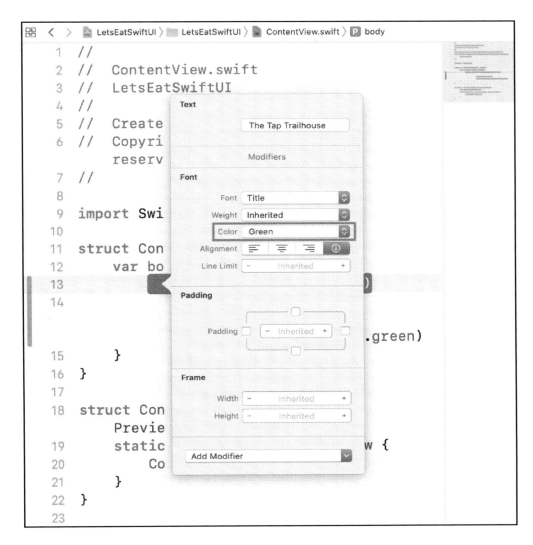

8. Change the **Color** to **Inherited.**

9. Inside `ContentView.swift`, the `.foregroundColor(.green)` modifier is automatically removed, and the code now looks like this:

```
struct ContentView: View {
    var body: some View {
        Text("The Tap Trailhouse")
            .font(.title)
    }
}
```

10. The color of the text displayed in the Preview area reverts to black as shown in the following screenshot:

Now, let's see how you can combine views using stacks to display the address and city of a restaurant together with the name. You will do this in the next section.

Combining Views using Stacks

You have added a single text view to the screen of your project. Now you'll learn how to add multiple text views and combine them. When using storyboards, you can combine multiple views by embedding them in a stack view. In SwiftUI, you combine and embed them in stacks, which are similar to stack views in storyboards. Like stack views, you can group views horizontally or vertically.

The original **Restaurant Detail** screen for the *Let's Eat* app shows the address of the restaurant, so you'll use a horizontal stack view to place the restaurant's address and city below the restaurant name. Perform the following steps:

1. *command* + click the text view's initializer to show the structured editing popover, then choose **Embed in VStack**:

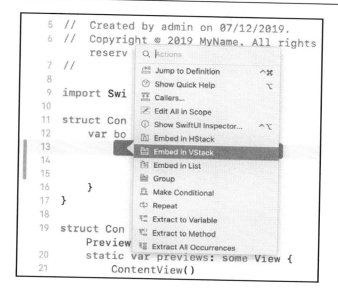

2. Note the code has been modified, and now looks like this:

```
struct ContentView: View {
    var body: some View {
        VStack {
            Text("The Tap Trailhouse")
                .font(.title)
        }
    }
}
```

3. Open the Object library by clicking the + button.
4. Type `text` in the filter field. A **Text** object appears in the results.

5. Drag the **Text** object to the place in your code immediately after the The
   Tap Trailhouse **text view:**

```
⟨ ⟩  🅻 LetsEatSwiftUI ⟩ ▦ LetsEatSwiftUI ⟩ 🅻 ContentView.swift ⟩ 🅿 body
1  //
2  //   ContentView.swift
3  //   LetsEatSwiftUI
4  //
5  //   Created by admin on 07/12/2019.
6  //   Copyright © 2019 MyName. All rights
       reserved.
7  //
8
9  import SwiftUI
10
11 struct ContentView: View {
12     var body: some View {
13         VStack {
14             Text("The Tap Trailhouse")
15                 .font(.title)
16         }
```

Q text

Control Views

Text   **Text**

Text Field

6. Your code should look like this. Note the addition of a new text view:

```
VStack {
    Text("The Tap Trailhouse")
        .font(.title)
    Text("Placeholder")
}
```

7. The Preview area should look like this:

8. Modify your code by replacing the new text view's placeholder text with 17 Union Street, which is the address of The Tap Trailhouse:

```
VStack {
    Text("The Tap Trailhouse")
        .font(.title)
    Text("17 Union St")
}
```

9. Set the address's font style to .subheadline by modifying the code as shown:

```
VStack {
    Text("The Tap Trailhouse")
        .font(.title)
    Text("17 Union St")
        .font(.subheadline)
}
```

10. Edit the VStack initializer to align the views by their leading edges as shown:

```
VStack(alignment: .leading) {
    Text("The Tap Trailhouse")
        .font(.title)
    Text("17 Union St")
        .font(.subheadline)
}
```

11. The Preview area reflects the changes:

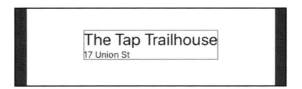

Next, you'll add another text view to the right of the location; this is for the city the restaurant is located in.

12. In the canvas, hold *command* + click on **17 Union St**, and choose **Embed in HStack**:

13. The code in `ContentView.swift` reflects the changes:

```
VStack(alignment: .leading) {
    Text("The Tap Trailhouse")
        .font(.title)
    HStack {
        Text("17 Union St")
            .font(.subheadline)
    }
}
```

14. Modify the code as shown to add a new text view after the address, change the placeholder text to `Boston`, and set its font to `.subheadline`:

```
VStack(alignment: .leading) {
    Text("The Tap Trailhouse")
    .font(.title)
    HStack {
        Text("17 Union St")
            .font(.subheadline)
        Text("Boston")
            .font(.subheadline)
    }
}
```

15. Note the Preview area shows the city next to the address:

16. Modify the code as shown by adding `Spacer()` between the restaurant's address and city. A spacer expands as required to make its containing view use all of the space of its parent view:

```
VStack(alignment: .leading) {
    Text("The Tap Trailhouse")
    .font(.title)
    HStack {
        Text("17 Union St")
        .font(.subheadline)
        Spacer()
        Text("Boston")
        .font(.subheadline)
    }
}
```

17. Note the Preview area shows the restaurant name, address, and city at the extreme edges of the screen:

18. To add space between the text views and the sides of the screen, modify the code as shown to use the `padding()` modifier method:

```
VStack(alignment: .leading) {
    Text("The Tap Trailhouse")
    .font(.title)
    HStack {
        Text("17 Union St")
        .font(.subheadline)
        Spacer()
        Text("Boston")
```

```
        .font(.subheadline)
    }
}
.padding()
```

19. The Preview area now looks like this:

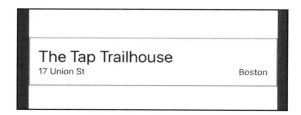

You have combined text views using vertical and horizontal stacks, and now you can see the restaurant address and city below the name. Now let's see how to add a picture of the restaurant and customize its appearance using modifiers in the next section.

Working with images

You have added the name and address of the restaurant to the screen. With the name and address views all set, the next thing you will do is add an image for the restaurant and customize its appearance. When using storyboards, you'll need to add an image to the `Assets.xcassets` file, use an image view to display the image, and use the Attribute inspector to modify its appearance. In SwiftUI, you still need to add an image to the `Assets.xcassets` file, but after that, you'll create a custom view that applies a mask, border, and drop shadow to the image. Note that this was not present in the original **Restaurant Detail** screen (restaurant images were shown in the **Restaurant List** screen), but let's do it here so you will know how it's done.

You'll start by adding an image to the project's asset catalog. Perform the following steps:

1. Find `taptrailhouse.jpg` inside the `resources` folder in the `Chapter25` folder of the code bundle downloadable from `https://github.com/PacktPublishing/iOS-13-Programming-for-Beginners`.

2. Click `Assets.xcassets` in the Project navigator. Drag `taptrailhouse.jpg` into the editor. Xcode creates a new image set for this image:

3. Now, you'll create a new SwiftUI view to display this image. Choose **File | New | File** to open the template selector.
4. iOS should already be selected. In the **User Interface** section, click to select **SwiftUI View** and click **Next**.
5. Name the file `CircleImage.swift` and click **Create**. It appears in the Project navigator.
6. Modify the code as shown to replace the text view with the image of `The Tap Trailhouse` by using the `Image(_:)` initializer:

```
struct CircleImage: View {
    var body: some View {
        Image("taptrailhouse")
    }
}
```

7. The Preview area displays the image:

8. Modify the code as shown to clip the image to a circle using the
   `.clipshape(Circle())` modifier:

```
struct CircleImage: View {
    var body: some View {
        Image("taptrailhouse")
            .clipShape(Circle())
    }
}
```

9. Modify the code as shown to overlay the image with a white border:

```
struct CircleImage: View {
    var body: some View {
        Image("taptrailhouse")
            .clipShape(Circle())
            .overlay(Circle().stroke(Color.white,
                lineWidth: 4))
    }
}
```

10. Modify the code as shown to add a shadow to the image with a 10-point
    radius:

```
struct CircleImage: View {
    var body: some View {
        Image("taptrailhouse")
        .clipshape(Circle())
        .overlay(Circle().stroke(Color.white,
            lineWidth: 4))
        .shadow(radius: 10)
    }
}
```

11. This completes the image view. The Preview area should look like this:

You've added an image to your project, and applied a custom mask, border, and drop shadow to it. Later, you will add it to your **Restaurant Detail** screen, but for now, let's see how you can use UIKit and SwiftUI views together to add a map to the **Restaurant Detail** screen. You will do this in the next section.

Using UIKit and SwiftUI Views together

At this point, you have learned how to create text views and image views for your app. Now let's see how to add a view that displays a map. When using storyboards, all you needed to do was to drag in a map view from the Object library to a view in storyboard. SwiftUI does not have a native map view but you can use the same map view that you used in storyboard to render the map. In fact, you can use any view subclass within SwiftUI by wrapping them in a SwiftUI view that conforms to the `UIViewRepresentable` protocol. You'll create a new custom view that can present a map view now. Do the following steps:

1. Choose **File** | **New** | **File** to open the template selector.
2. iOS should already be selected. In the **User Interface** section, click to select **SwiftUI View** and click **Next**.
3. Name the new file `MapView.swift` and click **Create**.
4. In `MapView.swift`, import `MapKit`, and make `MapView` conform to `UIViewRepresentable` as shown. Don't worry about the error, you'll fix that in the next few steps:

   ```
   import SwiftUI
   import MapKit

   struct MapView: UIViewRepresentable {
   ```

```
        var body: some View {
        Text("Hello World")
    }
}
```

5. You need two methods to conform to `UIViewRepresentable`, a `makeUIView(context:)` method that creates an `MKMapView` and an `updateUIView(_:context:)` method that configures it and responds to any changes.

   Modify your code as shown to replace the body property with a `makeUIView(context:)` method that creates and returns an empty `MKMapView`:

```
struct MapView: UIViewRepresentable {
    func makeUIView(context: Context) -> MKMapView {
        MKMapView(frame: .zero)
    }
}
```

6. Modify your code as shown to add an `updateUIView(_:context:)` method just below the `makeUIView(context:)` method. This sets the map view's region to center the map on `The Tap Trailhouse`. Note that this is the same method you used to make a region for the Map screen in the *Let's Eat* app:

```
func updateUIView(_ view: MKMapView, context: Context) {
    let coordinate = CLLocationCoordinate2D(
    latitude: 42.360847, longitude: -71.056819)
    let span = MKCoordinateSpan(latitudeDelta: 0.05,
                longitudeDelta: 0.05)
    let region = MKCoordinateRegion(center: coordinate,
                span: span)
    view.setRegion(region, animated: true)
}
```

7. The error is now gone, and a blank view appears in the Preview area. This is because the Preview area is in static mode and only renders SwiftUI views. You'll need to turn on live preview to see the map. Click the Live Preview button as shown:

8. You should see a map of Boston centered on **The Tap Trailhouse** in a moment:

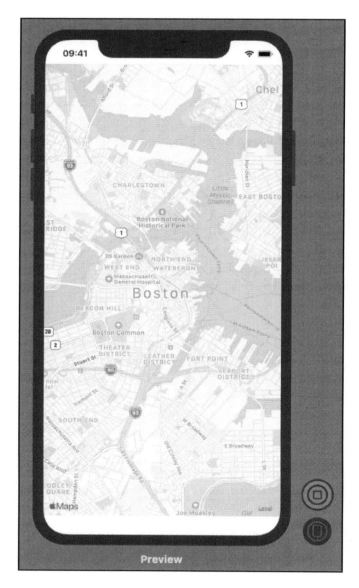

If it doesn't work, check your internet connection, and click the **Try Again** or **Resume** buttons above your preview.

You've created a map view that shows the restaurant's location. Now, let's see how to combine all the views you have created to make the complete **Restaurant Detail** screen in the next section.

Composing the Restaurant Detail screen

You now have the following SwiftUI components: a view displaying the name and location of a restaurant, a view displaying a circular image, and a view displaying a map. Now, you'll combine them to create the final design for the **Restaurant Detail** screen. Perform the following steps:

1. Click the `ContentView.swift` file in the Project navigator.

2. Modify your code as shown to embed the VStack that holds the three text views in another VStack:

```
var body: some View {
    VStack {
        VStack(alignment: .leading) {
            Text("The Tap Trailhouse")
                .font(.title)
            HStack(alignment: .top) {
                Text("17 Union St")
                    .font(.subheadline)
                Spacer()
                Text("Boston")
                    .font(.subheadline)
            }
        }
        .padding()
    }
}
```

3. Modify your code to add your custom `MapView` to the top of the stack. Set the size of the `MapView` with `frame(width:height:)` but with only height set to `300`. Since only the height parameter is specified, the view's width will automatically fill the available space:

```
var body: some View {
    VStack {
        MapView()
            .frame(height:300)
        VStack(alignment: .leading) {
            Text("The Tap Trailhouse")
                .font(.title)
```

```
                    HStack(alignment: .top) {
                        Text("17 Union St")
                            .font(.subheadline)
                        Spacer()
                        Text("Boston")
                            .font(.subheadline)
                    }
                }
                .padding()
            }
        }
```

4. The Preview area displays the map above the restaurant name and address, but does not render the map. As before, click the Live Preview button.

5. The Preview area displays the rendered map:

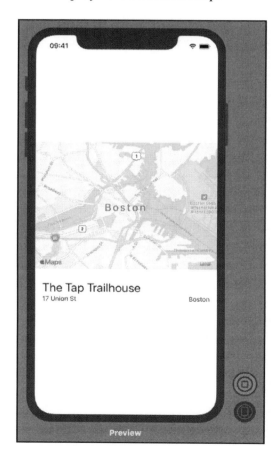

You can continue editing the view while showing a live preview.

6. Modify the code as shown to add `CircleImage` to the VStack:

```
var body: some View {
    VStack {
        MapView()
            .frame(height:300)
        CircleImage()
        VStack(alignment: .leading) {
            Text("The Tap Trailhouse")
                .font(.title)
            HStack(alignment: .top) {
                Text("17 Union St")
                    .font(.subheadline)
                Spacer()
                Text("Boston")
                    .font(.subheadline)
            }
        }
        .padding()
    }
}
```

7. The Preview area shows `CircleImage` between the map and the restaurant name and address. Modify the code as shown to place `CircleImage` on top of the map view, giving the image an offset of −130 points vertically, and a padding of −130 points from the bottom of the view:

```
CircleImage()
    .offset(y: -130)
    .padding(.bottom, - 130)
```

8. The Preview area shows the `CircleImage` partly overlapping the map
    view, with the text views under it:

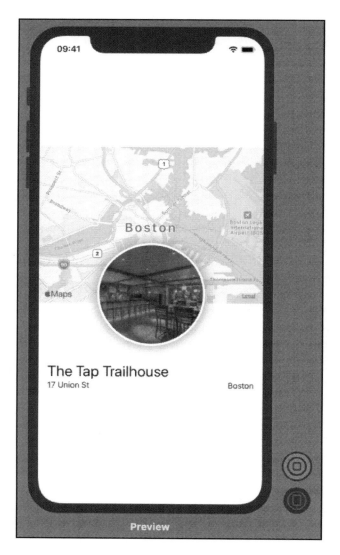

9. Modify the code as shown to add a spacer after the `.padding()` modifier
    to push the content to the top of the screen:

    ```
    .padding()
    Spacer()
    ```

10. Finally, modify the code as shown by adding the
    `edgesIgnoringSafeArea(.top)` modifier to the map view. This allows
    the map content to extend to the top edge of the screen:

```
MapView()
    .edgesIgnoringSafeArea(.top)
    .frame(height:300)
```

11. The Preview area displays the following:

12. Build and run your project in the iPhone 11 Simulator if you wish.

You've completed the implementation of the **Restaurant Detail** screen using Swift UI! Cool!

Summary

In this brief introduction to SwiftUI, you've seen how to build a **Restaurant Detail** screen using SwiftUI by compositing text, image, and map views.

You started by adding and configuring text views to a screen. Next, you combined the text views using stacks. After that, you created an image view by adding a photo to your `Assets.xcassets` file and configured it using SwiftUI. Then, you combined UIKit and SwiftUI views by adding and configuring a map view. Finally, you created the **Restaurant Detail** screen by combining all the views you created earlier.

You now know how to use SwiftUI to create a screen containing text views, stacks, image views, and UIKit views, which you can then use for your own projects.

In the next chapter, you will learn about Sign in with Apple, which allows you to uniquely identify users who use your app.

Getting Started with Sign In with Apple

26

This chapter will focus on **Sign in with Apple**, which allows the user to sign in to your app with their Apple ID. This offers you an easy way to uniquely identify your users and personalizes the app experience for each user. For example, after the user has signed in, you could show the user a list of the top five restaurants that are visited or the cuisines that are picked the most. It uses two-factor authentication to ensure security, though Apple doesn't track user activity. Note that, if you have implemented sign in using social media such as Facebook, you are required to implement Sign in with Apple for your app.

In this chapter, you will learn how to implement Sign in with Apple for your app. You'll start by adding a login screen to the `LetsEat` project you have been working on and then implement the code that's needed to display the **Sign in with Apple** button on that login screen. After that, you'll implement the delegate methods and actions that are required to make Sign in with Apple work. Finally, after the user has signed in, you'll pass the user information to `ExploreViewController` so that it can display a personalized greeting for the user in the **Explore** screen.

By the end of this chapter, you'll have learned how to implement Sign in with Apple for your own apps and will be able to personalize your apps for your users.

In this chapter, we'll cover the following topics:

- Adding a login screen
- Displaying a **Sign in with Apple** button
- Implementing delegate methods and button actions
- Passing user information to `ExploreViewController`

Technical requirements

You will continue working on the `LetsEat` project that you modified in `Chapter 24`, *Getting Started with Mac Catalyst.*

You will also need an Apple ID and a paid Apple Developer account to complete this chapter.

The completed Xcode project for this chapter is in the `Chapter26` folder of the code bundle for this book, which can be downloaded here:

`https://github.com/PacktPublishing/iOS-13-Programming-for-Beginners.`

Let's start by adding a login screen to the `LetsEat` app, which you will need later to incorporate the **Sign in with Apple** button.

Check out the following video to see the code in action:

`http://bit.ly/30MPBg5`

Adding a login screen

When you launch the `LetsEat` app, you'll immediately see the **Explore** screen. There is no way for the user to sign in. Due to this, you will need to implement a **Sign In** screen to allow the user to sign in. Initially, this **Sign In** screen will just display a button to allow the user to sign in in Guest mode, but you will add the **Sign in with Apple** button later. Follow these steps to do so:

1. Open the `LetsEat` project and build and run the app to make sure that it's working.
2. Go to **Xcode** | **Preferences** | **Accounts** and make sure that you have entered the Apple ID credentials for a paid Apple Developer account.
3. Click the `LetsEat` project in the Project navigator and click on **Signing and Capabilities**. Ensure the **Team** pop-up menu has been set for a paid Apple Developer account. If you get a **Failed to register bundle identifier** error, try changing the **Bundle Identifier** by adding some random characters to it, for example, `com.12345.myname.LetsEat`, and click the **Try Again** button:

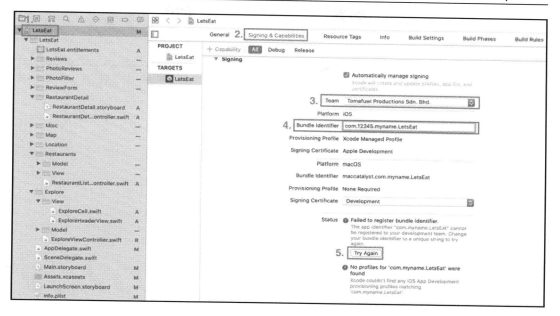

4. Click on the + button:

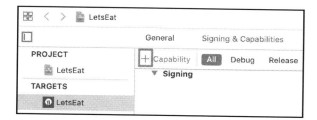

5. The Object library will appear. Type `sign` into the filter field. You should see **Sign in with Apple** in the list of results. Double-click it.

6. **Sign in with Apple** has been added to the **Signing and Capabilities** screen:

7. If you see any errors appear, fix them before continuing by clicking on the appropriate buttons:

8. Click on `Main.storyboard` in the Project navigator and click the **+** button to display the Object library:

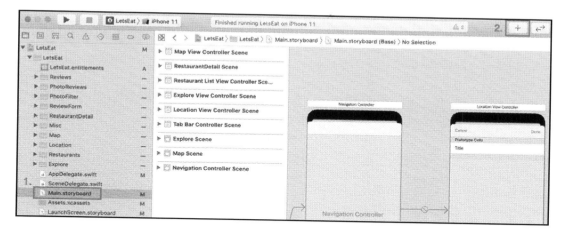

9. Type `viewcon` into the filter field. You will see a **View Controller** object as one of the results.

10. Drag it into the storyboard to the left of the **Tab Bar Controller**, as shown in the following screenshot:

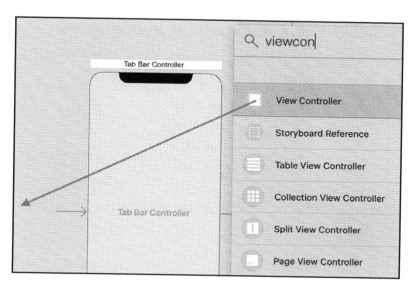

11. Move the arrow indicating the initial **View Controller** from the **Tab Bar Controller** to the newly added **View Controller**:

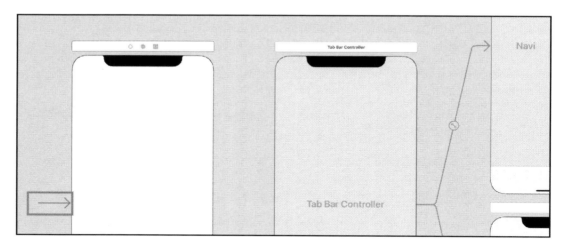

12. Click the **+** button to display the Object Library. Type button into the filter field. You will see a **Button** object as one of the results.

13. Drag it into the view of the newly added **View Controller**:

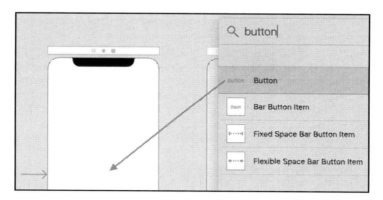

14. Change the button text to `Guest Mode`:

15. *Ctrl + Drag* from the `Guest Mode` button to the **Tab Bar Controller**. Choose `Present Modally` from the pop-up menu:

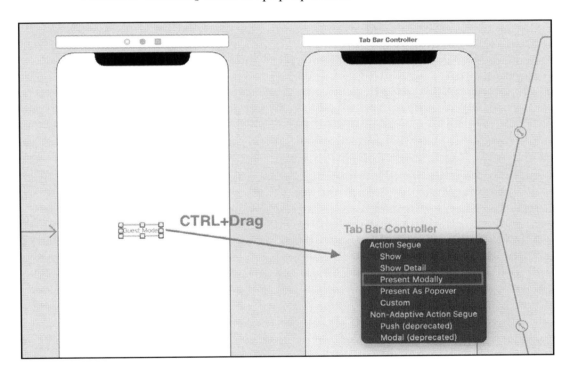

16. A segue will be created between the **View Controller** and the **Tab Bar Controller**. Click the segue to select it:

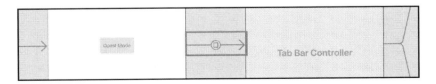

17. In the Attributes inspector, set the **Identifier** to `signin`, set **Presentation** to `Full Screen`, and set **Transition** to `Cross Dissolve`:

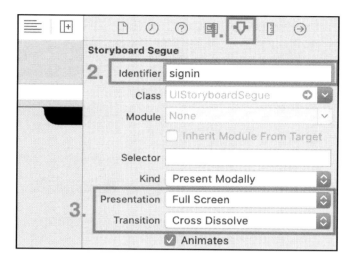

18. Select the **View** of the **View Controller** in the document outline. In the Attributes inspector, set **Background** to `Lets Eat Dark Grey`:

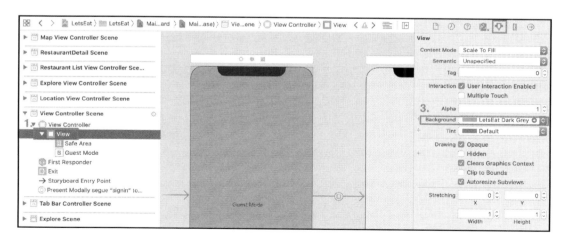

19. Select the `Guest Mode` button in the document outline. In the Attributes inspector, set the **Font** to `System Black 24.0`:

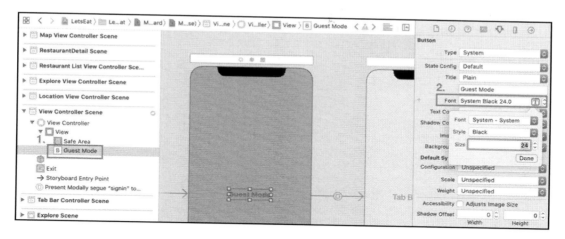

20. Set the button's **Text Color** to `System Red Color`:

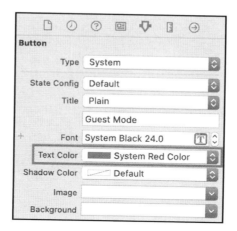

21. With the button selected, click the **Add New Constraints** button and add the following constraints:

- **Left**: 30
- **Right**: 30
- **Bottom**: 300

22. Build and run the app. Tap on the **Guest Mode** button:

23. The **Explore** screen will be displayed.

Now that you've implemented the **Sign In** screen, you have a place to display the **Sign in with Apple** button. You will implement a view controller for the **Sign In** screen with the necessary code to display the **Sign in with Apple** button in the next section.

Displaying a Sign in with Apple button

At this point, when the user launches your app, a **Sign In** screen is displayed and the user has to tap **Guest Mode** to see the **Explore** screen. In this section, you'll add a **Sign in with Apple** button to this screen. Apple has made it very easy to display the **Sign in with Apple** button, but you must do so programmatically.

 You can watch Apple's Sign in with Apple presentation at WWDC 2019 at `https://developer.apple.com/videos/play/wwdc2019/706/`.

You can learn more about implementing Sign in with Apple at `https://developer.apple.com/sign-in-with-apple/`.

In this section, you'll add some code to display the **Sign in with Apple** button on the **Sign In** screen you just added to `Main.storyboard`. Follow these steps to do so:

1. Right-click on the `Misc` folder in the Project navigator and choose **New File** from the pop-up menu.
2. **iOS** should already be selected. Choose **Cocoa Touch Class** and click **Next**.
3. Configure the options as follows:

   - **Class**: `SignInViewController`
   - **Subclass of**: `UIViewController`
   - Then, click **Next**

4. Click **Create**. The file will appear in the Project navigator.
5. The first thing you need to do is import the framework that's required for Sign in with Apple, so click `SignInViewController.swift` to select it and add the following code just after the `import` statement:

   ```
   import AuthenticationServices
   ```

   `Authentication Services` is the framework that supports Sign in with Apple.

6. Next, add the following method just after the `viewDidLoad()` method:

```
func displaySignInWithAppleButton(){
    let appleIDButton = ASAuthorizationAppleIDButton()
    appleIDButton.translatesAutoresizingMaskIntoConstraints =
false
    view.addSubview(appleIDButton)
    NSLayoutConstraint.activate([
        appleIDButton.centerXAnchor.constraint(equalTo:
view.centerXAnchor),
        appleIDButton.centerYAnchor.constraint(equalTo:
view.centerYAnchor),
        appleIDButton.widthAnchor.constraint(equalToConstant:
250)
    ])
}
```

This method creates the **Sign in with Apple** button and adds it to the view. The constraints for the button have been set so that the button will be placed in the center of the view. Note that the constraints are added programmatically instead of using the storyboard.

7. Call the `displaySignInWithAppleButton()` method inside `viewDidLoad()`, as follows:

```
override func viewDidLoad() {
    super.viewDidLoad()
    displaySignInWithAppleButton()
}
```

This calls the `displaySignInWithAppleButton()` method when the Sign in screen's view is loaded.

8. Go into `Main.storyboard`. Inside the Identity Inspector, set the **Identity** of the **View Controller Scene** you added earlier to `SignInViewController`:

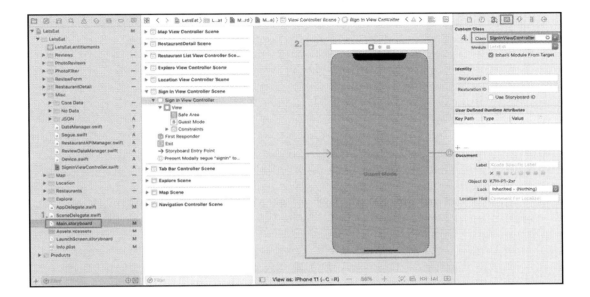

9. Build and run the app. You'll see the **Sign in with Apple** button in the middle of the screen:

At the moment, tapping this button does nothing. You'll add some code to `SignInViewController` to implement the sign in functionality with the user's Apple ID in the next section.

Implementing delegate methods and button actions

Now, your app is displaying a **Sign in with Apple** button on the screen when it is launched, but it doesn't work yet. To implement the functionality of the **Sign in with Apple** button, you'll need to make `SignInViewController` conform to the `ASAuthorizationControllerDelegate` and `ASAuthorizationControllerPresentationContextProviding` protocols.

`ASAuthorizationControllerDelegate` has two optional methods that you will implement:

- `authorizationController(controller: didCompleteWithAuthorization:)`: This will be executed if the user enters the correct Apple ID and password.
- `authorizationController(controller: didCompleteWithError:)`: This will be executed if the process was unsuccessful.

`ASAuthorizationControllerPresentationContextProviding` has a required method, `presentationAnchor(for:)`, which returns the view that will be used to display the various Sign in with Apple dialogs. To implement this, follow these steps:

1. Click on `SignInViewController.swift` in the Project navigator.
2. Add the following code after the class declaration to make `SignInViewController` conform to the `ASAuthorizationControllerDelegate` and `ASAuthorizationControllerPresentationContextProviding` protocols:

   ```
   class SignInViewController: UIViewController,
   ASAuthorizationControllerDelegate,
   ASAuthorizationControllerPresentationContextProviding {
   ```

   An error will appear; just ignore it for now.

3. Add the following code just before the final curly brace:

```
// MARK: - SignInWithApple

func authorizationController(controller:
ASAuthorizationController, didCompleteWithAuthorization
authorization: ASAuthorization) {

switch authorization.credential {

    case let credentials as ASAuthorizationAppleIDCredential:
        print(credentials.user)
        print(credentials.fullName?.givenName ?? "No given
name provided")
        print(credentials.fullName?.familyName ?? "No family
name provided")
        print(credentials.email ?? "No email provided")

    default:
        break
    }
}

func authorizationController(controller:
ASAuthorizationController, didCompleteWithError error: Error)
{
    print("AppleID Authentication failed", error)
}

func presentationAnchor(for controller:
ASAuthorizationController) -> ASPresentationAnchor {
    return view.window!
}
```

Let's break this down:

- `authorizationController(controller:didCompleteWithAuthorization:)`: This is executed when the user successfully enters their Apple ID and password and you get an `ASAuthorizationAppleIDCredential`. For now, you will just print the contents of this credential, which are as follows:
  - `user`: A unique identifier string
  - `fullName.givenName`: A string containing the user's given name

- `fullName.familyName`: A string containing the user's family name
- `email`: A string containing the user's email
  Note that with the exception of user, all these are optional, so you can provide some default strings if you don't get any values from the credential.
- `authorizationController(controller:didCompleteWithError:)`: This is executed if the process fails. For now, you'll just write an error message to the Debug area.
- `presentationAnchor(for:)`: This determines which view is used to display the various dialogs. Here, you set it to the view of **SignInViewController**.

The error should disappear at this point. Next, you need a property to store the user's given name, which will be passed to `ExploreViewController` at a later date.

4. Add the following property just after the class declaration:

    ```
    var appleIDGivenName: String?
    ```

5. Modify
    `authorizationController(controller:didCompleteWithAuthorization:)`, as follows:

    ```
    func authorizationController(controller:
    ASAuthorizationController, didCompleteWithAuthorization
    authorization: ASAuthorization) {

        switch authorization.credential {

        case let credentials as ASAuthorizationAppleIDCredential:
            print(credentials.user)
            print(credentials.fullName?.givenName ?? "No given
    name provided")
            print(credentials.fullName?.familyName ?? "No family
    name provided")
            print(credentials.email ?? "No email provided")
            appleIDGivenName = credentials.fullName?.givenName
            performSegue(withIdentifier: "signin", sender: nil)

        default:
            break
        }
    }
    ```

This sets `appleIDGivenName` to the user's given name and performs the `signin` segue.

Now, you'll implement the button action.

6. Add the following code after `displaySignInWithAppleButton()`:

```
@objc func appleIDButtonTapped() {
    let provider = ASAuthorizationAppleIDProvider()
    let request = provider.createRequest()
    request.requestedScopes = [.fullName, .email]
    let controller =
ASAuthorizationController(authorizationRequests: [request])
    controller.delegate = self
    controller.presentationContextProvider = self
    controller.performRequests()
}
```

This creates an `ASAuthorizationAppleIDProvider` request that will ask the user for their full name and email, set `SignInViewController` as the delegate and presentation context provider, and execute the request.

7. Modify `displaySignInWithAppleButton()` by assigning the button action, as follows:

```
func displaySignInWithAppleButton(){
    let appleIDButton = ASAuthorizationAppleIDButton()
    appleIDButton.translatesAutoresizingMaskIntoConstraints =
false
    appleIDButton.addTarget(self, action:
#selector(appleIDButtonTapped), for: .touchUpInside)
    view.addSubview(appleIDButton)
    NSLayoutConstraint.activate([
        appleIDButton.centerXAnchor.constraint(equalTo:
view.centerXAnchor),
        appleIDButton.centerYAnchor.constraint(equalTo:
view.centerYAnchor)
    ])
}
```

8. Build and run the app and tap the **Sign in with Apple** button, as shown in the following screenshot:

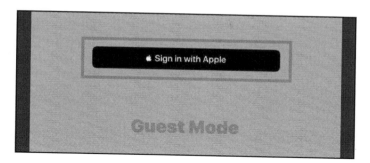

9. You'll see a prompt that asks you to enter your Apple ID settings. Tap **Settings**:

10. Go through the next few screens to enter your Apple ID username and password. Since this is running in the simulator, tap **Don't Merge** with iCloud when asked. After you have signed in successfully, stop the app:

11. Run the app and tap the **Sign in with Apple** button again.

12. You will see the following screen. Tap **Continue**:

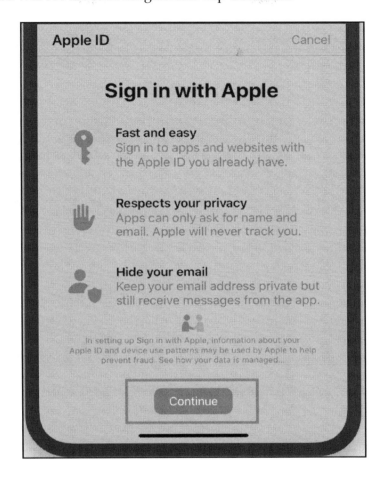

13. Tap the radio button next to **Share my email.** Then, tap **Continue with Password**:

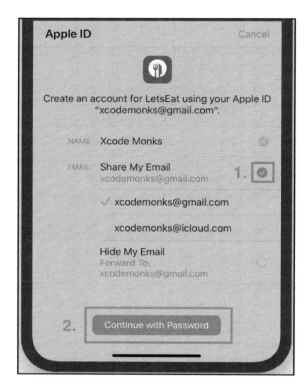

14. Enter the password for the Apple ID and tap **Continue.**

15. The **Explore** screen will appear.

16. If you look at the Debug area, you will see something similar to the following:

This shows that the process was successful and that the credentials for the user are now in the app.

Now, you can sign in successfully, but you still need to pass the user credentials to the **Explore** screen. You will modify `ExploreViewController` to get the necessary credentials and display the user's given name in the **Explore** screen in the next section.

Passing user information to ExploreViewController

You can now sign in successfully and the user's information is in your app. To display the user's given name in `ExploreViewController`, you need to implement the `prepare(for:)` method in `SignInViewController`. This is so you can pass the user's given name to `ExploreViewController` and use it to set the value of the large label in `headerView`. Follow these steps to do so:

1. Click on `ExploreViewController.swift` (inside the `Explore` folder) in the Project navigator.

2. Add a property just below the class declaration:

   ```
   var givenName:String?
   ```

3. Modify `collectionView(_:viewForSupplementaryElementOfKind:at:)` so that it prints `givenName` to the Debug area, as follows:

   ```
   func collectionView(_ collectionView: UICollectionView,
   viewForSupplementaryElementOfKind kind: String, at indexPath:
   IndexPath) -> UICollectionReusableView {
       let header =
   collectionView.dequeueReusableSupplementaryView(ofKind: kind,
   withReuseIdentifier: "header", for: indexPath)
       headerView = header as? ExploreHeaderView
       if let givenName = givenName {
           print("Hi, \(givenName)")
       }
       return headerView
   }
   ```

4. Click on `SignInViewController.swift` (inside the `Misc` folder) in the Project navigator.

5. Implement `prepare(for:)` like so (the boilerplate code should already be in the file; if it isn't, just type the following code before the `MARK:` – `SignInWithApple` methods):

```
// MARK: - Navigation
// In a storyboard-based application, you will often want to
do a little preparation before navigation

override func prepare(for segue: UIStoryboardSegue, sender:
Any?) {
    if let tabBarController = segue.destination as?
UITabBarController, let navViewController =
tabBarController.viewControllers?[0] as?
UINavigationController, let exploreViewController =
navViewController.viewControllers[0] as? ExploreViewController
{
        exploreViewController.givenName = appleIDGivenName
    }
}
```

This will set the value of `givenName` in `ExploreViewController` to `appleIDGivenName`.

6. Build and run the app and tap the **Sign in with Apple** button.

7. Repeat the same steps you performed earlier to sign in (*step 11 - 14* in the previous section, *Implementing delegate methods and button actions*). The **Explore** screen will appear.

8. You will see the following in the Debug area, indicating that the user's given name has been successfully passed to `ExploreViewController`:

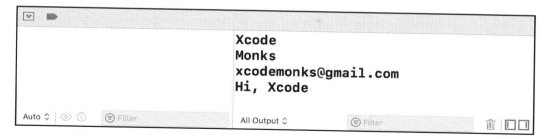

```
Xcode
Monks
xcodemonks@gmail.com
Hi, Xcode
```

Now, all you have to do is assign the given name to the **EXPLORE** label's text property. Follow these steps to do so:

1. Click on `ExploreHeaderView.swift` (inside the `View` folder in the `Explore` folder) in the Project navigator.

2. Add a property just below the `lblLocation` property:

   ```
   @IBOutlet weak var mainlbl:UILabel!
   ```

3. Click on `Main.storyboard` and select **Explore Header View** in the document outline. Click the Connections inspector. Drag from the `mainlbl` outlet to the **EXPLORE** label:

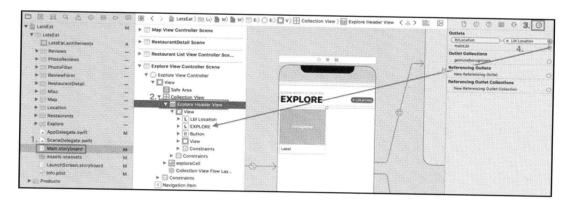

4. Confirm that the `mainlbl` outlet has been connected:

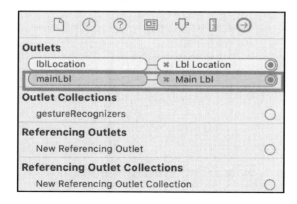

5. Click on `ExploreViewController.swift` in the Project navigator.

6. Modify
   `collectionView(_:viewForSupplementaryElementOfKind:at:)` in
   order to assign the given name to `mainlbl`:

```
func collectionView(_ collectionView: UICollectionView,
viewForSupplementaryElementOfKind kind: String, at indexPath:
IndexPath) -> UICollectionReusableView {
    let header =
collectionView.dequeueReusableSupplementaryView(ofKind: kind,
withReuseIdentifier: "header", for: indexPath)
    headerView = header as? ExploreHeaderView
    if let givenName = givenName {
        headerView.mainlbl.text = "Hi, \(givenName)"
    }
    return headerView
}
```

7. Build and run the app and tap the **Sign in with Apple** button.

8. Repeat the same steps you performed earlier (*step 11 - 14* in the previous section, *Implementing delegate methods and button actions*). The **Explore** screen appears with the user's given name displayed in the header, as shown in the following screenshot:

You have successfully implemented Sign in with Apple for your app. Excellent!

Summary

In this chapter, you learned how to implement Sign in with Apple for your app. You added a login screen to the *Let's Eat* app and then implemented the code that displayed the **Sign in with Apple** button on that login screen. After that, you implemented the delegate methods and actions that are required to make Sign in with Apple work. Finally, after the user signed in, you passed the user's information to `ExploreViewController` so that the user's given name appears in the **Explore** screen.

Now, you know how to implement Sign in with Apple for your own apps and can personalize your apps for your users.

In the next and final chapter, you'll learn how to publish your app to the App Store, as well as how to test your app with internal and external testers using TestFlight.

27

Testing and Submitting Your App to the App Store

Congratulations! You have reached the final chapter of this book.

Over the course of this book, you have learned about the Swift programming language and how to build an entire app using Xcode. However, you've only been running your app in the iOS Simulator or on your own device.

In this chapter, you will start by learning how to obtain an Apple Developer account. Next, you'll learn how to generate a certificate signing request to create certificates that allow you to test apps on your own devices and publish them on the App Store. You'll also learn how to create a bundle identifier to uniquely identify your app on the App Store and register your test devices. After that, you'll learn how to create development and production provisioning profiles to allow apps to run on your test devices and be uploaded to the App Store. Next, you'll learn how to create an App Store listing and submit your release build to the App Store. Finally, you'll learn how to conduct testing for your app using internal and external testers.

By the end of this chapter, you'll have learned how to build and submit apps to the App Store and conduct internal and external testing for your app.

The following topics will be covered:

- Getting an Apple Developer account
- Generating a certificate signing request
- Creating development and distribution certificates
- Creating a bundle identifier
- Registering your test devices
- Creating production and development provisioning profiles

- Creating an App Store listing
- Making the release build and submitting to the App Store
- Conducting internal and external testing

Technical requirements

You will need an Apple ID and a paid Apple Developer account to complete this chapter.

There are no project files for this chapter as it is meant to be a reference on how to submit apps and is not specific to any particular app.

Let's start by learning how to get an Apple Developer account, which is required for App Store submission, in the next section.

Getting an Apple Developer account

As you have seen in earlier chapters, all you need to test your app on a device is a free Apple ID. But the apps will only work for a few days, and you will not be able to add advanced features such as Sign in with Apple or upload your app to the App Store. For that, you need a paid Apple Developer account. Here are the steps to purchase an Individual/Sole Proprietorship Apple Developer account:

1. Go to `https://developer.apple.com/programs/` and click on the **Enroll** button.
2. Scroll to the bottom of the screen and click **Start Your Enrollment.**
3. Enter your **Apple ID** and **Password** when prompted.
4. On the **Apple ID & Privacy** screen, click **Continue.**
5. On the **Trust this browser?** screen, click **Not Now.**
6. On the **Confirm your personal information** screen, enter your personal information and click **Continue** when done.
7. On the **Select your entity type.** screen, choose **Individual/Sole Proprietor**. Click **Continue.**
8. On the **Review and Accept** screen, tick the checkbox at the bottom of the page and click **Continue.**
9. On the **Complete your purchase** screen, click **Purchase.**

10. Follow the onscreen directions to complete your purchase. Once you have purchased your account, go to `https://developer.apple.com/account/` and sign in with the same Apple ID that you used to purchase your developer account. You should see something similar to the following:

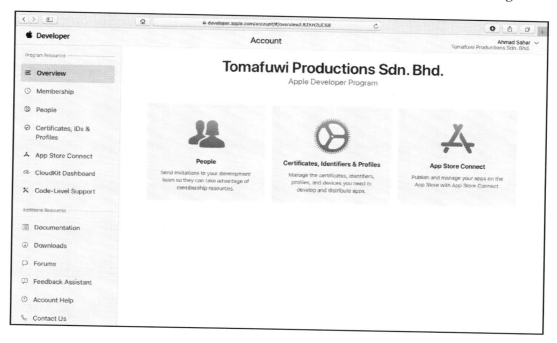

Now that you have a paid Apple Developer account, let's look at what you need to do to get your app on to the App Store. You'll start by learning about certificate signing requests, which are required to obtain Apple Developer certificates that you will install on your Mac, in the next section.

Generating a certificate signing request

Before you write apps that will be submitted to the App Store, you need to install a developer certificate on the Mac that you're running Xcode on. Certificates identify the author of an app. To get this certificate, you'll need to create a **Certificate Signing Request (CSR)**. Here's how to create a CSR:

1. Open the `Utilities` folder on your Mac and launch **Keychain Access**.

2. Choose **Certificate Assistant | Request a Certificate From a Certificate Authority...** from the **Keychain Access** menu:

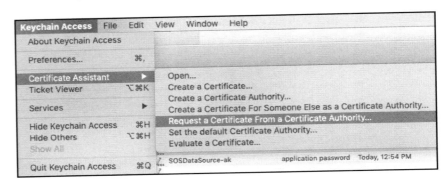

3. For the **User Email Address** field, enter the email address of the Apple ID that you used to register your Apple Developer account. In the **Common Name** field, enter your name. Select **Saved to disk** under **Request is:** and click **Continue**:

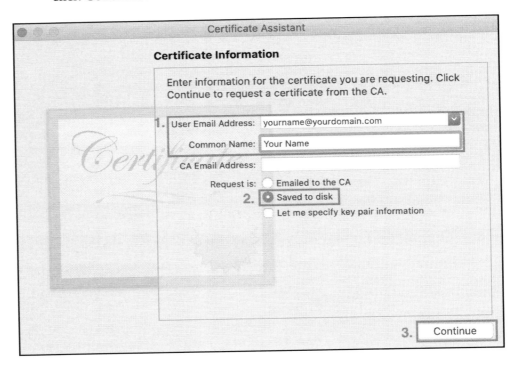

4. Save the CSR to your hard disk.

5. Click **Done.**

Now that you have a CSR, let's look at how you will use it to get development certificates (for testing on your own device) and distribution certificates (for App Store submission) in the next section.

Creating development and distribution certificates

Once you have a certificate signing request, you can use it to create development and distribution certificates. Development certificates are used when you want to test your app on your own iOS devices, and distribution certificates are used when you want to upload your app to the App Store. Here's how to create development and distribution certificates:

1. Log in to your Apple Developer account and click **Certificates, IDs & Profiles**:

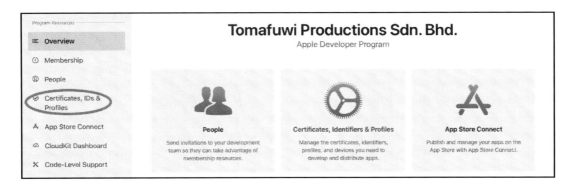

2. You'll see the **Certificates** screen. Click the **+** button:

3. Click the **Apple Development** radio button, and click **Continue**:

4. Click **Choose File**:

5. Upload the CSR by selecting **Choose File** under **Upload CSR file**, selecting the CSR file you saved earlier to your hard disk, and clicking **Choose**.
6. Click **Continue**:

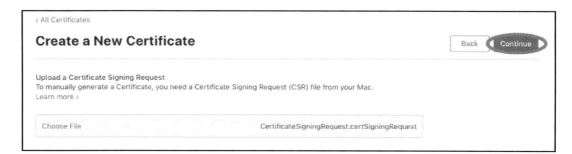

7. Your certificate will be generated automatically. Click **Download** to download the generated certificate onto your Mac:

8. Double-click the downloaded certificate to install it on your Mac.
9. Repeat *steps 3-9* again, but this time, choose **Apple Distribution** in *step 4*:

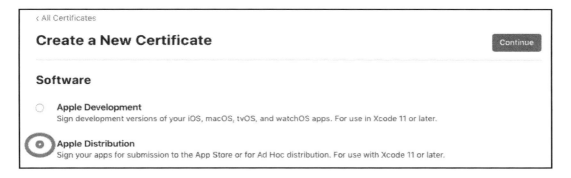

Great! You now have development and distribution certificates. The next step is to register the App ID for your app to uniquely identify your app on the App Store. You will learn how to do that in the next section.

Registering an App ID

When you created your project in Chapter 1, *Getting Familiar with Xcode*, you created a **Bundle Identifier** for it (also known as an **App ID**). An App ID is used to uniquely identify your app on the App Store. You'll need to register this App ID in your Developer account prior to uploading your app to the App Store. Here's how to register your App ID:

1. Log in to your Apple Developer account, and click **Certificates, IDs & Profiles.**
2. Click **Identifiers.**

3. Click the **+** button:

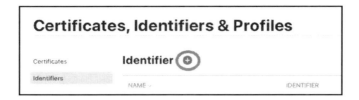

4. Click **App IDs** and click **Continue**:

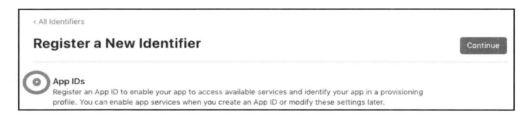

5. **iOS** should already be selected. Enter a description for this App ID, such as `Lets Eat Packt Publishing App ID`. Tick the **Explicit** button and enter your app's **Bundle ID** in the field. Make sure that this value is the same as the bundle identifier you used when you created the project.

   Click the **Continue** button when you're done:

6. Click **Register**:

7. Your App ID has now been registered.

Cool! You've now registered your App ID. Next, you'll register the devices you'll be testing your app on in the next section.

Registering your devices

To run the apps you write on your personal devices for testing, you will need to register them on your developer site. Here's how to register your devices:

1. Log in to your Apple Developer account, and click **Certificates, IDs & Profiles.**
2. Click **Devices.**
3. Click the + button:

4. The **Register a New Device** screen appears:

You'll need a **Device Name** and a **Device ID** to register your device.

5. Connect your device to your Mac. Launch Xcode and choose **Devices and Simulators** from the **Window** menu. Choose the device in the left pane and copy the **Identifier:**

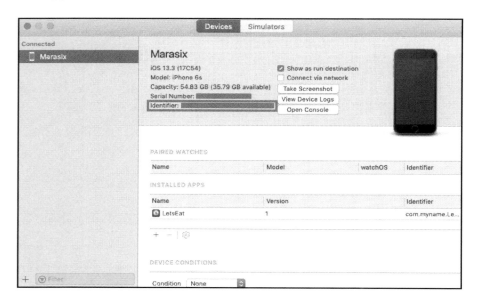

6. Type a name for the device in the **Device Name** field and paste the identifier into the **Device ID (UDID)** field. Click **Continue:**

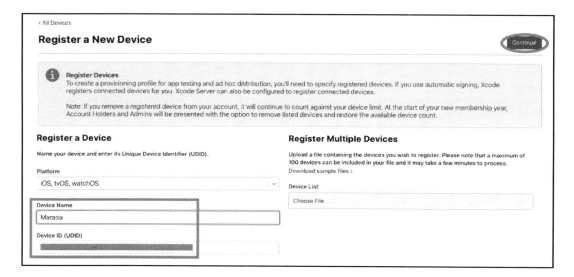

7. Your device is now registered.

You have successfully registered your test devices. Fantastic!

The next step is to create provisioning profiles. An **iOS App Development** profile is required so that your apps will be allowed to run on your test devices, and an **iOS App Store Distribution** profile is required for apps that will be uploaded on to the App Store. You will create development and distribution profiles in the next section.

Creating provisioning profiles

You will need to create two provisioning profiles. An **iOS app development** profile is required for apps to run on test devices. An **iOS App Store distribution** profile is used to submit your app to the App Store. Here's how to create the development profile:

1. Log in to your Apple Developer account, and click **Certificates, IDs & Profiles.**
2. Click **Profiles.**
3. Click the **+** button:

4. Click **iOS App Development** and click **Continue**:

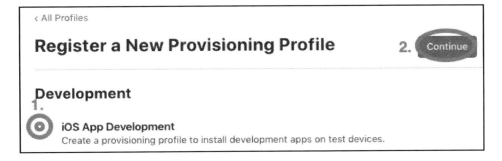

5. Select the **App ID** for the app you want to test and click **Continue**:

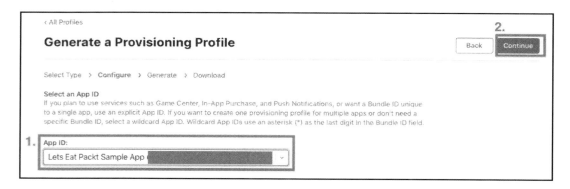

6. Select a **Development** certificate and click **Continue**:

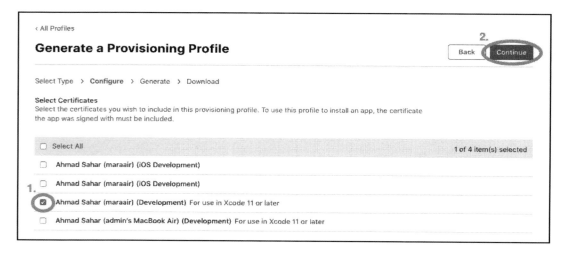

7. Tick all of the devices you will be testing this app on and click **Continue**:

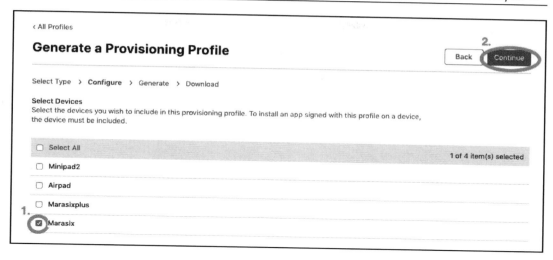

8. Enter a name for the profile and click **Generate**:

9. Click the **Download** button to download the **profile**:

10. Double-click the profile to install it.

Next, you'll create a distribution profile:

1. Click the **All Profiles** link to go back to the previous page:

2. Click the **+** button.
3. Click **App Store** and click **Continue**:

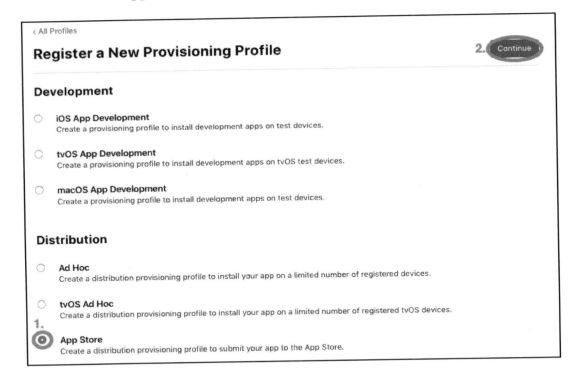

4. Select the **App ID** for the app you want to publish to the **App Store** and click **Continue**:

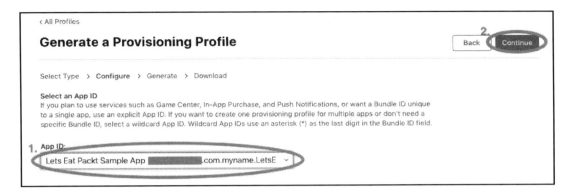

5. Select a **Distribution** certificate and click **Continue**:

6. Enter a name for the profile and click **Generate**:

7. Click the **Download** button to download the profile.
8. Double-click the profile to install it.

You've completed all of the steps necessary to submit your app to the App Store. But before you do, let's see how to create icons for your app, which will appear on the device screen when the app is installed. You will do this in the next section.

Creating icons for your app

Before you upload your app to the App Store, you'll need to create an icon set for it. Here's how to create an icon set for your app:

1. Create an icon for your app that is 1,024 x 1,024 pixels.
2. Use a website such as `appicon.co` to generate all of the different icon sizes.
3. Download the icon set.
4. Click `Assets.xcassets` in the Project navigator and click the `AppIcon` file. Drag in the icons from the icon set to the correct places based on their size:

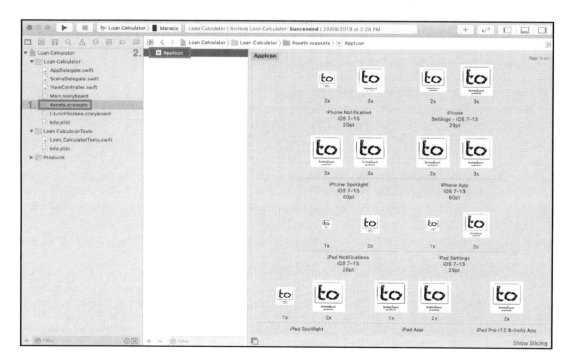

When you run your app in the Simulator or device and quit the app, you should be able to see the app's icon on the screen. Neat!

Let's look at how to create screenshots next. You'll need them for your App Store submission, so customers will know what your app looks like. You'll do this in the next section.

Creating screenshots for your app

You'll need screenshots of your app, which will be used in your App Store listing. Here's how to create them:

1. Run your app in the Simulator and choose **New Screen Shot** in the **File** menu. It will be saved to the desktop:

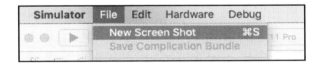

2. Use the iPhone 11 Pro Max and iPhone 8 Plus Simulators, and get few screenshots on each showing all of the different features of your app.

The reason why you have to use both simulators is that you will need screenshots of your app running on different screen sizes, which will be discussed in more detail in the next section, where you will learn how to create an App Store listing. The App Store listing contains all of the information about your app that will be displayed in the App Store, so customers can make an informed decision about downloading or purchasing your app.

Creating an App Store listing

Next, you're going to create the App Store listing. This allows customers to see information about your app before they download it. Perform the following steps:

1. Go to `http://appstoreconnect.apple.com` and select **My Apps**:

2. Click the **+** button at the top-left of the screen and select **New App**:

3. Enter your app details:

- **Platform**: **iOS** (should already be ticked)
- **Name**: The name of your app
- **Primary Language**: The language your app uses
- **BundleID**: The bundleID you created earlier
- **SKU**: Any reference number or string that you use to refer to your app
- **User Access**: **Full Access**

Click **Create** when you're done.

The app will now be listed in your account, but you still need to upload the app and all of the information about it. To upload the app, you need to create an archive build, and you will learn how to do that in the next section.

Creating an archive build

You need to create an archive build, which will be submitted to Apple for placement on the App Store. This archive will also be used for your internal and external testing. Here are the steps to create an archive build:

1. Open Xcode, select the project in the Project navigator and select the **General** tab. In the **Identity** section, you can change the **Version** and **Build** number as you see fit. For instance, if this is the first version of your app and the first time you have built it, you can set **Version** to 1.0 and **Build** to 1:

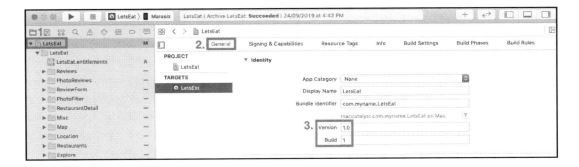

2. Select the **Signing & Capabilities** tab. Make sure **Automatically manage signing** is ticked. This will automatically resolve most issues with certificates, App IDs, device registrations, and provisioning profiles. Select your paid Developer account in the **Team** field:

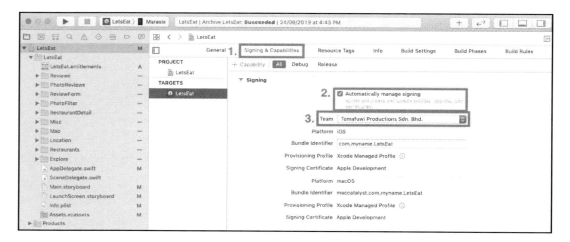

3. Select **Generic iOS Device** as the build destination:

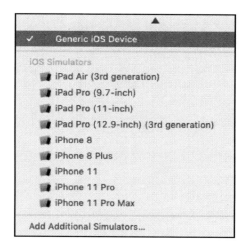

4. If your app does not use encryption, update your `Info.plist` file by adding `ITSAppUsesNonExemptEncryption`, **making its type** `Boolean`, and setting its value to `NO`:

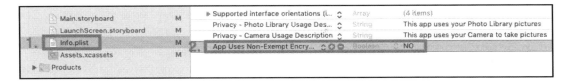

5. Select **Archive** from the **Product** menu:

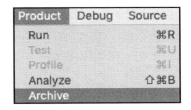

6. The **Organizer** window appears with the **Archives** tab selected. Your app will appear in this screen. Select it and click the **Distribute App** button:

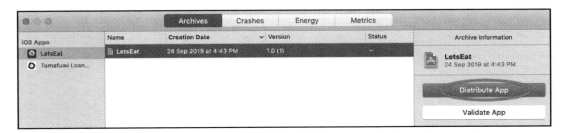

7. Select **App Store Connect** and click **Next**:

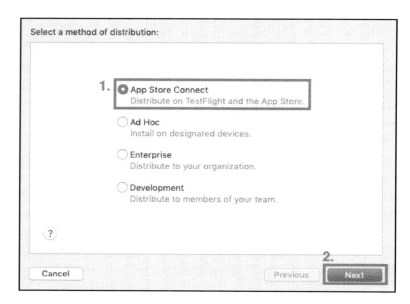

8. Select **Upload** and click **Next**:

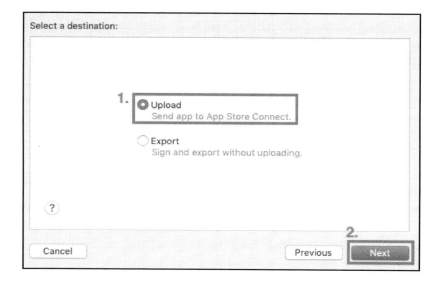

9. Leave the defaults as they are and click **Next**:

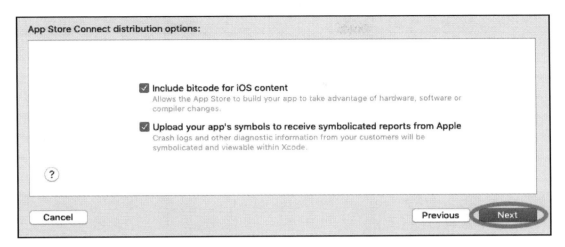

10. Select **Automatically Manage Signing** and click **Next**:

11. If you're prompted for a password, enter the Mac account password and click **Always Allow**:

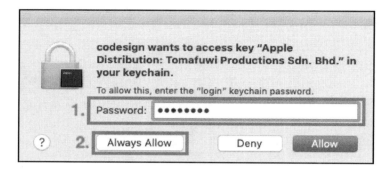

12. Click **Upload**:

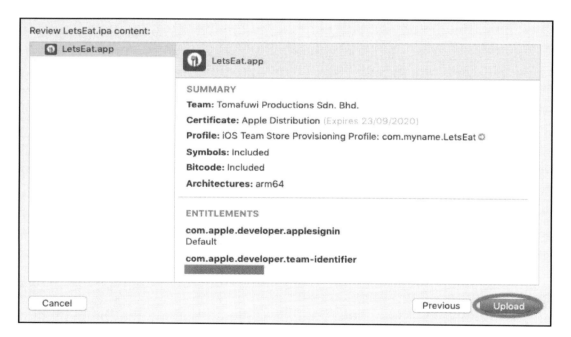

13. Wait for the upload to complete.
14. Click **Done**:

At this point, the build of the app that will be distributed by the App Store has been uploaded. In the next section, you'll learn how to upload screenshots and complete the information about your app that will appear on the App Store along with the app.

Completing the information in App Store Connect

Your app has been uploaded, but you will still need to complete the information about your app in App Store Connect. Here are the steps:

1. Go to http://appstoreconnect.apple.com and select **My Apps**.

2. Select the app that you just created:

3. Select **App Information** on the left side of the screen, and make sure all of the information is correct:

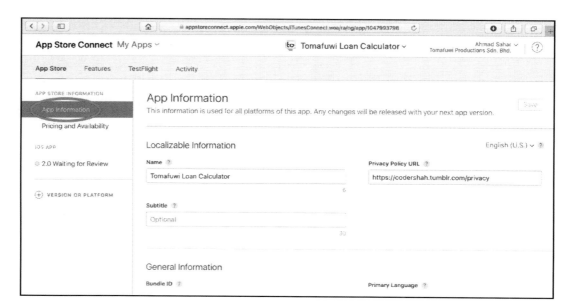

4. Select **Pricing and Availability** on the left side of the screen, and make sure all of the information is correct:

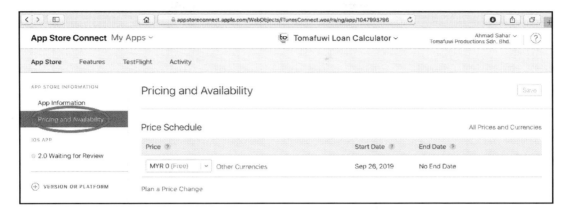

5. Select **Prepare for Submission** on the left side of the screen. Upload the screenshots that you took earlier here. Use the **iPhone 11 Pro Max** screenshots in the **iPhone 6.5" Display** section, and the **iPhone 8 Plus** screenshots in the **iPhone 5.5" Display** section:

6. Scroll down and fill in the **Promotional Text, Description, Keywords, Support URL**, and **Marketing URL** fields:

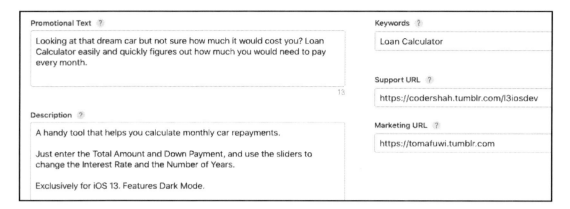

7. Scroll down to the **Build** section and you'll see the archive build you uploaded earlier:

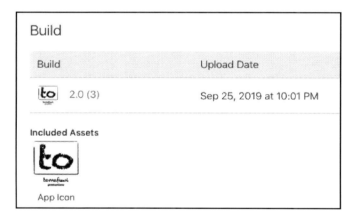

8. Scroll down to the **General App Information** section and fill in all of the required details:

9. Scroll down to the **App Review Information** section. If you would like to provide any additional information to the app reviewer, put it here:

10. Scroll down to the **Version Release** section and leave the default settings.

11. Scroll back up to the top of the screen and click the **Submit for Review** button:

12. Set the **Export Compliance** and **Advertising Identifier** settings appropriately. In the case of Let's Eat, encryption isn't used and there is no **Advertising Identifier**, so I would set both settings to **No**. Click **Submit**:

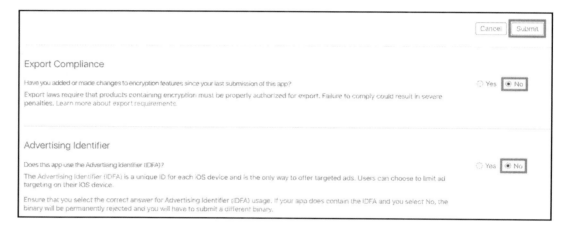

13. The **App Status** changes to **Waiting for Review**. You will need to wait for Apple to review the app, and you will receive an email if your app is approved or rejected. If your app is rejected, there will be a link that takes you to Apple's Resolution Center page, which describes why your app was rejected. After you have fixed the issues, you can then update the archive and resubmit:

You now know how to submit your app to the App Store! Awesome!

 To see Apple's presentation on App Store submission during WWDC 2019,
visit `https://developer.apple.com/videos/play/wwdc2019/304/`.
To see more information on how to submit your apps, visit `https://developer.apple.com/app-store/submissions/`.

In the next section, you'll learn how to conduct internal and external testing for your app, which is important in ensuring that the app is high quality and bug-free.

Testing your app

Apple has a facility named **Testflight** that allows you to distribute your apps to testers prior to releasing it to the App Store. You'll need to download the Testflight app, available from `https://developer.apple.com/testflight/`, to test your app. Your testers can be members of your internal team (internal testers) or the general public (external testers). Let's see how to allow internal team members to test your app first in the next section.

Testing your app internally

Internal testing is good when the app is in an early stage of development. It only involves members of your internal team. Apple does not review apps for internal testers. You can send builds to up to 25 testers for internal testing. Here are the steps.

1. Go to `http://appstoreconnect.apple.com` and select **My Apps.**
2. Select the app that you want to test.

3. Click the **Testflight** tab:

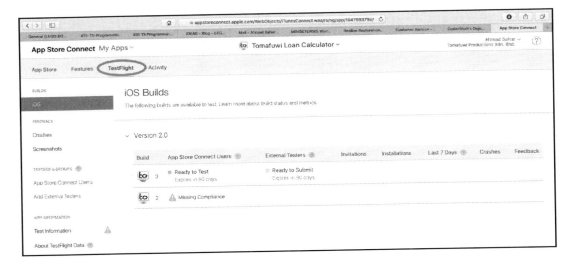

4. Select **App Store Connect Users**:

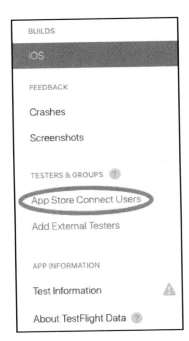

5. Tick all of the users that you want to send test builds to and click **Add**. They'll be invited to test all available builds:

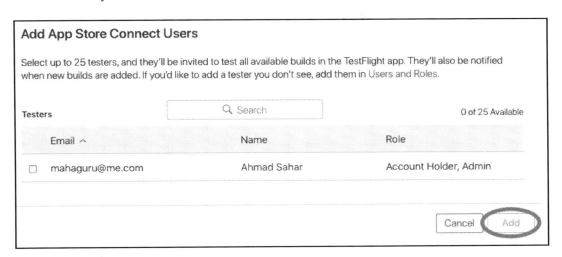

Internal testing will only involve members of your team. If you want to conduct testing with a large number of testers, you will need to do external testing, which is described in the next section.

Testing your app externally

External testing is good when the app is in the final stages of development. You can select anyone to be an external tester, and you can send builds to up to 10,000 testers. Apple may review apps for external testers. Here are the steps:

1. Go to `http://appstoreconnect.apple.com` and select **My Apps.**
2. Select the app that you want to test.

3. Click the **Testflight** tab:

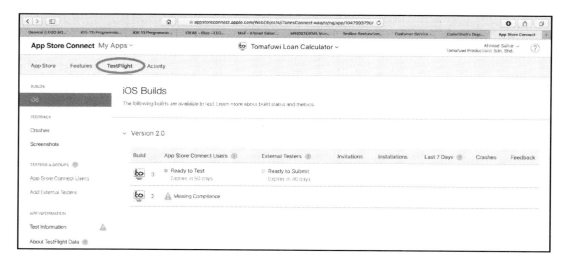

4. Select **Add External Testers**:

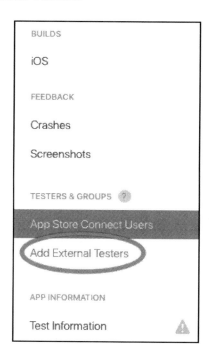

5. Type in a name for the test group and click **Create**:

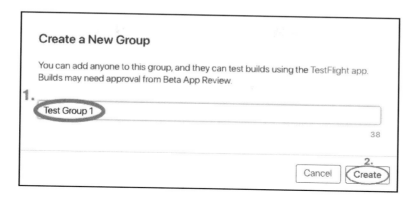

6. Click the + button next to **Testers** and choose **Add New testers**:

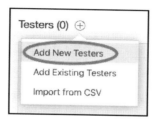

7. Enter the names and email addresses of your testers, and Apple will notify them automatically when a build is ready to be tested:

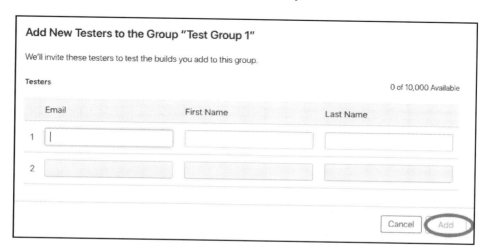

8. Click on **Builds**:

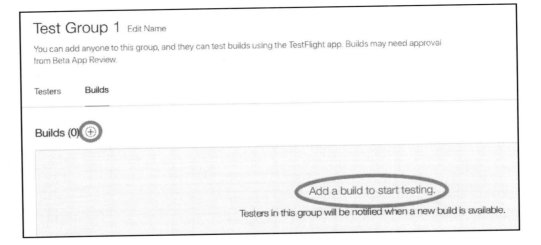

9. Click **Add a build to start testing**:

10. Choose one of your builds and click **Next**:

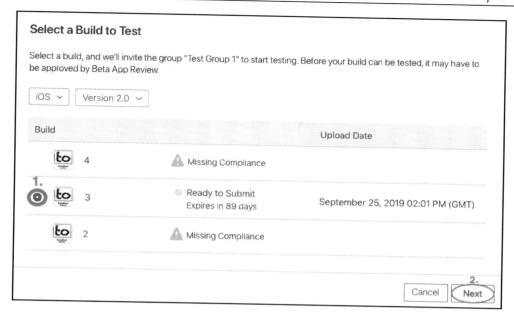

11. Enter **Test Information** and click **Next**:

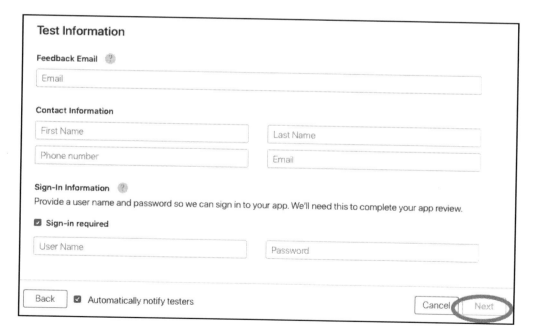

12. Enter **Testing Information** and click **Submit for Review**:

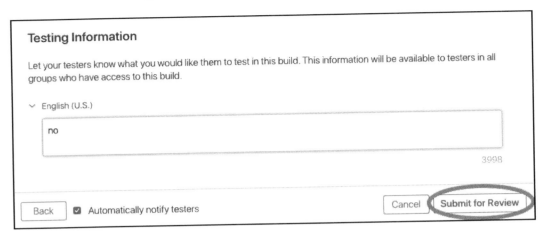

As with app submissions to the App Store, you will need to wait for Apple to review the app, and if your app is rejected, Apple's Resolution Center page will have the details on why your app was rejected. You can then fix the issues and resubmit.

Great! You now know how to test your apps internally and externally, and you have reached the end of this book!

Summary

You have now completed the entire process of building an app and submitting it to the App Store. Congratulations!

You started by learning how to obtain an Apple Developer account. Next, you learned how to generate a certificate signing request to create certificates that allow you to test apps on your own devices and publish them on the App Store. You learned how to create a bundle identifier to uniquely identify your app on the App Store, and register your test devices. After that, you learned how to create development and production provisioning profiles, to allow apps to run on your test devices and be uploaded to the App Store. Next, you learned how to create an App Store listing and submit your release build to the App Store. Finally, you learned how to conduct testing for your app using internal and external testers.

You now know how to build and submit apps to the App Store and conduct internal and external testing for your app.

Once an app has been submitted for review, all you can do is wait for Apple to review your app. Don't worry if the app gets rejected—it happens to all developers. Work with Apple to resolve issues via the Resolution Center, and do your research to know what is and what is not acceptable to Apple.

After your apps are on the App Store, feel free to reach out to me (@shah_apple) and Craig Clayton (@thedevme) on Twitter to let us know—We would love to see what you have built.

Other Books You May Enjoy

If you enjoyed this book, you may be interested in these other books by Packt:

Mastering Swift 5 - Fifth Edition
Jon Hoffman

ISBN: 978-1-78913-986-0

- Understand core Swift components, including operators, collections, control flows, and functions
- Learn how and when to use classes, structures, and enumerations
- Understand how to use protocol-oriented design with extensions to write easier-to-manage code
- Use design patterns with Swift, to solve commonly occurring design problems
- Implement copy-on-write for you custom value types to improve performance
- Add concurrency to your applications using Grand Central Dispatch and Operation Queues
- Implement generics to write flexible and reusable code

Swift Protocol-Oriented Programming - Fourth Edition
Jon Hoffman

ISBN: 978-1-78934-902-3

- Learn the differences between object-oriented programming and protocol-oriented programming
- Understand why value types should be prioritized over reference types
- Delve into protocols, protocol inheritance, protocol composition, and protocol extensions
- Learn how to implement COW (Copy-On-Write) within your custom value types
- Understand how memory management works in Swift and how to avoid common pitfalls
- Design applications by starting with the protocol rather than the implementation

Leave a review - let other readers know what you think

Please share your thoughts on this book with others by leaving a review on the site that you bought it from. If you purchased the book from Amazon, please leave us an honest review on this book's Amazon page. This is vital so that other potential readers can see and use your unbiased opinion to make purchasing decisions, we can understand what our customers think about our products, and our authors can see your feedback on the title that they have worked with Packt to create. It will only take a few minutes of your time, but is valuable to other potential customers, our authors, and Packt. Thank you!

Index

.

.plist file 327, 328

/

//MARK syntax
  using 430

A

annotations
  about 388, 389
  adding, to Map View 402
  creating 388, 389
  displaying, on Map View 407, 408, 409
app icon
  creating 766, 767
  URL 766
App ID
  registering 757, 758
app screenshots
  creating 767
App Store Connect
  information, completing 775, 776, 777, 778,
    779, 780, 781
  URL 775
App Store listing
  creating 768, 769
App Store
  Xcode, downloading 12, 13, 14, 16, 17
  Xcode, installing 12, 13, 14, 16, 17
app
  data, using from JSON files 444, 445
  executing, in Simulator 19, 20, 21, 22
Apple Developer account
  about 752, 753
  reference link 753
Application Programmer Interface (API) 440

archive build
  creating 769, 770, 771, 772, 773, 774, 775
arithmetic operators
  about 47
  using 47, 48
array of object types
  creating 117, 118
arrays
  about 72
  creating 72
  element, accessing 74
  item, adding 73
  item, removing from 74
  iterating over 75
  number of elements, checking 73
  reference link 84
  value, assigning to index 74
Auto Layout
  about 124
  reference link 163, 171
AutoLayout Constraints
  adding, to Explore screen section header
    267, 268, 269, 270, 271, 272
  adding, to restaurantCell 292, 293, 294,
    295, 296, 297, 298, 299, 300, 301

B

Build Only Device 23
bundle identifier 757, 758
button actions
  implementing 737, 738, 739, 741, 742, 743,
    744, 745

C

camel case 42
camera
  permission, requesting 573, 574, 575, 576,

577, 578
Cancel button
  unwind method, implementing 540
cell size 194
certificate signing request (CSR)
  about 753
  generating 753, 754, 755
CGRect
  reference link 527
class declaration
  creating 97
class instance
  creating 98, 100
classes
  about 96, 97
  exploring 309
  reference link 107
  using 107
closed range operator 64
closures
  about 92, 93
  reference link 94
  simplifying 93, 94
Cocoa Touch Class file
  adding, to project 172, 173, 174, 175
code
  organizing 427
collection view cell
  about 126
  configuring 193, 194, 195
collection view data source protocol 182
Collection View header
  button, adding 195, 196, 197
collection view
  about 310
  adding, to Explore screen 168, 169, 170,
    171
  data source methods, configuring 182, 183
Collection View
  data source methods, updating in
    ExploreViewController 346, 347
collection view
  data source methods, updating in
    ExploreViewController 343, 344, 345
  data source properties, setting of 183, 184

data, displaying 336, 337
delegate outlets, setting of 183, 184
outlets, connecting in exploreCell 338, 339,
  340, 342
Collection View
  reference link 309
  Section Header, adding 187, 188, 189
collection views 311, 312, 313, 315, 316, 317,
  318, 319, 320
collectionView method
  reference link 453
comparison operators
  about 49
  using 49
compound assignment operators
  about 48
  using 48
computed properties 393
conditionals
  about 54
  if statement, using 55, 56
  reference link 54
  switch statements, using 56
constants
  about 42
  examples 43
  exploring 42, 44
controllers
  exploring 309
Core Data manager
  creating 589, 590, 591
Core Data Stack
  about 580
  reference link 581, 582
Core Data
  about 580
  components, implementing 581
  reference link 580
Core Image
  reference link 550
custom annotations
  creating 410, 411, 412, 414
custom argument labels
  using 87, 88
custom color

creating 190, 191, 192
custom UIControl object
creating 520
stars, displaying 524, 525, 528, 531, 533
custom UIView
displaying, to indicate no data available 481,
482, 483, 484, 485, 486

D

Dark Mode colors
reference link 639
Dark Mode, simulator
turning on 632, 633, 634
Dark Mode
Explore screen, updating to work with 640,
641, 642, 643
Launchscreen.storyboard, updating to work
with 635, 636, 638, 639
NoDataView, updating to work with 653, 655
Photo Reviews View Controller scene,
updating to work with 655, 656, 657, 658
Restaurant Detail screen, updating to work
with 647, 648, 649, 650, 651, 652, 653
Restaurant List screen, updating to work with
644, 645, 646
Reviews View Controller scene, updating to
work with 653, 655
data manager 440
data manager class
implementing, to read data from .plist files
331, 332
data manager methods
implementing 342
data model
creating 582, 585
data source 182
data source methods
configuring, for collection view 182, 183
data source properties
setting, of collection view 183, 184
data source protocols
adopting 222, 223, 225, 226, 227, 228
data types
Boolean, storing 41
common data types, used in playground 41

exploring 39, 40
floating-point numbers, storing 40
integers, storing 40
reference link 40
strings, storing 41
data
displaying, in collection view 336, 337
passing, to Restaurant Detail screen 423,
424, 425, 426, 427
DataManager protocol
creating 397, 398, 399
DateFormatter
reference link 588
delegate method 745
implementing 737, 738, 739, 741, 742, 743,
744
delegate outlets
setting, of collection view 183, 184
delegate protocols
adopting 222, 223, 225, 226, 227, 228
Developer App certificate
on iOS device 29, 30
development and distribution certificates
creating 755, 756, 757
devices
registering 759, 760
dictionary
about 75, 76
creating 76
element, accessing 77
item, adding 77
item, removing from 78
iterating over 79
number of elements, checking 76, 77
reference link 84
value, assigning to key 78

E

enumeration
about 107, 108
creating 108, 109
reference link 109
error handling
exploring 118, 119
reference link 119

Explore screen section header
  AutoLayout Constraints, adding 267, 268,
    269, 270, 271
  AutoLayout, adding 272
  modifying 252, 253, 254, 255, 256, 257,
    258, 260, 261, 262, 264, 265, 266
Explore screen
  about 130
  collection view, adding 168, 169, 170, 171
  revisiting 321
  updating, to work with Dark Mode 640, 641,
    642, 643
  using 130
exploreCell collection view cell
  modifying 272, 274, 275, 276, 277, 278,
    279
exploreCell
  outlets, connecting 338, 339, 340, 342
ExploreDataManager
  refactoring 400, 401
ExploreItem instances
  initializing, with data manager 334
ExploreViewController
  data source methods, updating 343, 344,
    345, 346, 347
  refactoring 427, 428, 429
  section header's label, connecting 450, 451,
    452
  user information, passing 745, 746, 747,
    748, 749
extensions
  about 115
  array of object types, creating 117, 118
  protocol, adopting 116

F

filters
  about 550, 551, 552, 554, 555
for-in loop 66, 67
functions
  about 86
  creating 86, 87
  custom argument labels, using 87, 88
  guard statement, using to exist 91, 92
  nested functions, using 88, 89

reference link 92
using, as parameters 90
using, as return types 89, 90

G

Generic iOS Device 23

H

half-open range operator 65
Horizontally in Container 162

I

if statement
  using 55, 56
images
  working with 710, 711, 712, 713
index
  values, assigning 74
Interface Builder
  reference link 138
iOS 13 device
  Developer App certificate, on iOS device 29,
    30
  iOS device wirelessly, connecting 30, 31
  used, for development 23, 24, 25, 26, 27,
    28, 29
iOS App Development profile 761
iOS app development, terms
  about 124
  Auto Layout 129
  collection view controller 126
  Model-View-Controller (MVC) 129
  navigation controller 127
  segue 129
  stack view 124
  storyboard 129
  tab bar controller 128
  table view controller 125
  view 124
  view controller 124
iOS App Store Distribution profile 761
iOS app
  designing 660, 662, 663, 664, 665, 667,
    668, 669, 670
  device type, checking 672

ExploreViewController 675
ExploreViewController, updating, for iPad
   673, 674, 676, 678, 679
Restaurant Detail screen, updating for iPad
   686, 687, 688, 690
RestaurantListViewController, updating for
   iPad 680, 681, 682, 683, 684, 685
updating, to work on iPad 670
updating, to work on macOS 690, 691, 692,
   693
iOS device wirelessly
   connecting 30, 31
iPad
   iOS app, updating to work 670
   used, for Restaurant Detail screen 686, 687,
      688, 690
   used, for updating ExploreViewController
      673, 674, 675, 676, 678, 679
   used, for updating
      RestaurantListViewController 680, 681,
      682, 683, 684, 685

J

JavaScript Object Notation (JSON) 441
JSON files, parsing
   reference link 476
JSON files
   data, obtaining 440
   data, using in app 444, 445
   download link 440
JSON format 441, 442
JSONSerialization
   reference link 442

L

Launch screen
   updating, to work with Dark Mode 635
Launch screen
   background color, configuring 156, 157, 158
   creating 143
   logo and constraints, adding 158, 159, 160,
      162
   setting up 138, 139, 140, 141, 144
   updating, to work with Dark Mode 636, 637,
      638, 639

Let's Eat app
   Explore screen, using 130
   Locations screen, using 131
   login screen, adding 724, 726, 727, 728,
      729, 731, 732
   Map screen, using 135, 136
   Restaurant Detail screen, using 133, 134
   Restaurant List screen, using 132, 133
   Review Form screen, using 134, 135
   touring 130
location data, adding for table view
   about 372, 374
   data, adding to .plist file 375, 377, 378
   property list (.plist) file, creating 375
locationCell
   configuring, in table view cell 301, 302
LocationDataManager
   creating 379
   data, displaying in table view 380, 381
Locations screen
   about 131
   location, selecting 459, 461
   table view, adding 212, 213, 214, 215, 216
   using 131
LocationViewController
   creating 360, 361, 362, 363
   data source, adding 366, 367, 368, 371
   delegate methods, adding 366, 367, 368,
      371
   refactoring 432
   table view, connecting to 363, 364
   user-selected location, storing 445, 447,
      448, 449
logical operators
   about 49
   using 49
loops
   about 65, 66
   for-in loop 66, 67
   reference link 66
   repeat-while loop 68
   while loop 67, 68

M

Mac Catalyst WWDC 2019
  reference link 690
Mac Catalyst
  reference link 690
macOS
  iOS app, updating 690, 691, 692, 693
Map screen
  about 135
  implementing 244, 245, 246, 247, 248, 249
  using 135, 136
Map View region
  setting, to displayed 406, 407
Map View
  annotations, adding 402
  annotations, displaying 407, 408, 409
MapDataManager
  configuring, with RestaurantDataManager
    480, 481
  creating 395, 396, 397
  refactoring 399
MapViewController
  creating 402, 403
  refactoring 434, 436
memberwise initializer 105
methods 96
MKAnnotation
  about 389, 390
  reference link 389
MKMapView, regions
  reference link 388
model objects
  .plist file 327, 328
  about 324, 325, 326, 327
  data manager class, implementing 332
  data manager class, implementing to read
    data from .plist files 331
  data manager, using to initialize ExploreItem
    instances 334
  structure, creating to represent cuisine 328,
    329, 330, 331
Model-View-Controller (MVC) 324, 360
MVC design pattern
  about 308, 309

Controller 308
Model 308
reference link 308
View 308

N

Navigation Bar
  Cancel button, adding 205, 206, 207, 208,
    209
  Save button, adding 205, 206, 207, 208,
    209
nested functions
  using 88, 89
NoDataView
  updating, to work with Dark Mode 653, 654

O

one-sided range operator 65
operators
  arithmetic operators, using 47, 48
  comparison operators, using 49
  compound assignment operators, using 48
  exploring 46
  logical operators, using 49
  reference link 47
  string operations, performing 50, 51
optional binding
  using 59, 60, 61
optionals
  about 58
  using 59, 60, 61
Outlets in Storyboard
  connecting, to View Controller 176, 177,
    178, 179, 180, 181, 182
outlets
  connecting, for Map View to
    MapViewController 403, 404, 406

P

parameters 86
persistent store 582
Photo Filter screen
  View Controller, creating 561, 563, 564,
    567, 568, 569, 571
Photo Library

permission, requesting 573, 574, 575, 576, 577, 578
Photo Reviews View Controller scene
  updating, to work with Dark Mode 655, 656, 657, 658
PhotoFilterViewController
  updating, to save photos 606, 607, 608, 609, 610
photos
  loading 598, 599, 600
  saving 598, 599, 600
print() instruction
  using 51, 52
properties 96
protocol declaration
  creating 113, 115
protocols
  about 112, 113
  adopting, via extensions 116
  reference link 115
provisioning profiles
  creating 761, 762, 763, 764, 765, 766

R

range operators
  about 64, 65
  reference link 64
reference types
  about 105, 106
  versus value types 105, 106, 107
repeat-while loop 68
Restaurant Detail screen
  about 133, 414
  composing 717, 719, 720, 721
  data, passing to 423, 424, 425, 426, 427
  implementing 231, 232, 233, 234, 235
  rating, calculation 626, 627, 628
  saved photos, displaying 611, 612, 616, 617, 618, 620, 621, 622, 623, 624, 625
  saved reviews, displaying 611, 612, 616, 617, 618, 620, 621, 622, 623, 624, 625
  updating, to work with Dark Mode 647, 648, 649, 650, 651, 652, 653
  using 133, 134
Restaurant List screen

about 132, 217
data source protocols, adopting 222, 223, 225, 226, 227, 228
delegate protocols, adopting 222, 223, 225, 226, 227, 228
implementing 217, 218
list of restaurants, displaying 486, 487, 488, 489, 490, 491, 492, 493
presenting 228, 229, 230
RestaurantListViewController class, declaring 222
RestaurantListViewController, class declaring 220, 221
revisiting 321
updating, to work with Dark Mode 644, 645, 646
using 132, 133
View Controller, creating for cells 472
RestaurantAPIManager
  creating 442
restaurantCell
  AutoLayout Constraints, adding 292, 293, 294, 295, 296, 297, 298, 299, 300, 301
  modifying 279, 280, 281, 283, 284, 285, 286, 287, 288, 289, 290, 291, 292
RestaurantCell
  outlets, connecting 472, 473, 474, 475
RestaurantDataManager
  creating 476, 477, 479
  used, for configuring MapDataManager 480, 481
RestaurantDetailViewController
  outlets, setting up 496, 498, 499, 500, 502, 503, 505
restaurantID property
  adding, to RestaurantItem 601
RestaurantID
  passing, to ReviewFormViewController 602, 604, 606
RestaurantItem class
  creating 394
RestaurantItem
  class, creating 390, 391, 392
  restaurantID property, adding 601
RestaurantListViewController
  class, declaring 220, 221, 222

cuisine information, passing 461, 462, 463, 464, 465, 466, 467, 468, 469, 470, 471
data, passing to RestaurantDetailViewController 509, 510, 511, 512, 513, 514, 516
location, passing 461, 462, 463, 464, 465, 467, 468, 469, 470, 471
refactoring 431
RestaurantPhotoItem
    creating 588
return type 86
Review Form screen
    about 134
    implementing 236, 237, 238, 239, 240, 242, 243
    using 134, 135
ReviewDataManager
    creating 594, 596
ReviewFormViewController
    creating 541, 542, 543, 544, 546, 547
    RestaurantID, passing to 602, 604, 606
    updating, to save reviews 601
ReviewItem
    creating 586, 587, 588
Reviews View Controller scene
    updating, to work with Dark Mode 653, 654
reviews
    loading 598, 599, 600
    ReviewFormViewController, updating to save 601, 602
    saving 598, 599, 600

S

scene 129
scrolling list of filters
    creating 555, 556, 557
    View Controller, creating for filter cell 557, 559, 560
    View Controller, creating for Photo Filter screen 561, 562, 564, 567, 568, 569, 571
section header's label
    connecting, to ExploreViewController 450, 451, 452
section header, Explore screen
    view controller, adding 450

Section Header
    adding, to Collection View 187, 188, 189
section header
    size, configuring 193, 194, 195
    used, for adding view controller in Explore screen 449, 450
sets
    about 79
    checking, for specific item 81
    creating 80
    item, adding 80, 81
    item, removing from 81
    iterating over 82
    membership and equality 83, 84
    number of elements, checking 80
    operations 82, 83
    reference link 84
showDetail segue
    performing 419, 421, 422
Sign in with Apple button
    displaying 733, 734, 735, 736, 737
    reference link 733
simulated and physical devices, difference between
    reference link 23
simulator
    app, executing 19, 20, 21, 22
    build only device menu items 22, 23
    Dark Mode, turning on 632, 633, 634
    No Device menu items 22, 23
Size inspector 527
Stacks
    used, for combining Text Views 704, 705, 706, 707, 708, 709
Static Table View
    data, displaying 506, 507, 509
storyboard reference
    configuring 414, 416, 417, 418
    creating 414, 416, 417, 418
string interpolation 51
string operations
    performing 50, 51
strings
    reference link 50
structure declaration

creating 104
structure instance
creating 105
structures
about 103
reference link 107
using 107
subclass
creating 100, 101
superclass method
overriding 101, 103
Swift playgrounds
about 34, 36
fonts and colors, customizing 38, 39
SwiftUI project
creating 696, 698, 699, 700
SwiftUI tutorial
reference link 697
SwiftUI Views
using 713, 716, 717
switch statements
using 56

T

tab bar controller
Assets.xcassets file, adding 154, 155, 156
button title, configuring 145, 146, 147
icons, adding for Explore and Map button
163, 165
setting up 138, 139, 140, 141, 142, 144
view controller, embedding in navigation
controller 147, 148, 150, 151, 152, 153
table view cell
about 125
locationCell, configuring 301, 302
table view
adding, to Locations screen 212, 213, 214,
215, 216
connecting, to LocationViewController 363,
364
working 350, 351, 352, 353, 356, 357, 358,
359, 360
Testflight app
about 781
download link 781

externally, testing 783, 784, 785, 787, 788
internally, testing 781, 782, 783
Text Views
combining, with Stacks 704, 705, 706, 707,
708, 709
text
working with 700, 701, 702, 703, 704
touch events
support, adding 534, 535, 536, 537, 538,
539, 540
touches, handling
reference link 534
tuples
about 459
reference link 459
type annotation
used, to specify type 45
type inference 44
type safety 44, 46

U

UICollectionViewDataSource protocol
adopting 184, 185, 186, 187
reference link 310
UICollectionViewDelegate protocol
adopting 184, 185, 186, 187
reference link 310
UICollectionViewDelegate
reference link 572
UICollectionViewDelegateFlowLayout
reference link 567
UICollectionViewFlowLayout protocol
reference link 309
UIControl
reference link 522
UIImagePickerController
reference link 568
UIImagePickerControllerDelegate
reference link 569
UIKit
using 713, 716, 717
UITableViewDataSource protocol
reference link 351
UITableViewDelegate protocol
reference link 351

UIView
  reference link 526
unwind action method
  adding, to Done button 452, 453, 454, 456,
    457, 458, 459
unwind method
  implementing, for Camel button 540, 541
unwrapping 59
user information
  passing, to ExploreViewController 745, 746,
    747, 748, 749
user interface
  cleaning up 381, 382, 383, 384

V

value types
  about 105
  versus reference types 105, 106, 107
variables
  about 42
  examples 43
  exploring 42, 44
Version Control and Git
  reference link 16
Vertically in Container 162

View Controller scene
  adding 197, 198, 199, 200, 201, 202, 203,
    204, 205
view controller
  adding, section header in Explore screen 449
View Controller
  creating, for filter cell 557, 559, 560
  creating, for Photo Filter screen 561, 562,
    565, 567, 568, 569, 571
  Outlets in Storyboard, connecting to 176,
    177, 178, 179, 180, 181, 182
view modally
  presenting 195

W

while loop 67, 68

X

Xcode project
  creating 136, 137, 138
Xcode
  downloading, from App Store 12, 13, 14, 16,
    17
  installing, from App Store 12, 13, 14, 16, 17
  user interface 17, 18, 19

Printed in Poland
by Amazon Fulfillment
Poland Sp. z o.o., Wrocław